Anthology of Chinese Literature
Volume 2

Frontispiece

Tu Li-niang recalls her dream of love by the "peony pavilion." T'ang Hsien-tsu's play (see p. 87) was completed in the year 1598. This illustration from a contemporary edition shows the art of printing from carved pear-wood blocks at its late-Ming apogee.

The toiling peasants on the cover are those "trackers" of whom both Shen Ts'ung-wen and Mao Tun write in works translated below. These men whose straining muscles permit huge barges to inch along against the current are the subject of this 1934 woodcut by Lo Ch'ing-chen. It comes from a collection made by Lu Hsün, who was an enthusiastic promoter of this folk-art form.

Other Works by Cyril Birch
Published by Grove Press

Anthology of Chinese Literature, Vol 1: From Early Times
to the 14th Century (Donald Keene, Associate Editor)

Stories from a Ming Collection

Anthology of

Chinese Literature

Volume 2: From the 14th Century
to the Present Day

Edited and with an Introduction by
CYRIL BIRCH

GROVE PRESS, INC.
NEW YORK

Copyright © 1972 by Grove Press, Inc.
All Rights Reserved

Library of Congress Catalog Card Number: 65:14202

ISBN: 0-394-17766-5

No part of this book may be reproduced, for any reason, by any means, including any method of photographic reproduction, without the permission of the publisher.

First Evergreen Edition, 1972

First Printing

Manufactured in the United States of America
by Colonial Press Inc., Clinton, Massachusetts

Distributed by Random House, Inc., New York

Acknowledgments

The editor gratefully acknowledges his wife's unflagging assistance; the advice of Cheng Ch'ing-mao on textual problems; and the valued contributions of unpublished translations, some specifically requested for this volume, from A. C. Graham, J. R. Hightower, William L. Mac-Donald, Tao Tao Sanders, and William Schultz.

Acknowledgments are also made to the following: to Wayne Schlepp and the University of Wisconsin Press for material from *San-ch'ü*; to Chi-chen Wang for material from *Traditional Chinese Tales* and *Contemporary Chinese Stories*; to F. W. Mote and Princeton University Press for material from *The Poet Kao Ch'i*; to C. T. Hsia and Columbia University Press for material from *The Classic Chinese Novel*; to Ch'u Chai and Winberg Chai and Hawthorn Books for material from *Treasury of Chinese Literature*; to the late Arthur Waley and George Allen and Unwin for material from *Yüan Mei*; to Shirley M. Black for material from *Chapters from a Floating Life*; to Edgar Snow and John Day for material from *Living China*; to Tao Tao Sanders, Jonathan Cape and Grossman Publishers for poems by Wen Yi-to (soon to be published); to Jeannette Faurot and *Phi Theta Papers*, University of California, Berkeley, for poems by Feng Chih; to Yao Hsin-nung and the University of California Press for material from *The Malice of Empire*; to Eileen Chang and Cassell for material from *The Rouge of the North*; to Yip Wai-lim and the University of Iowa Press for material from *Modern Chinese Poetry*; and to the East Asiatic Library, University of California, Berkeley, for permission to reproduce the dust jacket and frontispiece illustrations.

Translators

CYRIL BIRCH

SHIRLEY M. BLACK

CH'U CHAI

WINBERG CHAI

JEANNETTE FAUROT

A. C. GRAHAM

JAMES R. HIGHTOWER

C. T. HSIA

JEREMY INGALLS

WILLIAM L. MACDONALD

F. W. MOTE

TAO TAO SANDERS

WAYNE SCHLEPP

WILLIAM SCHULTZ

EDGAR SNOW

ARTHUR WALEY

CHI-CHEN WANG

YAO HSIN-NUNG

YIP WAI-LIM

To the Memory of
Richard Gregg Irwin

Contents

MING DYNASTY (1368–1644)

CH'ING DYNASTY (1644–1911)

REPUBLICAN PERIOD (1911–

Anthology of Chinese Literature
Volume 2

Introduction

In a certain sense, there has never been a break in the literary tradition of China. A Chinese scholar of today, when he learns of the death of a friend, will turn aside from his research on *Finnegans Wake* to compose an obituary couplet whose language would have been acceptable to a fifteenth-century forebear, and whose content will probably include allusions to the *Book of Songs* of the sixth century before Christ. In another sense, the literary history of the past seven hundred years is a record of continual upheavals, of the periodic emergence of new forms, of the frequent substitution of one classical model for another, and (for the past half-century) of iconoclasm and innovation on the largest scale.

We may see the clearest break between the medieval and the pre-modern eras in the massive disruption inflicted by the Mongols in the thirteenth century. The period of their domination, the Yüan, is a time of literary florescence. It is the classical age of the Chinese drama and the seminal age of the novel: in our *Anthology of Chinese Literature: from early times to the fourteenth century* we included two Yüan plays and an extract from *The Men of the Marshes*, the great cyclic novel which took shape at this time. The Yüan poets excelled in the writing of lyrics (*tz'u*) and songs (*ch'ü*), two genres marked by lines of irregular length in complex metrical patterns. All these are relatively "popular" forms. As the traditional life-style of the scholar-official reeled under barbarian impact, there occurred a liberation of those creative forces which had already been gathering vitality in the urban centers of the preceding Sung dynasty, and men of letters drew new inspiration from girl entertainers and blind marketplace storytellers.

Perhaps only two subsequent ages, prior to the twentieth century, can compare in creativity with the Yüan. One, certainly, would be the generations which preceded and then witnessed the collapse of the Ming dynasty and the institution of the new alien domination of the Manchus. Charles Hucker says of China's imperial system of government that probably "no government ever served its people more effectively as a guardian of social stability, territorial integrity, and national dignity"; and the Ming, by its effective restoration of the system, had provided "one of the most notably tranquil interludes" of China's long history. As the tranquillity tottered, eaten away by the corruption it had engendered, new intellectual forces arose which in some ways prefigured the "Literary Revolution" of the early Republican period. On the establishment of the new Ch'ing (Manchu) dynasty men were faced again with the age-old dilemma of conflicting loyalties, the choice between service and seclusion. Many who made the latter choice turned to the craft of letters to console themselves or to justify themselves before the world.

The second great age is the Ch'ien-lung period (1736—1796), when China was as strong and stable as she had been weak and turbulent in the last decades of Ming rule. The Ch'ien-lung emperor is probably the only ruler in all of China's history whose reign title is widely familiar in the Western world. The history of art will explain this phenomenon by the exquisite porcelains manufactured in the imperial kilns and the remarkable collection of paintings assembled at the imperial behest. It was the last great age of the old nation, firmly founded on the territorial conquests of the K'ang-hsi emperor and not yet threatened by the gunboats from the West. It was a time of consolidation, symbolized by the comprehensive collection and editing of the entire literary heritage into the *Ssu-k'u ch'üan-shu*, the imperial "Complete Library in Four Categories," the assemblage of whose 36,000 volumes was finished in 1782. "Editing," in fact, may be read as a euphemism for the most fearsome censorship, as anything that might be construed as critical of the (still alien) Manchus was weeded out and its author, or even possessor, punished perhaps by death. Yet the Ch'ien-lung era saw the emergence of Yüan Mei, the greatest poet of recent centuries, and of Ts'ao Hsüeh-ch'in whose *Red Chamber Dream* is one of the half-dozen masterpieces of world fiction.

Some of the most eminent figures of seven centuries are missing from the present volume. In some cases this is because their major contribution lies outside the realm of "literature" as usually defined by the Western mind: this is true, for example, of the great eclectic philosopher Wang Yang-ming (1472–1528); and men like Ku Yen-wu (1613–1682) and Tai Chen (1723–1777) belong rather to the realm of classical scholarship than to creative literature. Such writers as Yao Nai (1732–1815), a leading practitioner of "ancient-style" or "plain-style" prose (*ku-wen*), have failed to attract the attention of translators; while major poets like Wang Shih-chen (1634–1711) may be full of interest but hard of access in the erudite and heavily allusive quality of so much of their work. We offer not a single specimen of the literary form most assiduously cultivated in the centuries preceding our own: the "eight-legged" (*pa-ku*) essay. This was a tedious rhetorical exercise which progressed (or regressed) in balanced or antithetical prose through prescribed sections, "broaching the theme," "taking up the theme," and so on. It was strictly an examination piece, and although major writers like Yüan Mei produced books of model "eight-legs" for the guidance of aspiring candidates, perhaps no one would claim ever to have expressed his innermost convictions in this form.

Until the "New Verse" of the nineteen-twenties Chinese poets continued to celebrate long-loved themes: friendship and the philosophic acceptance of time and change; pastoral tranquillity and the constant renewal of the seasons; the nostalgic recollection of antiquity and the honoring of historical models of ethical conduct. Occasional verse was a staple of social intercourse: to write a poem, for a Chinese educated in the classical tradition, was the natural response to a wide variety of life's situations. F. W. Mote, the biographer of Kao Ch'i, describes the embarrassment felt by the youthful poet when he could not afford the expensive preparations for his marriage to a daughter of the Chou family. On a visit one day Kao Ch'i was asked to provide a poem colophon to a painting of geese in the reeds which hung in the Chous' parlor. His poem read:

> The west wind tears at the blossoming water reeds.
> The good birds come flying past; a wing feather falls.
> The sandy beach is broad, and the water cold; no fish is to
>   be seen.
> I am covered with the frosty dew, so long have I been stand-
>   ing here waiting.

"Old Mr. Chou," writes Mote, "laughed when the poem was taken to him, for while it reads very well as a description of a fall scene at a river's edge with the wild geese flying, it is full of obvious allusions to Kao's own situation vis-à-vis his proposed marriage. In the standard symbolism, geese are the symbol of the marriage go-between, falling feathers are messages sent, the cold is the Kao family's declining fortunes, the fish is the bride who has not yet been seen, and the long waiting can be taken as a reference to Kao's own impatience with the delays forced upon him by circumstances."—In other words, the poem is an elaborate message in code from one educated man to another.

Scholar-officials were subject to a life of movement, and no one could travel very far without lighting on a place celebrated in the verse or prose of an earlier visitor. It might be a hilltop temple or a lakeside pavilion, a mountain pass or an ancient battlefield, a city gate or a particularly awesome cliff. A literary map of China would show a thick cluster of such famous sites in the lush vicinity of Soochow. When Kao Ch'i arrived at Maple Bridge on his way to the capital at Nanking he engaged in the common poetic practice of "variations on a theme." The T'ang poet Chang Chi had written a famous quatrain,

> Moonset, rooks caw, frost fills the sky,
> Maples and fishing lights, and sorrow before my bed.
> From Cold Mountain Temple, outside Soochow's walls,
> The sound of the midnight bell reaches the wanderer's
> boat.

Kao Ch'i, as Mote's following translation shows, "borrows half the phrases in Chang Chi's poem and turns them to his own uses":

> The ravens call through the frosty moonlight; the night is
> silent and lonely.
> I turn and look back at the city, left not yet far behind.
> This then is the night when homesick thoughts begin—
> The distant bell, the solitary boat, passing the night near
> Maple Bridge.

The typical early exemplar of the verse-form we call "lyric" (*tz'u*) was the plaint of the deserted courtesan. The great Sung masters had broadened the thematic scope of the lyric, and in Ch'ing times, late in the tradition, we find a wide variety of topics and moods. Two frequently-encountered kinds of lyric, contrasting and perhaps complementary in effect, are the idyll and the lament. Wang Fu-chih's poem "White Lotus" (p. 136 below) is an example of the idyll in its attempt to catch and hold a fleeting perception of beauty, perhaps to help the poet keep his sanity in a toppling world. Two hundred years later, Chiang Ch'un-lin looks at the stars and is reminded of the cold glitter of swordpoints in the endless nineteenth-century wars.

Throughout the Ming and Ch'ing periods, but especially in the sixteenth and seventeenth centuries, the drama offered poets unlimited scope for commentary on the human scene. In the "Southern" drama, the preferred form in Ming times, the strict conventions of the Yüan *tsa-chü* were relaxed or at least broadened. The *tsa-chü* was quite short, four acts with a prologue, each act consisting of a "song-set," a dozen or so arias (*ch'ü*) given to one singer only, the remaining players contributing only dialogue. Southern drama placed no limitation on singing parts, and thus each character in the play had at least the potential for full development. Length was vastly expanded, commonly to thirty or forty scenes upwards. The result was plays which resembled novels in their complexity of action and minuteness of detail: but novels filled with poetry, for their authors included the leading poets of their day, T'ang Hsien-tsu for example, and a particular scene might consist of song after song with very little dialogue. Great length offered scope for the unhurried exploration of every poetic nuance of a situation. Thus the entire scene "The Portrait," from *Peony Pavilion* (p. 106 below), is devoted to a young girl's reflections on the transience of her own beauty, and to philosophic contrast of her human frailty with the illusory permanence of the self-portrait she creates.

The predominant concerns of Ming drama are those which still exercise the "Peking Opera" of today: fidelity in family life and loyalty in service to the emperor. But against the stern Confucian ethic there may spring the tension of a more humane, more liberal morality, manifested in *Peony Pavilion* by the conflict between Li-niang's passion and her father's concern for her chastity. It is true that T'ang Hsien-tsu resolves this "triumph of heart over head," as we describe it in our introductory note to the extract below, respectably enough by resurrecting the girl and marrying her to her lover; but the fact remains that he has vindicated Li-niang's freedom of choice without reference to her good father, the Prefect, and justified her illicit liaison with her dream-lover.

A kind of proto-feminism is indeed an interesting undercurrent of late-Ming and Ch'ing writing, especially in drama and fiction. The prologue to the *Red Chamber Dream* announces the author's specific purpose: to commemorate the *women* he has known; and it is commonly noted that of the truly admirable characters in the novel almost all are women, while the men are a sorry lot (so pronounced is this that one critic took the novel as a Ming loyalist allegory, the male characters representing the hated Manchus while the women in the novel stood for the oppressed Chinese!).

The total output of fiction in China, since the late-Ming critics and editors consolidated the existing corpus, has been staggering. We regret that space precludes the representation of works of major importance, like *Chin-P'ing-Mei* or the satirical masterpiece *The Scholars*, not to speak of the voluminous library of heroic and chivalric fiction to which the nineteenth-century novelists contributed so heavily. *The Scholars*, by Wu Ching-tzu (1701–1754), turned the efforts of a whole group of writers of the last decades of the Ch'ing towards political and social satire: novelists like Wu Wo-yao, Li Po-yüan and Liu O were true precursors of the "May Fourth" writers, even though the more obvious influences on these last were from the Western world.

"May Fourth" is the name given to a political movement of the year 1919. The "Literary Revolution" two years before had adopted "write as you speak" and "reject the constraints of classical forms" as its principal slogans. Out of the reemergence of intellectuals as a force on the national scene came a new literature of remarkable vitality for all its excesses of formlessness and sentimentalism. The short story was its first preferred form. Neither the classical-style anecdote nor the old "promptbook" served as model for this new genre: the conventions and techniques which ruled it were developed rather by de Maupassant, Gogol, and Maxim Gorki.

The stories by Lu Hsün and Mao Tun included in the present volume offer an interesting contrast. Both show the new determination to bring to light the suffering of the peasant, so often a mere bucolic decoration in the literature of the past. But while Mao Tun's method is relatively objective and documentary, in his predecessor Lu Hsün we find that common persona of the fiction of the time, the deracinated or alienated intellectual, the superfluous man, who in this case can make no response to the old woman's "simple" question ("Is there such a thing as a *soul?*").

This self-tortured figure appears again and again, confessional in Yü Ta-fu, lachrymose in Pa Chin. The surprising thing is how quickly the new literature itself gains confidence. By the middle thirties there has come into existence a substantial body of serious work, much of which shows a high degree of technical control. Major novelists have emerged, Mao Tun with *Midnight*, Pa Chin with *The Family*, Lao She with *Rickshaw Boy*. These three works between them cover a broad spectrum of the principal concerns of the writers of the time. *Midnight* is a panoramic documentary of Shanghai in the grip of the Depression, and at the same time a penetrating study of its chief protagonist, the industrialist Wu Sun-fu. Agitators among the textile workers, bandits in the home village, gilded idlers of the younger generation, cutthroat competitors on the stock exchange, industrial spies and idealistic students, corrupt politicians and rivals in love; all surround the towering central figure of Wu Sun-fu, who is treated with remarkable compassion through to his final despairing cry, "Whom have I wronged, and how?"

Rickshaw Boy is excellent, but less complex, the story of the uphill struggle for survival of a strapping country lad who comes to Peking to "sell his strength." Pa Chin's *The Family* has been much the most influential of all the novels of its time. There is something formulaic, or mechanical, in its presentation of the varying responses of three brothers to the tyranny of parental domination in the old "big family system," and the Western reader is likely to find Pa Chin excessively sentimental. But there are scenes of real power, such as that of the death in childbirth (hastened by the enforced observance of old superstitious practices) of the wife of the eldest brother, Chüeh-hsin. Each of these three novels is reasonably available in English translation, and partly for this reason none is represented in this anthology.

In the hands of the lyric poets the "language of common speech" (or something quite close) has proved to be an instrument of great flexibility and forcefulness. As random instances of the new freedom we may cite Hsü Chih-mo's use of the tone-patterns of modern speech for imitative effect in a line like

> <u>*Pan-ts'an*</u>(*-ti*) <u>*hung-yeh*</u> *p'*<u>*iāo-yao*</u> <u>*tao*</u> *ti*
> (Half-faded red leaves sway down to the ground)

—the swaying, sliding motion of the leaves exactly caught by the cadence of the tones, with a device unavailable to the classical poet who had to follow prosodic rules based on general principles of euphony. Again, Pien Chih-lin's image of Peking on the eve of the Japanese War, city of Peking: flying kites on a dust-heap

is a line whose lexical content *could* be perfectly traditional, but whose striking juxtaposition has an unmistakably modern ring. (These examples are from poems not included in the selection below.)

There is some slavish imitation of Western models, to be sure. The European literary movements of a century past ripple across the Chinese pond at ever swifter intervals: from the English Romantics to the French Imagists takes a mere decade, and thereafter "isms" become "wasms" in a matter of months. But all the time there is going forward a reevaluation of the native heritage, and new ways are constantly found to incorporate into the new literary forms the modes of perception characteristic of China's unique culture.

Least successful are the dramatists. With the exception of a few short sketches, the classical drama of China was a musical art, or more precisely a fusion in a dramatic situation of music, poetry and dance. The "spoken drama" inspired by recent Western practice has had practitioners of outstanding talent, like Ts'ao Yü, but it has never won the hearts of large audiences.

The tragic disruption of the developing modern literature was simply one byproduct of the great national upheavals: the Japanese War, the Civil War, the establishment of the People's Republic. Some of the most gifted Chinese writers of today have no contact with their homeland. In Taiwan an unacceptable reality and a future difficult to envisage becloud literary creation with doubt and despair. And by a monstrous paradox, a mainland regime which has shown a more profound concern for literature even than Chinese governments of the past has succeeded at this time of writing in damming the flow of creation to the merest trickle.

In 1942, in their wartime base of Yenan in the arid northwest, the Chinese Communist leaders laid before their "literary and art workers" directives for the initiation of a new culture which would match, serve, and honor the new society a-building. Over three decades there have been many modifications in the directives, the sharpest during the years of the Revolution for a Proletarian Culture which began in 1965; but the basic requirements are unchanged. They begin from the definition of cultural activities, including literary creation, as a weapon in the class struggle and a tool in the construction of socialism. Reaffirm the rejection of the classical forms of the past (Mao Tse-tung apologized for the traditional form of his own poems, "written for his own amusement," and discouraged imitators); but reject also the bourgeois models of the May Fourth writers. Write for the worker-peasant-soldier masses and adopt their viewpoint; expose the past, celebrate the present, glorify the future; and be guided above all and always by the thought of Mao Tse-tung.

The Chinese term which would translate as "manipulate" literally reads as "grasp-and-release" (*ts'ao-tsung*). It exactly describes the situation of the writer, with all intellectuals, on the mainland today. From the tight grasp of governmental directives and control of literary associations and organs of publication the writer will from time to time be released to some degree, encouraged to diversify, to experiment, to criticize; but then inexorably the grasp will tighten again. The classic example of the process was the swift succession of the "Anti-Rightist" and other rectification movements to the "Hundred Flowers" interlude of 1956–57.

Under these conditions the craft of letters has been kept alive by men and women whose tenacious devotion to literature calls for our deep respect. To publish at all has meant denunciation, almost inevitable however long-delayed: virtually every major writer has been criticized, denounced, and silenced, certainly not physically, but by the sheer force of officially-engineered mass disapproval. Yet Ting Ling, Chao Shu-li, Chou Li-po, and others have interpreted the new society (in the villages especially) in novels and stories that offer some truthful insights beneath much glamorizing. Poets have brought back ballad and folk rhythms into the Chinese lyric; dramatists, almost the only writers currently productive, have turned aside from the never popular "spoken drama" to attempt the difficult task of bringing operatic modes to bear on contemporary themes.

The literature of China has been one of the most glorious achievements of the imagination of man. In its further development it will have to surmount the appalling obstacles raised by modern history and maintained by the irresistible demand for world power status. But it is impossible to visualize a society that is China without the poet's voice; and the voice will sing again.

—CYRIL BIRCH

Yüan Dynasty

1280-1367

Songs of the Yüan Dynasty

In the centuries preceding the Mongol conquest the preferred forms for Chinese verse were the metrically regular shih and the lyric (tz'u), whose lines were of irregular but prescribed length. The Yüan poets took with enthusiasm to a new form, the song (ch'ü), which offered a much wider and more exaggerated range of metrical patterns. These patterns, arising from the new music popular in the North, accommodated the colloquial language whose vocabulary and syntax were developing ever further away from the traditional literary diction. Tonal distinctions had altered, old rhymes no longer worked. The new songs developed conventions of their own, but the keynote was flexibility and hospitality to the lively new speech-patterns (vividly illustrated in the fourth poem of "Defy Old Age," below).

The songs in our selection are san-ch'ü, that is to say independent pieces rather than songs written for incorporation into plays. Most are separate units or hsiao-ling, though from the great poet-dramatist Kuan Han-ch'ing (ca. 1220–ca. 1300) we have examples of song-sets (t'ao-shu), clusters of songs within a particular musical mode which seem to be a sort of halfway stage between the unitary poem and the verse drama.

The folk origins of ch'ü are strongly evoked by our first two examples. The skillful use of prosodic convention is clearly apparent in Kuan Han-ch'ing's "Bedroom Scene" poems and in the much admired "Autumn Thoughts" of the equally celebrated poet-playwright Ma Chih-yüan. Chou Wen-chih's "Chattering Song" illustrates the fascination which onomatopoetic effects exercised on the writers of songs.

3

Teng Yü-pin's "Taoist Songs" are not the only ones in our selection to develop the popular theme of vanitas.

All the poets represented here were active in or about the year 1300.

●

Two Anonymous Songs

1. Tune: "Magpie on the Branch"

[*Ch'üeh t'a chih*]

> Sweetly the deft birds' voices blend,
> Lightly the white moths flutter,
> Busily bees fly through the flowers,
> Chattering, the swallows search for nests.
> Frolicking we seek the choicest herbs,[1]
> And there is laughter in lanes outside the town.

2. Tune: "Breaking Off the Cassia"

[*Che kuei ling*]

SEEKING A MATE

> Pretty maid in the spring wind,
> Lithe and graceful,
> A mere twist of waist,
> Countless charms,
> What one dreams of,
> Delightful face.
> I have poured out my heart to you:
> When you turn your back, don't change your mind,
> Pity me in my sufferings of love
> And from your gay life, steal a moment
> To comfort me a little.

---

[1] The prettiest girls.

Kuan Han-ch'ing

Tune: "Reining in to Listen"

[*Chu ma t'ing*]

> Many thoughts, much yearning
> Have weakened my body, haggard and thin,
> In idle sadness, idle gloom
> I tie the love knot on my willow belt.
> So gaunt, my red silken shirt is too large,
> Shy—afraid the girl next door will ask questions.
> If you say it's the dolor of spring,
> It's much worse this year than ever before.

TRANSLATED BY WAYNE SCHLEPP

Tune: "Half One Thing, Half the Other"

[*Yi-pan-erh*]

BEDROOM SCENE

I

> Cloudy at the topknot, misty at the temples, high piled,
>   deeper than raven. . . .
> Lotus feet just glimpsed rustle the red gauze.
> She's not like the common flowers outside the wall.
> To hell with you, pretty torment:
> Half the time you're teasing me, the other half having me on.

II

Outside the blue gauze window it's quiet, no one near:
She kneels at the bedside, eager to be kissed.
"How can you be so heartless, to turn your face from me?
Even if I did pretend to scold you
Half of me was willing though the other half said no."

III

The lamp on the silver stand is out, the wisp of smoke fades:
She's gone through the silk curtain alone, tears flood her
　　eyes.
"If you make me sleep by myself my love will soon grow
　　weary,
The single quilt's so thin.
Half the bed is warm and friendly, the other half is cold."

IV

"Little torment with so much love in you,
You're wearing me to death with all your tricks.
You took me in just now with those things you said."
How to understand her?
Half of her is the simple truth, the other half is lies.

Song Set: Defy Old Age

1. Tune: "One Sprig of Blossom"

[*Yi-chih hua*]

> I plucked from the wall so many flowers,
> Snapped from the wayside willow so many shoots:
> Plucked the flowers with the tenderest crimson buds,
> Snapped from the willow the softest green shoots.
> Man of pleasure, man of fashion,
> I'm proud that I plucked the flowers and snapped the wil-
>   low so deftly,
> Sad only that the flowers fade and the willow wilts.
> Half a lifetime now, snapping the willows, plucking the
>   flowers:
> I'll sleep out the ages on flowers beneath the willows.

2. Tune: "Seventh Liangchou Air"

[*Liang-chou ti-ch'i*]

> I'm the wide world's paragon of all gay lads,
> Not a rake on earth but learned his tricks from me.
> I want my red cheeks never to fade, always to be as I am,
> To linger out time among the flowers,
> In wine forget my cares,
> Sample the teas, shuffle the sticks,
> Play flog-the-horse and hook-in-the-palm.
> I know all the tunes, can play any music you please:
> Why fret my heart with useless cares?
> My playmates are the girls of the silver lute, who strum sil-
>   ver lutes on the silver terrace and smiling lean on silver
>   screens,

Houris of jade, jade hand in mine, jade shoulder to mine, as
　　they climb with me the jade stair,
Hair pinned with gold, who sing "Cloth of Gold," lift the
　　golden jar and fill to the brim the golden bowls.
You say I'm old now.
Enough of that.
There's no more debonair pacesetter of the wind and moon-
　　light:
Always look my best,
Keep my wits about me.
I command the blossoming camp, the brocaded warriors:
I've roved all the country and rambled all over the town.

3. Tune: "Third Coda"

[*San sha*]

Youngsters, you're fresh from the reed banks and sandy bur-
　　rows,
Baby rabbits, lambkins eager for your first hunt!
I've known all the traps and the nets, an old blue-feathered
　　cock pheasant,
A veteran wary of the trampling battle-horses.
Bows sprung in the snares have wounded me, stray arrows,
　　tin lances,
I was never the man to fall behind.
Don't say that there's no more fun in the middle years:
Am I to do nothing at all for the rest of my life?

4. Tune: "Yellow Bell Finale"

[*Huang chung wei*]

I'm a won't-soften-when-you-steam-me never-ready-when-
　　you-boil-me pounding-won't-flatten-me frying-won't-
　　cook-me dingdong ringing copper pea.
Youngsters, who was it taught you to drill

Those hoes-won't-slice-them hatchets-won't-crack-them-
won't-be-wrenched-open won't-be-worked-loose mad-
dening boxes within boxes inside the brocade box?
I play with the moon on the Liang Terrace,
Drink the wine of the East Capital,
Fancier of Loyang flowers,
Plucker of willows on the Chang Terrace.
I, too, can play chess like you, play football, beat for the
hunters, mime on the stage, sing and dance, blow and
strum, chant verses, play backgammon. . . .
You have made me toothless, wrymouthed,
Lamed my legs, cracked my knuckles,
Heaven's gifts to me are all these wretched ills,
And still I'm the one man who doesn't give up.

5. Tune: "Coda"

[*Wei-sheng*]

Till the King of the Dead in person sends me his summons,
And the devils are here to carry me off,
And my airy spirits return to the ground,
And my earthy spirits are lost in the dark,
Never till then, O Heaven!
Shall I give up running to the streets of mist and flowers.

Song Set: Get Out While You Can

1. Tune: "Stately Measure"

[*Ch'iao p'ai-erh*]

> Measure the world's ambitions, count their cost:
> The best life is to do as you please.
> Consider how fortunes veer, now up, now down,
> How good luck covers ill
> And ill luck darkens good.

2. Tune: "Sailing at Night"

[*Yeh hsing ch'uan*]

> Rich and noble, how long are we rich and noble?
> The sun declines from noon, the moon at the full is eclipsed.
> Earth dips in the southeast,
> Heaven is too high in the northwest:
> Even for Heaven and Earth there is no perfection.

everything changing into its opposite

3. Tune: "Felicity of Hsüan-ho"

[*Ch'ing Hsüan-ho*]

> Rack your brains till sunrise, run all day till dusk,
> You have all that matters when you're clothed and fed.
> The duck's short life and the crane's long can never be
>   made equal.
> Say no more of it:
> Which of us is right, which of us wrong?

11

4. Tune: "Brocade Flowers"

[*Chin-shang hua*]

> Unknit those fretful brows:
> When anger's vain, be reconciled.
> This day's countenance
> Will grow old like yesterday's,
> The past is gone, the present's here,
> Who can know all,
> Clever man, silly man,
> Poor man or rich man?

5. Tune: "Tiny One"

[*Yao p'ien*]

> At the last this one self
> Will not escape that one day.
> Each morning put to use
> You're the richer by one morning.
> A hundred years at most,
> Few live to seventy.
> Swiftly, swiftly, the passing years:
> The quick flood of the river rushes by.

6. Tune: "Clear River Prelude"

[*Ch'ing chiang yin*]

> Fallen blossoms fill the yard, spring is leaving again:
> When the last flower is gone, what remedy?
> In the dust of wheels, between horses' hooves,
> In the ants' nest, in the beehive,
> Find out a safe spot, a place to sit still.

7. Tune: "Green Jade Flute"

[*Pi yü hsiao*]

Crow and hare jostle each other,[1]
Sun and moon race east and west:
Man's life is parting,
Old friends with white heads are few.
The tireless months and years hurry,
Time like a colt gallops past the gap in the wall.
No more foolishness,
Be done with strife for fame and gain.
If you happen to have the price of a few cups
The best you can do is get drunk among the flowers.

---

[1] "Crow and hare": the crow in the sun, the hare on the moon.

8. Tune: "Finger Rest Coda"

[*Hsieh chih sha*]

In spite of all your vain cares,
Vain troubles,
Vain ties,
Vain appetites,
Vain disappointments,
Vain distractions,
The gold cock springs the trigger of disaster.
Find comfort while you can, leave the wrong road,
Reflect while pomp lasts that all music has an end,
Get out of the busy stream while you're young, look for a
way to get home.
Pick the wild herbs,
Wash off praise and blame,
Know that it's all equal.
Ch'ao and Yu, diligent ministers—
Was it they knew best, or these?
By chrysanthemums and pines, T'ao Ch'ien of Chin;
Fugitive on the river and the lakes, Fan Li of Yueh.

TRANSLATED BY A. C. GRAHAM

Hu Chih-yü

Tune: "Joy of Spring"

[*Hsi ch'un lai*]

THOUGHTS OF LOVE

Leisurely flowers brew honey for the bees,
Fine rain mixes mud for the swallows:
From my spring sleep by the green window I wake slowly.
Who rouses me?
Outside my window early the orioles sing.

Ma Chih-yüan

Tune: "Plum Blossoms in the Breeze"

[*Lo mei feng*]

I

Clouds encircle the moon
Breezes toy with the eave bells;
They make my sadness deeper,
But when I trimmed the lamp to write down the thoughts
    of my heart
My deep sighing blew it out.

II

EVENING BELLS AT A MISTY TEMPLE

Thin wintry smoke,
The old temple is tranquil,
Near dusk, all the worshipers have gone.
On the west wind three or four times the evening bell
    sounds:
How can the old monk practice *dhyana*?

TRANSLATED BY WAYNE SCHLEPP

Tune: "Sand and Sky"

[*T'ien ching sha*]

AUTUMN THOUGHTS

Dry vine, old tree, crows at dusk,
Low bridge, stream running, cottages,
Ancient road, west wind, lean nag,
The sun westering
And one with breaking heart at the sky's edge.

TRANSLATED BY CYRIL BIRCH

Chang Yang-hao

Tune: "Sheep on the Hillside"

[*Shan-p'o yang*]

T'UNG PASS

Peaks as if massed,
Waves that look angry,
Along the mountains and the river lies the road to T'ung
    Pass.
I look to the West Capital
My thoughts unsettled.
Here, where the Ch'in and Han armies passed, I lament
The ten thousand palaces, all turned to dust.
Kingdoms rise,
The people suffer;
Kingdoms fall,
The people suffer.

Teng Yü-pin

Tune: "Chattering Song"

[*Tao-tao ling*]

I

An empty skin sack filled with ambition,
A dried skull heaped with blame;
For daughters and sons I've schemed all I can
And used up all my strength for the family's fortune.
Do you understand this?
Do you see it at all?
Who really knows how to be an immortal?

II

Deep among white clouds in green mountains
A thatched and humble dwelling with neither winter nor
   summer;
In leisure I can talk with simple folk,
When tired, sleep under the gourd-vine trellis;
Do you understand this?
Do you see it at all?
It's better than bearing fear in a world of strife.

Hsü Tsai-ssu

Tune: "Breaking Off the Cassia"

[*Che kuei ling*]

THOUGHTS OF LOVE

All my life I knew not love.
Now that I know it
I am tormented by it.
Like floating clouds, my body,
My heart, like fluttering willow-down,
My soul like wafted gossamer.
Here, useless, a wisp of lingering fragrance;
Where is the longed-for noble wanderer?
Lovesickness comes. . . .
Just when *does* it come?
When the lamp is half-dim
When the moon is half-dark.

Tu Tsun-li

Tune: "Tipsy Sky"

[*Tsui-chung t'ien*]

TO A PRETTY GIRL WITH A MOLE ON HER CHEEK[1]

It must be Kuei-fei before me!
How did you escape your fate at Ma Wei?
It was the time you held the inkstone for Ming Huang—
Your beautiful face so bewitching—
When that hateful, heartless Li Po,
Drunk, snatched up the brush,
Spattered some "soot of pine"
    And blemished with one small spot your peachlike
    cheek.

---

[1] The allusion here is to the most popular of all imperial romances, the passion of the T'ang Emperor Hsüan-tsung (Ming Huang) for Yang Kuei-fei which led to her tragic self-strangulation on his unwilling command at Ma Wei. Compare Po Chü-yi's "A Song of Unending Sorrow," *Anthology of Chinese Literature, Vol. 1,* p. 266.

Chou Wen-chih

Tune: "Chattering Song"

[Tao-tao ling]

AUTUMN SADNESS

Ting-tang, ting-tang, eave bells' rattling-brattling noise,
Kree-kirr, kree-kirr, crickets' chirping-chirring cry,
Dripping, dripping, fine rain falling-flowing murmurs,
Rustling, rustling, *wu-t'ung* leaves lisping-whispering fall;
I'll never get to sleep!
Never get to sleep!
All alone, lying on the solitary pillow in silence.

Ch'iao Chi

Tune: "Water Sprite"

[*Shui hsien-tzu*]

A WATERFALL REVISITED

The loom of the sky has stopped working, the moon shuttle
    rests;
The stone cliff hovers, the silklike snow is cold,
Threads of ice carrying rain hang from the sky:
For thousands of years it has never dried up.
The dew is cold and I quail in my thin clothes.
It is like a white rainbow drinking at a stream,
Or a jade dragon descending the mountain,
Or snow by the river bank flying under a clear sky.

Chang K'o-chiu

Tune: "Red-broidered Slippers"

[Hung hsiu hsieh]

THE WATERFALL TEMPLE AT T'IEN-T'AI

At their very tops the peaks gather like swords of snow,
On the sheer cliff the stream hangs like a curtain of ice.
In the trees monkeys play with the tips of clouds.
Among the blood flowers the cuckoo calls,[1]
From dark caves the wind god howls. . . .
Compared to men's hearts, mountains hold no perils.

TRANSLATED BY WAYNE SCHLEPP

---

[1] The azalea is said to be stained red by the hawk-cuckoo which sings until it spits blood.

Ming Dynasty

1368-1644

Ghosts and Other Marvels

There is a tradition of tales of wonders dating back to the earliest times in China. Even the late tales here represented still employ the classical style of prose, the literary language: the swiftly developing genres of fiction and drama in colloquial language had as it were taken over themes of heroic biography or romantic love, and the classical-style short story "deteriorated" into what must be some of the best ghost stories ever set on paper.

Paradoxically, the earliest of the stories in our selection uses the most "modern" form of language. "The Jade Kuan-yin" is one of the oldest of "promptbook" stories, written in colloquial style on the basis of the work of the marketplace storytellers. It comes down to us thanks to its inclusion in "Penetrating Tales to Startle the World" (Ching shih t'ung yen), one of three collections by the great editor Feng Meng-lung (1574–?1645). In fact, however, the story had probably been changed very little since its original commitment to writing, which may have been as early as the thirteenth century. The story is prefaced in the original by eleven poems on the theme of the passage of spring. It was a convention of the promptbook to open with a prologue of some kind, in this case setting the scene for the prince's late-spring outing. It has been pointed out that such poems formed an important lyrical complement to the harsh realism of the events of the story (the ghosts themselves are appallingly "realistic" in their relentless pursuit of living companions). The verses may indeed have had a symbolic effect, the fading of spring presaging this tale of life's own transience. The long sequence makes a tiresome beginning, however, and is quite understandably omitted by the present translator.

Many early tales, and some later ones, too, are quite inconsequentially marvelous, or marvelously inconsequential. But as the genre advanced stylistically it developed also increasing scope for the didactic. Ch'ü Yu's story "A Record of the Land of the Blessed" is from his collection entitled New Tales by the Trimmed Lamp (Chien teng hsin hua). *Ch'ü Yu lived from about 1341 to 1427, Ma Chung-hsi from 1446 to 1512. Ma's "The Wolf of Chung-shan" is the prose version of a fable used by his contemporary, the dramatist K'ang Hai, as the material for a poetic play in the* tsa-chü *style. The story goes that K'ang Hai had risked his career to save the life of a political associate. This man later, when K'ang was dismissed from office, refused to raise a finger to help him, and the play was K'ang's protest against such ingratitude. Yet another version of the fable is in the form of a short sketch* (yüan-pen) *by K'ang's friend Wang Chiu-ssu.*

The Jade Kuan-yin

[Nien yü Kuan-yin]

I

In the Shao-hsing period (1131–1162) there lived in the capital a certain Prince of Hsien-an, a native of Yenanfu, Yenchou province. One day becoming conscious of the passing of spring he took his family out to enjoy the delights of the season. That afternoon, as he passed by the Carriage Bridge inside the Ch'ien-t'ang Gate on his way home, he heard some one in a picture mounter's shop say to his daughter, "Come, my child, and look at the Prince!" The Prince saw the girl and said to one of his orderlies: "I have been wanting to engage a girl like the one there. Now see that the girl is brought to the palace tomorrow." The orderly obeyed and set out to find the girl.

What sort of person was it that the Prince saw?

> Endless clouds of dust follow the traffic
> But sooner or later the bonds of love must break.

Under the Carriage Bridge the orderly saw a house with a sign on which was written: "The House of Ch'ü, Mounters of Painting and Calligraphy." Inside the shop there was an old man with his daughter. And what was his daughter like? Listen:

> Her hair was fashioned in a "cicada's wing."
> Her eyebrows like a mist over a mountain.
> Her lips were like a red cherry,
> Her white teeth like two rows of jade chips.
> Her lily feet were curved like tiny bows,
> Her voice was as clear as the oriole's.

This was the girl who had come to look at the prince.

The orderly went to a teahouse opposite and when the old woman in charge brought the tea he said to her, "Please go to the shop yonder

29

and tell Master Ch'ü that I would like to speak to him." She went and soon returned with the craftsman. "What do you have to command, Captain?" the latter asked after the two had exchanged greetings. "Nothing in particular," the orderly answered. "I just want to have a chat with you. Is the girl who came out to watch the Prince pass by your daughter?" "That is right," answered the craftsman. "There are only three of us in the family." "What is the age of your daughter?" the orderly asked. "Eighteen," the craftsman answered. "May I ask whether you intend her to marry soon or to enter service?" asked the orderly. "We are poor," the craftsman answered, "and unable to provide a dowry. We shall have to enter her into service." "What can the young lady do?" the orderly asked, and the father answered that she was a clever hand at embroidering.

"Just a while back the Prince saw from his sedan chair the embroidered vest that your daughter was wearing. It happens that we need an embroideress in the palace. Why don't you, venerable one, offer your daughter to the Prince?"

The craftsman went home and discussed the matter with his wife. The next day he had a petition drawn up and sent his daughter to the Prince. The latter paid him and gave the daughter the name of Hsiu-hsiu.

One day the Emperor bestowed on the Prince an embroidered warrior robe. Hsiu-hsiu was so clever with her needles that she made an exact copy of it. The Prince was greatly pleased, and said, "Since the Exalted One has given me this fine robe, what cunning object can I present to him?" He went to the storehouse and picked out a fine piece of translucent muttonfat jade; then summoning the jade carvers attached to the palace he said to them: "What can this piece of jade be made into?" "It will make a fine set of wine cups," said one. "It would be too bad to use such an excellent bit of jade for wine cups," said the Prince. "It will make a fine *māhākāla*[1] since it is pointed at the top and round at the bottom," said another. "A *māhākāla* is only suitable for the Double Seventh festival," the Prince said. "It is of no use for ordinary days."

Now among the jade carvers there was a young man about twenty-five years old by the name of Ts'ui Ning. He was a native of Chienk'ang, Shengchou province, and had been in the service of the

---

[1] A doll, rounded and heavy at the base, which cannot be tipped over.

Prince for several years. He stepped forward and said, "May it please Your Highness, the jade can be best made into a Kuan-yin of the South Sea."

"That's exactly what I am thinking," said the Prince, and commanded Ts'ui Ning to proceed with the task.

In about two months' time the jade Kuan-yin was completed and presented to the Emperor. The Dragon Countenance was greatly pleased and Ts'ui Ning was rewarded handsomely.

The days went by and soon spring returned. Ts'ui Ning and a few of his friends were in a wineshop near the Ch'ient'ang Gate after a spring outing. After a few cups they suddenly heard a commotion in the street, and on looking out of the balcony window they saw a throng talking excitedly about a fire in the direction of the Well Pavilion Bridge. They hurried out to the street themselves and this was what they saw:

At first it was like a firefly, then it was like lamp flames.
Soon it was brighter than a thousand candles and stronger than ten thousand buckets could extinguish.
It was as if the Liu Ting gods had emptied the celestial furnaces and the Eight Mighty Ones had kindled the mountain-consuming fire.
Could it be that another King Yu had set off the beacon fires to make his consort laugh,
Or another Admiral Chou Yü had made a conflagration of the enemy fleet?

"It is not far from the palace," the craftsman cried and dashed off in the direction of the fire. When he arrived at the palace he found that it was lit up like day and quite deserted. Then as he walked along the verandah on the left side a woman came out from the inside and ran straight into him. It was none other than Hsiu-hsiu, the bondmaid. He stepped back and greeted her.

Now the Prince had one day promised Ts'ui Ning that he would give Hsiu-hsiu to him in marriage after she had served her time, and every one had remarked what a fine couple they would make. Ts'ui Ning was a bachelor and looked forward to the union; Hsiu-hsiu liked the young man and was filled with hopes.

And now on the day of the fire Hsiu-hsiu ran into Ts'ui Ning as she came out from the inside with gold and jewels tied in a kerchief, and she said to him, "Master Ts'ui, I have been slow in getting away. You will have to help me and take me to a place of safety."

Thereupon Ts'ui Ning and Hsiu-hsiu left the mansion and walked along the river till they came to the Limestone Bridge. "I can't go on any farther, Master Ts'ui," Hsiu-hsiu said. "My feet hurt." "It will take only a few more steps to reach my house over there," Ts'ui Ning said, pointing ahead. "Why don't you come in and rest a while?"

So they went to Ts'ui Ning's house and sat down. Then Hsiu-hsiu said, "I am hungry. Won't you go out and buy some refreshments for me, Master Ts'ui? I should like to have some wine to quiet me after the fright I have received."

Ts'ui Ning got the wine and after two or three cups the wine began to work on them as the couplet says—

> After three cups of Bamboo Leaves pass through the lips,
> Two peach blossoms begin to mount the cheeks.

To say nothing of another couplet—

> Spring is the best tonic for flowers,
> Wine the matchmaker for men and women.

"Do you remember," Hsiu-hsiu said presently, "the night on the Moon Terrace when the Prince promised me to you in marriage? It was a moonlight night and you were so grateful to the Prince. Do you remember?" "Indeed I remember it," Ts'ui Ning answered. "Then," Hsiu-hsiu said, "why should we go on waiting? Why shouldn't we become man and wife tonight? What do you think?" "But I don't dare," Ts'ui Ning said. "If you won't do as I say," Hsiu-hsiu threatened, "I shall shout for help and ruin you. I shall go to the Prince tomorrow and say that you forced me to come to your house!" "I am perfectly willing," Ts'ui Ning said, "but there is only one thing: we cannot continue to live in this city. We must take advantage of the present confusion and flee from here." "It is as you say, since you and I are going to be man and wife," Hsiu-hsiu said.

And so they became man and wife that night. After the fourth watch, they took what gold and silver and valuables they had and slipped out of the city, and they "ate when they were hungry and drank when they were athirst, and rested by night and traveled by day," as wayfarers do, until they came to Ch'üchou.

"Where do we go from here?" Hsiu-hsiu said to Ts'ui Ning. "Five main roads lead out from this town. I think we might go to Hsinchou, for I am a jade carver and have there several acquaintances among the trade who might be of use to me."

And so they went to Hsinchou. But after a few days Ts'ui Ning became uneasy. "This is not a very safe place," he said. "Here people come and go from all over the empire and some one we know might see us and tell the Prince, and the Prince is bound to send men to seize us. It is better that we leave Hsinchou and go elsewhere."

And so they set out again and headed for T'anchow, a far-off place. There they rented a house and put up a sign reading: "Master Ts'ui, Jade Carver from the Capital."

"It is over two thousand *li* from the capital," Ts'ui Ning said to Hsiu-hsiu. "We ought to be safe. Let us put our minds at ease and be husband and wife always."

There were some retired officials at T'anchow and they all patronized Ts'ui Ning, seeing that he was a carver from the capital. Ts'ui Ning was thus seldom without occupation.

Ts'ui Ning sent some one to the capital to make inquiries and found that a bondmaid was found missing after the fire, that a reward had been posted for her, but that the matter had been dropped after a few days when no trace of the bondmaid was found. They knew nothing about Ts'ui Ning, nor that he and Hsiu-hsiu were then living at T'anchow.

"Time passes like the flight of an arrow and the sun and moon course through the sky like shuttles." More than a year soon passed. One day in the morning just after Ts'ui Ning had opened his shop front, two men dressed in the black costumes of official runners entered the shop and said to Ts'ui Ning: "We are runners from the Hsiangt'an District. Our magistrate has heard of a Master Ts'ui, jade carver from the capital, and wishes to have some work done by him."

Thereupon Ts'ui Ning left his wife in charge of the shop and went to Hsiangt'an with the runners. He was taken to the magistrate and given some pieces of jade to take home to work. On his journey home a carrier passed him on the road. Ts'ui Ning did not note who the man was, but the man saw Ts'ui Ning. He stared at him for a moment and then turned around and followed him.

> What naughty children have cast the stone
> That scattered the Mandarin ducks apart?

II

> Along the bamboos the morning-glories climb
> Through the hedge the moonlight peeps.
> In the glass cups there is crude wine
> And in the jade dish salted beans.
> > Regret not
> > But be gay
> For laughter is life's best pay;
> Once you rode at the head of a hundred thousand men
> While no one remembers who you are today.

This song was written to the tune of "Partridges Across the Sky" by a certain General Liu of the Hsiungwu troops. After the battle of Shunch'ang he lived at Hsiangt'an in very modest circumstances, for he was a general who cared nothing about money. He used to go to the country wineshops to drink, but no one remembered him and few paid him any respect. And so he composed this poem to express how he felt.

Now this poem was seen by certain important personages in the capital and they all felt sorry for the general. Among these were the Prince of Yangho and the Prince of Hsien-an, Ts'ui Ning's erstwhile master, who both sent money and presents to General Liu. It was the messenger of the Prince of Hsien-an that Ts'ui Ning passed on the Hsiangt'an road. His name was Kuo Li, one of the Prince's bodyguards. He followed Ts'ui Ning to his house and surprised both Ts'ui Ning and Hsiu-hsiu, saying, "So you are here, Master Ts'ui! And Hsiu-hsiu here, too!"

Ts'ui Ning and his wife were frightened to death and implored Kuo Li not to betray them. "Why should I betray you?" Kuo Li said. "The Prince knows nothing about you two and it is not for me to meddle in other people's affairs." Then he partook of the feast that Ts'ui Ning set out for him, thanked his hosts, and went away.

After he had reported to the Prince he said, "Your Highness, I saw two persons at T'anchow that Your Highness would probably like to know about." "Who are they?" the Prince asked. "The bondmaid Hsiu-hsiu and Ts'ui Ning the jade carver," Kuo Li answered. "They invited me to a feast and begged me not to tell Your Highness about them."

Thereupon the Prince commanded the prefect of Lin-an to have

Ts'ui Ning and Hsiu-hsiu arrested. The prefect obeyed and sent an official note to the prefect of T'anchow. In due time Ts'ui Ning and Hsiu-hsiu were returned to the Prince. Thereupon, the Prince went into his great hall to confront the fugitives. Now when the Prince was in the wars against the barbarians he carried in his right hand a sword called Great Blacky and in his left hand a sword called Little Blacky and many were the barbarians who had perished under those swords. The swords were now hanging on the wall. At the sight of Ts'ui Ning and Hsiu-hsiu the Prince became very angry. With his left hand he took Little Blacky down from the wall and with his right he unsheathed it. His eyes were opened wide as when he slaughtered the barbarians, and he gritted his teeth so that the grinding sound they made echoed in the great hall.

Luckily for Ts'ui Ning and Hsiu-hsiu, the Princess was at that moment standing behind the screen. "Your Highness," she said from behind the screen, "you mustn't kill them! For we are now living under the shadow of the Emperor's carriage, not on the frontier. The two should be sent to the prefect's yamen and punished according to law." "They deserve death for escaping together," the Prince said, "but since you intercede for them, let Hsiu-hsiu be taken to the garden in the back and Ts'ui Ning sent to the prefect's yamen."

At the trial Ts'ui Ning confessed the true circumstances, and when the Prince found that he had not been the instigator of their escape, he did not insist on the extreme punishment. Ts'ui Ning was sentenced to exile at Chienk'ang-fu.

Ts'ui Ning and his guard had just gone out of the North Gate when they noticed a sedan chair following them. Then Ts'ui Ning heard the voice of Hsiu-hsiu calling to him, saying, "Master Ts'ui, wait a while for me!" He wondered what Hsiu-hsiu was up to but "like a bird that has had experience with the bow," he did not dare to get further involved and so went on without answering. But soon the sedan chair overtook him and out came Hsiu-hsiu, saying, "Master Ts'ui, what am I to do now that you are going to Chienk'ang?" "I don't know," Ts'ui Ning said. "Let me go with you," Hsiu-hsiu said. "The Prince had me given thirty strokes of the bamboo and dismissed from his service." "In that case, you can come along with me," Ts'ui Ning said.

They hired a boat and soon reached Chienk'ang. The guard returned to the capital. Now if the guard had been a telltale, Ts'ui Ning and Hsiu-hsiu would have been in for more trouble, but he was a sensible man and decided to mind his own business, especially since he had no connection with the Prince's palace. Moreover, Ts'ui Ning had been very generous to him, providing him with food and wine all along the way, and he was inclined to say nothing of what he had seen.

To return to Ts'ui Ning. He had now nothing to fear as he had been tried and sentenced. As before, he opened a jade turner's shop. Then said his wife to him, "We are now happy together, but my parents have suffered many anxieties on account of us. Let us send for them and have them live with us." To this Ts'ui Ning said, "Excellent," and immediately sent a messenger to the capital to get his parents-in-law, giving him their address. Arriving at the capital, the mesenger went to the street to which he had been directed and inquired of the neighbors for old Ch'ü and his wife. He located their house but found the door locked from the outside. From the neighbors he learned that they had been in great distress when their daughter was captured and that they had not been seen since.

In the meantime, as Ts'ui Ning was sitting home one day he heard someone say outside, "This is where Master Ts'ui lives." He went out to see who it was and who should it be but old Ch'ü and his wife! "It took us a long time to find you here," they said. After that the four of them lived together at Chienk'ang.

Now one day the Emperor was looking over his curios in one of the palace rooms. He took up the jade Kuan-yin that Ts'ui had made and noticed one of the bells broken off. "How can we have this repaired?" the Emperor asked. One of the attendants examined the Kuan-yin and noticed the words "Made by Ts'ui Ning" carved at the bottom. "It is easy," the attendant said. "It is only necessary to summon the man who made this Kuan-yin."

The Prince of Hsien-an was commanded to produce Ts'ui Ning, and the latter was accordingly summoned to the capital. He was presented to the Emperor and given the Kuan-yin to mend. He found a piece of jade of the exact color and texture of the Kuan-yin and did such a clever job of repairing that no one who did not know would have noticed that it had been broken. Ts'ui Ning was handsomely rewarded and commanded to live in the capital.

"Since I have nothing to fear should any one run into me," Ts'ui Ning said, "I shall rent a house by the side of the Clear Lake River and open up another jade shop."

Coincidences will occur. Only two or three days after Ts'ui Ning opened his shop who should come in but Kuo Li! "So you are here, Master Ts'ui," he said. "Congratulations, Master Ts'ui," he said. But when he saw Hsiu-hsiu behind the counter, his countenance changed and he hastily withdrew. "Call that man back," Hsiu-hsiu said to her husband. "I want to ask him a few questions." Well says the couplet:

> If one does nothing to cause the arching of eyebrows,
> He will have no one to spit in his face.

Ts'ui Ning ran after Kuo Li and soon caught up with him. "How strange, how strange!" Kuo Li was murmuring to himself. He went back to the shop with Ts'ui Ning and there Hsiu-hsiu said to him: "We have been good to you and invited you to drink wine with us, but you betrayed us to the Prince. We are now in the Emperor's favor and no longer afraid of what you might say." Kuo Li had nothing to say to this accusation; he made his apologies and went away.

He went back to the palace and said to the Prince: "I have seen a ghost!" "What are you talking about?" said the Prince. "Please, Your Highness, I have seen a ghost," Kuo Li said. The Prince asked, "What ghost?" Kuo Li said, "I was walking along the Clear Lake River and passed by Ts'ui Ning's shop. I went inside and there behind the counter I saw the bondmaid Hsiu-hsiu." The Prince said impatiently, "What nonsense! Hsiu-hsiu was beaten to death and is buried in the garden. You saw it happen yourself. How could you have seen her? Are you trying to make fun of me?" Kuo Li answered, "How dare I jest with Your Highness? I did indeed see her, and she spoke to me. If Your Highness does not believe it I am ready to sign a 'martial order.'"[2] The Prince said, "Sign a martial order then and produce Hsiu-hsiu if you can."

The luckless Kuo Li signed the order and gave it to the Prince. The latter ordered a sedan chair to go with Kuo Li, saying, "Go and get the girl! If she is really where you say she is I shall put her to death with my sword; if you cannot produce her, I shall put you to death with the same sword."

Kuo Li was a foolish and impetuous man; he should have known that it was no light matter to sign a martial order.

He and the two sedan bearers went directly to Ts'ui Ning's shop

---

[2] Failure to carry out such an order would mean death.

and there said to Hsiu-hsiu, "We have the Prince's order to take you to him." Hsiu-hsiu said, "I shall come with you as soon as I get myself ready." She went inside, washed and changed her clothes, came out and got into the sedan chair. Soon they arrived at the palace and Kuo Li went inside first and reported to the Prince that he had brought Hsiu-hsiu. The Prince said, "Bring her in." Kuo Li went out to the sedan chair and said, "Hsiu-hsiu, the Prince wants you to come in." Receiving no answer he lifted the curtain and thereupon he felt as if a bucket of cold water had been poured on him, and his mouth dropped open. For there was no Hsiu-hsiu to be found in the sedan chair! He asked the sedan bearers but they said that they had not stirred from the place. Kuo Li rushed into the palace, shouting and mouthing excitedly, and said to the Prince, "May it please Your Highness, she must be a ghost!" The Prince said, "I have no patience with your jokes!" Then to the attendant he said, "Seize this man. I have his order and shall put him to the sword."

Kuo Li was frightened and said, "I have told the truth as the sedan bearers will bear witness." The bearers were summoned and they said that they did see Hsiu-hsiu getting into the sedan chair but that she had then disappeared without a trace. Then Ts'ui Ning was summoned and he told the story over from beginning to end. The Prince said, "Let him go since he knows nothing about it." But he had Kuo Li given fifty strokes of the penal rod.

On his part Ts'ui Ning went home and confronted his parents-in-law with what he had just found out. The couple looked at one another and then walked out of the shop and *plop, plop* both jumped into the river one after the other. Ts'ui Ning summoned help but the bodies could not be found. The truth was that the old couple had committed suicide by drowning soon after they heard of their daughter's death and it was their ghosts that had been living with Ts'ui Ning.

After a fruitless search for the bodies, Ts'ui Ning went home and found Hsiu-hsiu sitting on the bed. Ts'ui Ning said, "Please, sister, spare my life!" Hsiu-hsiu said, "I died because of you, and my body was buried in the garden. I could not rest in peace because I wanted to take revenge on Kuo Li. Now that he has been punished and I am known for what I am, I can no longer stay here." After saying this she rose and laid her hands on Ts'ui Ning and then uttering a sharp cry she fell to the ground. When the neighbors arrived on the scene they found—

Her pulse had sunk until it was quite still,
And she herself well on the way to the Yellow Springs.

Ts'ui Ning, too, had been dragged away by her so that he could be her husband in the other world. Posterity summed up the incidents thus:

The Prince of Hsien-an could not suppress his fiery temper;
Kuo Li could not hold his evil tongue.
Hsiu-hsiu could not bear to leave her mate in life;
Ts'ui Ning could not shake off his wife in death.

TRANSLATED BY CHI-CHEN WANG

Ch'ü Yu

A Record of the Land of the Blessed

[San shan fu ti chih]

Yuan Tzu-shih was a native of Shantung. He was naturally slow-witted and a stranger to learning. The family was fairly well to do, deriving its income from its farm lands. In the same district was a gentleman named Miao who had been appointed to an office in Fukien. He lacked the money for traveling expenses and borrowed 200 ounces of silver from Tzu-shih. Since the two families lived in the same village and were on good terms, Tzu-shih did not ask for a promissory note, but simply let him have the sum he requested. Toward the end of the Chih-cheng period (1367) there was civil war in Shantung and Tzu-shih lost all his property to the rebels. At that time Ch'en Yu-ting was Governor of Fukien, which remained undisturbed by the war. So Tzu-shih took his family and went there by boat, intending to apply to Miao for help. On his arrival he found that Miao was indeed in Ch'en Yu-ting's service, holding an important administrative position, exercising great power, and living in style. Tzu-shih was delighted. However, after the hardships he had suffered and the long journey, his clothes were in tatters and his body emaciated, so that he did not venture to present himself for an interview directly. He rented a room in the city where he lodged his family, put his clothes in order, and chose a lucky day for his visit. He arrived just as Miao was leaving his gate, and bowed low before his carriage. At first Miao did not seem to recognize him, but when Tzu-shih told him his name and where he had come from Miao made surprised apologies and invited him into his house, where he treated him as an honored guest. After some time tea was served and Tzu-shih left. He returned on the morrow, when the entertainment was much more perfunctory. Miao was rather distant and inattentive, nor did he say anything about the money he owed.

Tzu-shih went back to his bleak room, where his wife scolded him angrily, "Here you have come a thousand miles to get help from this man and what do you do? You sell out for three cups of wine and don't say a word. What are we to do now?" Tzu-shih had no choice but to go again the next day.

Before he could open his mouth, Miao interposed, "I shall never forget the money you loaned me long ago. It's just that in this out of the way post my income is very small. But I would never think of being ungrateful to an old friend from afar. If you will give me back my note, I will pay you the full sum right now."

Tzu-shih was horrified. "We are fellow townsmen and have been friends since childhood. When you said you needed the money I gave it to you; there never was any note. How can you talk like this?"

Miao was unperturbed. "Surely there was a note, but I suppose you must have lost it in the civil war. I don't know whether you have it or not, but I will give you more time to try to locate it."

Tzu-shih went out mumbling assent and marveling at the deceit and ingratitude of the man. He was nonplussed and could see no way out of the impasse. Half a month later he paid Miao another visit and was received politely enough, but not a cent did he get. In this way he was put off for half a year.

In the market there was a little shop which Tzu-shih always passed on his way to Miao's residence, and where he was accustomed to stop and rest. The proprietor, Hsien-yüan, a pious man, became quite well acquainted with him during his frequent trips. As the winter passed and it was nearly New Year's time, Tzu-shih's plight became desperate, and weeping and bowing outside Miao's house he cried, "The New Year is about to begin, and my wife and children are starving. I have not a cent in my purse and no rice in my stores. I don't dare ask for the money I loaned you, but I do beg for a little help now when my need is desperate, as a kindness to an old friend. On my knees I ask you, have pity, have compassion." And he crawled forward on his knees.

Miao helped him to his feet. Counting the days on his fingers he said, "Ten days from now is New Year's Eve. You wait at home and I will send you two hundred pounds of rice and two ingots of silver from my salary for your New Year's expenses. I hope you will not take offense that it is not more." And he repeatedly instructed him not to go out, but to wait for it at home. Tzu-shih thanked him and went home to console his wife with Miao's promise.

When the appointed day came the whole household watched expectantly. Tzu-shih sat straight in his chair and had his youngest son keep watch at the gate. In a minute he came running in, "A man is coming with a load of rice!" They all went out to wait for him, but he went right past their house without turning his head. Tzu-shih thought the messenger did not know the house and ran after him to ask, but the man said, "His honor Chang is sending this rice to a guest at the inn." Tzu-shih returned in silence. In a little while his son came in to say that a man was coming with the money. They rushed out again, and again the man went past their house. Tzu-shih also went after him and was told that this was a gift for a retainer of Prefect Li's. Ashamed and disappointed, he kept asking the messengers that passed until evening, but there was never a sign from Miao. Next day was New Year's, and he had neither food nor livelihood. His wife and children looked at him and wept. Unable to contain his rage, Tzu-shih concealed a knife and sat waiting for the dawn. At cockcrow he went directly to Miao's gate, waiting for him to come out so that he might stab him.

Now just at that time, before it was light and while no one was abroad, old Hsien-yüan was sitting inside his shop door reading a sutra by candlelight. He saw Tzu-shih walk past, followed by an extraordinary mob of dozens of outlandish demons, holding knives and gouges. Their heads were split and their skeletons exposed, altogether a most evil-looking crew. In the time it takes to eat a meal, he saw Tzu-shih coming back, and now he was followed by a hundred or more men wearing golden caps and jade ornaments, carrying banners and flags. Their appearance was dignified and composed, and the whole gave the impression of peace and harmony. Hsien-yüan was unable to understand what had happened and thought Tzu-shih must have died. When he had finished reciting the sutra he went at once to his house to find out, and there was Tzu-shih, whole and unharmed. When they had sat down Hsien-yüan asked, "Where were you going this morning in such a hurry and why did you return so slowly?"

Tzu-shih did not venture to lie, but told about Miao's outrageous behavior. "I was at my wits' end, and this morning I put a dagger in my pocket and was on my way to kill him. When I got to his gate it suddenly occurred to me: although he has certainly done me an injury, of what are his wife and children guilty? What's more, his old mother is still alive. If I kill him, what will become of his family? Better that another should wrong me than that I should wrong another. So I gave up my plan and came home."

When Hsien-yüan heard this, he bowed to congratulate him. "You will have your reward; the spirits know what you did." Tzu-shih asked how he knew and the old man said, "When your heart was set on evil, baleful demons assembled, and when you decided on the good, beneficent spirits surrounded you. It is as certain as shadow follows form and echo sound; verily, neither in the privacy of one's room nor in the urgency of the act can evil go unpunished or good unrequited." He went on to tell what he had seen. He tried to console him and gave him enough money and rice to meet his immediate needs. But Tzu-shih remained depressed and unhappy. That night he threw himself into the well at the foot of San-shen Mountain.

The water suddenly parted. On both sides were smooth stone walls between which led a narrow path just wide enough for him to pass. Tzu-shih groped his way for several hundred paces, when the wall stopped and the path came to an end at a narrow opening. Once through that he found himself in another world, with its own sky and earth, sun and moon. Before him was a great palace with a sign that read "Land of the Blessed." Staring about him Tzu-shih entered. The large hall was deserted, nothing stirred in the palace. He hesitated, looking in all directions, but no one was to be seen anywhere. Then he heard the far-off sound of a bell. Overcome with hunger and fatigue he was unable to go farther, and lay down beside a stone dais. Suddenly a Taoist priest appeared, wearing a green-cloud robe with moon-jade ornaments, and called to him to rise and asked, "Does the Academician know the taste of travel?" Tzu-shih bowed and replied, "I have had altogether too much of the taste of travel, but how could you make such a mistake as to call me Academician?"

The Taoist said, "Don't you remember drafting the decree to the Tibetans in the Palace of Abundance?"

"I am an uneducated man from Shantung, a commoner, forty years old and illiterate. I have never in my life been in the capital; how could I have drafted any decree?"

"You have been so concerned about making a living that you have had no time to remember your past." And the priest took several dates and pears from his sleeve and gave them to him to eat, saying, "These are magic fruits. When you have eaten them you will know the past and the future."

As soon as Tzu-shih had eaten them his eyes were opened and he could remember when he was a Han-lin official and had drafted the decree to the Tibetans in the Palace of Abundance in the capital as though it were yesterday. He asked the priest, "What crime did I commit in a past life that I should be punished in this way?"

"It was no crime, but when you were an official you so prided yourself on your literary skill that you were unwilling to give a place to younger men. As a consequence in this life you were born to be stupid and illiterate. Because you were too proud of your rank and would not give lodging to a homeless wanderer, in this life you have been forced to drift about without any support."

Tzu-shih mentioned a high minister of the time and asked, "A prime minister who is insatiably avaricious and overtly accepts bribes —what will be his recompense in the other world?"

"In the underworld the king of the insatiable demons has ten furnaces to melt down his ill-gotten wealth. Today his good fortune is at its peak, but he will suffer the tortures of hell."

Tzu-shih asked further, "There is a certain governor who does not control his soldiers but lets them kill the people; what will be his recompense?"

"The king of the murderous demons has three hundred hellish soldiers with copper heads and iron foreheads who aid him in his atrocities. Today his life span, too, is running out, and he will suffer the slicing torture."

"There is a judge who sentences unjustly, a prefect who levies taxes and corvée inequitably, an inspector who never makes a report, a military advisor who never offers a plan—what will be their recompense?"

"These will all be fettered and bound to await punishment until their flesh rots and their bones decay—they are not worth mentioning."

Then Tzu-shih recounted the story of Miao's ingratitude. The priest said, "He is General Wang's treasurer, and is in no position to make free with his property." He went on to say, "Within three years there will be a revolution and a great disaster, much to be feared. You should choose a place to live, otherwise you will suffer like a fish in a pool when the water runs out." Tzu-shih asked where he could go to avoid the fighting. "Fu-ching would do, but Fu-ning is better." Then he said, "You have been here for a long time and your family is worried; you should go home now."

Tzu-shih protested that he did not know the way, and the priest showed him a path to follow. Tzu-shih bowed and left, and after he had gone about a mile he came out of a cave in the mountain. When he got home he found he had been gone half a month. In all haste he moved his family to Fu-ning, where he lived as a farmer. One day when he was wielding his hoe he struck something metallic, and on digging found four ingots of silver. After that his family was in more comfortable circumstances.

Later Chang usurped the throne and Prime Minister Ta was taken prisoner. As the revolting armies approached the city Governor Ch'en Yu-ting was captured, and few of his subordinates could preserve their heads. Miao was killed by General Wang, who confiscated all his property. When reckoned up, this occurred just three years after the priest had made his prediction.

Ma Chung-hsi

The Wolf of Chung-shan

[*Chung-shan lang*]

Chao Chien-tzu held a great hunting party on Chung-shan. The foresters led the way, falcons and dogs in their wake. There was no counting the swift birds and fierce beasts that fell before their arrows. There was a wolf in the road standing upright like a man and howling. Chien-tzu spat on his hands and mounted his chariot. He drew his great bow, pinching a Su-shen arrow, and let it fly. The arrow buried itself to the feathers; the wolf stopped howling and fled. Chien-tzu in anger drove his chariot in pursuit. The sound of the horses' feet sounded like thunder. The dust they raised veiled the sky, so that at a distance of ten paces neither man nor horse could be distinguished.

At the time there was a Mohist, Master Tung-kuo, on his way north to Chung-shan to seek employment. He was spurring a lame donkey and carrying a bagful of books. In the early morning he had lost his way, and he was startled to see the cloud of dust. The wolf ran up to him in all haste and raised its head to say, "Is it not your aim to help all creatures? Of old Mao Pao set free the turtle and later when in need was ferried across the river. The Marquis of Sui saved the serpent and so got the pearl. Surely turtles and snakes are no more intelligent than wolves. In my present extremity could you not let me quickly get into your bag, so that I may prolong my threatened life? Later on if I get out alive, I will be indebted to you for saving my life, and I will certainly do everything in my power to repay your kindness, no less than did the snake and the tortoise for their benefactors."

Master Tung-kuo said, "Hah! If I helped you in defiance of the powers that be and in opposition to the mighty, there is no guessing the disaster I would court; would I be looking for recompense? But the basic principle of Mohist teaching is universal love, so after all I should

46

try to preserve your life. If there are consequences, I shall certainly not avoid them." He took out his books, emptying the bag, and carefully put the wolf inside. He was anxious lest he drop on his head and concerned that he might fall on his tail. In three attempts he had not succeeded, and hesitated undecided while the pursuers drew nearer. The wolf pled with him, "Matters are urgent. Do you expect to save a person from fire or water by scraping and bowing? Or oppose bandits by ringing a bell? Hurry and think of a way!" And the wolf flexed his four legs for him to bind with a cord. He lowered his head to his tail, crooking his back until his spine pressed against his dewlap, curling and twisting like a hedgehog or an inchworm, coiling like a snake and holding his breath like a turtle, waiting for Master Tung-kuo to act. The master did as the wolf indicated, and thrust him into the bag. Then he closed the bag, and hoisting it to his shoulder, mounted the donkey and guided it to the side of the road to wait for the hunters to pass by.

In a moment Chien-tzu arrived, seeking the wolf. Furious at not finding it, he drew his sword and slashed off the end of the chariot pole and showed it to Master Tung-kuo. "This is what will happen to you if you fail to tell me the direction the wolf went!"

Master Tung-kuo fell to the ground and prostrated himself, crawled forward and spoke from his knees, "Stupid wretch that I am, I am seeking my fortune. Coming from afar, I have lost my way. How could I find the track of a wolf, to put your dogs and falcons on its trail? But I have heard it said that a sheep gets lost on a highway with many forks. A child can take care of a sheep, it is so docile, and still the sheep will get lost if left on a road with many forks. A wolf is hardly comparable to a sheep, and even a sheep has every chance to get lost on the turnings of these Chung-shan roads. Sticking close to the highway to look for a wolf is rather like climbing a tree to look for a fish, or waiting for a rabbit to knock his brains out by running against a stump. Hunting is the business of the foresters; why don't you ask them? How is a mere passer-by to blame? Now I may be stupid, but at least I know about wolves. They have a greedy, fierce disposition, ruthless as jackals. To help you destroy such a creature, I would peer into every corner to contribute my bit;—would I be willing not to tell you, if I knew?"

Chien-tzu in silence turned his chariot and drove off. Master Tung-kuo for his part urged his donkey quickly along the road. After some time, when the banners of the party faded from view and the sound of their chariots and horses could no longer be heard, the wolf calculated that Chien-tzu was far away and spoke up inside the bag.

"Master, don't forget me! Let me out of this bag, loosen my bonds, and draw the arrow from my leg, or I perish!"

Master Tung-kuo let the wolf out. The wolf growled and said, "When I was pursued by the hunters and they were hot on my trail, it was my fortune that you preserved my life. I am starving. If one who is starving does not get food, in the end he will die, too. Rather than die of hunger by the roadside and become the prey of beasts, I should prefer to have died at the hands of the hunters, when I would have become an offering to a noble house. Since you are a Mohist, prepared to be ground to powder if it would be of the slightest use to anyone, surely you will not grudge me your body to eat, thus completing the job of saving my life?" And he turned on Master Tung-kuo with smacking lips and stretched-out claws. The master hastily struck him with his fists, and alternately striking and retreating managed to get behind the donkey, and then continued to keep the donkey between them. The wolf was unable to get at him, the master using all his strength to keep away. When both were exhausted, they stopped to rest, the donkey still between them. The master said, "You are ungrateful, ungrateful!"

The wolf said, "I have no desire to be ungrateful to you. Heaven created your species to supply food for mine." Time passed as they argued, and the sun moved toward the west. The master thought to himself, "Dark is coming, and when the wolf pack arrives I will die for sure." So he tricked the wolf by saying, "It is a custom when in doubt to consult the local elders. Let's go look for the local elders and ask them. If they say it is all right to eat me, then you may; if not, then that's an end to it." The wolf was delighted and they set out together.

They went along for some time, but there was no one on the road. The wolf was terribly hungry, and when he saw an old dead tree trunk by the roadside he said to Master Tung-kuo, "You might ask this elder."

Master Tung-kuo said, "Plants have no understanding; what's the use of asking?"

"Just ask; it should have something to say."

There was nothing else for it, and saluting the old tree, Master

Tung-kuo recited the whole story. "That being the situation, should the wolf eat me?" he asked.

Inside the tree there was a rumbling sound and it addressed the master, "I am an apricot tree. Years ago when the gardener planted me I cost him only a single fruitstone. The following year I put out blossoms, and the next year I bore fruit. In three years I had grown to a handbreadth; in ten years I was to be measured by an embrace. That was twenty years ago. The gardener ate me, his wife ate me, even to their guests and their servants, they all ate me. What's more they sold some of my fruit in the market and so made a profit on me. My services to the gardener were very considerable. Now that I am old and unable to bloom and bear fruit, the gardener in anger has cut my branches and stripped my leaves. What's more, he is going to sell me to a carpenter for what he can get for me. Alas! Old and worthless as I am I cannot escape the executioner's axe. What have you done for the wolf that you expect to get off? Certainly he should eat you."

At the end of the speech the wolf turned with smacking lips and outstretched claws on the master, who cried, "The wolf is violating the agreement! We agreed to consult the local elders. So far we have met only an apricot tree; how does that justify him in pressing me?" And they continued to walk along together.

The wolf was getting increasingly desperate when he saw an old cow inside a broken fence standing exposed to the weather. He said, "You might ask this elder."

"Last time it was an ignorant plant that spoiled things with its irresponsible talk. Now this is only a beast; what's the point of asking it, too?"

"Just ask. If you don't, I will eat you."

There was nothing for it, and saluting the old cow he again recited the whole story and asked for a judgment. The cow wrinkled her brows and stared, licked her nose and opened her mouth. She addressed the master, "There is nothing wrong with what the old apricot tree said. When I was young and my horns had just begun to grow, I was strong and vigorous. A farmer traded a knife for me and put me to work in the southern field helping his oxen. As I grew to maturity the oxen became daily older and more worn out until I was doing everything. When the farmer was in a hurry to go some place, I would draw him in the farm wagon, choosing the shortest route to take him to his destination. When he wanted to plow I left the wagon and walked before him in the fields to open a way through the weeds and brambles. The farmer loved me as his right hand. He depended on me for his food and clothing, he was able to marry only because of me, he payed his taxes through my efforts, his granary was full because of me. I also assumed that in return I would be given a mat to cover me, like any horse or dog. In former times he had hardly enough to eat, now he harvests ten more bushels of wheat than he needs. Formerly he lived in poverty with no friends; today he complacently swaggers in the town hall. Then his wine cups were filled with nothing but dust, his parched lips never touched even an earthen pot filled with wine. Today he brews his own millet wine, sits behind his wine jars, and brags to his wife and concubine. In the past he wore coarse clothes and lived as a rustic. He was boorish and uneducated. Now he keeps company with the village literate, wears a straw hat, and a leather belt; his clothes are full cut: and every grain and every thread comes from my work. In spite of that he has taken advantage of my being old and weak to drive me out into the country, where the sharp wind lashes my eyes, as I stand solitary in the cold sun. I am so thin my bones stick out like hills, my old tears fall like rain. My spittle drops and I cannot stop it; my legs are bent, and I cannot raise them. My hair is all gone, my skin covered with sores that will not heal. The farmer's wife is a shrew. She is always telling him, 'No part of a cow's whole body need be wasted. The flesh can be dried, the hide can be cured, the bones and horns can be carved to make useful vessels.' Then she points to her eldest son, 'You have studied for a year to be a butcher, why don't you get busy with your knife and whetstone?' None of this promises well for me; I may be put to death at any time. Now I have been of real service to him, and yet he is heartless enough to do me an injury. What have you done for the wolf that you should hope to escape?"

As the cow finished speaking, the wolf again turned with smacking lips and outstretched claws on the master, who said, "Don't be in such a hurry!" In the distance he saw an old man who approached supporting himself on a staff. His beard and eyebrows were white, his garments refined. In all he appeared to be a person of some parts. Master Tung-kuo was delighted and eagerly went ahead, leaving the wolf behind. He knelt down and said weeping, "Venerable Sir, a word from you will save my life." The man asked what the matter was. He answered, "This wolf was hard-pressed by hunters and asked me to save him. I actually did save his life; then he turned around and wanted to eat me, and I was as good as dead. Wishing to prolong my life a little bit, I got him to agree to let the matter be settled by the village elders. First, we met an old apricot tree. He forced me to ask the tree, but a plant has no understanding, and nearly condemned me to die. Next we met an old cow. He forced me to ask the cow, but an animal has no understanding, and nearly caused my death. Now we have met you, sir. This must be because Heaven is unwilling to destroy the truth that must die with me. Let me beg of you a word to save my life." And he knocked his head before the old man, waiting for his judgment.

On hearing this, the old man sighed again and again, and raised his stick to beat the wolf saying, "You are in the wrong! There is nothing more wicked than to be ungrateful for favors. The Confucians say, 'a man who cannot bear to be ungrateful will be a filial son.' They also speak of parents and children among tigers and wolves. Ingratitude like yours is a denial of even the elementary relationship of father and son." Then he shouted, "Wolf, begone! If you don't, I will beat you to death."

The wolf said, "Sir, you know only one side of the story. Let me lay my complaint; I hope you will deign to listen. When the master first went about rescuing me, he bound my feet and shut me up in the bag with his books pressing down on top of me. I was so bowed and bent I hardly dared breathe. Then he spun out his conversation with Chao Chien-tzu. Probably his idea was to let me die in the bag so that he would have the profit all to himself. So what's wrong with my eating him?"

The old man turned to the master and asked, "If that's it, then you are as much at fault as was the Archer Yi."

The master was not at all satisfied and depicted in detail his concern for the wolf when he was inside the bag. For his part the wolf strove very cleverly to convince the old man, who said, "There is not sufficient evidence to decide the truth. Let us make a trial of putting the wolf in the bag, so that I can see for myself whether he is painfully cramped there." The wolf gladly agreed, and stretched out his legs for the master, who tied them up again and put him inside the bag. Shouldering the bag, he got on the donkey without the wolf's knowing what they were up to. The old man leaned close to his ear and said, "Have you a knife?" The master said, "Yes," and took out a knife.

The old man signaled with his eyes that the master should stab

the wolf with the knife. The master said, "Won't it hurt the wolf?"
The old man laughed, "If you still can't bear to kill an animal that has
been as ungrateful as this, you are humane indeed, but also stupid to a
degree. To save a man from a well, to give your clothes to preserve a
friend's life, are procedures that have a good result for the recipient
but what about the benefactor, if he dies in the process? Humaneness
pushed to the point of stupidity is something the superior man does
not condone." As he finished speaking he gave a great laugh, and the
master laughed with him. Then he helped the master wield the knife
and together they killed the wolf, threw the carcass on the road, and
departed.

TRANSLATED BY JAMES R. HIGHTOWER

A Poet of the Early Ming

Kao Ch'i lived from 1336 to 1374. Although the new Ming authority had been officially established only six years when its founder cruelly took Kao's life, he has been ranked foremost among the poets of the entire dynasty.

The pieces in this selection employ traditional shih forms, and many recall the work of the T'ang masters; the "Song of the Man of the Green Hill" is in a form known as "long and short lines"—mostly couplets of five or seven syllables.

Like his preface itself, Kao Ch'i's poems are often concerned with the age-old question of duty versus inclination. He relishes the tranquillity of rustic retirement, but there is usually the sense that at these times he is "sharpening his native powers, conserving his native energies," as he says, against the time of summons to the service of the emperor.

He leaves full of "firm purpose" when the call does come, but before much time has passed he is longing again for the quiet life ("Winter Hardship in the Capital"). Our selection ends with the serene detachment of the late sequence "Four Poems from the Eastern Cottage."

In times of despotic rule even the writing of an occasional poem could lead to desperate consequences. The reign of the first Ming emperor was such a time. Kao Ch'i's tragic death illustrates the hazards of the pursuit of letters. He wrote a set of apparently harmless lines to congratulate his superior "On Raising the Roof Beams of the Prefectural Hall." But the site of the prefectural offices whose restoration he ap-

53

plauded had been in more recent years the base of the principal rival to the new Ming authority. The rebuilding on this spot was declared a seditious act, Kao Ch'i's poem bore witness to his "complicity," and he was summarily executed.

●

Kao Ch'i

Preface to His Own Poems

[Ch'ing-ch'iu shih-chi hsu]

In an age when the world is not troubled, scholars possessing vast and outstanding abilities and who find no place to utilize them often go off to mountains or forests or wastelands of grass and marsh, to keep the company of farmers and old rustics; they drink until deep in their wine, and sing aloud, and in these things find pleasures that satisfy them. But because of this they never become known abroad in the world. However when the world is troubled, such persons can join together in the common cause, the brave ones utilizing to the full their strength, the learned ones applying all their stratagems, and those skilled in speech winning others to their views. Such activities all display the ways by which men can utilize whatever abilities they possess to advance their careers and gain for themselves merit and fame. Nor, in such times, could they restrict themselves to the company of farmers and old rustics and be content with idle pleasures. But in either case they would be acting in accord with the times.

Today the world is in a state of disintegration and collapse. Campaigns and military expeditions are underway on all sides. This can indeed be called an age of troubles. Persons who are capable of presenting invincible stratagems in the council tents, or of performing warlike deeds within the military forces, or of carrying out important missions beyond the borders, all are needed by the rulers. All of these await the appearance of scholars who are wise and brave and skilled in speech. If such were to exist in the mountains or forests or wastelands of grass and marsh in a time like this, who among them would *not* be willing to come forth, in response to the needs of the ruler, to utilize his special talents? Who would willingly remain to shrivel up and die of old age, wearing only rough homespun and eating only coarse foods?

I live in such an age, but I am truly lacking in those abilities. Even though I might want to rouse myself into action, it would be like a man who lacked a strong carriage and good horses yet wanted to set out on a journey of a thousand miles—would not that be too difficult? Therefore it is that I have ensconced myself on the banks of the Lou River, and content myself with mean status.

Sometimes I climb a hill and gaze out where the Yangtze's waters race past for a hundred miles, to pour into the sea. The tumbling and tossing of its waves, the dark mysteries of its mists and haze, the flowering and dying of plants and trees, the soaring and drifting of birds and fishes, in fact all sorts of things that can move the mind and entice the eye have been here set forth in poetry. For it is in this way that I have been able to dispel disquieting sadness by forgetting both myself and the world, granting to matters of gain and loss no more than a laugh.

From the first I paid no attention to the matter of these poems' poetic workmanship; they have just accumulated until they fill a volume. I have named this a "Draft of Poems from the Lou River." If one finds himself in a rustic cottage or under a thatched roof, where there is mellowed wine and a fattened pig, and he drinks with farmers and old rustics until all are drunk together, and should he then strum on an old pot and sing these verses, that will be enough to bring out all that they have to say. Thus my preface, by way of introduction, in which to make known that I have turned myself out to dwell among the rivers and lakes because I am a man of no ability; it is not as if I had ability but would not utilize it.

On Hearing the Sound of Oars, When Leaving the East Gate of the City at Dawn

[*Hsiao ch'u ch'eng-tung-men wen lu sheng*]

> The city gate opens at sunrise; the road lies at the water's
>   edge.
> Through the mist come human voices; a fish market is
>   nearby.
> Whose oars, unseen in the fog's expanse, move with such
>   flying speed?
> Still half in a dream a startled duck flies up from the wa-
>   ter's edge willows.

At the crossing point, chill waves lap against the sand.
From the distance I hear the creaking of wheels, and again the
    splash of oars.
A traveler's cart winds along the twisting hillside road.
Looms whir where women work, in houses behind the bam-
    boo.
I am but a wanderer from the wilds,
Dropped by chance into the Yellow Dust, to set forth on my
    travels at dawn.
These sounds, I am vaguely reminded, I have heard some-
    where before.
Was it in a boat, on waking after drinking, just as the east grew
    light?

The Song of the Man of the Green Hill

[*Ch'ing-ch'iu-tzu ko*]

*By the Yangtze's edge there is the Green Hill (Ch'ing-ch'iu). I've moved
my home to the south of it, and so have adopted the cognomen, "the
man of Ch'ing-ch'iu." This man lives there in idleness, with nothing to
do. All day long he works earnestly at making poems, and while there
he happened to write this "Song of the Man of Ch'ing-ch'iu" in which
he sets forth his mind, in the hope of dispelling the ridicule of him for
his addiction to poetry.*

The man of Ch'ing-ch'iu, he is thin and unsullied—
Originally he was a genie-courtier at the Pavilion of Five-col-
    ored Clouds.
What year was he banished to this lower world?
He tells no one his real name.
He wears rope sandals, but he has wearied of distant roam-
    ing.
He shoulders a hoe, but he is too lazy to till his own fields.
He has a sword, but he lets it gather rust.
He has books, but he leaves them piled in disorder.
He is unwilling to bend his back for five catties of rice,
He is unwilling to loosen his tongue to bring about the fall
    of seventy cities.
But, he is addicted to the search for poetic lines.

He hums them to himself, he sings them for his own pleasure.
He wanders through the fields, dragging his cane, wearing a
    rope-belt.
Bystanders, not understanding him, laugh and ridicule,
Calling him a "muddleheaded scholar of Lu," a veritable
    "madman of Ch'u."
The man of Ch'ing-ch'iu hears it but cares not at all—
Still the sound of poetry chanting comes in unbroken gurgle
    from his lips.
He chants poetry in the morning till he forgets to eat;
He chants poetry in the evening till he has dispersed all ill-
    feelings.
When intent on his poetizing
He groans like a man sick from too much drinking;
He finds no time to comb his hair,
And has no time to attend to family affairs.
His children cry, and he knows not to pity them.
Guests call, and he shows them no hospitality.
He is not concerned that shortly he will be destitute;
He envies not at all the way the thrifty Mr. Yi prospered.
It grieves him not to wear rough uncut homespun;
He longs not at all for the colored tassels of an official's hat.
He pays no attention to the bitterly fought duel of dragon and
    tiger,
Nor gives he notice to the frightened scurryings of the golden
    crow and the jade rabbit.[1]
Instead, he sits alone, facing the shore.
He walks alone, in the grove.
He sharpens his native powers, he conserves his native ener-
    gies.
None of creation's myriad creatures can conceal their nature
    from him.
Through the vast, misty realm of the eight farthest limits he
    wanders in his imagination.
Sitting there, he makes the formless become real.
He has acquired the sensitivity of the one who could shoot an
    arrow through a suspended flea,

---

[1] Sun and moon.

The strength of one who could behead a great whale.
He becomes pure as one who drinks the nourishing dew,
Lofty as the ranks of soaring crags and cliffs.
Towering above, the bright clouds open to him;
Luxuriantly the frozen plants again grow.
He ascends to clutch at the roots of Heaven, seeking out the
     caves of the moon.
With rhinoceros horn magic lens he scans the Oxen Ford,
     seeing the myriad wonders in its depths.
Wonderful, suddenly, to be in the company of gods and spir-
     its!
Grand spectacle, vaster than the expanse of rivers and moun-
     tains!
The stars and the rainbows lend him their radiance;
The mists and the dews nourish his heroic spirit.
The sounds he hears are divine harmonies,
The tastes, the flavors of the unearthly broth.
"In this world below there is no object which delights me;
Even instruments of bronze and jade emit harsh clanking
     sounds.
In my thatched hut, by the river's edge, the storm clears;
Behind my barred gate, now I've slept out my sleep, and I've
     just finished a poem.
So I strum the wine pot and sing a joyous song,
Giving no thought to startled mundane ears.
I want to call to the old man of Mount Chün, to bring out the
     long flute of magic powers
And accompany this song of mine, under the bright moon.
But then I think sadly how the waves would suddenly rise,
Birds and beasts would shriek in fright, the very hills shake and
     crumble.
The Lord of Heaven would hear it and be angered,
Would send a white heron to fetch me back.
He would let me go on no longer with these tricks of this
     world;
I would don again my jeweled waist pendants, and go back
     to the City of Jade."

Written on Seeing the Flowers, and Remembering My Daughter

[*Chien hua yi wang nü shu*]

I grieve for my second daughter,
Six years I carried her about,
Held her against my breast and helped her eat,
Taught her rhymes as she sat on my knee.
She would arise early and copy her elder sister's dress,
Struggling to see herself in the dressing table mirror.
She had begun to delight in pretty silks and lace
But in a poor family she could have none of these.
I would sigh over my own recurring frustrations,
Treading the byways through the rain and snow.
But evenings when I returned to receive her greeting
My sad cares would be transformed into contentment.
What were we to do, that day when illness struck?
The worse because it was during the crisis of war;
Frightened by the alarming sounds, she sank quickly into
    death.
There was no time even to fix medicines for her.
Distraught, I prepared her poor little coffin;
Weeping, accompanied it to that distant hillside.
It is already lost in the vast void.
Disconsolate, I still grieve deeply for her.
I think how last year, in the spring,
When the flowers bloomed by the pond in our old garden
She led me by the hand along under the trees
And asked me to break off a pretty branch for her.
This year again the flowers bloom;
Now I live far from home, here by this river's edge.
All the household are here, only she is gone.
I look at the flowers, and my tears fall in vain.
A cup of wine brings me no comfort.
The wind makes desolate sounds in the night curtains.

Called for the Compilation of the Yüan History and about to Leave for the Capital, I Take Leave of My Wife

[*Chao hsiu Yüan-shih chiang fu ching-shih pieh nei*]

In receipt of the imperial command, I hasten to prepare
my carriage;
Comes the dawn, I must depart for the capital.
Is not this fine commission a thing imparting honor?
I hesitate only because I must bid you farewell.

Ever since you came into my household
You have long shared my humble poverty.
Yet within your rooms joy and happiness have prevailed;
I honor all your goodness; I do not judge only by a stand-
ard of beauty.

The season is cold and the house empty of provisions.
How can I bear to go off so far like this?
But the ruler awaits me to work on the archival records—
I have no time to be concerned about my own affairs.

As I rush about, I'm touched by your devoted aid,
And that you've cooked the setting-hen for me.
Leading our children by the hand, you see me off in tears
And ask when the homeward journey will be.

The journey is to be a distant one.
Moving clouds gather low on the river's edge.
The Sages forbade pleasant idleness;
Would I dare linger on at ease in my thatched hut?
It has been my firm purpose gladly to serve my country;
That it has come about in this way is my good fortune.

'Eat well and take care until we meet again—
Don't give way to loneliness and sad thoughts.

Winter Hardship in the Capital

[*Ching-shih k'u han*]

The north wind rages, the scudding clouds are dark;
Deep winter's cruelty saddens both Heaven and Earth.
Dragons and serpents burrow deep in the mud, and wild animals hide in their caves.
Misshapen stones freeze and crack, and are marked by broken lines.

Below Lin-ts'ang Temple the air is filled with swirling snow;
At the Yangtze ferry-crossing frightened waves race by.
In the deserted mountains the trees stand all stark and dead
Awaiting the sun's warmth to penetrate deep to their roots again.

By his thatched hut there sits an old man without even a rough coat,
He raises his head and looks hopefully where the dawn is about to break.
Bitter cold like this is worst of all for the traveler;
I sigh that at the year's end I'm still a wandering soul.

Usually, at home, we could find pleasures indeed.
By the bedstead there would be a pot of well-aged wine,
In our mountains the charcoal is cheap, and the floor stove always warm,
With the children we'd sit encircling it, forgetting formalities of rank.
The flight of birds even stopped, let alone the visits of friends—
For ten days at a time we might not dare even open our gate.

But now, having come to the capital, I get up and go out at dawn
Forcing my way, by cart and horse, to get to the palace gates.

By the time I return my face is the color of earth.
In my shabby room in the evening I perch like a hungry fal-
    con.
At the corner wine-shop the wine is mercilessly dear;
Yet who could argue about the price, even if it cost three
    hundred cash the pint.
I can't wait to get drunk, then fling myself down to rest,
But the padding is thin in my cotton blankets, and warmth
    never comes.

Then I think about those husky fellows, now campaigning
    off in the Northwest—
There for a thousand miles the snow stretches, all the way
    to the K'un-lun Mountains.
The ice of frozen rivers is splintered by the hooves of their
    horses.
By night they storm firm fortresses, capturing armies of
    ch'iang and *hun*.

But scholars like me only know how to use their jaws;
I lack the strength to repay the court's gracious favor.
Would it not be better to submit tomorrow a petition to re-
    sign?
Then as an old commoner I could go home and fish in my
    southland village.

Four Poems from the Eastern Cottage

[*Ch'u chiao ti Tung-t'un*]

I

My old village, and that little patch of land
Left to me by my forebears,
Relying on it I can be lazy—
I don't till, yet can sit and wait to be fed.
Frost and dew cover the cold countryside;
This is the season when the harvest is gathered.
I have come to collect my scanty incomes
And to take my rest, here on the eastern slope.

Although the harvest this year is not abundant
Still there's enough to keep me from hunger.
I know that a vast salary from high office carries its own
    difficulties;
If I can just retain this, what more should I demand?

II

I'm but a commoner from this eastern slope
Who happened to go away and live in the prefectural city.
Returning now to rest again in my farm house
I am suddenly overcome by the mood of the countryside.
I am like a fish who has returned to his own deep pool
Overwhelmed again by the joy of life.
Before leaving again, I go to thank my old host's wife;
But next time I come I'll cook my own simple fare.
I am not a tax-collector, come to hasten payment;
When I knock at your gate you need feel no fright.

III

My court robes have long been laid aside;
I have the wan look of a thin hermit in the wilds.
I want to keep company with the rustics of the country-
    side,
Share in their pleasures, forgetting distinctions of "wise"
    and "foolish."
Since early morning I've been here at this river's edge
Singing aloud, wandering with slow steps.
Suddenly I encounter an old country man
Who has left his field to come and greet me with courtesy.
He thinks perhaps I may be a high official
But is puzzled by my unexpected appearance.
I have already forgotten everything
But he has not forgotten what I should be.
I can't keep him from too polite expressions
And I am only ill at ease that he should be so respectful.

IV

After sitting a long time my body is cramped,
I close my book away and wander out my garden gate.
Coming to the stream, I unconsciously look to the west:
Suddenly, squarely before me, I see the Ch'in-yü Mountain.
The wilds are stilled, the bare trees stand sparse;
The stream flows far on, and the birds of dusk return.
Instantly a poem forms itself in my mind—
In a wave of good feelings my cares all disappear.
Then I go along home with the woodcutters and herdsmen
And we sing and laugh as the evening sun goes down.

TRANSLATED BY F. W. MOTE

A Hilarious Buddhist Allegory

The "real Tripitaka" (this is the title of his biography by Arthur Waley) was a Buddhist monk named Hsüan-tsang who between the years 629 and 645 journeyed overland to India to bring back a vast collection of holy sutras. Hsüan-tsang's own factual record of his adventures is remarkable enough; it is hardly surprising that legends of fantastic exploits grew up around his name in succeeding centuries. Before long the legends introduce the figure of a magically gifted monkey-protector who bears striking resemblance to the monkey-general of the Indian epic, the Rāmāyana.

On the basis of promptbook and perhaps other fictional versions of the quest, Wu Ch'eng-en (ca. 1506–1582) created an allegorical romance which makes a poor lackluster preachment out of Bunyan's Pilgrim's Progress. The range of Wu's humor is prodigious. From gross slapstick to the keenest satire there are few opportunities, verbal or visual, that he lets slip. The Buddhist gospel—the need for compassion, the importance of "emptiness," the vanity of the senses, the enlightenment which shows this world as snare and delusion—comes through a gale of laughter: perhaps the gale is the gospel.

One half of Wu's great novel Journey to the West is well known to Western readers in Waley's translation under the very appropriate title of Monkey. We have chosen an episode which Waley did not include.

•

Wu Ch'eng-en

From Journey to the West

The Temptation of Saint Pigsy

[*Hsi yu chi,* XXIII]

The four of them, master and disciples, resumed the highroad that led westward. Through green hills they passed and over blue waters, past meadows of wildflowers and endless grassy plains. Time flew by, and autumn was upon them again. They saw:

> Hillsides red with maple leaves,
> Chrysanthemums stirring in the evening breeze;
> As the old cicada's humming fades
> The crickets start their endless plaint.
> Lotus unfold their green silk fans,
> Oranges cluster gold and fragrant;
> Sad to see the wild-goose columns
> Dotting the distant sky.

Evening began to overtake the pilgrims, and Tripitaka said, "It's getting late, disciples; where shall we find shelter for the night?"

"That's not the right thing to say, Master," said Monkey. "Any place is home to us who have left the world. We feed on wind and rest on water, lie in the moonlight and sleep in the frost. What is this talk of 'shelter for the night'?"

"It's all right for you, brother," said Pigsy, "you travel light, what do you care about other people's problems? It's been heavy going for me, with this load on my back, up one ridge and down another ever since we left the River of Flowing Sand! It's only fair that we should look for somebody's house where we can get something to eat and drink and a place to rest up a while."

But Sandy objected: "The way you talk, fool, it seems you've still got something on your mind. But you can't keep on the way you were back at the Kao Farm, sunk deep in your own idle comforts. You've joined the priesthood now, and if you're going to be a worthwhile disciple you'll just have to put up with a few hardships."

"Do you know how much this baggage weighs?" asked Pigsy.

"How would I know?" replied Monkey. "I've never carried it since you and Sandy joined us."

"Then let me tell you," said Pigsy:

"Four little rattan splints,
Eight short lengths of cord.
But you don't want the rain to get in,
So you wrap it in three or four rugs;
Then you fear it might spill at the ends,
So you bang in a handful of nails;
Then protect the whole thing with copper-shod staffs
Propping up a massive great bamboo awning.

—All this pile of baggage, and Old Porker here to carry it for you all day long, it's all very fine for you to talk about being a disciple when you've got me for a hired hand!"

"Fool, who are you talking to?" laughed Monkey.

"You," said Pigsy.

"Then you've got the wrong person," said Monkey. "My job is to look after the master, it's up to you and Sandy to deal with the horse and the baggage. But just you slip up on this, and you'll get a taste of my cudgel!"

"Don't talk about 'cudgels,' brother, it isn't right to use physical force on people," said Pigsy. "I know very well how high and mighty you are, you'd never be willing to carry the stuff; but look at that horse Master's riding, a great stout creature with no more of a load than one solitary priest: it would be a kindness to me if you'd get *him* to carry a few bits and pieces."

" 'Horse,' you call him," said Monkey. "He's no common horse, let me tell you, he's the son of Ao-jun, Dragon King of the Western Sea, and his name is Third Prince Dragon-steed. He was responsible for a fire which destroyed the magic pearl which lit the palace, and his father accused him of rebellion and had him convicted of breaking the laws of Heaven. But luckily for him the Goddess of Mercy came to save him. He had to wait for ever so long at Eagle Grief Ford, until at last the Goddess came in person, took away his scales and horns and plucked the pearl from under his chin, and changed him into this horse form you now see. Then he took his vow to carry Master to the west to pay homage to the Buddha. He's working out his own salvation, don't interfere with him."

"Is he really a dragon, brother?" asked Sandy.

"He's really a dragon," said Monkey.

"There's an old saying I once heard," said Pigsy:

> " 'Dragons can spit cloud, snort fog,
> Furrow earth, scatter rock,
> Pick up the mountains and toss them around,
> Roil and broil the rivers and the sea.'

—How can he plod along as slowly as he does now?"

"If you want him to speed up," said Monkey, "I'll have him show you what he can do."

Dear Great Sage! He took a tight grip on his magic iron cudgel, and the sky suddenly filled with tinted clouds. Seeing the cudgel in Monkey's hand the horse feared there was a blow coming and took off in fright, his four hooves clear of the ground, swift as lightning and with a sound like a swish of the wind. Tripitaka lacked the strength in his wrists to rein him in, but had to give him his head until he slowed down of his own accord as he mounted a slope.

When Tripitaka had got his breath back and was able to look about him he noticed in the distance a pine wood within which stood a cluster of imposing dwellings:

> Verdant cedars shade the gate,
> A dwelling close by the green hill slope.
> A grove of rustling pines,
> A clump of speckled bamboo.
> Wild asters sparkle in the fence's shade,
> Cool iris reflect their colors below the bridge.
> Whitewashed walls,
> Walks paved with brick,
> In nobly soaring halls
> A dwelling most serene.
> No cattle, dogs, or chickens to be seen:
> The harvest must be in, the farmers resting.

Monkey and the others came up as Tripitaka sat there gazing, reins in hand. "You didn't fall off then, Master?" said Monkey.

Tripitaka scolded him: "I don't know how I managed to stay in my seat, you thoughtless ape, when you startled him so!"

"Don't take me to task, Master," said Monkey with a smile. "It was Pigsy saying the horse was too slow—I just wanted to speed him up a little."

That fool had had to race to catch up to the horse, and now panted and puffed as he mumbled: "Enough, enough! All very well for you, free as the air—here's me with a load so heavy I can hardly lift it, and you make me charge around chasing a horse!"

Tripitaka said, "Look across there, my disciples: there is a farm where I believe we might well spend the night."

Monkey at once raised his head and stared up into the sky: and there sure enough he saw felicitous clouds riding above the spot, a shining mist enveloping the scene. It was obvious to him that these "dwellings" were a transformation brought about by Buddhist divinities; but being reluctant to divulge the secret workings of Heaven, he said no more than "Good! Splendid! Let's stay the night there then."

Tripitaka dismounted by a gatehouse where passionflowers trailed like elephants' trunks over carved and painted pillars. Sandy set down his load, Pigsy led the horse up. "From the look of it," said Pigsy, "I'd say these people were quite nicely-off, thank you."

Monkey was for going in at once, but Tripitaka said, "That won't do, priests like we should show a little diffidence and not go pushing our way in. We must wait until someone comes out and formally invites us."

Pigsy tied up the horse and propped himself up against the wall. Tripitaka seated himself on a stone drum, Monkey and Sandy on the edge of a low terrace. Some considerable time passed with no sign of anyone coming out, and at last Monkey's patience gave out and he jumped up and strode through the gate to look around. The principal room was of fair size and faced south, the blinds rolled up high. Across the door screen was mounted a horizontal scroll bearing an auspicious landscape of hills and sea; gold-lacquered pillars at either side offered a "spring couplet" in large characters on bright red paper:

Evening by the low bridge, floss floats from gentle willows;
Spring in the little court, snow bedecks the fragrant plum.

Right in the middle of the room stood an incense table of gleaming black lacquer, with a burner of ancient bronze in the shape of an animal. Six armchairs were set out, and at either end of the room hung painted screens of the four seasons.

Monkey was in the middle of his uninvited investigation when suddenly footsteps sounded from inside the house and through the doorway came a lady of middling years who asked playfully,"Who can this be who comes forcing his way in at this widow's gate?"

Taken aback, the Great Sage stammered his apologies: "I am a poor priest from the land of Great T'ang in the distant East. I am under commission to travel to the western regions, to pay homage to the Buddha and receive the holy sutras. There are four of us altogether. Our journey brought us past your gate, blessed Bodhisattva, and since it is growing late we turn to you for the kind favor of a night's lodging."

"Well, sir pilgrim, and where are your three companions?" asked the woman with a welcoming smile. "Bring them in!"

"Come in, Master," called Monkey at the top of his voice, and Tripitaka now came forward with Sandy and Pigsy, horse, baggage, and all. The woman stepped forward to greet them, and Pigsy's greedy eye took in every detail of her appearance:

> Brocaded coarse-weave jacket in mandarin green,
> Over her shoulders a riding-cloak of deep pink;
> Gosling-yellow skirt embroidered and tasseled,
> Deep-soled patterned slippers peeping beneath.
> Modish coiffure like fine silk gleaming black
> With "coiling dragon" braids bound with colored threads;
> Ivory "palace" combs brilliant with feathers, red and emerald,
> A pair of jeweled hairpins set aslant.
> The hair at her temples slightly greying, brushed into "phoenix wings,"
> Earrings with pendants set with precious gems.
> Her face lovely without need of paint or powder,
> Glamor not to be matched by tenderer years.

The woman's pleasure increased when she saw the three new arrivals, and she welcomed them courteously into her reception room.

The greetings over she invited them to be seated and to take tea. And now a serving-girl appeared from behind the door screen, hair-tufts adorned with decorative threads and in her hands a golden tray with jade cups. To the warm fragrance of fine tea was joined the delicate scent of exotic fruits. Slim bamboo-shoot fingers slipped out from gaily-colored sleeves as she raised a jade bowl of tea to each of the pilgrims in turn. No sooner had they drunk the tea than orders were given for a vegetarian meal to be prepared.

Tripitaka raised his hands in salutation and asked, "May I ask your name, blessed Bodhisattva, and the name of this place?"

"This is the Western Land of Ox-greet," said the woman. "My maiden name was Chia[1], my husband's name was Mo.[2] My husband's parents died, alas, when we were very young, and it fell to us to continue the management of this estate, which is a substantial one: ten thousand strings of cash, a thousand *ch'ing* of fertile land. It was not in our fate to be granted a son, only three daughters were born to us. Then two years ago I suffered a new bereavement, that of my husband. I have been living as a widow: my mourning will be fulfilled this year. My husband left all this property with no other heir or relative, just my daughters and myself to carry it on. I should like to marry again, but would find it difficult to give up the estate. But now comes this great good fortune of your visit. I understand there are four of you in all, master and disciples: exactly the right number for my three daughters and myself to invite you to become our husbands and 'take over the mountain'—I should be grateful to know how this would appeal to you."

When Tripitaka heard these words he pretended to be deaf and dumb, shut his eyes tight to compose his thoughts, and sat on in total silence. The woman then continued: "The estate comprises over three hundred *mou* of wet paddy, over three hundred *ch'ing* of dry, with over three hundred *ch'ing* also of hillside orchard land. We have a thousand or so water buffalo, herds of horses and mules, pigs and sheep beyond my ability to count. Our farmsteads lie in every direction, some sixty or seventy in all; we have grain in the house that we shall be unable to use for eight or nine years to come, silks that we shall not wear for another ten years, gold and silver that will take more

---

[1] "Unreal."
[2] "No such person."

than our lifetimes to spend. Nowhere will you find such a place, where 'brocade hangings make perpetual spring,' and 'jeweled beauties wait on either hand.' If the four of you, master and disciples alike, could see your way to changing your minds, marrying us and settling here, you would live at ease in the fullest luxury imaginable. Would not this be an improvement over toiling on to the West?"

Tripitaka sat on, stupid and vacant and without a word. Again the woman resumed: "The time of my birth was early evening on the third day, third month, year *ting-hai*. I am forty-five, my husband was three years older than I. My eldest daughter's name is Truth, and she is twenty. Love, the second, is eighteen; Pity, my youngest, is sixteen; and none of them is promised in marriage. Though I am quite ill-favored, my daughters have some good features, and there is nothing beyond their capacities in the way of needlework and the feminine accomplishments. Since no boy was born to us, my late husband and I brought up these girls like sons: we had them read the classics when they were quite small, and they are skilled in the composition of verses and couplets. Despite its rustic nature, this has not been an uncultivated environment for them, and I believe they could make suitable companions even for exalted elders like yourselves. If you could only open your hearts to us, let your hair grow and become the masters of this estate, then you could wear silks and satins and lead a life surely superior to that of the earthenware begging-bowl, the homespun robe, the hat, and pattens of straw!"

Tripitaka sat on his seat like a child frightened by thunder or a toad drenched with rain, idiotically rolling his eyes. But the talk of such wealth and such gorgeous beauty had set up an uncontrollable itching in Pigsy's heart. He twisted left and right as if the chairbottom were sticking pins in his backside. Then he marched forward and seized Tripitaka by the arm: "Master! Why do you pay no attention to what this lady is saying? It's only polite to at least acknowledge her proposal."

Tripitaka threw up his head and made Pigsy jump back with the force of his expostulation: "Ill-omened beast! A monk like myself— what would happen if thoughts of wealth should move my heart, sensual joys seduce my purpose?"

"Poor thing, poor thing!" the woman laughed. "What's so fine about being a monk?"

"And what is so fine, blessed Bodhisattva," asked Tripitaka, "about your domestic joys?"

"Be seated, sir pilgrim," said the woman, "and I will tell you what are the joys of the domestic life. They are expressed in a poem:

> Our new spring wardrobe is finest silk,
> In summer's light gauze we view the lotus;
> Fall brings the harvest and sweet new wine,
> Winter, flushed cheeks in closet's warmth.
> So to each season its special joys,
> Festival pleasures the year around:
> The bridal chamber's silken sheets
> Will muffle the trudging pilgrim's chant."

"Blessed Bodhisattva," responded Tripitaka to this recital, "the householder's is indeed a good life, with wealth to dispose of and luxury to enjoy, plenty to wear and good things to eat, and children gathered about his knee. But you fail to realize that the life of a mendicant monk has its own rewards. I have a poem, too:

> A rare achievement, to leave the world,
> To loose affection's tender bonds.
> When worldly goods cause no more strife
> The heart has a fortune of its own.
> Road's end is our report to the Throne,
> Hearts new-illumined, home once more:
> Who'd lust for meat, waiting for age
> To swallow this stinking sack of flesh?"

Hearing this the woman became very angry and said, "What insolence from an ill-mannered monk! If it weren't for the fact that you are pilgrims from the distant east I would drive you out of my house. In all sincerity I was inviting you to be my sons-in-law and to enjoy my property, and you dare to make fun of me with your sarcasm. Even if you have embraced the discipline and taken the vow and won't ever return to lay life, there's nothing wrong if I invite one of your disciples to join my family. Why are you so strict?"

Tripitaka could only turn very apologetic under this wrath. He appealed to Monkey: "Aware-of-Vacuity, how about you staying here?"

Monkey replied, "This is rather out of my line. Let Pigsy stay."

Pigsy said to Monkey, "Elder brother, don't make fun of me. Let's take more time to think this over."

Tripitaka then suggested, "Since you two are unwilling, let Sandy stay on."

But Sandy replied, "Master, what words are these! Your disciple was honored to be converted by Kuan-yin and to embrace the discipline and await your arrival. Since then I have been further privileged to become your disciple and receive instruction from you. It's not even two months and I haven't yet accomplished any meritorious deeds. How dare I seek this wealth and honor? I would rather risk death faring forward to the Western Paradise than do such a dishonorable thing."

Seeing them all make excuses, the woman swiftly turned around and disappeared behind the door screen. She further slammed the side door leading to the parlor as she went in. The master and disciples were left by themselves, without refreshments. No one came out to wait on them.

Highly vexed, Pigsy complained to Tripitaka, "Master, how undiplomatic of you to have refused her so flatly. If you had given her some ground for hope with a vague yes, we should have got a free meal from her and had a jolly evening. Each of us could surely give her a definite answer tomorrow. As it is, she has shut the door on us and won't come out. We are as short of food as a stove with nothing in it but cold ashes. How can we get through the night?"

Sandy suggested, "Second brother, then you stay on as her son-in-law."

Pigsy said, "Younger brother, don't tease me—let's take time to deliberate this."

Monkey said, "What's there to deliberate? If you are willing, then let our master and that woman sponsor your marriage and let you be her son-in-law and stay with her family. She is so fabulously wealthy she would certainly provide you with a dowry and prepare a wedding banquet for all the relatives. We would certainly enjoy this while you return to 'lay' life here. Wouldn't that be nice for all concerned?"

"Finely said," replied Pigsy. "Only to return to lay life after you have forsaken it, to marry again after you have severed ties with your first wife—that's kind of difficult."

"So our second brother was once married?" asked Sandy.

"You wouldn't have guessed," replied Monkey. "He was originally the son-in-law of old Mr. Kao of the Kao Farm at Wu-ssu-tsang. After I had subdued him—he had earlier received the discipline from the Bodhisattva Kuan-yin—we managed to rope him in to serve as a monk. So he abandoned his first wife and became a disciple of our master to go westward to pay homage to Buddha. Probably he has been away from home too long and is again itching with desire. Just now he has heard this offer—undoubtedly he is tempted." Then he turned to Pigsy, "Fool, you stay here as a son-in-law. Only don't forget to give proper thanks to old Monkey; so I won't make trouble for you."

The fool said, "Nonsense, nonsense. All of us are tempted, don't just single me out for ridicule. As the saying goes, 'Monks are sex-starved fiends.'—Who isn't like that? If we all act so damned coy, we shall only ruin our evening. No tea, and no lights either! I suppose we can survive the night, but that poor horse has to carry our master tomorrow and has a whole day's journey ahead of it. If it is famished in the night, the only good we shall get from it will be to strip its hide. You stay here and I'll put the horse to pasture."

In a great hurry the fool loosened the reins and led the horse out. Monkey said, "Sandy, you stay here and keep Master company. I'll follow him and see where he is grazing the horse."

Tripitaka said, "It's all right if you go and watch him. Only don't plan on just teasing him."

"I know," said Monkey. The Great Sage then left the hall and, giving his body a shake, turned himself into a red dragonfly, darting out of the front gate to catch up with Pigsy. Pulling the horse, the fool didn't stop where there was grass, but shooed it and dragged it toward the back door. That woman was standing there with the three girls, idly enjoying the sight of the chrysanthemums. Seeing Pigsy approach, the three girls swiftly disappeared behind the door. The woman, however, stood there and asked him, "Little priest, where are you going?"

The fool dropped the reins and came forward with a bow, saying, "Mother, I'm pasturing the horse."

The woman said, "Your master is too goody-goody. Won't it be much better to stay on as my son-in-law than to be a mendicant monk trudging westward?"

Pigsy smiled, "They are doing this by the order of the T'ang Emperor; so they daren't disobey and won't consent to settling down here. Just a moment ago they were even making fun of me in the hall. But for my part, I am kind of diffident—I'm afraid Mother will object to my long snout and big ears."

The woman said, "I don't mind, really. Since there is no man in the house, it won't be a bad idea to take in a son-in-law. But I am afraid my daughters may object to your ugliness."

Pigsy replied, "Mother, please tell your honored daughters not to be so picky. The T'ang monk may be good to look at, but he is no good on other counts. I may be ugly, but there is a poem. . . ."

The woman asked, "How does it go?" and Pigsy recited:

> "Though I am ugly
> My industry is commendable:
> A thousand *ch'ing* of land
> Needs no oxen to plough it;
> I rake it once, and
> The seeds will sprout in season.
> No rain and I am a rainmaker,
> No breeze and I will summon the wind.
> If the house is too low
> I will add two or three stories;
> The unswept floor I will sweep,
> The clogged sewers I will unclog.
> Household chores big and small
> I can manage all."

The woman said, "Since you can manage the chores around the house, why don't you go back to consult your master? If nothing goes wrong, we'll have you."

"No need to consult him," said Pigsy, "he is not my father or mother. The decision rests entirely with me."

The woman said, "All right, I'll talk it over with my daughters." She then darted inside, shutting the back door behind her.

Pigsy didn't even bother to pasture the horse, but pulled it round to the front door again. How was he to know that Monkey had observed everything? Monkey flew back, changed into his real shape, and told Tripitaka, "Pigsy is leading the horse back."

The elder said, "If the horse is not led, he may get excited and wander away."

Monkey couldn't help laughing as he told from the beginning

about the transactions between Pigsy and that woman. Tripitaka wasn't sure whether he should believe the whole story. Presently the fool pulled the horse in and tied him to a post. "Did you graze the horse?" asked the elder.

Pigsy replied, "There's no good grass and I didn't graze it."

"You may not have found a place to graze it," said Monkey, "but I'm sure you found the *bridal* path."

Hearing this, the fool knew for sure that the news had leaked out. He hung his head and twisted his neck, puckered his snout and creased his brows, and said not a word.

Then the side door swung open and in came the woman with her three daughters, who carried with them two pairs of red gauze lanterns and a pair of portable censers. The pendants at their waists tinkled while the censers exhaled clouds of fragrance. The woman led Truth, Love, and Pity forward and bade them make obeisance to the pilgrims. The girls stood in a row in the center of the hall and bowed to them. Truly they were beautiful:

Their moth-brows curved and penciled,
Powder-white faces fresh as spring,
Seductive with beauty that could topple a kingdom,
Graceful with charm that could pierce one's heart;
The flowers and adornments on their hair, how gorgeous,
The embroidered sashes floating about their dresses, how
   elegant;
Cherry lips half-open with a smile,
Feet stepping daintily with odor of orchid and musk.
Their tall coiffures studded with jewels
And countless precious hairpins;
Their bodies exuding rare fragrance
And decked with flowers made of golden threads;
The beauties of Ch'u,
Hsi-shih of the West Lake
Could not compare with them:
Truly, they are fairies descending from the Ninth Heaven
Or moon goddesses emerging from the Palace of Wintry
   Vastness!

Tripitaka placed his palms together and bowed while Monkey pretended not to notice them and Sandy turned his back on them. But not so Pigsy: his eyes were glued on the sight and his lustful heart was turbulent with uncontrollable desire. With simpering gallantry he spoke softly: "It is an honor that you celestial ladies have descended to visit us. Mother, please ask our sisters to retire."

The three girls went out behind the door screen, leaving behind them a pair of gauze lanterns. The woman then asked, "Have you four elders made up your minds as to which one of you is to be matched with one of my daughters?"

Sandy replied, "We have. That one called Pigsy is to be your son-in-law."

Pigsy said, "Younger brother, please don't make fun of me—let's deliberate together."

"What's there to deliberate?" asked Monkey. "Haven't you concluded everything at the back door, and haven't you even called her 'Mother'? Our master will represent the groom's family, and that woman the bride's family. Old Monkey will serve as a guarantor and Sandy as a matchmaker. There will be no need to consult the almanac either, since today is an auspicious day blessed with Heaven's favors. First bow before your master and then go in as groom."

But Pigsy protested, "This can't be done, can't be done! How could I do such a thing!"

"Fool, stop protesting," said Monkey. "What can you mean by 'This can't be done' when you have already called her 'Mother' so many times? Quickly get on with the ceremony so that we may attend your wedding banquet, there's a good boy." With one hand he grabbed Pigsy and with the other he pulled at the woman, saying, "Dear mother-in-law, take your son-in-law inside."

Pigsy was now quite eager to go in and so the woman gave orders to the boys, "Wipe clean the table and chairs, and spread out a vegetarian dinner to entertain my three relatives while I take my son-in-law to his room." She also gave orders to the cooks to prepare a feast next morning in honor of the relatives. The servants took their orders. Soon afterwards, the three pilgrims ate their vegetarian supper and in no time at all they went to sleep where they sat.

In the meantime Pigsy followed his mother-in-law through he didn't know how many suites of rooms. Most of the way he bumped his head against the walls and stumbled over the doorsills. The fool said, "Mother, please go slower. I am new here and you'd better guide me."

The woman said, "We are now passing by the granaries, store-rooms for money and valuables, and flour mills. We haven't reached the kitchen yet."

"What a big place!" Pigsy exclaimed. Again bumping and stumbling, he managed to get through many more narrow passages and turns until he finally reached the chambers of the inner court.

The woman said, "Son, your elder brother said that today is an auspicious day blessed with Heaven's favors, and so I have made you my son-in-law. But in our hurry we haven't brought along a fortune-teller to guide the rites of worshipping Heaven and Earth and throwing coins and balls of colored silk against the bed curtains. You'd better kneel eight times before the seat of honor."

"Mother is right," replied Pigsy. "Please sit in the seat of honor and let me prostrate myself a few times before you. This will serve the dual purpose of thanking Heaven and Earth and thanking you. Two things done at once, isn't that simple?"

His mother-in-law smiled, "All right. I can see you are a practical man, a really efficient son-in-law. I'll sit here and you pay your respects to me."

In a hall refulgent with the silvery glitter of candles, the fool prostrated himself before her. That done, he asked, "Mother, which one of the sisters is to be mine?"

His mother-in-law replied, "That's precisely what's bothering me. If I let the eldest marry you, the second might complain. If I marry you to the second, the third might complain. And the eldest might complain if I marry you to the third. So I haven't decided yet."

"If you're afraid they might fight over me," said Pigsy, "then give all three to me. That would prevent bickerings and quarrels and preserve propriety."

His mother-in-law said, "How absurd! Do you mean to say that you want to possess all three of my daughters?"

"The way you talk, Mother!" said Pigsy. "Who doesn't have three or four wives? Even if there are a few more, your son-in-law will be happy to receive them. In my early youth I learned the art of staying firm in battle. I guarantee I can please every one of them."

"That can't be done," said the woman. "I have with me a handkerchief. Place it on your head and cover your face, and let luck decide your marriage. I'll let my daughters pass before you and you stretch your hands out to grab. Whoever you get hold of will be your bride." The fool agreed, took the handkerchief, and placed it on his head. There is a poem commenting on this:

The crazy and foolish, ignorant of their essence, cherish
The sex-sword that injures their health and causes their de-
    struction:
Formerly there were the rites of the Duke of Chou,
Today a bridegroom wears a handkerchief on his head.

His head securely wrapped, the fool said, "Mother, please ask the sisters to come out."

His mother-in-law called, "Truth, Love, and Pity, all of you come out to try your luck. See who gets married." Then the tinkling of the jade ornaments announced their arrival, and the fragrance of orchid and musk pervaded the room as if celestial fairies were flitting to and fro. The fool stretched out his hands to grab them. He rushed to the left and right, but to no avail. There seemed to be many, many girls passing by him, but he couldn't get hold of any one of them. He dashed west only to embrace a pillar, and he dashed east only to encounter a wall. With so much running around he finally got dizzy and began to fall and stumble all the time. Going forward he would knock himself against the leaf of a door, and turning back he would bump into a brick wall. He was bumped and banged so often that his mouth became swollen and his head was covered with black-and-blue bruises. Finally, sitting on the floor, he panted, "Mother, your daughters are all so slippery I can't get hold of them. What am I supposed to do now?"

That woman removed his wrapping and told him. "Son, it is not that my daughters are all so slippery. They are all too modest to want to marry you."

Pigsy said, "Mother, since they won't have me, then you marry me."

"My good son-in-law, how shocking!" said the woman. "How could you think of marrying your mother-in-law! But my three daughters, they are all very clever. Each has made a brocade shirt embroidered with pearls. Let the one whose shirt fits you marry you, how about that?"

"Good, good," said Pigsy. "Let me try all three; if they all fit, let me marry them all."

The woman went to an inner chamber, brought out only one shirt and handed it to Pigsy. He stripped off his blue gown, took the shirt, and put it on right away. He had not yet tied the sashes together when, thump! he suffered another fall and down on the floor he went. What had happened was that the fool had been tightly bound by several ropes and was now suffering unendurable agony. But the woman and her three daughters had vanished.

Now the story goes that Tripitaka, Monkey, and Sandy woke up from a sound slumber, not realizing that the east had turned white. They stared hard all around them, but where could they see any large mansion or tall hall, carved beams or storied pillars? They had slept in a grove of pines and cypresses. Frightened, the elder called for Monkey. And Sandy also called, "Elder brother, we are finished. We have met with ghosts."

Monkey, who had known it all along, now asked with a smile, "What's the trouble?"

The elder said, "Just see where we have been sleeping."

"It was fun to be in the pine grove," said Monkey. "Wait till we find where the fool has been tortured."

"Who's been tortured?" asked the elder.

Monkey smiled: "I don't know which Bodhisattvas appeared before us yesterday in the guise of those ladies. Probably they left in the middle of the night after putting poor Pigsy to the torture."

Monkey's words made Tripitaka press his palms together in salutation. Then, on looking round, they saw a slip of paper fluttering from an ancient cypress behind them. Sandy ran to get it, and Tripitaka saw that it was a monitory verse:

No mortal desires brought the Goddess Mother of Li-shan,
But a plea from the Bodhisattva of the Southern Sea.
Manjusri, Samantabhadra were of my company,
Here in this grove disguised as maidens fair.
The holy monk has risen above fleshly snares,
But Brother Pigsy still wallows unenlightened.
He must compose himself, correct his faults:
Backsliding makes the road so much the harder!

Just as the elder, with Monkey and Sandy, was in the midst of reading out these lines, he was interrupted by a yelling from deep within the grove: "Master, these bonds are strangling me! Save me, save me, I'll never do it again!"

"Could that be Pigsy calling?" asked Tripitaka.

"That's who it is," said Sandy.

Monkey said, "Don't take any notice of him, brother, let's be on our way."

But Tripitaka said, "That fool is stupid and stubborn, it's true; but he's an honest enough fellow, and has a good strong back for carrying the baggage. Since he did after all make his vow to the Bodhisattva we should rescue him and take him along. I don't believe he'll dare go wrong again."

So Sandy rolled up their bedding and packed the baggage, and the Great Sage untethered the horse and led Tripitaka into the trees to search. There soon enough they found Pigsy bound to a tree trunk, struggling in agony and bellowing at the top of his voice. Monkey strolled up to him, laughing: "What sort of a son-in-law do you think you are, fooling about here at this time of the morning instead of getting up to greet your in-laws and 'share your bliss' with the master? Hey, where's your mother-in-law? Where's your missus? A great son-in-law you are, all strung up for a flogging!"

That fool responded to Monkey's raillery by hanging his head, gritting his teeth, swallowing his pain, and ceasing to bellow. Sandy could bear the sight no longer, and set down the baggage to loose Pigsy from his bonds. The fool set himself to kowtowing and making obeisances before them, thoroughly overcome with shame. There is a poem to the tune of "Moon on the West River":

> Desire is a wounding sword,
> Give in and you will suffer.
> A maiden so fair, just sweet sixteen,
> More vicious than a hungry *yaksha*.
> One body is all you have,
> Capital only, no interest.
> Guard your capital with care,
> Don't let it run to seed!

Pigsy scraped some soil together and stuck in incense sticks, then made obeisance in the direction of the heavens. Monkey asked, "Do you know who those Bodhisattvas were?"

"I've been dizzy and unconscious here, blurry-eyed and bewildered," said Pigsy, "how am I supposed to know who they were?"

Monkey handed over the slip of paper. Pigsy's shame grew even deeper as he read the monitory verse. But Sandy laughed: "What a fine character you must have, Second Brother, to prompt four Bodhisattvas to seek you in marriage!"

"Please don't speak of this any more, brothers," said Pigsy. "I'm so ashamed of myself. But I'll never behave so foolishly again, ever. I don't care if it breaks every bone in my body, I'm going to set that burden back on my shoulders and follow the master to the Western Paradise."

"That's the way, that's the way," said Tripitaka.

Monkey led them back on to the highroad. They traveled on for some considerable time, when suddenly a high mountain blocked their path. . . .

TRANSLATED BY C. T. HSIA AND CYRIL BIRCH

A Masterpiece of Ming Drama

Peony Pavilion (Mu-tan t'ing [the play is also known as The Soul's Return, Huan hun chi]) was completed in 1598, the masterpiece of the poet-dramatist T'ang Hsien-tsu (1550–1617). It was very long even by contemporary standards: its total of fifty-five scenes would have taken several days to perform, before a birthday or festival audience which would be free to wander in and out as the musical or comic highlights succeeded each other. The following are scenes 7, 10, 14, and 20. Modified versions of the first two of these are still performed under the rubric of k'un-ch'ü. The esoteric poetry of the songs and the virtuosity required for the flute accompaniment place k'un-ch'ü in an unfavorable position vis-à-vis the more robust "Peking Opera," but connoisseurs highly prize the delicacy of lyric, melody, and movement, and the Schoolroom Scene is a popular vehicle for the comedienne who plays Spring Fragrance.

The great theme of T'ang Hsien-tsu's play is expressed by the heroine's abigail in the death scene, below: "What has the world to show more puissant than passion?" The playwright found his device in the rather crude and fantastic story of a girl who dies of unfulfilled longings and is brought back to life by the power of her own passion and the devotion of her lover. After rebellion and separation the lovers win through to acceptance by the girl's stern Confucian father, in a triumph of heart over head. But despite its overall character of romantic comedy, T'ang's play is best known for its moving portrayal of the cloistered maiden in all the pathos of her pining for love.

●

T'ang Hsien-tsu

From Peony Pavilion

[*Mu-tan t'ing*]

THE SCHOOLROOM

CH'EN TSUI-LIANG (*recites*): Droning verses, re-revising
        lines composed last spring
  pondering, my belly filled,
        the taste of the noontime tea;
  ants climb up the table leg
        to skirt the inkslab pool
  bees invade the window screen
        to raid the blooms in my vase.

Here in the prefect's residence I, Ch'en Tsui-liang, have "hung my bed-curtain" so that I may instruct the daughter of the house in the *Book of Songs*. The mistress, Madam Chen, is treating me with the greatest kindness. Now that breakfast is over I shall immerse myself for a while in the *Songs*.

(*He intones.*) "*Kwan-kwan* cry the ospreys
  on the islet in the river.
  So delicate the virtuous maiden
  A fit mate for our Prince."

"Fit," that is to say, "fit"; "mate," that is to say, "seeking."

(*He looks about.*) How late it gets, and still no sign of my pupil. Horribly spoilt! Let me try three raps on the cloud-board.

(*He raps the cloud-board.*) Spring Fragrance, summon the young mistress for her lesson.

(*Enter* TU LI-NIANG *followed by* SPRING FRAGRANCE *bearing books.*)

LI-NIANG (*sings*): Lightly adorned for morning
        to library leisurely strolling;
        low tables bathe in rays of window's brightness.

SPRING FRAGRANCE: *Words of Worth from the Ancients*
        —what a deadly thought!
  but when I'm through
        I'll be able to teach the parrot to order tea.

(*They greet* TUTOR CH'EN.)

LI-NIANG: Our best respects, esteemed sir.

SPRING FRAGRANCE: We hope you're not vexed, esteemed sir.

CH'EN: As the *Rites* prescribe, "it is proper for a daughter at first
cockcrow to wash her hands, to rinse her mouth, to dress her hair,
to pin the same, to pay respects to father and mother." Once sun
is up then each should attend to her affairs. You are now a pupil
and your business is to study: you will need to rise earlier than
this.

LI-NIANG: We shall not be late again.

SPRING FRAGRANCE: We understand. Tonight we won't go to bed so
that we can present ourselves for our lesson in the middle of the
night.

CH'EN: Have you rehearsed the portion of the *Songs* I presented yesterday?

LI-NIANG: I have, but await your interpretation.

CH'EN: Let me hear you.

LI-NIANG (*recites*): "*Kwan-kwan* cry the ospreys
        On the islet in the river.
        So delicate the virtuous maiden
        A fit mate for our Prince."

CH'EN: Now note the interpretation.

    "*Kwan-kwan* cry the ospreys":
the osprey is a bird; "*kwan-kwan*," that is to say, its cry.

SPRING FRAGRANCE: What sort of cry is that?

(CH'EN *imitates the call of the osprey.* SPRING FRAGRANCE *ad libs an imitation of* CH'EN *imitating the osprey.*)

CH'EN: This bird, being a lover of quiet, is on an islet in the river.

SPRING FRAGRANCE: Quite right. Either yesterday or the day before, this year or last year some time, I lost a needle when I was sewing down by the stream. Then an osprey got trapped in the young mistress' room and she set it free and it found my needle for me, and when we looked there it was, on an eyelet in the river.

CH'EN: Rubbish. This is a "detached image."

SPRING FRAGRANCE: What, a graven image? Who detached it?

CH'EN: To "image," that is to say, to introduce thoughts of. It introduces the thought of the "delicate virtuous maiden," who is a nice, quiet girl waiting for the Prince to come seeking her.

SPRING FRAGRANCE: What's he seeking from her?

CH'EN: Now you are being impudent.

LI-NIANG: My good tutor, to interpret the text by means of the notes is something I can do for myself. I should like you rather to instruct me in the overall significance of the *Book of Songs*.

CH'EN: Of all Six Classics
the *Book of Songs* is the flower
with "Airs" and "Refinements" most apt for lady's chamber:
for practical instruction
Chiang-yuan bears her offspring
"treading in the print of God's big toe";
warning against jealousy
shine the virtues of queen and consort.
And then there are the
"Song of the Cockcrow,"
the "Lament for the Swallows,"
"Tears by the Riverbank,"
"Longings by the Han River"
to cleanse the face of rouge:
in every verse an edifying homily
to "fit a maid for husband and for family."

LI-NIANG: How long is the book?

CH'EN: "The *Songs* are three hundred, but their meaning may be expressed in a single phrase":

> no more than this,
> "to set aside evil thoughts,"
> and this I pass to you.

End of lesson. Spring Fragrance, fetch the "four jewels of the scholar's study" for our calligraphy.

SPRING FRAGRANCE: Here are paper, ink, brushes, and inkstone.

CH'EN: What sort of ink is this supposed to be?

LI NIANG: Oh, she brought the wrong thing. This is "snail black," for painting the brows.

CH'EN: And what sort of brushes?

LI-NIANG (*laughing*): Mascara brushes.

CH'EN: Never did I see such things before! Take them away, take them away. And what sort of paper is this?

LI-NIANG: Notepaper woven by a famous courtesan.

CH'EN: Take it away, take it away. Bring such as was woven by the noble inventor of paper, the ancient Ts'ai Lun. And what sort of inkstone? Is it single or double?

LI-NIANG: It's not single, it's married.

CH'EN: And the "eye" patterns on it—what sort of eyes?

LI-NIANG: Weeping eyes.

CH'EN: What are they weeping about?—Go change the whole lot.

SPRING FRAGRANCE (*aside*): Ignorant old rustic! (*To* CH'EN.) Very well. (*She brings a new set.*) Will these do?

CH'EN (*examining them*): All right.

LI-NIANG: I believe I could copy some characters. Spring Fragrance, the brush, please.

CH'EN: Let me see how you write. (*As* LI-NIANG *writes, he watches in amazement.*) Never did I see writing of this quality! What is the model?

LI-NIANG: The model is "The Beauty Adorns her Hair with Blossoms," the style transmitted by the Lady Wei of Tsin times.

SPRING FRAGRANCE: Let me do some characters in the style of "The Maid Apes Her Mistress."

LI-NIANG: Wait a while.

SPRING FRAGRANCE: Master, I beg leave to be excused—to leave the room and excuse myself. (*She exits.*)

LI-NIANG: Esteemed tutor, may I inquire what age your mother has attained?

CH'EN: She will shortly reach the age of sixty.

LI-NIANG: If you would let me have the pattern, I should like to embroider a pair of slippers for her birthday.

CH'EN: Thank you. The pattern should be from Mencius, "to make sandals without knowledge of the foot."

LI-NIANG: Spring Fragrance isn't back yet.

CH'EN: Shall I call her? (*He claps thrice.*)

SPRING FRAGRANCE (*entering*): Clapping like that—I'll give him the clap!

LI-NIANG (*annoyed*): What have you been doing, silly creature?

SPRING FRAGRANCE (*laughing*): Peeing. But I found a lovely big garden full of pretty flowers and willows, lots of fun.

CH'EN: Dear, dear, instead of studying she is off to the garden. Let me fetch a bramble switch.

SPRING FRAGRANCE: What do you want a bramble switch for?
  How can a girl
  take the examinations and fill an office?
  All it's for is to
  read a few characters and scrawl a few crow's-feet.

CH'EN: There were students in ancient times who put fireflies in a bag or read by the moon.

SPRING FRAGRANCE: If you use reflected moonlight
    you'll dazzle the toad up there
    as for fireflies in a bag
    just think of the poor things burning!

CH'EN: Then what about the man who tied his hair to a beam to keep from nodding off, or the scholar who prodded himself awake with an awl in the thigh?

SPRING FRAGRANCE: If you were to try
    tying your hair to a beam
    you wouldn't have much left,
    and pricking your thighs
    you'd be even scabbier than you are.
    What's so glorious about that?

(*A flower-vendor's cry comes from within.*)

    Listen, young mistress,
    a flower-vendor's cry
    drowns out the drone of studies.

CH'EN: Again she distracts the young lady. This time I shall really beat her.

(*He moves to do so.*)

SPRING FRAGRANCE (*dodging*): Try and beat me then
    poor little me
    —this "peachlike plumlike pupil"
    will make you look such a fool,
    you who carry a "burden of thorns"
    like a criminal craving pardon!

(*She grabs the bramble switch and throws it to the floor.*)

LI-NIANG: You wicked creature, kneel at once for such rudeness to the tutor. (SPRING FRAGRANCE *kneels.*) Since this is her first offence, sir, perhaps it will be enough if I give her a scolding:

Your hands must not touch the garden swing
nor your feet tread the garden path.

SPRING FRAGRANCE: But just come and see.

LI-NIANG: If you answer back, we shall have to
scorch with an incense stick
these lips of yours that blow breezes of malice
blind with a sewing needle
these eyes that blossom into nothing but trouble.

SPRING FRAGRANCE: And what use would my eyes be then?

LI-NIANG: I insist that you
hold to the inkstone
stand fast by the desk
attend to "it is written in the *Songs*"
be there when "the Master says"
and do not let your thoughts wander.

SPRING FRAGRANCE: Oh, do let's wander a little!

LI-NIANG (*seizing her by the hair*): Do you want as many
weals on your back
as there are hairs on your head?
I'll have you show respect for the "comptroller of the household."
—the whip Madame Chen, my mother, keeps in her room!

SPRING FRAGRANCE: I won't do it again.

LI-NIANG: You understand then?

CH'EN: That will be enough, we shall let her go this time. Get up.
(SPRING FRAGRANCE *rises to her feet*.) Except she lacks ambition
for the fame of office, instruction of the girl pupil parallels the
boy's.

Now that your lesson is ended you may return to the Prefect's residence while I exchange a few words with your father.

ALL THREE: What a waste of
this new green gauze on the sunlit window.

(*Exit* CH'EN TSUI-LIANG.)

SPRING FRAGRANCE (*pointing scornfully at his retreating back*): Ignorant old ox, dopey old dog, not an ounce of understanding.

LI-NIANG (*tugging at her sleeve*): Stupid creature, "a tutor for a day is a father for a lifetime." Do you think he is incapable of beating you? But tell me, where is this garden of yours?

(SPRING FRAGRANCE *refuses to speak.* LI-NIANG *gives an embarrassed laugh and asks again.*)

SPRING FRAGRANCE (*pointing*): Over there, of course!

LI-NIANG: What is there to look at?

SPRING FRAGRANCE: Oh, lots to look at, half a dozen pavilions, one or two swings, a meandering stream one can float winecups down, weathered T'ai-hu rocks on the other bank. It's really beautiful, with all those prize blooms and rare plants.

LI-NIANG: How surprising to find such a place. But now we must go back to the house.

THE INTERRUPTED DREAM

LI-NIANG: Orioles dream-waking coil their song
      through all the brilliant riot of the new season
      to the listener in the tiny leaf-locked court.

SPRING FRAGRANCE: Burnt to ashes the aloes wood
      cast aside the broidering thread
      no longer able as in past years
      to quiet stirrings of the spring's passions.

LI-NIANG: Like one "eyeing the plum-flower to slake her thirst"
      at dawn, cheeks blurred with last night's rouge
      I gaze at Plum-flower Pass.

SPRING FRAGRANCE: The coils of your hair
      dressed with silken swallows in the mode of spring
      tilt aslant as you lean
      across the balustrade.

LI-NIANG: Rootless ennui

"where are the scissors can cut
the comb can untangle this grief?"

SPRING FRAGRANCE: I have told the oriole and the swallow
to leave their urging of the flowers
and with spring as their excuse
to come look at you.

LI-NIANG: Spring Fragrance, have you given orders for the paths to be swept?

SPRING FRAGRANCE: Yes.

LI-NIANG: Now bring my mirror and my gown.

SPRING FRAGRANCE (*reentering with mirror and gown*):
"Cloud coiffure set to perfection
        still she questions the mirror
robe of gauze soon to be changed
        still she dabs on perfume."

I've brought your mirror and gown.

LI-NIANG: The spring a rippling thread
of gossamer gleaming sinuous in the sun
borne idly across the court.
Pausing to straighten
the flower heads of hair ornaments
I tremble to find that my mirror
stealing its half-glance at my hair
has thrown these "gleaming clouds"
into alarmed disarray.

(*She takes a few steps.*)

Walking here in my chamber
how should I dare let others see my form!

SPRING FRAGRANCE: How beautifully you are dressed and adorned today!

LI-NIANG: See now how vivid shows my madder skirt
how brilliant gleam these combs all set with gems

—you see, it has been

always in my nature to love fine things.
And yet, this bloom of springtime no eye has seen.
What if my beauty should amaze the birds
and out of shame for the comparison
"cause fish to sink, wild geese to fall to earth,
petals to close, the moon to hide her face"
while all the flowers tremble?

SPRING FRAGRANCE: Please come now, it's almost breakfast-time. (*They begin to walk.*)

Look how

while on the lacquered walkway
            traces of gold dust glitter
there on the lodge at pool's edge
            mosses make a green mass.
Timid lest the grass stain
            our newly broidered socks
we grieve that the flowers must bear
            the tug of tiny gold bells.

LI-NIANG: Without visiting this garden, how could I ever have realized this splendor of spring!

See how deepest purple, brightest scarlet
open their beauty only to the dry well's crumbling parapet.
"Bright the morn, lovely the scene," listless and lost the heart
—where is the garden "gay with joyous cries"?

My mother and father have never spoken of any such exquisite spot as this.

LI-NIANG *and* SPRING FRAGRANCE: Flying clouds of dawn, rolling storm at dusk
pavilion in emerald shade against the sunset glow
fine threads of rain, petals borne on breeze
gilded pleasure-boat in waves of mist:
sights little treasured by the cloistered maid
who sees them only on a painted screen.

SPRING FRAGRANCE: All the flowers have come into bloom now, but it's still too early for the peony.

LI-NIANG: The green hillside
　　　　bleeds with the cuckoo's tears of red azalea
　　　　shreds of mist lazy as wine fumes thread the sweetbriar.
　　　　However fine the peony
　　　　how can she rank as queen
　　　　coming to bloom when spring has said farewell?

SPRING FRAGRANCE: See them pairing, orioles and swallows!

SPRING FRAGRANCE *and* LI-NIANG: Idle gaze resting
　　　　there where the voice of swallow shears the air
　　　　and liquid flows the trill of oriole.

LI-NIANG: We must go now.

SPRING FRAGRANCE: Really, one would never weary of enjoying this garden.

LI-NIANG: How true. (*They begin to walk back.*)

　　　　Unwearying joy—how should we break its spell
　　　　even by visits each in turn
　　　　to the Twelve Towers of Fairyland?
　　　　But better now, as first elation passes
　　　　to find back in our chamber
　　　　some pastime for idle hours.

(*They reach the house.*)

SPRING FRAGRANCE: Open the west chamber door,
　　　　in the east room make the bed,
　　　　fill the vase with azalea,
　　　　light aloes in the incense-burner.

Take your rest now, young mistress, while I go to report to Madam.

(*She exits.*)

LI-NIANG (*sighing*): Back from spring stroll
　　　　　　　　to silent room

what to do but try on
    the spring's new adornments?

Ah spring, now that you and I have formed so strong an attach-
ment, what shall I find to fill my days when you are past? Oh this
weather, how sleepy it makes one feel. Where has Spring Fragrance got to? (*She looks about her, then lowers her head again,
pondering.*) Ah, Heaven, now I begin to realize how disturbing
the spring's splendor can truly be. They were all telling the truth,
those poems and ballads I read which spoke of girls of ancient
times "in springtime moved to passion, in autumn to regret."
Here am I at the "double eight," my sixteenth year, yet no fine
"scholar to break the cassia bough" has come my way. My young
passions stir to the young spring season, but where shall I find an
"entrant of the moon's leaf-palace"?[1] Long ago the Lady Han
found a way to a meeting with Yu Yu, and the scholar Chang met
with Miss Ts'ui by chance. Their loves are told in the "Poem on
the Red Leaf" and the *Western Chamber,* how these "fair maids
and gifted youths" after clandestine meetings made marital un-
ions "as between Ch'in and Tsin"—(*She gives a long sigh.*)
Though born and bred of a noted line of holders of office, I have
reached the age to "pin up my hair" without plan made for my
betrothal to a suitable partner. The green springtime of my own
life passes unfulfilled, and swift the time speeds by as dawn and
dusk interchange. (*She weeps.*) O pity one whose beauty is a
bright flower, when life endures no longer than leaf on tree!

From turbulent heart these springtime thoughts of love
will not be banished
—O from what spring, what hidden source
comes this sudden discontent?
I was a pretty child, and so
of equal eminence must the family be
truly immortals, no less
to receive me in marriage.
But for what grand alliance
is this springtime of my youth
so cast away?

---

[1] A scholar successful in the examinations.

Who may perceive
these passions that lie dormant in my heart?
My only course this coy delaying
but in secret dreams
by whose side do I lie?
—hidden longings roll with the spring-swelling stream.
Lingering
where to reveal my true desires!
Suffering
this wasting
where but to Heaven shall my lament be made!

I feel rather tired, I shall rest against this low table and drowse for a while. (*She falls asleep and begins to dream of* LIU MENG-MEI, *who enters bearing a branch of willow in his hand.*)

LIU MENG-MEI: As song of oriole purls in warmth of sun
so smiling lips open to greet romance.
Tracing my path by petals borne on stream
I find the Peach Blossom Spring[1] of my desire.

I came along this way with Miss Tu Li-niang—how is it that she is not with me now? (*He looks behind him and sees her.*) Ah, Miss Tu! (*She rises, startled from sleep, and greets him. He continues.*) So this is where you were—I was looking for you everywhere. (*She glances shyly at him but does not speak.*) I just chanced to break off this branch from a weeping willow in the garden. You are so deeply versed in works of literature, I should like you to compose a poem to honor it. (*She starts in surprised delight, and opens her lips to speak but checks herself.*)

LI-NIANG (*aside*): I have never seen this young man in my life—what is he doing here?

LIU (*smiling at her*): Lady, I am dying of love for you! I am the
partner born of fairest line
for whom you wait as the river of years rolls past.
Everywhere I have searched for you
in compassion for you, secluded in your chamber.

Lady, come with me just over there where we can talk. (*She gives*

---

[1] Cf. T'ao ch'ien's allegory in *Anthology of Chinese Literature, Vol. 1,* p. 167.

him a shy smile but refuses to move; he tries to draw her by the sleeve).

LI-NIANG (*in a low voice*): Where do you mean?

LIU: There, just beyond this railing peony-lined
    against the mound of
    weathered T'ai-hu rocks.

LI-NIANG (*in a low voice*): But sir, what do you mean to do?

LIU (*also in a low voice*): Open the fastening at your neck
    loosen the girdle at your waist
    while you
    screening your eyes with your sleeve
    white teeth clenched on the fabric as if against pain
    bear with me patiently a while
    then drift into gentle slumber.

(LI-NIANG *turns away, blushing.* LIU *advances to take her in his arms, but she resists him.*)

LIU *and* LI-NIANG: Somewhere at some past time you and I met.
    Now we behold each other in solemn awe

but do not say

    in this lovely place we should meet and speak no word.

(LIU *exits carrying off* LI-NIANG *by force. Enter* FLOWER SPIRIT *in red cloak strewn with petals and ornamental headdress on piled up hair.*)

FLOWER SPIRIT: Commissioner of the Flowers' Blooming
        come with new season
    from Heaven of Blossom-Guard
        to fulfill the springtime's labors.
    Drenched in red petal rain
        the beholder, heartsore
    anchors his yearnings
        beyond the shining clouds.

In my charge as Flower Spirit is this garden in the rear of the prefectural residence at Nan-an. Between Li-niang, daughter of Prefect Tu, and the young graduate Liu Meng-mei there exists a marriage-affinity which must some day be fulfilled, and now Miss Tu's heart has been so deeply moved by her spring strolling that she has summoned the graduate Liu into her dream. To cherish in compassion the "jadelike incense ones" is the special concern of a Flower Spirit, and that is why I am here to watch over her and to ensure that the "play of clouds and rain" will be a joyous experience for her.

> Ah, how the male force surges and leaps
> as in the way of wanton bee he stirs
> the gale of her desire
> while her soul trembles
> at the dewy brink of a sweet, shaded vale.
> A mating of shadows, this,
> consummation within the mind
> no fruitful Effect
> but an apparition within the Cause.
> Ha, but now my flower palace is sullied by lust.

I must use a falling petal to wake her.

(*Scatters petals in the entrance to the stage.*)

> Loth she may be to loose herself
> from the sweet spellbound dream of spring's delight
> but petals flutter down
> like crimson snow.

So, graduate Liu, the dream is but half-complete. When it is over, be sure to see Miss Tu safely back to her chamber. I leave you now. (*Exits.*)

(*Enter* LIU MENG-MEI, *leading* LI-NIANG *by the hand.*)

LIU: For this brief moment

> nature was our comforter
> leaves for pillow, our bed a bed of flowers.

Are you all right, Miss Tu? (*She lowers her head.*)

> Disarrayed the clouds of her hair
> combs set with ruby and emerald
> falling aslant.

O Lady, never forget

> how close I clasped you
> and with what tenderness
> longing only to make
> of our two bodies one single flesh
> but bringing forth
> a glistening of rouge raindrops in the sun.

LI-NIANG: Sir, you must go now.

LI-NIANG *and* LIU: Somewhere at some past time you and I met.
Now we behold each other in solemn awe

but do not say

> in this lovely place we should meet and speak no word.

LIU: Lady, you must be tired now. Please take a rest. (*He sees her back
to the table against which she had been drowsing, and gently taps
her sleeve.*) Lady, I am going now. (*Looking back at her.*) Lady,
have a good rest now, I shall come to see you again.

> Rain threatened the spring garden as she approached
> and when she slept the "clouds and rain"
> broke over Wu-shan, hill of fairy love.

(*He exits.*)

LI-NIANG (*waking with a start, and calling in a low voice*): Young sir,
young sir, oh you have left me.

(*She falls asleep again.*)

MADAM CHEN (*entering*): Husband on prefect's daïs
daughter in cloistered chamber
—yet when she broiders patterns on a dress
above the flowers the birds fly all in pairs.

Child, child, what are you doing asleep in a place like this?

LI-NIANG (*waking and calling again after* LIU): Oh, oh.

MADAM CHEN: Why child, what is the matter?

LI-NIANG (*startled and rising to her feet*): Mother, it's you!

MADAM CHEN: Child, why aren't you passing your time pleasantly with needlework or a little reading? Why were you lying here sleeping in the middle of the day?

LI-NIANG: Just now I took an idle stroll in the garden, but all at once the raucousness of the birds began to distress me and so I came back to my room. Lacking any means to while away the time I must have fallen asleep for a moment. Please excuse my failure to receive you in proper fashion.

MADAM CHEN: The rear garden is too lonely and deserted, child. You must not go strolling there again.

LI-NIANG: I shall take care to do as you bid, Mother.

MADAM CHEN: Off to the schoolroom with you now for your lesson.

LI-NIANG: We are having a break just now, the tutor is not here.

MADAM CHEN (*sighing*): There must always be troubles when a girl approaches womanhood, and she must be left to her own ways. Truly,

> moiling and toiling in the children's wake
> many the pains a mother needs must take.

(*She exits.*)

LI-NIANG (*watching her leave and sighing heavily*): Ah, Heaven, Li-niang, what strange adventures have befallen you today! Chancing to visit the garden behind the house I found a hundred different flowers in bloom everywhere, and the beauty of the scene set my heart in turmoil. When my elation passed and I came back I fell into a midday slumber here in my incense-laden chamber. Suddenly a most handsome and elegant youth appeared, of age just fit for the "capping ceremony" of the twentieth year. He had broken off a branch from a willow in the garden, and he smiled and said to me, "Lady, you are so deeply versed in works of literature, I should like you to compose a poem in honor of this willow branch." I was on the point of replying when the thought came to me that I had never seen this man in my life before and did not even know his name. How should I so lightly enter into conversation with him? But just as this was in my mind he came close and began to speak fond words to me; then taking me in his arms he carried me to a spot beside the peony pavilion, beyond the railings which the tree peonies line, and there together we found the "joys of cloud and rain." Passion was matched by passion, and indeed a thousand fond caresses, a million tendernesses passed between us. After our bliss was accomplished he led me back to where I had been sleeping and many times said, "Rest now." Then, just as I was about to see him off, suddenly my mother came into my room and woke me. Now perspiration chills all my body—it was no more than a "dream of Nan-k'o, the human world in an anthill." I hastened to greet my mother with the proper decorum, and was duly given a good talking-to. Though there was nothing I could say in my defence, how can I now free my mind from memories of all that happened in my dream? Walking or sitting still I find no peace, all I can feel is a sense of loss. Ah Mother, you tell me to be off to the schoolroom to my lesson—but what kind of book has lessons to lighten this heavy heart?

(*She weeps, screening her face with her sleeve.*)

> Through scudding of "clouds and rain"
> I had touched the borders of dream
> when the lady my mother
> called me, alas! and broke
> this slumber by window's sunlit green.
> Now clammy cold a perspiration breaks
> now heart numbs, footsteps falter
> thought fails, hair slants awry
> and whether to sit or stand
> is more than mind can decide
> —then let me sleep again.

SPRING FRAGRANCE (*entering*): Against the coming of night
> rid cheeks of powder's traces
> against the damp of spring
> add incense to the burner.

Young mistress, I have aired the bedclothes for you to sleep now.

LI-NIANG: For heart spring-burdened, limbs

> now lax from garden strolling
> no need of incense-aired
> brocaded covers to entice to slumber.

Ah, Heaven,

> let the dream I dreamed be not yet fled too far.

THE PORTRAIT

LI-NIANG: By winding walks I left my dream
> and lost him, fading
> now jadelike charms grow chill in chamber's depth
> where soul must languish
> while as the mist the petal
> or the moon the cloud
> a flicker of untold love
> touches the morning.

SPRING FRAGRANCE: Dreading some glimpse of amorous butterfly
> leaf-lost in quest of fragrance
> weary she rises, paints her face
> and listens to the harshness of the shrike.
> Spring passes, though crimson sleeves still beckon.

LI-NIANG: No man was there at the peony pavilion
> and yet as I recall my dream
> there is one who holds my longings.

SPRING FRAGRANCE: In the curving of her eyebrows
> shows her beauty, spring-tormented
> —but who should depict these "slopes of distant hills"?

LI-NIANG: In my thin gown I tremble
> wrapped against the morning chill
> only by regrets
> to see red tears of petals shake from the bough.

LI-NIANG *and* SPRING FRAGRANCE: How to depict the fairy maid of
> Wu-shan
> whether by sun or rain
> against the cloud and shadow of Kao-t'ang?

SPRING FRAGRANCE: My young mistress: ever since you took that stroll in the garden you have been careless of your meals and careless of your rest. Do you think it can be the disturbance of the spring that is causing you to pine and grow thin? I am too stupid to be offering advice to such as yourself, but I do not think you should visit the garden any more from now on.

LI-NIANG: Ah, but how are you to know what lies behind this? You must understand how
> vernal dreams mysteriously
>> flower with the third month
> lightly the chill of dawn
>> thins out the blossoms.

(*She sings softly.*)

> So chill the spring's leave-taking
> daily my thoughts grow idler
> my will more feeble.
> My toilet made at last, I sit alone
> listless as the incense-smoke I watch
> no peace of mind
> until the choking weeds that breed distress
> are rooted out, and the shoots of joy can grow.
> Whom to please if I mask my sorrow with smiles?
> —My vision quivers in a blur of tears.

SPRING FRAGRANCE: My young mistress
> if your fever cannot be cooled
> then why doesn't it dry the cold tears?
> It's clear that in these spring roamings
> you have had no defence
> from the upsetting chatter of oriole and swallow.
> Just think
> what anxiety you will cause madam your mother.
> Go on with this grieving
> and folks will be far from perfectly enchanted
> with this perfect beauty of yours.

LI-NIANG (*with a gesture of alarm*): Oh dear, from what Spring Fragrance tells me I must have become completely haggard. Let me see in the mirror what has really happened. (*She looks in the mirror and sobs.*) Alas, when before I could boast of an enticing soft fullness, how could I have grown as thin and frail as this? Before it's too late let me make a portrait of myself to leave to the world, lest the worst should suddenly befall me and no one then ever learn of the beauty of Tu Li-niang who came from Western Shu! Spring Fragrance, bring plain silk and colored inks, and attend on me while I sketch.

SPRING FRAGRANCE (*returning with silk and brushes*): Easy to sketch
　　　　　　　　　　　freshness of youth
　　　hard to portray
　　　　　　　the pain at heart.

The silk and the colored inks are ready for your use.

LI-NIANG (*weeping*): How can it be that Tu Li-niang must sketch with her own hand the grace of her sixteen years! Ah, that time should have etched

　　　these peachbloom cheeks of youth
　　　so swiftly with lines of care!
　　　I ask no "blessed lot never to fail"
　　　—but why must it be "fairest face first to age"?
　　　Many the beauty has been praised as peerless
　　　only for time to erase the bright vision—so soon.
　　　Now to damp down the burning
　　　of desire in the soul's brief resting-place of flesh
　　　take brush and paper, ink and inkstone
　　　the "four jewels of the study," of quality
　　　such as is found in chambers of princely consorts
　　　and render eyebrows to rival the Western Maid's
　　　which arched above the West Lake's loveliness
　　　twin crescent moons.
　　　With a silk cloth
　　　lightly wipe the mirror.
　　　Hairs' tip lightly brushing, deftly limning;

ah, mirror-semblance
you must be my close model
for cheeks with teasing smile
and cherry mouth
and willow leaf of brow
and now in washes of drifting mist
the cloud of hair.
The fine dark tip of eyebrow still to draw
already the eyes, with light of autumn stream
personify the sitter;
hair ornaments bright with feathers and gems
set off the forehead gentle as hills of spring.

SPRING FRAGRANCE: Best fit to smile
slender waist poised to breath of spring breeze
yet sensing too the sorrows the east wind brings.

LI-NIANG: For background, hills and stream
a dwelling or two
and my self-portrait
is complete in miniature;
put in my hand a "green sprig of plum"
ready to tease a lover
—here see me lean
in a dawn dream against a rocky mound
grace of bearing to match the wind-stirred willow;
to lines so fine-drawn
add last for contrast broad green leaves of the plantain.

Spring Fragrance, hold it up so that we may see whether I have
caught a likeness.

SPRING FRAGRANCE: Easy enough to sketch her aspect
in hues red or dark;
harder to portray the rare individual self
when the image reflects the reality
like flowers seen behind closed lids
or the moon on water.

LI-NIANG (*pleased with her work*): But it will make a charming picture. Ah,

> surely my painting promises well
> with a sweet appeal more marked than in the model!

SPRING FRAGRANCE: All it lacks is a husband by your side. If only
> your marriage destiny could be soon fulfilled
> and a fine handsome husband found

then we should see

> a happy couple limned against clouds of bliss!

LI-NIANG: Spring Fragrance, I have something to confess to you: that time I was strolling in the garden—I found a man.

SPRING FRAGRANCE (*startled*): Oh, my young mistress, how could you be so fortunate?

LI-NIANG: Why, in a dream!

> There he stood smiling
> and I could recall his living likeness
> catch with the fine lines of my brush
> the very essence of his soul
> but that I fear to reveal my secret love.

Oh, his ardent gaze

> lone crescent of an autumn moon
> rising in space where peak is touched by cloud
> —is this the cloud that frames the honored guest
> in the moon's toad-palace?

Now take good note of this, Spring Fragrance: the young scholar who appeared in my dream had broken off a branch of willow to present to me. Surely this must be a sign that the husband I shall meet in time to come will have the surname Liu, for "willow"? What would you say to my making up a poem now, to inscribe at the head of this scroll, which would contain hints of my spring yearnings?

SPRING FRAGRANCE: That would be a clever plan.

LI-NIANG (*inscribes the poem, reciting it as she does so*):

> However close the likeness
> > viewed from near at hand
> from farther off one would say
> > this was an airborne sprite.
> Union in some year to come
> > with the "courtier of the moon"
> will be beneath the branches
> > either of plum or willow.

(*She sets down her brush with a sigh.*)

Spring Fragrance, many a beautiful maiden in past or present time has married early in her youth a loved and loving husband who has painted her portrait; whilst many another has taken up the brush herself to send her own likeness to a lover. But who should receive this portrait of Tu Li-niang?

> Pleasure yields to pain:
> pleasure in the bright vision
> elegantly demure
> as fairy pendants sway;
> pain to predict, as the years deepen
> the fading of tint from eye and lip
> of this A-chiao, locked up in golden chamber.
> Vain labor
> when to no lover's eye this lovely image
> unrolled will bring a tear
> when there is none to call
> the living Chen-chen from the painted scroll.

(*She weeps.*)

> O melancholy fate
> that this most imminent presence must stay hid
> for latter days to witness.

Spring Fragrance, call softly now for the flower-lad, I have an errand for him.

(SPRING FRAGRANCE *calls.*)

GARDENER'S LAD (*entering*): Honored like Ch'in-kung I have lived
                            among flowers all my days
                   but this lady no longer as Ts'ui Hui
                            rivals the beauty of the scroll!

What is your errand, miss?

LI-NIANG: I want you to take this self-portrait of mine to the scrollmak-
er's to be mounted, and tell him I want it done with care:

> Who shall mount this portrait, so to enhance
> the happy capture of the living model?
> Let the material be flowered damask
> bleached to a gemlike gleam of white
> and have the margins slender.
> Let there be no blabbing
> should anyone enquire the painter's name.
> Lining and mount must survive
> burning of sun and buffeting of breeze
> for "finest things are least enduring"
> and the delicacy of red stroke or of black
> must not be sullied.

GARDENER'S LAD: Young mistress, the scroll is all complete now, where
shall I hang it?

LI-NIANG: To the gentle boudoir none will come to enjoy its beauty

SPRING FRAGRANCE: more fit to be enshrined in the fairy temple of Wu-
shan

LI-NIANG *and* SPRING FRAGRANCE: or will it take its flight
                            in transformations between cloud and rain?

KEENING

SPRING FRAGRANCE: Nightlong the harshness of wind and rain
                   and she so frail

so wasted in her sorrow.
The gods no help
herbs no effect.

A time for frowns
a time for smiling:
alas, for one so young
neither to smile nor frown!

I have waited on my young mistress while her "spring sickness"
has lasted deep into autumn. Tonight, full moon, is the beloved
Midautumn Festival, but outside a bleak wind buffets the rain.
Still I must help my young mistress here, to distract her from the
gloom of her worsening sickness. Truly,

when rain threatens the Midautumn moon
the Ever-Burning Flame flickers in the wind.

(*She exits, and reenters supporting the dying* LI-NIANG.)

The moon-viewing hall is vacant
as clouds jostle down the pathways of the sky.
The chill in the bone
presages a passing, life like an autumn dream.
What has the world to show more puissant than passion?
—Soul cast adrift, heart aching, all is done.

LI-NIANG: Wasting sound of water clock
has worn my pillow through;
one who lies as drunk or stupid
finds it not hard to die.
A dark thread of fragrance
lost in the night of rain
my body wholly worn
dreading the autumn cold.

I have been so sunk in sickness, Spring Fragrance, tell me what
night is this?

SPRING FRAGRANCE: It is the middle of the eighth month.

LI-NIANG: So, tonight is the Midautumn Festival! Have my father and
mother been too distressed by my condition to enjoy viewing the
moon?

SPRING FRAGRANCE: You must not worry about that.

LI-NIANG: I remember when Tutor Ch'en made a prognostication for me, he said the important thing was to get past the Midautumn. But it seems that my sickness is growing more severe, and tonight I feel a little worse. But open the window for me, so that I can see the moon.

(SPRING FRAGRANCE *opens the window.*)

LI-NIANG (*gazing*): Where does the ice-toad moon
　　　swim in this sea of sky?
　　　The jade pestle stands in an autumn blankness
　　　—who now will steal herbs to offer Ch'ang-o?
　　　What western wind has "scattered all trace of dreams"?
　　　Once gone, hard to find him again
　　　unless the tricks of sprites or demons may help.
　　　"Vanishing from the brow
　　　a new pain enters in the heart below."

(*She gestures her listlessness.*)

SPRING FRAGRANCE: How callous the spring, to leave in passing such
　　　　　　torment,
　　　its mists and vapors each more horrid than the other.
　　　A human life, the high concern of heaven
　　　might win a brief respite
　　　yet must dwindle so soon.
　　　Whose to enjoy
　　　this beauty of form so carelessly cast aside?

Let me try to divert her a little: my young mistress, the moon has risen!

　　　The moon clearing the sky
　　　must surely flood the dark dreams from your bed.

LI-NIANG (*sighing as she gazes at the moon*):
　　　Hour by hour, week by week
　　　　　　longing for Midautumn
　　　yet the Midautumn finds me
　　　　　　still unfree.

No light of new orphan moon
        shall touch my life
which in the rain
        of this sad night must end.

But, however fair you may shine,
    whose happiness do you bring, Midautumn moon
as plane trees sheared by west wind
    drip tears of rain?
My shrunken limbs, feebler than before;
and at the sky's edge, melancholy geese
hasten their departure.
"Wintry crickets where the grass ends";
the windows rustle their paper panes.

(*She faints, then cries in alarm.*)

A floating numbness:
hands and feet wilt and will not move.

SPRING FRAGRANCE (*in alarm*): The chill in my young mistress' body has
numbed her limbs—I must ask Madam to come.

MADAM CHEN (*entering*): My husband eminent
        in old age hale and strong;
So delicate my daughter
        her short life filled with pain.
How is your sickness progressing, my child?

SPRING FRAGRANCE: She is worse, Madam.

MADAM CHEN: How can this be!

In the garden of the rear court
an unguarded dream
but how to explain
this continued failure to wake?
Her heavy head droops in deep slumber.

(*She weeps.*)

Oh, why did we not have you long ago

"mount the dragon" of a successful match!
Nightly the lone wild goose
strips the soft feather sheen
from this my "fledgling phoenix."
All becomes void
and time now also for your mother's life to pass.

LI-NIANG (*revives*): Now my spirit stirs
like the air of a mirage
as the breeze sets to tinkling
the pendants below the eaves.

Mother, I make obeisance to express my gratitude.

(*Stumbling to her knees in prostration.*)

From my first years you have prized me
as your "thousand gold pieces"
but I, unfilial
cannot serve you to the end of your days.

Mother, this is Heaven's decree. In this life

a flower no sooner red. . . .
ah, let me only serve anew
these parents, lily and cedar, in the lifetime to come.

ALL (*making gestures of weeping, and singing*): O cruel west wind
so sudden, so callous
to scatter green leaf and red petal.

MADAM CHEN: Lacking sons
still I was sent a child all fragrant charm
to smile her joy about me.
Grown now to womanhood, she was to care
for us, her revered elders, at our end
but now, alas, childless and lost shall we
remain at the rim of the sky.

My child, very soon

from the clash of moon and year
a void of time
shall quench your troubled spirit.

ALL: O cruel west wind
    so sudden, so callous
    to scatter green leaf and red petal.

LI-NIANG: Mother, if the worst befall, what will become of my body?

MADAM CHEN: We shall take you back to your native place for burial,
    child.

LI-NIANG (*weeping*): My spirit, coffin-borne, will see in dream
    the thousand thousand folded ranges
    that bar the road to home.

MADAM CHEN: It is indeed a far journey.

LI-NIANG: Far as it is, your daughter has one request to make. I have
    come to love one tree, a plum, in the rear court. It is my wish that
    you bury my body beneath that tree.

MADAM CHEN: Why do you ask this?

LI-NIANG: I can become no
    ailing Ch'ang-o, immortal
    in the moon's cassia grottoes

yet I should wish

    my bones to powder white
    the caverns at the ancient plum tree's roots.

MADAM CHEN (*weeping*): See how her
    eyes blur with tears
    as she strains to raise her head
    and the cold sweat pours
    a chill to her very heart

oh, could I only

    offer my life for hers now
    to appease the demon of death!

ALL: A cruel empyrean that sends
    the flower-despoiling storm
    when the moon is at her brightest.

MADAM CHEN: I must go now to arrange with your father for a great mass to be held. Ah, child,

> in vain the silver toad
> > mixes one herb with another;
> now paper charms are followed
> > by burning of paper ingots.

(*She exits.*)

LI-NIANG: Spring Fragrance, do you think a time can come when I may return to life?

(*She sighs.*)

> Always you have observed my slightest wish,
> what I desired you would design.

Spring Fragrance, take good care of my father and mother.

SPRING FRAGRANCE: Indeed I shall.

LI-NIANG: One thing I have to tell you. That portrait scroll on which I inscribed the poem: when rolled it does not present a very pleasing appearance. When I am buried, put it in a box of red sandalwood, to be placed beneath the weathered T'ai-hu rock.

SPRING FRAGRANCE: What is your purpose in this?

LI-NIANG: That portrait and those brush strokes
> telling my heart's desire
> may reach some day someone who understands.

SPRING FRAGRANCE: Mistress, set your mind at rest. If the worst should befall now, and the lone grave-mound cast a single shadow, then let me bear a message to your honored father, that he take into the family a young graduate by the name of Mei or Liu, "Plum" or "Willow," who can be your "companion in life or death." Would not this be an excellent plan?

LI-NIANG: I fear it is too late. *Ai-yo, ai-yo!*

SPRING FRAGRANCE: How to locate the root of this sickness
> how find healing for the heart?

LI-NIANG: When I am dead, Spring Fragrance, stand often before my spirit-tablet and call to me!

SPRING FRAGRANCE: Syllable after syllable
strikes my heart with pain!

BOTH: A cruel empyrean that sends
the flower-despoiling storm
when the moon is at her brightest.

(LI-NIANG *faints away.*)

SPRING FRAGRANCE: Oh, she is going, she is going! Master, mistress, hurry!

(*Enter the* PREFECT TU PAO *and* MADAM CHEN.)

TU PAO *and* MADAM CHEN: Drum's triple boom
ten thousand echoes of sorrow
cold rain at window
unlit by lamp's red glow.
The serving-girl brings word that our daughter worsens.

SPRING FRAGRANCE (*weeping*): Oh, my young mistress!

TU PAO *and* MADAM CHEN (*a joint gesture of weeping*): Ah, daughter,
laying aside your own life
us also you abandon
as our road's end approaches;
you were the one we looked to
to see us off.

ALL: So soon, so soon
trackless as stream-borne duckweed
shadow of passing sea wave
hibiscus flower like gleaming jade
by the wind cut low.

(LI-NIANG *revives.*)

TU PAO: See, her senses quicken! Child, your father is here.

LI-NIANG (*recognizing him*): Oh Father, help me into the inner hall.

TU PAO: Lean on me, child.

(*He supports her.*)

LI-NIANG: Head to foot the tree stripped
  "ere ever the dawn wind blows."

Set me a

  tablet upon my youthful grave
  telling I died of longing.

Father, tonight is the Midautumn.

TU PAO: Yes, child, it is the Midautumn.

LI-NIANG: How can the nightlong rain be stopped?

(*She sighs.*) Why is it

  the moon must set
  but it can rise again
  the lamp can be relit!

(*All exit.*)

SPRING FRAGRANCE (*reenters, weeping*): Oh, my young mistress,

  "No more than in cloud-patterns of the sky
  is there a constancy in the fates of men."

My young mistress is dead of her spring-sickness, and the master
and mistress are themselves near death in their grief. Oh, you who
watch, what is there we can do?—But let me now make a keening
for her. . . . No more will you tell me, my young mistress

  to burn incense sticks in the shape of the "heart" character
  for the sweetening of your linen

no more will you tell me

  when the lamp is trimmed
  to wipe away the red tears from the candle

no more will you tell me

  to tease with a smile and a proffered flower
  the singing-bird

no more will you tell me

turning your face to the mirror, to paint
with crimson your peachbloom lips.

I shall remember how you would

lay down your sewing scissors
as the night deepened
or in the clear dawn light
take up your sketching brush.

—But that reminds me of the self-portrait she made. When the
master saw it he ordered me to bury it with the corpse for fear
that the sight of it would distress Madam Chen. But bearing in
mind my young mistress' dying words, I shall have her, as she did
in life,

lean once again by the rocky mound

—although I fear

the garden-strolling youth
may find the colors faded when he comes.

Oh, it's you, Sister Stone!

SISTER STONE (*entering*): You're making a good job of your wailing and
I've come to help you. Now, Spring Fragrance, no more will she
make your

painted lips grow warm
as you follow her on the pipes.

SPRING FRAGRANCE. That's true.

SISTER STONE: No more will she need your company as

like the fairy of the River Hsiang
skirt soaking wet
you pick a random flower.

SPRING FRAGRANCE: Quite right.

SISTER STONE: Now that your young mistress is gone you will find
things a lot easier.

SPRING FRAGRANCE: How is that?

SISTER STONE: She won't be making you

> cosset her, fuss her, chitter-chatter
> summer and winter alike

she won't be making you

> stay awake late at night
> get up with the dawn.

SPRING FRAGRANCE: Well, I'm used to that.

SISTER STONE: And there are other ways you'll be saved a lot of trouble. You won't have to

> pull a wry mouth when you pick her corns

or

> stop your nose when you empty the chamber pot.

(SPRING FRAGRANCE *spits in disgust.*)

SISTER STONE: There's another thing, too: a young mistress in the bloom of youth, no telling when she might have been at it,

> when she might have been at it
and madam her mother would have

> broken your back for taking her into that garden.

SPRING FRAGRANCE: Stop your nonsense! Here's the mistress.

MADAM CHEN (*enters, weeping*): Oh, my own daughter, day by day
> a hundred times you would pass before me
and never once did I see
> irreverent levity in your eyes.
She had studied by heart
> Pan Chao's "Four Precepts" from end to end
no need had she for Mencius' mother's
> "three changes of dwelling" to mend her ways.
We feared to see her
> so slender-soft, so delicate
but who could foresee
> a wasting sickness never to mend.
> (*She wails.*)

From this time forth
a mother none will call for
—every inch of my bowels a hundred inches of fire.

(*She falls in a faint.*)

SPRING FRAGRANCE (*calls in alarm*): Master, the mistress is dead of grief! Come at once, hurry!

TU PAO (*enters, weeping*): Oh, my child! What—my wife lying here in a faint! Madam, either it was your fate

to meet with some forsaken day when Aries was obscured

or I

who sit as judge must pay
myself the penalty for past sins.
Better to be old Shun-yü Yi of Han
with all his daughters—and one
who saved his life by her pleading;
or why was there none like that other
ancient doctor of Lu
to save my daughter's life?

Ah, Heaven, Heaven, my years advance, my head is white, and

where now to seek in mist dissolving
the lineage I established?
I live to see
my little edifice torn down!

Madam, you must be careful of your own health. For even if

your bowels every inch were shattered
into a thousand fragments

still you could no more

call back your daughter's soul
than that of Wang-ti, changed into a cuckoo.

MAJOR-DOMO (*enters*): The startled crows fly off
                with old mortal woes
now magpies, harbingers of joy,
                bring word of celestial favor.

Your honor, here is the gazette announcing your promotion.

TU PAO (*reads*): Orders of his sage Imperial Majesty, transmitted by the Board of Civil Office: "Observing the Chin brigands sneaking south, we hereby appoint Tu Pao, Prefect of Nan-an, to be Pacification Commissioner charged with the defense of Huai-yang. He is to proceed to his post forthwith, and neither delay nor error will be countenanced. By imperial command." (*He sighs.*) My lady, in view of these orders from the court to proceed north, it will not be possible to make the westward journey for the burial of our daughter. Major-domo, send for Tutor Ch'en.

MAJOR-DOMO: Tutor Ch'en, the master wishes to see you.

CH'EN (*enters*): A single ditch claims the venerable P'eng
               and the child dead ere his teens;
    the same hall witnesses mourning
           and joyful felicitation.

(*He greets* TU PAO.)

TU PAO: Tutor Ch'en, my daughter has excused herself from your presence for the last time.

CH'EN (*weeping*): True indeed. I grieve that the young lady has passed to the realm of the spirits, leaving myself, Ch'en Tsui-liang, bereft of a place. I rejoice, sir, in your elevation, yet by the same token I lose my job!

(*All weep.*)

TU PAO: Tutor Ch'en, I have something to discuss with you. I am under imperial orders and dare not delay my departure. But I recall my daughter's dying wish, that she be buried beneath the plum tree in the rear garden. Anxious to avoid inconvenience to my successor during his residence here, I have given orders that a part of the garden be set aside and a "Plum-flower Shrine" built thereon, for the keeping of my daughter's spirit-tablet. I shall ask Sister Stone here to see to the upkeep of the shrine. Sister, would you be willing to do this?

SISTER STONE (*kneels*): I will see to it that the incense is replaced and the water kept fresh. But for all the comings and goings in the maintenance of the shrine, someone else will be needed in addition.

MADAM CHEN: Then let us ask Tutor Ch'en if he will be so kind.

CH'EN: I shall be happy to do my utmost in carrying out my lady's orders.

MADAM CHEN: My lord, there should be some lands assigned to furnish the expenses.

TU PAO: There are some thirty acres of grace and favor land lying fallow whose yield will supply the costs of the shrine.

CH'EN: These grace and favor fields will grease and flavor my diet!

SISTER STONE: When you see a Taoist sister, it's your duty to assist her; but I can't see any of this coming to you, Mister "Ch'en No Food!"

CH'EN: As a lay priest I "eat in eleven directions." You're only one spinster, but I am a bachelor and a Bachelor of Arts, too, so it's mine should be the greater portion.

TU PAO: Let us have no squabbling, the income and expenditures shall be Tutor Ch'en's responsibility. Sir, during the years of my tenure here I have highly favored the schools.

CH'EN: As we well know. And now that your honor has received promotion I shall have your scholars, in accordance with time-honored practice, compose a Record of your Fatherly Benevolence, together with a commemorative inscription. Then upon reaching the capital you will find these most useful to include with the gifts you will be making to your superiors and colleagues.

SISTER STONE: Hey, "Ch'en No Food," is this Record of Fatherly Benevolence some kind of a keepsake of his daughter's to show what a good father he was?

CH'EN: It's a eulogy of his honor's administration—what's it got to do with his daughter?

SISTER STONE: Well, and what might a "commemorative inscription" be?

CH'EN: We build a hall of worship and carve a statue of his honor to receive our homage there, and then over the entrance we write "Hall of the Lord Tu."

SISTER STONE: But wouldn't it be better to put the young lady there, too, at the side, so that we could all pay our respects to her?

TU PAO (*annoyed*): Stop this nonsense! Even if these are time-honored practices, I'll have none of them. Tutor Ch'en, Sister Stone,

> our thoughts, like sunset clouds, rise not
> above the three-foot mound of our daughter's grave
> and this one task my wife and I bequeath you:

we dare not ask that you should hour by hour watch over her

> but at the Feast of the Tombs, on the day of Cold Food
> let her at least receive a bowl of rice.

TRANSLATED BY CYRIL BIRCH

Ch'ing Dynasty

1644-1911

Early Ch'ing Lyrics

The chill pillows, guttering candles, and falling petals of several of the following poems recall the early greatness of the lyric (tz'u) in the Five Dynasties and early Sung. This is especially true of Ch'en Tzu-lung and Singde. Ch'en Tzu-lung (1608–47) drowned himself after last-ditch attempts in support of the Ming: the "swallows" of his "Spring Sorrows" are those who collaborated with the Manchus. Singde (Na-lan Hsing-te or Na-lan Jung-jo, 1655–85), himself a Manchu, when he died so prematurely had already established himself as the dynasty's most brilliant lyricist.

Other poets in this section include Ming loyalists like Chin-shih Tan-kuei (1614–80), whose name was Chin Pao before he became a monk, and the philosopher Wang Fu-chih (1619–92), who went into seclusion; eminent scholars like Wu Wei-yeh (1609–72) and Chu Yi-tsun (1629–1709); and romantics like Ch'en Wei-sung (1626–82).

●

Ch'en Tzu-lung

Tune: "Youthful Roamings"

[*Shao-nien yu*]

SPRING LOVE

Flowering trees in the court were bright with dew
As hand touched hand in the moonlight.
Now the glazed pillow strikes chill
Scent fades from the kerchief token
And still no way to join her lover.

What help from tears he shed at parting
When dreams must stay unfulfilled?
A moment's pleasure,
A measure of pining
Turn by turn till the third watch of night.

Tune: "Crimson Lips Adorned"

[*Tien chiang ch'un*]

THOUGHTS ON A SPRINGTIME STORM

Glory of spring as far as eye could see:
To the east wind, scattering blossoms is an old game.
The mists came down
And these poor petals none could protect.

Dreams fill with longings
For the land that is lost, and the ways of its royal line.
But spring obeys no man
And where the cuckoo calls
Its tears leave stains of blood.

Tune: "Mountain Wildflowers"

[*Shan hua tzu*]

SPRING SORROWS

Willows standing spare in morning mist
Almonds shedding to the clang of the fifth watch,
The moon across the silent Palace of Sunlight
Still touches the lingering petals.

Gold-broidered robes, fragile as butterfly wings, are rent
     apart,
Roaches strip the paint from empty bowers.
Only the hardened swallows, pairing off,
Dance in the east wind.

Wu Wei-yeh

Tune: "River Red with Blossom"

[*Man chiang hung*]

CHERISHING ANTIQUITY AT GARLIC HILL[1]

Buying wine at Nan-hsü,
Hearing a thousand feet away the night rain on the river,
I recall the Eastern Expedition of Wang Chün long ago
And later the Toba lord, the "Buddha Fox," striking south.
What use the pale-faced scholar?
—And yet the young dandy disdains his foe,
Hsieh Hsüan cuts a dash as he jokes with his staff,
Plays at war, and wins.

Events shift and swirl,
Winter clouds pile white.
Old forts crumble,
Crows gather at the Toba lord's temple.
Spearpoint and broken halberd
Sink in the wave-washed sand.
The sun set on war junks bursting through iron chains,
The west wind tore down halls of lords and princes.
Yellowing reeds, hoary bamboos, the cold tide beating
And notes of the fisherman's flute.

---

[1] From a pun on the word for "garlic," *suan,* this place was also known as "Reckoning Hill," for it was here in the third century that Sun Ch'üan's general Chou Yü devised his tactics for the defeat of Ts'ao Ts'ao—compare Chu Yi-tsun's poem below, "The Temple to Sun Ch'üan." Wang Chün's expedition compelled Sun Ch'üan's grandson to surrender to the Tsin dynasty, in whose service Hsieh Hsüan won fame as a brilliant strategist.

Tune: "The Fairy by the River"

[*Lin chiang hsien*]

OLD FLAME

Racketing round the landscape, one vintage to the next,
Ten misspent years, and here's Yün-ying again.
Complaisant as ever, tiny, dance-on-your-palm,
One quick smile in the lamplight
And she's fumbling with her waistband.

Ah, but the feelings I had are worn as my face,
I've nothing for you, sweetie, not in this life.
The moon fades, at Soochow, over the city wall,
By her green window some pass, some stay,
And crisscross go the pink-stained tears.

Tune: "Joy to the Groom"

[*Ho hsin-lang*)

IN TIME OF SICKNESS

The world presses, and white hairs multiply.
Kung Sheng refused to serve, "died young" at eighty
And left a name imperishable.
Medicine knows no cure for this sickness of mine,
This bright flame of blood in my breast.
Can I sprinkle it here in offering to west wind and waning
    moon,
Take out my heart and lay it on the ground,
Ask the magician Hua-t'o to loosen the knot in my entrails?
I think on past follies
And sob aloud.

So many stalwart friends, men of high constancy;
And I, because I wavered at the crucial moment,
I hide in the reeds on borrowed time.
Burn moxa between the brows, clear the nose with gourd
    stalks,
Nothing brings relief
As old disasters come again thousandfold.
Too hard to sacrifice wife and children, cast them off like
    an old shoe,
And still I can boast not a penny to my name.
Why are some lives so flawed
When others find wholeness?

Chin-shih Tan-kuei

Tune: "River Red with Blossom"

[*Man chiang hung*]

White horses rage on the river
But like him you ride the wind and smash the wave.
Your quayside clamor quivers as frost clashes with ice,
Thunder itself sounds feeble.
Speak not of perilous places, Antler Gorge and Wolf's Head,
When it was here that Heaven foiled his dragon dream.
Who named you for Huang Ch'ao?
Is the name truth or slander?

The clouds' persistence
Forces rain,
The river's pride
Blocks the sea's advance.
All's in ruin, laugh it off,
Myriad schemes have failed.
Old age forgets the acts once planned
And sickness mocks retirement's dream.
I lay aside chain mail to don the cassock
And keep you company.

135

Wang Fu-chih

Tune: "Tranquil Joys"

[*Ch'ing-p'ing lo*]

RAIN

Cries of homing birds fill the dusk,
The path to the south is curtained off.
Pearls, tears, burst from the weeping willows
Sending their spatter across the lotus acres.

Rain-risen ripples tease the fish to distraction,
Invest the clear pool with a duckweed cover.
Hard to believe, where turquoise clouds are deepest
The setting sun still rests on the horizon.

Tune: "Spring by the Jade Tower"

[*Yü-lou ch'un*]

WHITE LOTUS

Slender moon-sliver plunged in autumn shadows,
Flickering reflection close on silver pool.
Freshly powdered against soft clouds of hair,
Dew sprinkled clear as jade, and a fragrance self-aware.

Against the wind from the reeds, and the cold of the au-
    tumn waves
She guards her rust gold heart, with a glance in the mirror
    of dawn.
When the time comes we will ask where her spirit wanders
Between green waters and cloudless skies in the long, pure
    night.

Tune: "The Butterfly Woos the Blossoms"

[*Tieh lien hua*]

SENTRY FIRES AT T'UNG-KUAN

[*T'ung-kuan Inlet is 30 li north of Changsha. Reed beds stretch along the banks, and the approach of evening brings the scent of water iris. Against the gathering dusk the fishermen's lanterns and the fires of the customs guards strike reflections like wintry stars.*]

Drumbeats announce our sailing to the customs guards.
This endless voyage home
Marked by remembered cloud-high forests.
Sunset on Changsha, and in the swift dusk
Hunters' torches light the shrouding mist through the central lands.

Where is this, that oars cease and voices mutter in the night?
The river black, clouds too thick
To sail on to the sky's edge.
Here long ago came the wandering Tu Fu
To climb a rise, look down on the water and rhyme his grief.

Ch'en Wei-sung

Tune: "Water Music Prelude"

[*Shui-tiao ko-t'ou*]

GIRL ON A SWING

Yesterday evening, lustration rites,
Today a gaming session claimed her.
Beyond the whitewashed wall, through the red gate
Lies Bronze Camel Lane.
From high silk ropes with love-knots tied
The patterned seat an inch in depth
Flaps like a banner in the breeze.
She looks down, tightens her sash,
Adjusts a comb or two.

Soar and swoop
Sweep the green grass
Whisk away the mosses.
Pink skirts coyly refuse to flutter
But flirt with her envious shadow.
Now a falcon stooping on the wind
Now a young swallow skimming the waves
As everywhere plum blossoms swirls.
With evening, the waxing moon
Catches a jade comb where it lies.

Chu Yi-tsun

Tune: "Messages"

[*Hsiao-hsi*]

CROSSING THE PASS AT WILD-GOOSE GATE[1]

Who ever crossed these folded leagues
Of passes, but the wildgoose bearing
Reeds to his lonely resting-place?
Above the turbulent Hu-t'o waters
Through cloud packs of ice and snow
Bird trails link our path to Kou-chu Peak.
The post horn is a wail of gloom,
Windborne sand strikes the cheek
And yet men travel up this road and down:
They ask the distance, then, on failing mount in failing light
Leave the shelter
Into the pass again.

General Li Kuang, old "Ape Arms,"
Military Governor Ch'en, "the Crow"—
Heroes both, but who could hold for ever?
Prince by right of conquest

---

[1] Each of the first three poems recalls certain heroes of early times. Li Kuang of the early Han period, referred to in the first poem, is the subject of the biography by Ssu-ma Ch'ien in *Anthology of Chinese Literature, Vol. 1*. (See, on page 127, the story of the drunken watchman who held General Li all night in his watch station and was later executed for his pains.) Chou Yü, general of the "Lord of Wu" at the time of the Three Kingdoms (third century A.D.), is the subject of an allusion by Su Tung-p'o (*Anthology, Vol. 1*, page 356). Kao Huan, of Chu Yi-tsun's third poem, was a kingmaker in the bewilderingly swift succession of royal houses during the sixth century. He received his own royal title only posthumously, after his son assumed the throne of the Northern Ch'i Dynasty.

Or watchman drunkenly righteous,
All go the way of fortune in this world.
The garb of spring is soon laid aside,
Mountain inns are few here,
Drinking companions only a vain hope.
Willows droop with age,
The east wind blows indifferent
And rain threads the mist.

Tune: "River Red with Blossom"

[*Man chiang hung*]

THE TEMPLE TO SUN CH'ÜAN, THE LORD OF WU

White stone benches are lichen-clad
But as I kneel his beard juts red as yesterday.
An age resounded to their names:
Chou Yü, Lu Sun, his generals;
Lordly in his favors, he chided Chang Chao
For begging, but gave wine to Kan Ning.
Splitting the empire with his rivals, Ts'ao and Liu
For him was matter for a casual chat.

He straddled the great River,
Moat between North and South;
Set up his watchtowers,
Conquered by feigning surrender.
Ah, but of all the Six Dynasties here established
Was ever one that matched him?
Halls added before his time still stand in this lair of drag-
ons,
Chickens and hogs are slaughtered yet in spring and au-
tumn rites.
Beyond the empty battlements, grass withers on the hillside
And the cold tide laps the wall.

Tune: "Summer Approaching"

[*Hsia ch'u lin*]

AT THE HEAVENLY DRAGON TEMPLE, WHERE KAO HUAN
BUILT HIS SUMMER PALACE

Here came Kao Huan,
Warlord who at Kettle Pass
Drew his share of the royal aura.
Tales of those days
Recall a pleasure palace built where the clouds take root.
Smoke of cooking fires misted the valley over:
Surely these tiles are relics of his Hsiang-chiang Hall.
But where are the *p'i-pa* players?
A snatch of the Ch'ih-lo tribesmen's song
Would melt the heroic heart.

The hoary eagle is gone,
Ospreys soar aimlessly.
By the Well of Ice stood painted pavilions,
Twelve, and left not a single trace.
Only the scented grasses
Forever rustle their skirts to spring's seductive breeze.
As the sun declines I ride
Toward vesper bells and the dusk incense burning,
To watch, in the dwindling company of mountain monks
The cool moon from the gate framed with pines.

Tune: "Long Halt Lament"

[*Ch'ang-t'ing yüan-man*]

WILD GEESE

Uncounted company of the autumn-stricken
Joined in annual purpose
To plane the northern winds.
Wild-goose Gate is the loneliest pass,
The moon is cold on Gold River
But who will tell their griefs?
The river flats twist and turn
But longings linger
In valleys of the South.
They light at will on level sands
Their ragged line like the stepped frets of the zither.

Leaving the bank,
Wary as always, never a fixed place,
Timid before rain spatters on year-end lotus.
Threaded by wisps of cloud
In calligraphic forms: "dewdrops," "poised needles."
The writing wavers as they lose strength, flutter low,
Merge at the eye's limit in turquoise dusk.
Still inarticulate
But charged afresh from the cold waves, off they fly.

TRANSLATED BY CYRIL BIRCH

Singde

Tune: "Dream Song"

[*Ju meng ling*]

In countless arched shelters of felt, drunken men;
Abroad, starry shapes twinkle, as if to tumble down.
　　These dreams of home, sundered by White Wolf River,
Die, shattered by its thunderous sound.
　　　　Come, sleep!
　　　　Come, sleep!
Though surely I'll waken to tasteless days.

Tune: "Long Thoughts"

[*Ch'ang hsiang-ssu*]

　　　　Through the hills, a march;
　　　　By the sea, a march;
Bodies turned towards Elm Pass, to the border we go.
　　Deep in the night, a thousand tents aglow.

　　　　In the wind, a watch;
　　　　In the snow, a watch;
All a'clamor, shattered my village heart, undone my
　　dreams:
　　Sounds my old garden never knew.

Tune: "Remembering the South"

[*Yi Chiang-nan*]

I

Beautiful is the south
Here in Chien-yeh, this ancient Ch'ang-an.
Purple canopied barges, emblazoned with sea birds, heave quickly
into view;
Imperial kingfisher banners press forward, and six dragon-horses,
Martial, magnificent, and yet austere, remote.

II

Beautiful is the south
Where towered walls are like jagged peaks.
Before the tomb, an ancient relic, a solitary stone charger;
Along the highway, a vestige of the past, a bronze camel;
"Song of the Jade Trees" is heard deep in the night.

III

IMPRESSIONS OF A NIGHT'S STAY AT SHUANG-LIN TEMPLE

Heart turned to ashes,
Hair long, not yet a monk am I.
Wind and rain melt and scour—life-and-death partings;
Only a solitary candle, but how like an old companion,
Emotions endure, insurmountable.

IV

Spring has gone,
Yet people stay on at the Eastern Mansion.
Luxuriant grasses, green spot beneath a corner of the sky,
Fallen blossoms redden the pool, three bow-lengths wide;
A lovely scene, but who to share it with?

Tune: "Heavenly Immortal"

[*T'ien hsien-tzu*]

In a dream: a swath of deer parsley, green;
The young man away a year now, but not a word.
A shadowed bell rings in the moonlight; he does not return.
     Swallows on the rafters,
     Sheer gauze door screens,
A pleasant breeze; again peach blossom petals begin to fall.

Tune: "Picking the Mulberry"

[*Ts'ai sang tzu*]

I

Who will peruse the *Folk Songs*, those mournful tunes?
     Swish, swish—the wind;
     Swish, swish—the rain;
Candle wasted away, another night has passed.

Not knowing what it is you cherish.
     Sobriety is cheerless,
     Drunkenness is cheerless.
When in dreams will I visit Hsieh Bridge again?

II

In the Hsieh family courtyard, we lingered at watch's end;
     Swallows nesting on carved beams,
     The moon crossing silvery walls,
Flowers, in clusters, indistinct, even their fragrance vague.

Of itself, this love has become a memory for reflection;
     Mandarin ducks scatter,

The rain gives way to a mild chill;
Eleven years gone—nothing but a dream.

III

Ever more will I know the error of those days;
Heart strings sadly tangled,
Red tears falling furtively,
The spring wind turns everything awry before my eyes.

Knowing we were not fated to meet again,
Bravely we spoke the time.
Such is separation:
Gone, the pear blossoms, westering the moon.

Tune: "Song of the Golden Thread"

[*Chin lü ch'ü*]

I

THOUGHTS ON THE ANNIVERSARY OF MY WIFE'S PASSING

This grief, when will it all end!
Dripping on the vacant stairs,
The rain ceases, the night turns cold:
Weather fit only to bury flowers.
These past three years, a somber, dolorous dream,
A dream from which I should have awakened long ago.
Certain is it that
The world of man is savorless.
The mansion of night unattainable, blocked by this too
solid earth,
Cold, unsullied,

A plot of ground to inter my woe.
    Upon this bauble a pledge was said,
    But now it is cast away!

Were there a pair of messenger fish to contact the nether
        springs,
    Then would I know
  Who has given you comfort
  These past few years, in sorrow and in joy.
Throughout the endless nights I toss and turn,
  Enduring the "Song of the Hsiang," over and over.
    I wait for our reunion—
  In another life may we meet again;
I fear however that we two are ill-fated.
    Slight chance we should meet
  Under the slivered moon, or in the fading breeze.
    Crystal tears vanish,
    Paper ashes drift away.

II

TO LIANG FEN (KU CHEN-KUAN)

O! Mad is this man Singde,
    Whose clothes, by chance,
  Reek of the dusty odors of the court,
  Of the mansions of the Wu-yi nobility.
Had I wine, I would sprinkle it only on the soil of Chao,[1]
  But, where is he who can embody these ideals?
    And yet, to my surprise,
  I've met one who understands me.
Clear of eye, full of voice, neither of us old.
    Here before our cups,
  We wipe away the tears of heroes brave.
    Milord, don't you see,
    The moonlight like water!

---

[1] Ruled (in the third century B.C.) by a famous patron of art and letters.

With you, Milord, I will drink my fill this night.
        Pay them no mind,
    The mothlike eyebrows must gossip,
    But, yesterday or today, they are despised.
Troubles are endless: why bother with people?
    Give them a cold smile, and no more.
            Think, though, of this:
        Expel regret from your mind,
One day's desires gained, one thousand hurts remain;
        After this life, our fates
    Will surely unite in another existence.
            Promise me again;
            Remember this, you must.

Tune: "Joy Fills the Sky"

[*Ch'i t'ien lo*]

BEYOND THE BORDER ON THE SEVENTH NIGHT

North along White Wolf River, autumn comes early;
    Again the Bridge of Stars welcomes the Cowherd.
        Faster drips the water clock,
        Small clouds threaten showers,
    Just at this time of golden breezes, jade dews.
        Eyebrows knitted in concern,
        Waiting to return to tread the elm blossoms;
        Then, I'll be able to explain,
        Though I fear when next we meet,
    Surely, face to face, I'll have nothing to say.

Partings among men occur without number.
    Beyond a table set with melons, fruit,
        The azure heavens hold my gaze.
        Flowers on branches intertwined,
        Leaves of the love-seed tree,
    In the end, where will they follow the wind?
        A traveler, deep in sadness,
        And yet, this is not an empty room
            Full of cold fragrance!
            Tonight, the Weaving Girl
    Smiles, while melancholy is my mood.

TRANSLATED BY WILLIAM SCHULTZ

On the Art of Living

From Ming and Ch'ing times we have an abundance of sui-pi, the "random jottings" of men of letters on every subject under the sun. The modern scholar Lin Yutang has carried the tradition forward to our day in books like My Country and My People and The Importance of Living. The latter work includes Lin's translation of the celebrated "Thirty-three Happy Moments" recalled by Chin Sheng-t'an during ten days he once spent with a friend, imprisoned in a temple by heavy rain. Chin was an unconventional scholar and critic who lived from about 1610 to 1661, one of the first men to devote serious consideration to works of the popular tradition of literature, notably the novel Men of the Marshes (Anthology of Chinese Literature, Vol. 1, pp. 449–487) and the Yüan play Romance of the Western Chamber. His happy reminiscences include hearing his children fluently recite the classics, "like the sound of water pouring from a jar"; seeing someone's kite-line broken; watching, in the early morning, men under a mat-shed sawing a large bamboo pole; bathing, "with hot water behind closed doors," the spots of eczema he has deliberately allowed to remain in an intimate part of his person.

Chin's contemporary, the famous dramatist Li Yü or Li Li-weng (1611–ca. 1680), left a collection of Random Relaxations which again vividly exemplify the humane aesthetics of late imperial China. The work is most importantly concerned with Li's theories and observations on the writing and production of plays; but it offers also his detailed recommendations on architecture, medicinal herbs, and feminine charm as well as the subjects indicated by the following extracts.

●

Li Yü

Random Relaxations

[*Hsien ch'ing ou chi*, extracts]

ON FRUITS AND SWEETMEATS

Wine has fruit for a rival and tea for an enemy; it is determined by fate that the wine-drinker will have little liking either for tea or for fruit. Should a new guest join you, who has not previously drunk in your company and the depth of whose capacity is therefore an unknown factor, he may be tested with a dish of fruits or a plate of sweetmeats. If he should pop such things straight into his mouth, brightening with enthusiasm as he does so, then you are in the presence of a tea-drinker, not a wine man. If he takes them but refrains from eating, or does start to eat them but shows signs of boredom before the fourth mouthful, then this is a guest of heroic capacity, one to whom wine is the staff of life. Try this test on your honored guests and you will fail in less than one case out of a hundred.

ON EATING MEAT

We despise meat-eaters not for eating meat but for being slow-witted. And the reason meat-eaters are slow-witted is that their breasts are blocked with greasy secretions, congealed into solid fat, like reed beds round the heart whereby the channels of intelligence are closed.

This is not merely my personal prejudice, but a verifiable fact. Those animals which subsist on grasses, shrubs, and so forth are without exception crafty and wise. The tiger alone lives on human flesh, or if he cannot obtain this, on the flesh of other beasts. He alone, the tiger, will eat nothing unless it be meat: and the tiger is the stupidest of beasts. How do we know this? Written sources of every kind bear witness.

The reason the tiger will not eat a small child is not that he does not wish to, but that the child is too ingenuous to fear the tiger, who consequently mistakes him for a brave warrior and keeps his distance. The reason the tiger will not eat a drunken man is not that he does not wish to, but that taken in by his boisterous revelry he avoids him as a redoubtable foe.

The tiger will not enter on a winding path: if a man meet with a tiger, he need only lead him to a winding path to make good his escape. The reason the tiger avoids a winding path is not that, like Confucius' disciple T'an-t'ai Mieh-ming, he "would never take a shortcut": it is because he is too stiffnecked to be able to look behind him. . . .

ON AGE IN TREES

In the hoary pine and ancient juniper, beauty grows in proportion to age. Blossoming trees and bamboos of all kinds are valued for their youth and freshness; only pine, juniper, and plum, these three, are more highly prized when they have grown old than when they are young. If one wishes to enjoy the company of this venerable trio, then he must buy an old house for his dwelling; for to plant such trees is to plan for one's sons and grandsons rather than to indulge one's own anticipations.

I have sometimes teased young people by suggesting that if they wished to appear as figures in a painting they must wait until they grew old, for they would win no respect while still in their teens. Questioned, I would explain: "You must have noticed that whenever a landscape painter inserts a human figure, the person will inevitably be depicted as leaning on a staff. Or if he is seated on the ground, gazing at a far hillside or overlooking a lake, it is sure to be some hardy old scoundrel rather than a handsome youth. There may indeed be young people somewhere about: but they will be carrying the zither or holding up the painting scroll, fetching the food-hamper or passing the winecups, one way or another they will be performing some slavish service for the gentleman in the painting."

Try as they might to disprove my theory, the youngsters would never be able to find any evidence in their favor. Now it seems fitting to apply my observation to the pine and juniper. Fill a garden with seasonal flowers and tender plants, but neglect to provide a dozen solid, mature trees to preside over it, and it can be a playground for one's children all day long, but not a place to meet with friends or to sit at the feet of a tutor.

ON THERMOSTATIC SEATING

There are three articles of furniture designed for sitting, to wit: the chair, the stool, the bench. Historically, the modern era excels antiquity in the manufacture of these items; geographically, the north is surpassed by the south. Yangchow for wooden pieces and Soochow for bamboo are preeminent among all places and periods.

What call have I, then, to append this present note? Simply that two lacunae have existed which I have now filled with appropriate inventions. One of these I will call the "self-warming chair," the other the "self-cooling stool."

When summer's heat is at its most intense glue will run and metals melt, whatever one touches almost burns one's hand, and even wood is not entirely exempt. My "self-cooling stool" is like any ordinary stool, except that its seat is replaced by a kind of rectangular box whose bottom and four sides are sealed with putty. The cover is a tile, which must be specially ordered from the kiln. The best tiles to use are from Kiangsi or Fukien; Yi-hsing ware is next best. It will depend on where one is situated: but the cost may be reduced if several like-minded friends can be induced to club together to engage a carrier.

Now fill the interior of the stool with cold water and set the tile cover in place: but the under surface of the tile must be in contact with the water, which will make it ice-cold. When the water warms up, change it. This will be no great effort since only a few ladlefuls are needed.

The reason for the preference of stool over chair is that each object removed from one's proximity during the summer months represents one less source of heat: the absence of obstacles about one will permit the circulation of air. Since the panels of a chair consist of wood, they form obstructions to one's arms and back; but this stool of mine makes provision for the buttocks only, and concerns itself not at all with the rest of the body.

When I am at my writing during the winter months I suffer great distress from chilled limbs and frozen inkslab. If I install more braziers so as to heat my entire study the result is not only soaring expense but the accumulation of dust on the surface of the desk, so that before the day ends I am living in a world of ashes. If I limit myself to a large stove for my feet and a small one for my hands, then my four extremities enjoy preferential treatment over the rest of my body: in my own person I house both summer and winter at once, and ears and nose and brain itself could well style themselves spurned ministers or rejected offspring. The rationale, therefore, for my "self-warming chair" is the need for a comprehensively satisfactory provision.

My chair resembles but is somewhat wider than the usual armchair or "Grand Tutor's chair," since the latter undertakes to house only the buttocks whilst my chair accommodates the entire body. It resembles also the reclining chair or "dozing elder's chair," but is somewhat more upright since it is designed for either sitting or lying, with sitting as the primary function. Entrances are provided at front and rear, and the two sides are enclosed by panels. Seat itself and footrest are constructed of bars. The reason for the bars is to give passage to the heated air; the panels insure that no breath of warmth is permitted to escape; the front and rear doors are to admit the occupant and the coals respectively. If one wishes to save trouble, however, the rear door may be omitted from the design and the coals introduced via the same entrance as the occupant.

The beauty of this chair lies in the insertion of a drawer beneath the bars of the footrest. This single provision is sufficient to banish winter's cold; equally and insensibly its benefits are suffused throughout the five organs and the four limbs. An additional refinement is a box on which the hands may rest, twice the size of that provided inside a palanquin. When one enters to take one's seat, this box is placed before one in lieu of a table, so that one has twice the space furnished by a palanquin for the disposition of books, brushes, and inkslab.

The lower drawer is constructed of panels, the bottom thinly tiled and the sides brass-lined. The charcoal used should be very fine, of the type used in incense burners. If a layer of ash is spread on top of the coals, then the whole structure will be warmed without fierce heat at any point, and in the very depth of winter one enters another world. Moreover, the cost is most economical: four small pieces of charcoal will suffice from morn till night, if two are lighted in the early morning and supplemented by two more at noon. The total weight of these four pieces need not reach four ounces, and yet one may enjoy all day the joys of a room warm enough to hold the winter at bay.

This then is the benefit to one's person. But if the benefit were only to one's body and not to one's work, then we should have here merely an aid to repose; and this is not at all the case. For one may cut a hole the size of the palm of the hand in the "desk-top," insert a very thin Tuan-ch'i inkslab and lacquer it in place. It will then go without saying that as the warm air rises the inkslab will be kept warm, absolving one from the need to be eternally breathing on the tip of one's writing brush to thaw it out. And this is the benefit to one's work.

Nor is this all. Just as ash is spread over the coals, so may incense be placed on top of the ashes: then daylong the nose of the occupant will be visited by nothing but the sweetest of fragrances. Thus the chair has the additional function of replacing the incense burner: for the burner dissipates incense whilst the chair concentrates it. From this point of view, indeed, the chair not only replaces the burner but improves upon it. For there is no man but must bear a body, and no body but must wear clothing. And as this incense burns and ascends from below its gentle vapors suffuse one's very bones. Thus the chair has the additional function of replacing the clotheshorse used for perfuming garments; and since a clotheshorse can accommodate only a few items, whereas the chair accommodates everything one is wearing, then by this token it replaces not one but several clotheshorses.

When one grows tired and drowsy the chair may be equipped with a pillow for a short nap: it then becomes a bed with a seat. When one intends to eat, the meal may be served on the desk-top, so that the chair becomes a legless table. To take a turn in the hills or visit a friend, no need to look elsewhere for a sedan chair; one need only attach carrying-poles and furnish an awning to brave cold winds and driving snow with warmth and to spare.

Ancient worthies like Wang Hui-ch'ih, sailing down a freezing river to visit a friend, or Meng Hao-jan, crossing the bridge on his donkey in the snow, could have used such a chair and saved themselves much trouble. For my chair is also a palanquin in which one may sit or sleep as he chooses.

When evening draws on, place pillow and sheets inside the chair and in a short while your bedding will be heated through; before rising at dawn, have your clothing set therein and in a twinkling your jacket and trousers will be warm enough to don in comfort. Thus one and the same object brings ease to one's body and assistance to one's work; replaces bed, table, palanquin, incense burner, clotheshorse; and serves one as filial son with respectful greeting at dawn and dusk, and as dutiful wife with loving protection from frost and cold.

When Ts'ang Chieh invented writing, the heavens rained down grain and demons wailed by night that the sources of divine inspiration were thereby spent to the last breath. In putting forward this notion of mine, however, I believe I need not emulate the man of Ch'i who feared the sky would fall.

ON BEING HAPPY THOUGH POOR

The recipe for being happy when one is poor contains nothing more arcane than the simple prescription, "one step back." I may consider myself poor; but there will be other men poorer than I. I may count myself lowly; but there will be other men lowlier than I. I may regard my wife as an encumbrance; but there are widows and widowers, orphans, and childless folk who strive in vain to acquire just such an encumbrance. I may deplore the calluses on my hands; but there are men in the jails and in the wild lands who long without prospect for a livelihood with plough or shovel.

Rest in such thoughts as these, and the sea of sorrows gives place to a land of joy; but if all your reckoning is in a forward direction, weighing yourself against your betters, then you will know not a moment's peace but live fettered forever in a prison cell.

A man of substance once spent the night in a courier station. The humid summer was at its height and his bed-curtains admitted swarms of mosquitoes which would not be driven off. He fell prey to reminiscences of home, of a lofty hall arching like the sky itself over him, of bamboo matting cool as ice, and a whole bevy of fan-wielding concubines. There he would hardly be aware of summer's presence; how had he ever managed to get himself into his present predicament? Thoughts of bliss increased his frustrations, and the upshot was a night of total sleeplessness.

The station sergeant had lain down on the steps outside where clouds of mosquitoes gnawed at him until it seemed his bones must be exposed. In desperation at last he began running up and down the yard, his arms and legs ceaselessly flailing so as to afford no foothold to his attackers. His movements back and forth were those of a man bothered and annoyed, yet the sighs he gave were sighs of relief and satisfaction, as though he had found a source of pleasure in the midst of his misery.

The rich man was puzzled, and called him over to question him. "Your sufferings," he said, "are a dozen or a hundred times more severe than mine, yet I am miserable and you seem to be enjoying yourself. Can you explain this?"

"I was just remembering," said the sergeant, "the time some years ago when an enemy of mine brought charges against me and had me thrown into jail. That was summer, too, and the jailor to prevent my running away bound my wrists and ankles every night so that I could not move. There were more mosquitoes then than tonight, and they bit me at will, for however I longed to dodge and hide I could make no effort to do so. But see how tonight I can run up and down, moving my arms and legs just as I wish—it's like comparing a living man with a devil in hell. Thinking of the past I realize how pleasant things are now, and I can ignore whatever sufferings there might be."

His words roused the rich man to the understanding of his own error; for what he had heard was the secret of being happy though poor.

TRANSLATED BY CYRIL BIRCH

More Ghosts and Fantasies

The moralizing tendencies observed in our earlier section "Ghosts and Other Marvels" recur in P'u Sung-ling (1640–1715). His literary style is regarded as exceptionally elegant, and although the translations which follow are more recent, P'u Sung-ling's stories of ghosts, fox-fairies, and dragon princesses have been well known to Western readers through the charming versions made long ago by Herbert Giles under the title Strange Stories from a Chinese Studio.

The three anecdotes by Yüan Mei (1716–1798) are from a large collection to which he gave the wry title "What the Master Would Not Discuss" (Tzu pu yü) in allusion to the disclaimer in the Analects *of Confucius, that "the Master never talked of wonders, feats of strength, disorders of nature, or spirits." Yüan Mei remedies the deficiency with an obvious pleasure in wonder for wonder's sake and a noticeable interest in what one might term super-natural history, indicated for example by his description of the approach to food of the ghost named Wang.*

In contrast, we may observe in Li Ju-chen (ca. 1763–ca. 1830) the highly effective satirical use to which tales of marvels were put by some later writers. "In the Country of Women" is a very brief extract from a long, rambling novel, Flowers in the Mirror *(Ching hua yüan). Lin Chih-yang in this novel is a T'ang merchant who travels Gulliver-fashion to strange lands which offer splendid opportunities for satirical comment on home institutions and practices.*

P'u Sung-ling

The Rakshas and the Sea Market

[*Liao-chai chih yi: Lo-sha hai-shih*]

Ma Chün, also known as Lung-mei, "Dragon Match," was the son of a merchant. He was a handsome, unconventional youth, and loved singing and dancing. He used to associate with actors and to wear a silk handkerchief on his head, so that he looked as beautiful as a fair maiden. Hence he won the pet name of "Handsome." At the age of fourteen he entered the county school and began to make a name for himself.

His father, growing old and weak, retired and stayed at home.

"Son," said the old man, "books cannot be turned into food when you are hungry, nor into clothes when you are cold. You had better follow your father's trade."

Accordingly, Ma Chün from that time on turned his hand to business.

While on a sea voyage with other traders, Ma Chün was carried off by a typhoon. After several days and nights he reached a city where all the people were extremely ugly. When they saw Ma Chün, they all exclaimed in horror and fled as if he were a monster. At first Ma Chün was frightened of their ugly looks; but as soon as he discovered they were even more afraid of him, he took advantage of their fears. Whenever he found them eating and drinking, he would rush upon them, and when they scattered in alarm, he would regale himself upon what they left behind.

Later Ma Chün went to a mountain village, where the people had some resemblance to ordinary men. But they were all in rags and tatters like beggars. As he rested under a tree the villagers gazed at him from a distance, not daring to approach. After some time, when they realized that he would not eat them, they began to come nearer to him, and Ma Chün addressed them with a smile. Although their language was different, he could make himself understood. And when Ma Chün told them whence he had come, the villagers were pleased and spread the news that this stranger was not a man-eater. However, the ugliest of them would turn away after he had looked at him, not daring to approach. Those who did go up to him had a mouth, a nose, and other features not much different from those of the Chinese. As they brought food and wine to him, Ma Chün asked why they were afraid of him.

"We have heard from our forefathers," they said, "that some twenty-six thousand *li* to the west there is a country called China, and its people are most extraordinary in appearance. Before we knew this by hearsay only, but now we believe it."

"Why are you so poor?" asked Ma Chün.

"In our country, what we value is not literary accomplishments, but beautiful appearance. Our most handsome men are made ministers of state, those coming next are governors and magistrates, while the third class have noble patrons and receive pensions for the support of their wives and children. But we, from our very birth, are regarded as inauspicious, and our parents nearly always abandon us, only keeping a few of us in order to continue the family line."

"What is the name of the country?"

"It is the Great Kingdom of Rakshas, and our capital is some thirty *li* to the north."

Then Ma Chün requested to be guided there for a visit. The next day they set off with him at cockcrow and reached the capital at dawn. The city walls were made of black stone—as black as ink—with towers and pavilions about one hundred feet high. There were no tiles, and red stones were used instead. Picking up a fragment, Ma Chün found that it marked his fingernail like vermilion. They arrived just as the court was retiring, in time to see all the equipages of the officials coming out. The villagers pointed at one and said, "This is the prime minister." And Ma Chün saw that his ears drooped forward in flaps; he had three nostrils, and his eyelashes covered his eyes like a screen. Then some riders came out, and the villagers said, "They are ministers." The villagers told Ma Chün of each man's rank; and, although all the officials were ugly, the lower their rank, the less hideous they were.

Ma Chün soon turned to leave and the people in the street, at the sight of his appearance, exclaimed in terror and started running and stumbling as if he were an ogre. Only when the villagers reassured them with various explanations did these city people stand at a distance to look at him. By the time he got back to the village, there was not a man, old or young, in the kingdom, who did not know that a monster was among them. All the gentry and officials were curious to see him and asked the villagers to fetch him. However, when he went to any of their houses, the gatekeeper would slam the door in his face, while man and woman alike would peep at him through cracks and comment on him in whispers. All day no one dared to invite him in.

"There is a captain of the imperial guard, who has been sent abroad on an official mission by our late king," said the villagers. "Having seen many kinds of men, he may be unafraid of you."

When they called on the captain, he was delighted to meet Ma Chün, treating him as a guest of honor. Ma Chün saw that his host was about eighty or ninety years of age; his eyes protruded and his beard curled up like a hedgehog's.

"In my youth," said the captain, "His Majesty sent me to many countries, but never to China. Now at the age of one hundred and twenty years, I meet one from that honorable country. It will be my duty to report to His Majesty. I am living in seclusion now, and have not been in the court for more than ten years, but I will go there on your behalf early tomorrow morning."

Then he treated Ma Chün with food and wine, showing him every courtesy. After they had drunk a few cups of wine, some scores of girls came in to dance and sing. They looked like devils and wore white silk turbans and long red dresses which trailed on the ground. Their songs were unintelligible, and the music was very queer. The host, however, seemed to enjoy it very much, and asked, "Is there equally fine music in China?"

"Yes," answered Ma Chün.

Then the host asked Ma Chün to sing a song, and beating time on the table Ma Chün obliged with a tune.

"How strange!" said his pleased host. "It is like the cry of a phoenix or the thundering of a dragon. I have never heard such music before."

The following day the captain went to the court and recommended Ma Chün to the king, who at once decided to summon him for an audience. Some of the ministers, however, protested that Ma Chün's hideous appearance might frighten His Majesty, and the king accordingly reversed his decision. The captain, quite upset, returned to tell Ma Chün of the failure of his mission.

Ma Chün stayed with the captain for some time, and one day when he was in drink he smeared his face with coal dust in the stage guise of the general Chang Fei, and performed a sword dance. The captain considered the disguise pretty and said, "You must see the prime minister with your painted face. He will certainly be glad to employ you and procure you a high remuneration."

"Oh, no!" said Ma Chün, "I just disguised myself for fun. How can I change my appearance for the sake of seeking glory?"

However, he gave in when the captain insisted.

Then the captain invited some of the high officials to a banquet, and asked Ma Chün to paint his face in readiness. When the guests arrived and Ma Chün was called out to meet them, they were all amazed, exclaiming, "How strange! How is it that he used to be ugly, but now is quite handsome?"

Then they drank together with great pleasure. When Ma Chün started to dance and sing a popular Yi-yang tune, they were all delighted. The next day they recommended him to the king, who was glad to summon him to court. In his audience, the king questioned Ma Chün about the ways of maintaining order in China. And Ma Chün made a very detailed report, which pleased the king so much that a banquet was held in Ma Chün's honor in the imperial residence.

"I hear that you are skilled in fine music," said the king, who was in drink. "Will you kindly let me hear you?"

Ma Chün immediately rose to dance and, wearing a white silk turban, to sing vulgar tunes. The king was so pleased that he at once made Ma Chün a minister. Thereafter, he often invited Ma Chün to dinner and showed him special favor.

As time went on, the other officials found out that Ma Chün's face was disguised. Wherever he went, people would whisper behind his back and avoid associating with him. He was thus isolated and felt very uneasy. He then submitted a petition to the king for permission to retire, but the king refused. Then he asked for a vacation, and the king granted him three months' leave. Therefore Ma Chün went back in a carriage loaded with gold and jewels to the mountain village, where the villagers went down on their knees to welcome him as, amid thunderous applause, he distributed his wealth among his old friends.

"We are humble people," said the villagers, "and yet Your Honor has treated us so kindly. Tomorrow we shall go to the Sea Market and look for some treasures and gems to repay your kindness."

"Where is the Sea Market?" asked Ma Chün.

"It is a market in the middle of the sea, where mermaids from the four seas bring their pearls and jewels, and merchants from all the twelve countries around come to trade. Deities flock there among the colored clouds and tossing waves. Nobles and royalty will not risk this great danger, but commission us to buy treasures for them. The season for the market is now at hand."

Ma Chün asked them how they knew the date.

"When we see red birds flying back and forth, we know that in seven days the market will be held."

Ma Chün asked them when they would start and whether he might go with them, but the villagers begged him not to take such a risk.

"I am a sailor," said Ma Chün, "and I am not afraid of the wind and waves."

Soon after this, people came with money to buy treasures, and the villagers loaded their wares and boarded a vessel capable of carrying several scores of people. This was a flat-bottomed boat with a high taffrail; with ten men at the oars it cut through the water like an arrow. After a voyage of three days they could see in the distance, between the clouds and the water, pavilions and towers one after another, and the busy traffic of trading junks. They soon arrived at a city, the walls of which were made of bricks as long as a man's body. The watchtowers of the city soared up to the clouds. Here they moored the boat and went ashore to find all kinds of rare pearls and precious stones, seldom seen in the world of men, displayed in the market, dazzling the eyes.

Then there came a young man riding on a fine steed, and the market people hastened to make way for him, saying that this was the Third Prince of the Eastern Ocean. When the Prince passed by, he noticed Ma Chün and said, "Isn't this a foreigner?" And immediately a guard came to ask Ma Chün his name and country, and Ma Chün, bowing at the roadside, told them.

The Prince was pleased and said, "Since we are favored by your visit, it is our destiny to meet you here." He then gave Ma Chün a horse and bade him follow. They went out the West Gate, and when they came to the seashore their steeds neighed and leapt into the sea. Ma Chün was greatly frightened and cried out, but the sea parted in the middle to form a wall of water on either side. In a little time a magnificent palace came into sight, with rafters of tortoiseshell and tiles of fish scales. The four walls were made of bright crystals, dazzling the eyes and reflecting everything around them. Here they dismounted, and Ma Chün was invited to go in. When they saw the Dragon King seated on his throne, the Prince reported, "When I was in the market, I came across a distinguished scholar from China. I have brought him here before Your Majesty."

Ma Chün stepped forward to make a bow.

"You are a great scholar, sir," said the Dragon King, "not inferior to Ch'ü Yüan and Sung Yü. I venture to ask for a poem on our Sea Market. Pray do not spare your gemlike verses."

Thereupon Ma Chün kowtowed and accepted the King's command. As soon as he was given a crystal inkslab, dragon-beard brush, paper as white as snow, and ink as fragrant as orchids, he dashed off one thousand characters, which he presented to the throne.

Beating the rhythm of the poem, the Dragon King said, "Your great talent glorifies our watery kingdom, sir." Then he summoned all his royal kinsmen to feast at the Rainbow Palace, and when the wine had circulated for several rounds the Dragon King toasted the guest.

"My beloved daughter has not yet been promised in marriage," said the King. "I would like to marry her to you, if you are willing to accept her."

Ma Chün, blushing, stood up and stammered his thanks. The Dragon King turned to give orders to his attendants, and presently palace maids led in the Princess, whose jade ornaments tinkled, while the drums and trumpets sounded forth. After the nuptial obeisance, Ma Chün stole a glance at her and saw that the Princess was a fairy beauty. When the ceremony was over she retired, and as soon as the feast came to an end two bridesmaids, holding painted candles, escorted Ma Chün into the bridal chamber. The Princess, magnificently dressed, was sitting on the bridal couch, which was of coral studded with the eight jewels. The curtains were adorned with colored silk flowers and decked with huge pearls, and all the bedding was velvety and scented.

The next morning at dawn chambermaids rushed into the room to offer their services, and Ma Chün got up and went off to the court to thank the King. He was duly received as the royal son-in-law and was made an official at court. Copies of his poem were distributed to all seas, and the dragon rulers of the various seas sent special envoys to offer their congratulations to the King and vied with each other in their invitations to Ma Chün. Then, dressed in magnificent robes and riding on a green dragon, he went forth with a grand retinue, accompanied by scores of well-armed knights with carved bows and white staffs. They formed a glittering cavalcade, with musicians on horseback and in chariots playing jade instruments. Thus for three days Ma Chün visited the different seas, and the name of Lung-mei became known throughout the four seas.

In the palace there was a jade tree, so large that a man could barely encircle it with his arms. The trunk was as transparent as glass, and pale yellow in the middle; the branches were slighter than a man's arm; the leaves were like green jade, little thicker than a coin, and cast a fine checkered shade. Ma Chün and his bride often chanted poems under this tree, which was in full bloom with flowers like gardenias. When a petal fell it made a ringing sound. When he picked it up it looked like a carved red agate, very bright and pretty. A strange bird would often come to sing here; its feathers were gold and green, its tail was longer than its body, and its song was like the tinkling of jade, so plaintive that it moved a man's heart. Whenever Ma Chün heard the bird sing he thought of his old home.

"I have been wandering abroad for three years," said Ma Chün to his princess, "separated from my parents. Whenever I think of them, tears flow and perspiration runs down my back. Will you accompany me to my home?"

"Immortals and mortals live in different worlds," answered the Princess. "I cannot go with you, but neither would I let the love of husband and wife stand in the way of your love for your parents. Let us consider this again later."

Hearing this, Ma Chün could not refrain from weeping.

"It is clear that nothing can be perfect," said the Princess with a sigh.

The next day when Ma Chün came back from an outing the

Dragon King said to him, "I hear that you are thinking of your old home. Would you like to take your leave tomorrow?"

"Your servant came here as a stranger," said Ma Chün, gratefully, "and yet you have conferred honors upon me. I am indeed overwhelmed with heartfelt gratitude. I shall pay my family a short visit and try to return again."

That evening the Princess prepared a farewell feast, and Ma Chün made plans for his return, but she said, "Our marital life will be at an end."

Ma Chün was greatly grieved to hear these words.

"Go back to your parents to show your filial piety," continued the Princess. "As for our meetings and separations, a hundred years pass like a single day; then why should we weep like children? Hereafter, if I stay true to you and you faithful to me, even in two different worlds our hearts will be united as husband and wife. Why should we remain together morning and night to await the approach of old age? If you break this pledge, your next marriage will be inauspicious; but if you need someone to look after you, you may take a maid as your concubine. I have something else to tell you, too. As we have lived together, it seems that I am now with child. I pray you to choose a name for it."

"If it is a girl," said Ma Chün, "call her Lung-kung ('Dragon Palace'). If a boy, call him Fu-hai ('Happy Sea')."

Then the Princess asked him for a token of his pledge, and he gave her a pair of red jade lilies which he had obtained in the land of the Rakshas.

"Three years from now, on the eighth of the fourth moon," said the Princess, "when you sail into the South Sea, I shall give you your child."

Then she handed him a fish-scale bag filled with pearls and jewels.

"Guard this well," said she. "It will be a provision for several generations."

At dawn the Dragon King prepared a farewell feast for Ma Chün and bestowed many rich gifts on him. When Ma Chün bade them all adieu with a bow and left the palace, the Princess escorted him in a carriage drawn by white rams. As soon as they reached the seashore Ma Chün dismounted and stepped ashore.

"Farewell!" called the Princess and turned swiftly away. Soon the sea waves closed over her and she vanished. Then Ma Chün returned home.

Since he had gone into the sea, all had believed that he was dead. So his family was amazed at his return. Happily his parents were still well, but his wife had remarried. He then realized that when the Dragon Princess spoke to him of keeping faith, she must have already known this. His father urged him to marry again, but he refused and only took a concubine. He kept in mind the date, and after the three years had passed he sailed south again until he saw two children floating over the sea and splashing about in the waves. As he drew near and leaned over them, one of them seized him by the arms with a smile and sprang into his breast, while the other cried out as if to reproach him for not taking it up. When he pulled the second child aboard, he saw that one was a boy and the other a girl. They were beautiful children, wearing embroidered caps adorned with the red jade lilies. On the back of one of the children was an embroidered bag, in which he found the following letter:

I know your parents are well. Three years have quickly passed; you and I are permanently separated by the vast space of water, with no bluebird to carry our messages. I am longing for you in my dreams and gazing in grief at the blue sky! Yet even Ch'ang O, fleeing to the moon, pines under her cassia tree, and the Weaving Maid laments over the Milky Way. Why should I alone enjoy eternal happiness? When I think of this, my tears often turn into smiles.

Two months after you left, I gave birth to twins, who now prattle and laugh at my breast, and look for dates and grasp pears. As they can live on without a mother, I am sending them to you, with the red jade lilies which you gave me attached to their caps so that you may know them. When you take them on your knees, you may imagine that I am sitting by your side.

I am happy to know that you have kept your pledge, and I shall remain true to you until death. I no longer keep orchid cream in my dresser, nor do I rouge or powder my face before the mirror. You seem to be a wanderer, but I am not a wicked woman; even though we cannot live together, how can it be said that we are not husband and wife? However, your parents will take their grandchildren upon their knees without meeting their daughter-in-law—I feel there is something improper in this. Next year when your mother comes to the end of her days, I shall visit her grave as her daughter-in-law. From this time on, if all goes well with Lung-kung, it may be possible for us to meet again. When Fu-hai grows up, he may find a way for us to visit each other. Please take good care of yourself. I cannot express all I want to say.

Ma Chün read this letter over and over again, his tears flowing all the time. His two children put their arms around his neck and said "Let us go home!"

Ma Chün was much grieved and patted them, asking, "Ah, my children, don't you know where our home is?"

The children wept bitterly, crying in their longing to return home, and Ma Chün gazing at the great ocean stretching away to the horizon found no trace of the Princess, nor could he see any road through the misty waves. Then he embraced his children and proceeded sorrowfully to return. As he knew that his mother would not live long, he made everything ready for her funeral and planted a hundred pine trees in the ancestral graveyard. The next year the old lady died, and when the interment took place a woman clad in heavy mourning dress appeared by the side of the grave. As everyone stood there astonished, suddenly a wind sprang up, thunder crashed, and rain poured down, and the woman instantly vanished. Many of the pine trees which Ma Chün had planted, and which had withered, were brought back to life.

When Fu-hai grew bigger, he often thought of his mother, and suddenly he went into the sea, returning only several days later. Lung-kung being a girl could not go, but often wept in her room. One day the sky grew dark, and the Dragon Princess suddenly came in and bade her daughter stop weeping.

"You will have your own home soon," said she. "Don't cry, my child!"

She then gave her daughter as her dowry a coral tree eight feet high, a packet of Baroos camphor, one hundred pearls, and a pair of gold boxes inlaid with the eight gems. When Ma Chün heard of her coming he rushed in and took her hands in tears. But with a violent peal of thunder that shook the building the Princess vanished.

The author comments: "Men must put on painted, ugly faces to please others—such is the hypocritical way of the world. Odd ways of life have been followed all over the world. 'What one feels a little ashamed of may win praise; what one feels greatly ashamed of may win much greater praise,' but the world seldom fails to be shocked at those who dare to reveal their true selves in public. Where would that fool of Ling-yang take his priceless jade to weep? [1] Alas! Honors and riches can be found only in castles in the clouds and mirages of the sea!"

Ying-ning

[*Liao-chai chih yi: Ying-ning*]

Wang Tzu-fu, a native of Lotien in the county of Chü, lost his father when he was a child. He was very intelligent and passed the district examination at the age of fourteen. His mother loved him so much that he was not allowed to stray far from home. He had been betrothed to a girl of the Hsiao family, who died before they could be married. Therefore he was in search of a match, and still remained unwed. On the Lantern Festival his cousin Wu invited him out for a stroll. Hardly were they outside the village when his uncle's servant called Wu back, but Wang, seeing bevies of pleasure-bent girls, proceeded cheerfully alone. Among these girls was a young lady, attended by her maid, and toying with a sprig of plum blossom. She was the prettiest girl in the world and had a charming smile. He stared and stared at her, regardless of manners. When the girl passed by she remarked to her maid, "That lad has a wicked look in his eyes!" She tossed her flowers to the ground and walked away, laughing and talking.

Blankly, Wang picked up the flowers and turned back disconsolately, as if he had lost his wits. Once home he hid the flowers under his pillow and bowed his head to sleep. He would neither talk nor eat, and his mother, in her anxiety about him, called on the aid of priests. However, his illness became worse, and his weight decreased rapidly. Physicians examined him and prescribed remedies; still he seemed bewildered in his mind. Though his mother tenderly inquired as to the

---

[1] A man who in ancient times presented a piece of uncut jade to the King of Ch'u. The King thought it worthless and cut off the donor's feet. The allusion illustrates the difficulty of recognizing a man's true worth.

cause of his illness, he made no reply. One day when Wu came, he was asked to sound him out. At the sight of Wu approaching the bed, Wang shed tears. Wu comforted him and gradually led the conversation into inquiries, at which Wang told him the truth and appealed to him for assistance.

"What a fool you are!" said Wu with a smile. "What difficulties are there in the matter? I'll make inquiries for you. The girl who went out alone can't belong to a noble family. If she is not betrothed, the match is as good as made. Even if she is, we can carry out our plan by the use of money. But first of all you must make haste to get well, and leave the rest to me."

On hearing this Wang relaxed and smiled. Wu went out and reported this to Wang's mother, then set about looking for the whereabouts of the girl. All inquiries, however, proved in vain. Wang's mother was distressed and did not know what to do, although Wang himself looked better and began to take some food. A few days later, when Wu called again, Wang asked how the plan was going.

"We have traced the girl," Wu lied. "Do you know who she is? My aunt's daughter, who is also your cousin. She is not yet betrothed, and although you are rather closely related to marry, if you tell her the truth you can win her over."

Wang's face lit up and he asked, "Where is she living?"

"In the southwest hills," lied Wu, "just over thirty *li* from here."

Wang begged him again to do his best, and Wu promised and took his leave. After this Wang's appetite improved daily and he soon recovered. Then he took a look at the flower under the pillow. It had faded but its petals had not fallen off. He played with this flower and imagined that he saw the girl. When Wu failed to come he wrote inviting him over, but Wu excused himself on various pretexts. Thereupon Wang became so angry and depressed that his mother, fearing a relapse, wanted to find him a wife without delay. When she hinted at what she had in mind, he shook his head and would not agree. He waited day after day for Wu, but Wu failed to appear. This intensified his grief and anger. Then it occurred to him that thirty *li* was not such a great distance that he had to rely on others. So, slipping the flower into his sleeve, he went off in a huff by himself without letting his family know it.

All alone, with no one to lead the way, he headed straight to the south hills and after thirty *li* or more found himself in the midst of ex-quisite, refreshing verdure without a single soul on the narrow path. But down in the valley below, almost buried among densely luxuriant trees and flowers, he glimpsed a small village. He descended the hill and made his way to the village, where he found only a handful of thatched dwellings, which however were graceful and pleasant to look at. On the north there was a house, and outside its gate grew willow trees, while within were peach and apricot trees in plenty, inter-spersed with fine bamboos where wild birds were chirping. As he thought that it might be a private garden, he dared not venture inside. He turned back and saw a smooth, clean boulder outside the gate, on which he sat down to rest. Presently he heard a girl's voice inside the wall calling "Hsiao-jung!" The voice was sweet and charming. As he pricked up his ears, a girl came from the east, with head lowered that she might pin an apricot flower in her hair. Looking up and seeing Wang, she stopped pinning the blossom but went inside smothering a laugh and playing with the flower. Looking at her closely, he found that she was none other than the girl of the Lantern Festival. He was in raptures, but did not know how to introduce himself. If he asked for this aunt, whom he had never met, he might make some blunder. Since there was nobody at the door whom he could ask, he stayed there ei-ther sitting down or wandering to and fro from morning till afternoon. In his eagerness to see the girl he forgot hunger and thirst. From time to time the girl peeped out and seemed very much astonished to find him still there. Suddenly an old woman with a stick came out.

"Where are you from, sir?" asked she. "I hear you have been here ever since early morning. What do you want? Aren't you hungry?"

Wang sprang up and made a bow.

"I came here to see a relative," he replied.

The old woman was deaf, so he had to repeat his answer loudly. "What is the name of your honorable relative?" she asked again. But Wang would not answer.

"Strange enough!" said the old woman with a laugh. "How can you call on someone whose name you don't even know? I think you are but a bookworm. You had better come in for a simple meal. We'll give you a bed and you can go home tomorrow. When you find out their names, it will not be too late for you to come and visit them."

As Wang was very hungry and, besides, eager to get closer to his beauty, he was only too glad to follow the old woman in. They walked

along a path paved with white stones. Crimson petals were scattered
about on the sidewalks and steps. Then they turned to the west and
passed through another gate into a courtyard full of trained creepers
and trellises covered with flowers. He was shown into a chamber with
white walls as bright as mirrors. From outside the windows branches
of crab-apple blossom reached into the chamber. All the bedding and
furniture was also nice and neat. When he sat down, he glimpsed
someone peeping through the window.

"Hsiao-jung!" called the old woman. "Hurry up and get dinner!"

The maid outside gave a loud answer. Meanwhile Wang, seating
himself, began to speak of his ancestors and family.

"Was your maternal grandfather named Wu?" asked the old
woman.

"Yes," said Wang.

"Then you are my nephew!" exclaimed she. "Your mother is my
younger sister. In recent years, because of poverty, and having no man
in the house, we have kept quite to ourselves. You have grown up
without my ever having known you."

"I came to see you, aunt," said Wang, "but in my hurry I forgot
your name."

"My name is Ch'in," said the old woman. "I have no son, only a
daughter, the child of my husband's concubine who married again and
left her in my care. She is very intelligent, although she has not had
much education; she is full of fun and ignorant of sorrow. I'll send for
her shortly to make your acquaintance."

The maid then brought in the dinner of plump chicken, and the
old woman urged him to eat. The maid came to clear away.

"Call Mistress Ning here," said the old woman.

The maid went off to do so. After some time giggling could be
heard outside the door.

"Ying-ning!" called the old woman. "Your cousin is here!"

The giggling outside the door went on. Even when the maid
pushed her in, the girl, keeping her hand over her mouth, could not
help laughing.

"We have a guest here," said the old woman, staring at the girl.
"Tittering and giggling—where are your manners?"

So Ying-ning controlled her laughing and stood there while Wang
bowed to her.

"This is Mr. Wang," said the old woman, "your aunt's son. And yet oddly enough we have never met."

"How old is my young cousin?" asked Wang.

The old woman did not hear, and Wang had to repeat the question, which sent the girl into another fit of laughter.

"As I told you," said the old woman, "she has not had much education—now you see it. She is sixteen years old, but she has no more sense than a baby."

"Just one year younger than I am," said Wang.

"So you're seventeen already," said the old woman. "Were you born in the year of *keng-wu*—the year of the horse?"

Wang nodded his head.

"Who is your wife?" asked the old woman.

"I have no wife," answered he.

"As intelligent and handsome as you are," said the old woman, "at seventeen why have you not yet been betrothed? Ying-ning is not betrothed either. You'd make a good match if it weren't for being so closely related."

Wang said nothing, just gazed at Ying-ning without looking at anyone else. The maid whispered to the girl, "He still has that wicked look in his eyes!"

"Shall we see if the peaches are in bloom yet?" said Ying-ning to the maid, with a gurgle of laughter.

Then she got up, covering her mouth with her sleeve, to slip out. Once she got outside she burst into a hearty fit of laughter.

The old woman rose, too, and ordered the maid to get a bed ready for Wang to rest.

"It is not easy for you to come here," said the old woman to Wang. "You must stay several days with us, and then we'll send you home. If you are bored, there is a small garden in the back where you can amuse yourself. There are also books to read."

The next day Wang went to the back of the house, where he found a garden half a *mou* in size, covered with fine grass and strewn with willow catkins. There were three thatched houses surrounded by flowers and trees. Strolling among the flowers he heard a rustling from the trees, and looked up to see Ying-ning, who at the sight of him at once burst out laughing and nearly tumbled down.

"Don't!" he cried. "You'll fall!"

She came down laughing, quite unable to stop, until when she was near the ground, she lost her grasp and fell. Wang helped her up, surreptitiously squeezing her wrist. Ying-ning laughed again and was obliged to lean against a tree for support. It was some time before she was able to walk. Wang waited till she stopped laughing, and then drew the flower from his sleeve and handed it to her.

"It's dead," she said. "Why do you keep it?"

"You dropped it during the Lantern Festival," said Wang, "and so I have kept it."

"What is the purpose of keeping it?"

"This is to show my love and that I do not forget you. Since I met you on the Lantern Festival, I have been so lovesick I thought I was going to die. I did not expect to see you again. Pray have pity on me!"

"Such a trifle!" said the girl, "Why should I begrudge a close relative? When you leave I'll ask the old gardener to cut you a whole bundle of flowers."

"Are you so dense, cousin?" said he.

"Why am I dense?"

"It's not the flower that I love, but the girl who picked it."

"There should be love between relatives; you needn't tell me that."

"The love which I am talking about is not that between relatives, but the love between husband and wife."

"What's the difference?"

"They share one pillow at night."

The girl lowered her head and meditated for a while.

"I'm not used to sleeping with strangers," said she.

Before they could finish talking the maid came up, and Wang beat a hasty retreat. Presently they met again in the old woman's room.

"Where have you been?" asked the old woman.

"We were chatting in the garden," said the girl.

"Dinner has been ready for a long time," said the old woman. "What has kept you talking so long?"

"My cousin wanted me to sleep with him."

Wang was much embarrassed, and shot her a look at which she smiled and became silent. Luckily the old woman had not heard and repeated her question. Wang immediately made an evasive answer and then whispered a reproach to the girl.

"Shouldn't I have said that?" the girl asked.

"That's a secret between us!"

"It may be a secret from others, but can it be a secret from my mother? Sleeping is a common affair; what harm is there in it?"

Wang was annoyed by her naïveté but knew no way to make her understand. By the time dinner was over, some of his family servants with two donkeys came looking for him. For when Wang's mother found that he was missing she had become alarmed and searched the whole village, but discovered no trace of him. Then she went to see Wu, who remembering what he had told Wang advised her to look in the southeast hills. The servants had passed several villages before they reached this place. As Wang, going out, happened to meet them, he returned to ask the old woman if he might take the girl back with him. The old woman was delighted.

"I have long had the intention of visiting your family," she said, "but my feeble body is unable to travel far. Now it is really good of you to take your cousin to see her aunt." Then she called Ying-ning, who came in laughing.

"Why do you always laugh so much?" asked the old woman. "You would be a very good girl if only you could stop laughing."

She looked at the girl in some annoyance and continued, "Now your cousin wants to take you with him. Go and get ready."

After she had entertained the servants with food and wine, the old woman came out to see them off.

"Your aunt's family has plenty of land and can afford to support you," said she to her daughter. "You may as well stay there and learn a little about refinement and etiquette, so that you can serve your elders well. Meanwhile I'll ask your aunt to find you a good match."

So the young people took their leave, and when they reached the hills and looked back they could discern the old woman leaning against the gate and gazing towards them. When they reached home Wang's mother, seeing this lovely girl, asked in amazement who she was. He told her she was his aunt's daughter.

"But what Wu told you was his own invention!" said his mother. "I have no elder sister; how could I have such a niece?"

Then she questioned the girl.

"I am not my mother's real daughter," said the girl. "My father, by the name of Ch'in, died when I was too small to remember anything."

"I had a sister," said Wang's mother, "who married a man named

Ch'in, that's true; but she died long ago—how could she be alive again?"

However, on inquiring about the facial appearance and distinctive features of the old woman, Wang's mother had to acknowledge the identity of her sister, although she was still bewildered.

"It does sound like her," she said. "But my sister died years ago—how could she come back to life?"

She was still puzzling when Wu arrived and the girl retired to an inner room. When he heard the story, he remained for some moments lost in astonishment.

"Is the girl named Ying-ning?" asked Wu.

Wang replied that she was. Wu exclaimed that it was a strange affair and went on to give his explanation.

"After the death of our aunt in the Ch'in family," said Wu, "Uncle Ch'in was bewitched by a fox-fairy, and later died. The fox gave birth to a daughter named Ying-ning, whom all my family saw in her swaddling clothes. After our uncle's death, the fox kept on coming back till we asked the Taoist priest for charms to put on the wall, and then at last the fox took the girl away. Can this be the same girl?"

While they were thus speculating, peals of laughter were heard from the inner room; this was the laughter of Ying-ning.

"What an uncouth girl she is!" remarked Wang's mother.

Wu asked to be introduced, but when Wang's mother went into the room, the girl simply laughed. Urged to come out, she tried hard to restrain herself from laughing and turned her face to the wall. No sooner had she curtsied to Wu than she rushed back in fresh fits of giggling, to the great amusement of all the women in the house. Wu offered to find out about the girl and to arrange the marriage. But when he reached the village, all the houses had gone, and nothing was there except a hillside stream with flowers. He recollected that his aunt was buried nearby, but the grave mound had been razed and he could no longer locate it. Not knowing what to make of it he returned home.

Suspecting that the girl was a spirit, Wang's mother told her what Wu had seen, but the girl was not at all surprised. When condoled with for having no home, the girl was not upset either but only laughed as hilariously as ever. None of them could understand her. Wang's mother got a maid to sleep with her, and the girl came to pay respects to Wang's mother each morning. When it came to needlework the girl was unsurpassed in her exquisite workmanship. But her laughing once started could not be restrained. Wild as it was, her laughter was nevertheless charming, a joy to hear, and all the girls and young wives in the neighborhood wanted to meet her.

Wang's mother selected an auspicious day for the wedding, but she was still afraid that the girl might be a spirit. So she secretly watched the girl in the sunlight till she found that she had a shadow. When the wedding day came they dressed her in the splendid clothes of a bride, but she laughed so much that she could not kneel down and so was excused from completing the wedding ceremony.

Wang was afraid that her naïveté might make her disclose their secrets of the bedchamber. Never a word of these things passed her lips, however. When Wang's mother was upset or out of temper, the girl would come to comfort her with her laughter. When the maids did wrong and feared a whipping, they would beg her to intercede for them with their mistress, for she always got them off.

Ying-ning had a passion for flowers. She got all she could from her relatives and neighbors, and even secretly pawned her gold trinkets to buy rare specimens; thus in a few months the steps and fences were all covered with flowers. Behind the house was a trellis of climbing roses which overlooked the neighbor's house on the west. She often climbed up to pick roses for her hair, in spite of her mother-in-law's attempt to stop her. One day the neighbor's son saw her and was captivated. She did not hide herself, but just laughed. Thinking that he had won her he grew bolder, whereupon she pointed to the bottom of the wall and climbed down with a smile. The young man was greatly delighted, thinking that she had made an assignation. As soon as night fell he presented himself at the wall where he found Ying-ning waiting. As he tried to take her in his arms, such a piercing pain shot through his heart that he fell with a cry to the ground. When he looked round, there was no girl, only a withered tree stump by the wall, rotted by rain. His father, hearing his cry, rushed to see what was the matter, but the young man simply groaned until his wife came, and then he told her something of the truth. When they lighted a torch to look into the hollow trunk they found in it a huge scorpion, the size of a crab. The old man smashed the stump and killed the scorpion before carrying his son home, but the youth died at midnight. Then this neighbor accused Wang of having a witch for a wife. The local magistrate, who admired Wang's talents and knew him to be a good scholar, dismissed this as a false accusation and would have had the neighbor beaten with bamboos had Wang not spoken up for him and procured his release.

"What has happened is due to your wild ways!" Wang's mother said to Ying-ning. "I knew all along that too much joy would bring sorrow. But for our enlightened magistrate, we would have got into trouble. A hawklike official would arrest women and interrogate them in public. If that had happened, how could you have held up your head to face relatives and neighbors?"

At that Ying-ning looked grave and swore never to laugh again.

"One must laugh sometimes," said Wang's mother. "Only there must be a limit."

After that Ying-ning never laughed, no matter how hard they tried to amuse her. Yet she did not look gloomy. But one night she wept, and Wang was surprised.

"When we were married," she said with sobs, "I dared not tell you the truth for fear of shocking you. Now that mother and you both love me so well, I can tell you all without fear. I am the daughter of a fox-fairy. When she went away, she put me in the care of a ghost-mother, with whom I remained for more than ten years. I have no brothers; I can only rely on you. Now my old mother is lying on the lonely hillside with no one to have pity on her and bury her with her dear ones. She must often grieve at this in the nether regions! If you don't mind taking some trouble to rid her of this grievance, she will know that her daughter has not forgotten her."

Wang agreed, but worried that the grave might be lost in the brambles. Ying-ning told him not to worry. Soon afterwards husband and wife set out with a coffin, and amid a thicket of brambles she pointed out the burying place, where they found the body not yet turned to dust. Ying-ning wept bitterly over the remains, which they carried back in the coffin and interred in the Ch'in family graveyard. That night Wang dreamed that the old woman came to thank him, and when he woke he told Ying-ning.

"I saw her last night," said she, "but she told me not to disturb you."

Wang regretted not having detained her.

"She is a ghost," explained the girl. "There are too many living beings here and the presence of too much life would overpower her. How could she stay long?"

Then Wang asked about Hsiao-jung.

"She is also a fox-fairy," said she, "but very clever. My fox-mother left her to look after me, and I shall always be grateful for the cakes and fruit she gave me. I learned from my mother that she has married."

After that every year on the day of the Spring Festival Wang and Ying-ning would go without fail to the Ch'in family graveyard to visit her parents' graves. A year later the girl gave birth to a son, who while still at her breast was unafraid of strangers but laughed at anyone, just like his mother.

The author comments: "On observing her steady foolish laughter one felt that she was lacking in feelings, and the wicked trick by the wall displayed her deceitful cunning. However, her grievous longing for her ghost-mother, turning laughter into tears, shows that Ying-ning concealed her true feelings under laughter. I have heard of a herb in the hills called 'laughing grass,' the smell of which makes people laugh without stopping. A plant of this sort in the house would beat all other flowers."

TRANSLATED BY CH'U CHAI AND WINBERG CHAI

Yüan Mei

Three Ghost Stores

[From *Tzu pu yü*]

I

A certain Mr. Yeh had a friend called Wang, and on Wang's sixtieth birthday Yeh mounted his donkey and rode off to congratulate him. At dusk, when he was crossing the hills southwest of Peking, he was caught up by a big fellow on horseback, who asked him where he was going. When Yeh told him, he said, "How fortunate! Wang is my cousin and I too am going to visit him on his birthday. Let us keep each other company!"

Yeh was delighted to have a companion, and readily assented. After a time he noticed that the big fellow continually lagged behind. He invited him to lead the way, and the other pretended to accept the suggestion. But in a few minutes he had fallen behind again. Yeh began to suspect that the man was a bandit and kept on glancing at him over his shoulder. It was soon pitch dark, and he could no longer see his companion. But presently a storm began, there was a flash of lightning and by its light Yeh saw that the fellow was now hanging from his saddle head downwards, his feet moving in space, as though he were walking; and at every step he took there was a peal of thunder, each thunderclap being also accompanied by a black vapor which issued from the fellow's mouth. Yeh saw that he had an immensely long tongue, red as cinnabar. He was of course much startled and alarmed; but there seemed to be nothing for it but to ride on as fast as he could to Mr. Wang's house.

Wang was delighted to see them both and at once asked them to have a drink. Taking Wang aside, Yeh asked him if it was a fact that he was related to the person he had met on the road. "Oh, yes," said Mr.

181

Wang. "That's quite right. It's my cousin Mr. Chang. He lives in Rope-makers' Lane in Peking and is a silversmith by trade."

This reassured Yeh, and he began to think that what he had seen during the night was simply an hallucination. However, when the time came for going to bed, he did not much like the idea of sharing a room with the fellow. But the other insisted upon it and Yeh was obliged reluctantly to concur, only taking the precaution of getting an old servant of Mr. Wang's to sleep in the same room. Yeh could not manage to get to sleep. At the third watch, though the candle had gone out, the whole room was suddenly filled with light, and Yeh saw the man sitting up in bed; the light came from his huge protruding tongue. He then came over and sniffed at Yeh's bed-curtains, saliva dripping from his jaws. But seeming to realize that Yeh was awake, he changed his mind and seized the old servant, devouring him almost to the last bone.

It so happened that Yeh was a devotee of Kuan Yü, the God of War, and he now hastened to call out, "Great Sovereign, subduer of demons, where are you?" At once there was a resounding boom as though a gong had been struck, and Kuan Yü appeared from between the rafters, with a huge sword in his hand. He struck at the monster, who at once turned into a butterfly as big as a cart wheel which spread its wings to parry the blow. After the combatants had pranced round one another for a moment or two, there was a loud crash, and both the butterfly and the god vanished.

Yeh fell fainting to the floor and was still lying there at noon when Mr. Wang came to see what had happened to him. He had now recovered sufficiently to tell Wang the whole story, and Wang indeed saw for himself that there was fresh blood on the servant's bed. But both Mr. Chang and the servant had disappeared, though Chang's horse was still in the stable. They at once sent a messenger to Peking, who on reaching Chang's workshop found him at his stove melting silver. He had been in Peking all the time and had never gone to Mr. Wang's to congratulate him on his sixtieth birthday.

II

In the year *hsin-mao* of the Ch'ien-lung period (1771) my brother Yüan Shu went to the capital in company with his examination-mate Shao. They reached Luan-ch'eng on the twenty-first of the fourth month. All the inns at the Eastern Barrier were crammed with travelers and their equipages. But presently they found an inn where there seemed to be no guests at all, and decided to stay here for the night.

Shao took the outer room and my brother the inner room. When it was beginning to get late they went to bed each in his own room, but kept the lamps burning and continued for a time to talk to each other through the partition wall. Suddenly my brother saw a man about ten feet high, with a green face and green whiskers, dressed and shod all in green, come in at the door. He was so tall that his hat made a rustling sound as it brushed against the paper of the top-light in the ceiling. Soon a dwarf not so much as three feet high also appeared at my brother's bedside. He had a very large head, and he too had a green face and was dressed all in green. He moved his sleeves up and down, and postured like a dancer. My brother tried to call out, but found he could not open his mouth. Shao was still talking to him from the next room but he was unable to say anything in reply. To add to his bewilderment another man now appeared, sitting on the low stool beside his bed. He had a pock-marked face and a long beard; on his head was a gauze cap, and he was wearing a very wide belt.

This man pointed at the giant and said to my brother, "He's not a ghost." Then he pointed to the dwarf with the big head, and said, "But that one is." Then he waved his hand towards the giant and the dwarf, saying something that my brother could not catch. They both nodded and began to salute my brother with their hands folded in their sleeves. At each salute they retreated one step. The last salute brought them to the door, and they disappeared through it. The man with the gauze cap then saluted in the same way, and also disappeared.

My brother leapt up and was just on the point of leaving the room when Shao, screaming wildly, came rushing in, saying that he had been visited by apparitions. "Was it two green men, one big and one little?" asked my brother.

"Nothing of the kind," said Shao. "When I lay down I at once felt a draught that seemed to come from a small closet close to my bed. It was so ice-cold that my hair stood on end. I was too uncomfortable to sleep, and that was why I went on so long talking to you, though after a time you did not answer. Presently I saw that in the closet there were about twenty men, some large, some small, with faces round as bowls, moving restlessly about. I made sure it was only my fancy, and took no notice. But suddenly their faces, big and little, appeared at the doorway, in rows, one above the other, till the whole opening was blocked up with faces, the topmost place of all being taken by a huge face as big as a grinding-pan. When all these faces began grinning at me it was more than I could bear, and throwing aside my pillow I jumped up and came here. But of your 'green men' I saw nothing at all."

My brother then told him of what he had seen, and they agreed to leave the place at once without even getting fodder for their horses. At dawn they heard one groom whisper to another, "That place we stayed at last night is said to be a ghost-inn. A lot of people who have stayed there have afterwards gone mad, or even died. The officials of the district got tired of having to inquire into all these cases, and more than ten years ago they ordered that the place was to be closed down. If these two gentlemen stayed the night there without coming to any harm, it must either mean that the haunting has ceased, or that the gentlemen are destined by fate to rise high in the world."

III

A student called Li was going up to Peking for the examinations. At Soochow he hired a launch and had got as far as Huai-an, when there suddenly appeared at the cabin-door a certain Mr. Wang, who had formerly been Li's neighbor. He asked if he might join him. Li consented, and they traveled together for the rest of the day.

At nightfall, when they anchored, Wang asked him with a smile, "Are you easily frightened?"

The question surprised Li. He paused for a moment, and then said, "I don't think so."

"I was afraid that I might scare you," said Wang. "But as you have assured me that you are not easily scared, I had better tell you the truth at once. I am a ghost, not a live man. It is six years since you and I last met. Last year the crops failed, prices soared, and driven by hunger and cold I rifled a tomb, in order to get something valuable to sell for food and firing. But I was arrested, found guilty, and executed. And now I am a ghost, hungry and cold as before. I boarded your boat and asked you to take me with you to Peking, because I have a debt to collect there."

"Who is it that owes you money?" asked Li.

"A certain Mr. Piao," said Wang. "He is employed by the Board of Punishments, and he promised that when my papers passed through his hands he would erase the death-sentence and substitute something milder, in consideration for which I was to give him five hundred ounces of silver. I managed to collect the sum, but once it was in his hands he ignored his side of the bargain, and the sentence was duly carried out. So now I am going to haunt him."

This Mr. Piao happened to be a relative of Li's. He was very much upset that a member of his family should have behaved in this way. "The sentence pronounced upon you was of course perfectly in order," he said. "But my kinsman had no right to rob you in this way. How would it be if I were to take you with me to his house and point out to him how badly he behaved? He would then probably give you your money back and you would no longer feel so bitterly against him. But by the way, as you are dead, I don't quite see what use the money would be to you."

"It is true that I do not now have any use for it," said Wang, "but my wife and children are still living quite close to your home, and if we recover the money I shall ask you to give it to them for me."

Mr. Li promised to do this. Several days later, when they were approaching the capital, Wang asked leave to go on ahead, saying, "I'm going off to your relative's house to haunt him. If he has already realized that he is in my power, he is more likely to listen to what you say when you put my case to him. If you were to go there straight away he would certainly take no notice, for he is a man of extremely avaricious disposition."

So saying, Wang disappeared. Li went on into Peking, found himself a lodging, and a few days later went to his kinsman's house. On arriving, he was told that Mr. Piao was suffering from a "possession." Shamans, soothsayers, everything had been tried, but all to no purpose. As soon as Li reached the door the "possession," speaking through the sick man's mouth, shouted out, "Now's your chance, people! Your star of deliverance has arrived." The people of the house all rushed out to meet Li, asking him what the madman's words meant. Li told them the whole story, and Piao's wife at first suggested burning a considerable quantity of paper money in payment of the debt. At this the sick man roared with laughter. "Pay back real money with make-believe money?" he said. "Nothing in this world can be disposed of quite so conveniently as that! Count out five hundred ounces of silver at once, and hand them over to our friend here. I shan't let go of you till you do." The Piaos produced the money, and Mr. Piao at once recovered his senses.

Some days later the ghost turned up at Li's lodging and urged him to set out for the south at once. "But I have not sat for my examination yet," said Li.

"You are not going to pass," said the ghost, "so there is no point in sitting."

Li, however, insisted on remaining at Peking. After he had sat for the examination the ghost again urged him to start for home. "Do let me just wait till the results are out," said Li.

"You haven't passed," said the ghost, "so what is the point of waiting for the results?" When the results were published, Li's name was not on the list. "Now perhaps you'll consent to start," said the ghost, laughing. Ashamed of having kept him waiting for nothing, Li agreed to start immediately. On the boat he noticed that Wang sniffed at things to eat and drink, but never swallowed them, and that if he sniffed at anything hot, it at once became icy-cold.

When they got to Sutsien, the ghost said, "They are giving a play in that village over there. Let's go and look on." When they had watched several episodes, the ghost suddenly disappeared. But Li heard somewhere nearby a sound of sand flying and pebbles rolling. He thought he had better go to the boat and wait till the ghost came back. It was getting dark when the ghost at last reappeared, dressed up very grandly. "Goodbye," he said, "I'm staying here. I've got the job of God of War."

"How have you managed that?" asked Li, very much surprised.

"All the so-called Goddesses of Mercy and Gods of War down here in this world are merely ghosts passing themselves off as divinities. The play we saw was given in pursuance of a vow to the God of War. But the local 'God of War' is in fact the ghost of a scamp who did far worse things than I ever did. I suddenly made up my mind I would oust him from his job, so I went and had a scuffle with him and drove him away. I dare say you heard the noise of sand flying and pebbles rolling."

With these words the ghost bowed his thanks and vanished. Li went on down the canal, and eventually handed over the five hundred ounces of silver to the ghost's family.

TRANSLATED BY ARTHUR WALEY

Li Ju-chen

In the Country of Women

[*Ching hua yüan*, XXXIII]

[*The voyager Lin Chih-yang has observed with amusement the antics
of the inhabitants of one fantastic realm after another. He enters now a
situation in which he becomes personally involved, to his great discomfort. His travels have brought him to the Land of Women, where the
traditional roles of the sexes are exactly reversed. Women rule the roost,
and Lin, unprotected male, is seized and bound for the delectation of
the female ruler of the country.*]

The palace maidens were all immensely strong, and seized hold of Lin
Chih-yang as a hawk seizes a sparrow—there was no question of his
being the master. As soon as they had taken off his shoes and un-
dressed him, fragrant water was brought for his bath. They changed
his coat and trousers for a tunic and skirt, and for the time being put
socks of thin silk on his dainty great feet. They combed his hair into
plaits, pinning it with phoenix pins, and rubbed in scented oils. They
powdered his face and smeared his lips with bright red lipstick. They
put rings on his hands and bangles on his wrists, and arranging the curtains of the bed invited him to take his seat upon it.

Lin Chih-yang felt as though he were dreaming or drunk, and could
only sit there in misery. Closely questioning the palace maidens, he
discovered for the first time that the ruler of the country had chosen
him to be a royal concubine, and that he was to enter the palace as
soon as an auspicious date had been picked.

As he was reflecting on this alarming news, more palace maidens
came in. These were of middle age, all tall and strong, and with jowls
covered in hair. One of the maidens, who had a white beard and held
in her hand a needle and thread, advanced before the bed and there

knelt and said, "Gracious lady, with your permission, I have been ordered to pierce your ears." Already four maidens had come forward
and were gripping him firmly. The white-bearded maiden approached
and took hold first of his right ear. She rolled a few times between her
fingers the lobe where the needle was to go, and then straight away
drove the needle through. Lin Chih-yang shrieked out, "The pain's
killing me," and would have fallen over backwards had the maidens
not been supporting him. She then got hold of his left ear, rolled it a
few times and stuck the needle through. The pain brought continuous
shouts and cries from Lin Chih-yang. Both ears pierced, white lead
was smeared on them and rubbed in, after which a pair of golden earrings of the "eight jewel" design was fixed to them.

When the white-bearded maiden had finished her task she withdrew, and another maiden, this time with a black beard, came up. This
one had in her hand a roll of thin white silk. Kneeling before the bed,
she said, "Gracious lady, with your permission, I have been ordered to
bind your feet." Two more maidens approached, and kneeling on the
floor to support his dainty feet proceeded to take off the silk socks. The
black-bearded maiden seated herself on a low stool. Tearing off a strip
of silk, she first set Lin Chih-yang's right foot on her lap and sprinkled
alum between the joints of the toes. Then she drew all five toes tightly
together and, forcibly bending the whole foot over till it took on the
shape of a drawn bow, swiftly bound it up with the white silk. When
she had wound the silk round a few times, another of the palace
maidens brought a needle and thread and began to sew up the ends
tight, and so they continued, one binding while the other sewed.

With the four palace maidens pressing closely against him and the
two others holding on to his feet, Lin Chih-yang could not move an
inch. When the bindings were in place he felt his feet burning like a
charcoal brazier. Wave upon wave of aching swept over him, and soon
sharp pains began to shoot and forced out a loud cry: "I am dying in a
fiery pit!"

Having finished binding his feet, the maidens hurriedly made a pair
of large red slippers with soft soles and put them on for him. Lin Chih-
yang's tears flowed for a long time. His thoughts flew back and forth,
but he could think of no plan, all he could do was entreat the palace
maidens: "My brothers, I beseech you, put in a word for me before
your ruler: I am a married man, I have a wife, how can I become a
concubine? And these big feet of mine are like a wandering student

who has spent years without presenting himself for examination and has grown accustomed to a life of abandon—how can they bear restriction? I beg you, let me go, and then my wife as well will be filled with gratitude."

But the maidens replied, "Our ruler has just now given us the order to bind your feet and then invite you into the palace. Who then would dare to raise her voice in protest?"

TRANSLATED BY CYRIL BIRCH

A Poet of the Ch'ien-lung Period

The Ch'ien-lung reign (1736–96) was some of the last full blooms of the ancient culture so soon and so roughly to receive the graftings from the West. Among its poets Yüan Mei (1716–98: his adult life was almost coterminous with the reign) was regarded in his lifetime as preeminent. His fame has endured, deservedly, but in part at least because of the tinge of scandal to some of his eccentricities, such as his enlightened encouragement of girl pupils.

Though he passed the highest examinations and became a scholar of the Han-lin Academy at the early age of twenty-three, he held office for only a few years before retiring to his famous "Sui Garden." This Nanking residence "when finished," says Arthur Waley, "consisted of twenty-four pavilions, standing separately in the grounds, or built round small courtyards. Behind the pavilions was a piece of artificial water, divided into two parts by a meandering causeway, with little humped bridges that enabled a boat to pass from one part of the lake to the other. It was a miniature imitation of the causeways over the Western Lake at Hangchow." Yüan Mei himself believed it was the model for the Grand View Garden of Ts'ao Hsüeh-ch'in's Red Chamber Dream, but scholars now are doubtful of this identification.

Arthur Waley seems to have found Yüan Mei no less attractive than the great T'ang poet Po Chü-yi, and indeed their poems show strong similarities. Waley describes Yüan as "a lovable, witty, generous, affectionate, hot-tempered, wildly prejudiced man; a writer of poetry that even at its lightest always has an undertone of deep feeling

191

and at its saddest may at any moment light a sudden spark of fun."

In form, all the poems in this selection belong to the various sub-categories of the five- or seven-syllable shih.

Yüan Mei

On a Picture Called "Returning Boat," Painted for Him by His Friend Ni Su-feng

[*Ni Su-feng kuei chao t'u*]

I had long had it in mind to make a boat
That should skim the waves quick as any bird
Yet never carry people away from their friends,
But only carry people back to their homes.
Its misty sails and bamboo paddles existed only as a dream;
Year after year, a traveller afar, I was plagued by
    winds and sands.
Su-feng, brush in hand, looked at me and laughed,
Then bending over his painting-paper he chortled
    to himself.
What before was only a dream has today become a picture;
Now I really *have* come home; suddenly I realize it!

The Bell

[*Chung*]

No monk lives at the old temple, the Buddha has toppled to
    the floor;
One bell hangs high, bright with evening sun.
Sad that when only a tap is needed, no one now dares
To rouse the notes of solemn music that cram its ancient
    frame.

On the Funeral of His Carpenter, Who Had no Family

[*Yi tzu-jen shih*]

Life has a pattern, has its retributions;
Such things cannot be mere chance.
It fell to you to make my house;
It fell to me to make your coffin.
I buried you in a corner of the garden,
And having done so, felt at peace with myself,
For I felt as though you still came and went
Among the things your own hand had made.
A fresh wind fans your mortal form;
The wild wheat makes you its offerings—
Happier here than if pious sons and grandsons
Had carried you off to the dismal fringes of the town.
Here forever you shall be our Guardian Spirit,
Unsaddened by the murky winds of Death.

On His Chair-Bearers — a Case of Misplaced Sympathy

[*Yü-fu t'an*]

Today my carriers have had a double task;
We have gone up a mountain and then down into a valley.
For the moment they are through with all their hardships
    and dangers;
Night is falling, and at last they can rest their feet.
I was quite certain that directly they put down their bur-
    den
Tired out, they would sink into a heavy sleep.
To my great surprise they re-trimmed the lamp
And all night long played at games of chance.
A quarrel began; feeling ran high.
One of them absconded; another went in chase.
All the fuss was about a handful of pence;
Hardly enough to pay for a cup of gruel.
Yet they throw down those pence with as high and mighty
    an air

As if they were flinging a shower of golden stars.
Next day when they shouldered their burdens again
Their strength was greater than that of Pen and Yü.
The same thing happened five nights on end;
It was almost as if some demon had possessed them.
Can it be, I wonder, that when the dice are thrown
The Owl and the Black[1] have the power to cure fatigue?
But different creatures have their different natures;
What suits the fish will not please the bear.
The simplest folk and the most learned men
Cannot possibly be measured by the same rules.
Rather than sorrow over other people's sorrows
It is better, when one can, to enjoy one's own pleasures.

On the Rock, Near Kiukiang, on Which the Poet T'ao Ch'ien Lay When Drunk

[*Kuo Ch'ai-sang . . . kuan T'ao-kung tsui shih*]

It was not unusual for T'ao to get drunk,
And on one such occasion he slept on this rock,
With the strange result that a scrubby piece of stone
Has been cherished and admired for more than a thousand
    years.
Golden couches and jade stools have always existed in
    plenty;
But does anyone know the names of those who have taken
    a nap upon them?
They cannot compare with this rock that dominates Ch'ai-
    sang
More completely than an obelisk ten thousand cubits high.

---

[1] Names of dice-throws.

On Returning from a Journey

[*Yu kuei*]

When I reached the steps a fluttering snow of blossom struck
my face;
What a joy, amid such fragrance, to take off one's travelling
dress.
My old wife says with a smile, pointing at my concubines:
"If it had not been for the plum blossom, you would never
have come home!"

On Books

[*various titles*]

I

If one opens a book, one meets the men of old;
If one goes into the street, one meets the people of today.
The men of old! Their bones are turned to dust;
It can only be with their feelings that one makes friends.
The people of today are of one's own kind,
But to hear their talk is like chewing a candle!
I had far rather live with stocks and stones
Than spend my time with ordinary people.
Fortunately one need not belong to one's own time;
One's real date is the date of the books one reads!

II

Everything else in life is easy to break with;
Only my books are hard to leave behind.
I want to go through them all again,
But the days hurry by, and there is not time.
If I start on the Classics I shall never get to history;

If I read philosophy, literature goes by the board.
I look back at the time when I purchased them—
Thousands of dollars, I never worried about the price.
If passages were missing, the pains I took to supply them,
And to fill out sets that were incomplete!
Of the finest texts many are copied by hand;
The toil of which fell to my office clerks.
Day and night I lived with them in intimacy.
I numbered their volumes and marked them with yellow
     and red.
How many branches of wax-candle light,
How many drops of weary heart's blood!
My sons and grandsons know nothing of this;
Perhaps the book-worms could tell their own tale.
Today I have had a great tidy-up,
And feel I have done everything I was born to do. . . .
It is good to know that the people in the books
Are waiting lined up in the Land of the Dead.
In a little while I shall meet them face to face
And never again need to look at what they wrote!

Seven Poems on Aging

[*various titles*]

I

For the present I am happy to wield a feather fan
While I cross the river, singing the *A-t'ung*.[1]
To drink my health there are no companions or guests;
To row me on, plenty of hands at the oars.
Wave on wave the grey waters flow;
Gust on gust, the breeze from the distant hills.

---

[1] The *A-t'ung*, "boy's-song," supposed to date from the third century:
     A-t'ung and again A-t'ung!
     Sword in mouth he swam across the river.
     He had never feared the tigers on the bank,
     But was frightened of the dragons in the river.

There is no one to point at the misty waves and say,
"Out in the offing is an old man of fifty."

II

On this night year after year I have listened eagerly,
Never missing a single sound of the crackers till dawn
    came.
But this year on New Year's Eve I cannot bring myself to lis-
    ten,
Knowing that when the cock crows I shall enter my sixtieth
    year.
The mighty din of the celebrations has already died away;
If a little time is still left, it is only a last scrap
But the cock, as though feeling for my plight, is slow to
    open its mouth,
And I that write this am still a man of fifty-nine!

III

If at seventy I still plant trees,
Lookers-on, do not laugh at my folly.
It is true of course that no one lives forever;
But nothing is gained by knowing so in advance.

IV

When one is old, one treasures every minute;
A single day is precious as a whole year.
And how seldom, even in a whole year,
Does a true rapture of the senses come one's way!
Man is born to get pleasure where he can;
How he sets about it depends on how he is made.
All that matters is to find out in good time,
Each for himself, which things he really enjoys.
I was born with many strong cravings;
Now that I am old they are gradually slipping away.
There are only left two or three things
That still delight me as they did in former days—

To spread out a book beside a bamboo stream,
To run my fingers along an ancient jade,
To climb a hill with a stout stick in my hand,
To drink wine in the presence of lovely flowers,
Talk of books—why they please or fail to please—
Or of ghosts and marvels, no matter how far-fetched.
These are excesses in which, should he feel inclined,
A man of seventy-odd may well indulge.

v

Writing poems is like the blossoming of flowers;
If there is too much blossom the flowers are generally small;
And all the more, with a man nearing eighty,
Whose powers of invention have long withered away.
Yet all the same, people wanting poems
Continue to clamor for them all day long.
They know that the silkworm, till the moment of its death,
Never ceases to put out fresh threads.
I do my best to turn out something for them,
Though secretly ashamed to show such poor stuff.
Yet oddly enough my good friends that come
All accord in praising what I produce.
I am not the least shaken in my own belief;
But all the same I keep a copy in my drawer.
Can it be that though my body sinks to decay
My writing brush alone is still young?

vi

Now that I am old I get up very early
And feel like God creating a new world.
I come and go, meeting no one on the way;
Wherever I look, no kitchen-smoke rises.
I want to wash, but the water has not been heated;
I want to drink, but no tea has been made.
My boys and girls are behind closed doors;
My man-servants and maid-servants are all fast asleep.
At first I am cross and feel inclined to shout;
But all of a sudden remember my young days—

How I, too, in those early morning hours
Lay snoring, and hated to leave my bed.

VII

The east wind again has brought the splendor of spring
    flowers;
The willows gradually turn more green, the grass gradually
    sprouts.
When I look into the stream I must not repine at the snow
    on my two brows;
How few people have lived to see the flowers of four
    reigns!
Every moment I am now given comes as a gift from
    Heaven;
There is no limit to the glorious things that happen in the
    spring.
If you want to call, you need only pause outside the hedge
    and listen;
The place from which most laughter comes is certain to be
    my house!

TRANSLATED BY ARTHUR WALEY

Red Chamber Dream

The Red Chamber Dream *is one of the world's truly great novels. Sensitive, complex, and profound, it is preeminent in the Chinese tradition.*

Readers of the book tend to become addicts, a part of their minds invaded and under permanent occupation by the host of characters created by Ts'ao Hsüeh-ch'in (?1715–1763). They may take the book in one or more of several ways: as the recherche du temps perdu *of a middle-aged Bohemian, as a merciless analysis of a great family in decline, or as an allegorical statement of the Buddhist-Taoist vision of love and life in the "red dust" of this world.*

Existing translations of the novel abridge not only by excluding entire episodes (as Waley abridged Monkey*) but by constant compression of the text to speed the narrative. But Ts'ao Hsüeh-ch'in's forte is the unhurried exploration of every nuance of a situation. In the following extract, therefore, we move at the author's own pace as he builds up phrase by phrase the vivid mosaic of Phoenix's vengeance. Our story of Phoenix (Wang Hsi-feng) and Second Sister Yu links together passages drawn from a middle section of the novel, seven chapters in length.*

Between Chia Lien's taking of Second Sister Yu as his secondary wife and the discovery of this act by Phoenix, his first wife, there occurs in the novel the pathetic suicide of the third of the Yu sisters. This Third Sister also has come under the baneful influence of the all-powerful Chia family: it is her association with the Chia men that flaws her reputation in the eyes of her fiancé, and his doubts in turn that drive her to self-destruction. It is unfortunate that considerations of space

201

prevent the inclusion of this episode, for there is great ironic force in the contrast between Third Sister and the weaker Second Sister: the one is resistant to the blandishments of the corrupt Chia menfolk, the other succumbs, but the fate of each is inevitably tragic.

On her first encounter with Second Sister Yu in our extract, Phoenix presents an unforgettable image in her glitter of white and silver. At this point we need to recall that this mourning garb is not only a subtle reproach to Second Sister (whom Chia Lien improperly took as his concubine during the period of double mourning, for his uncle Chia Ching and for the deceased Imperial Consort from the Chia family, Cardinal Spring). It is no less subtle an allusion to the fate which has overtaken Third Sister Yu—the mourning may be said to be for her as well.

●

Ts'ao Hsüeh-ch'in

From Red Chamber Dream

How To Be Rid of a Rival

[*Hung-lou-meng*, LXIII–LXIX, extracts]

For some time past Chia Ching, the master of the Peace Mansion of the Chia family, had been cultivating the Way in the Mystic Truth Temple outside the city. Now suddenly there came swift messengers from the temple to report that Chia Ching had died in the night of no known cause.

Madam Yu was thrown into confusion by this news of her father-in-law's death. Her husband Chia Chen, their son Jung, and their cousin Chia Lien were all away from home, and for the time being there was not a single close male member of the family to help her. Her first act was to remove her jewelry, her next to send servants to the Mystic Truth Temple with orders to lock up every one of the Taoist priests there so that Chia Chen could question them on his return. This done she had a carriage hastily prepared and made her way out from the city with Lai-sheng and a number of the older servants both male and female. She also summoned doctors to determine the cause of death. Since he was already dead the doctors had no scope for pulse-taking and so on. But the absurdity of Chia Ching's Taoist yoga practices had long been common knowledge. He had overexerted both mind and body in all kinds of vain and foolish activities, greeting the stars and saluting the Dipper, fasting on days numbered *keng-shen*, and swallowing mercuric sulphide. It was these things that had taken his life, and now in death his belly was hard as iron and there were the purple fissures of burn marks about his mouth. The doctors reported to the women servants: "He has died all burnt and swollen from swallowing gold and dosing himself with sulphide of mercury in his Taoist pursuits."

The Taoists, however, in some panic said, "What went wrong was that he took cinnabar according to a secret formula. We priests had warned him that it shouldn't be taken before the time was ripe. He surprised us by taking it without our knowledge, last night during his *kengshen* fast. And now he has made his 'sylph ascension,' with devout heart he has attained the Way, emerged from the ocean of bitterness and cast aside the fleshly sack."

Madam Yu took little notice of what they said but ordered that they be locked up until her husband returned. Then she sent messengers on the swiftest mounts while she looked into what was to be done. The cell was too cramped for the body to be held there and it was not the time yet to move him into the city. So she made haste to have the corpse dressed and carried in a soft palanquin to the Buddhist Monastery of the Iron Sill. She reckoned it up: it would be at least two weeks before Chia Chen returned. The weather just now was certainly too hot to wait so long and so she had to take it upon herself to consult the astrologers as to the proper day for the encoffinment.

By a convenient chance the "longevity boards" had been made ready years previously and deposited in the monastery. On the third day she entered deep mourning and had the masses begun. In the Glory Mansion Phoenix was still too sick to leave her room, the widow Li Wan had the young girl cousins to look after, and Pao-yü was out of touch with things. So Madam Yu had to entrust all the outside dealings to some of the more subordinate family members. Chia Pien, Chia Ling, and others all had their work to do. Since Madam Yu was too busy to go home she had her stepmother come to look after the Peace Mansion. And to ease her own mind the stepmother brought her two unmarried daughters along with her.

When Chia Chen heard the news of his father's death he at once requested leave of absence for himself and his son. Knowing the emphasis placed by the present incumbent of the throne on the virtues of filial piety, the Board of Rites rather than deciding the case on their own initiative submitted a request for instructions. The goodness and piety of the Son of Heaven were indeed boundless, and furthermore he set a high value on the descendants of men distinguished for their service to the nation. On receipt of the memorial he inquired what office

Chia Ching had held. "He had attained the *chin-shih* degree," was the submission of the Board, "but the hereditary offices of the family had been assumed by his son Chia Chen. In advancing years and sickness Chia Ching himself had dwelt in seclusion in the Mystic Truth Temple outside the walls of the capital, where now he lies dead of an illness. His son Chia Chen and grandson Chia Jung, currently members of the imperial cortege to conduct the mourning for their deceased relative, the Imperial Consort Cardinal Spring, now petition for leave of absence to bury their progenitor."

The Son of Heaven responded at once with an edict of special grace: "Despite commoner status and lack of service record, Chia Ching is hereby posthumously awarded the fifth official rank in recognition of the achievements of his grandfather. His son and grandson will escort the coffin into the capital via the North Gate. Mourning ceremonies will be conducted in the family residence. When the coffin has been further escorted to the family tombs, memorial services will be held at the Light of Prosperity Monastery in due accord with the above-stipulated rank. Permission is given for court personnel from the princely and ducal ranks down to participate in the mourning ceremonies. By imperial command."

The edict was heard with profound gratitude by the Chia family and indeed was lauded for its conspicuous generosity by high officers of the court one and all.

Chia Chen hurried back with his son Jung, traveling day and night. At one point they met with Chia Pien and Chia Kuang who galloped up with a group of servants and leapt out of their saddles to greet Chia Chen.

Questioned on their errand, Chia Pien replied, "Your wife knew that you had already set out and she was afraid that her stepmother, old Dame Yu, would have no one to escort her. So she sent the two of us to look after her."

Chia Chen praised his wife's thoughtfulness and asked how things were being handled at home. Chia Pien told him how they had seized the Taoist priests and moved the body to the monastery. He gave also the details of how Madam Yu, reluctant to leave the house empty, had brought in her stepmother to live there together with her two half-sisters. Chia Jung had also dismounted by this time and when he heard of the arrival of his two aunts he glanced at his father with a smile. Chia

Chen murmured a few rapid "Very good's," then whipped up his horse again and was off. They did not even bother about inns but rode through the night on relays of mounts.

At last they were approaching the gate of the capital. They did not enter the city, but went straight to the Iron Sill Monastery. It was the fourth watch and as soon as the watchman saw them he roused everyone. Chia Chen and Chia Jung dismounted and gave themselves over to loud wailing. They began to crawl on their hands and knees from as far away as the main gate. When they reached the coffin they banged their foreheads against the floor until the blood ran. They wailed right through until day dawned and their throats were too dry to allow them to continue. Madam Yu and the rest greeted them and then father and son made haste to change into mourning garb in accordance with the rites and took up their stations before the coffin. Unfortunately they had certain things to attend to themselves and so were not quite able to "close the eyes to sight, the ears to sound." They were obliged to reduce the extremity of their grief just enough to be able to give directions to the servants and to announce the imperial grace to family and friends. Then Chia Jung was sent back home to prepare for the reception of his grandfather's body there. Chia Jung eagerly mounted and rode off. Once home he gave swift orders to rearrange the furniture in the reception rooms, set up partitions, hang the mourning drapes, erect tents for the musicians and a memorial arch outside the gate, and so on and so forth. Then he went bustling in to greet Dame Yu and her two daughters. Now the fact was that Dame Yu was very old and fond of sleep so that she was well out of the way as usual. Second Sister Yu and Third Sister Yu were at their embroidery attended by the little slave-girls. When he entered they gave him a polite greeting.

But Chia Jung said with a giggle, "Are you here, too, Second Sister? My father was just longing to see you."

Second Sister blushed and scolded him: "A fine one you are, little Jung. If I don't give you a good scolding every other day you're impossible. And now you're worse than ever, with no regard for what's proper at all. And you the son of a noble father in such a great family, studying and learning the rites day after day. Look at you, getting further and further behind even the humblest of people."

With these words she took a playful swipe at his head with a flatiron. Chia Jung clutched his head in mock terror, then cuddled up to her begging forgiveness. Third Sister Yu tried to "tear his mouth" to shut him up: "Wait till our sister, your mother, gets home. We'll tell her all about it."

Chia Jung laughed and knelt on the bed-platform seeking forgiveness. Then he tried to snatch one of the cardamoms that Second Sister was chewing. She had her mouth full of the juice and spat it in his face, whereupon he stuck his tongue out and licked it off and swallowed it. The little slave-girls couldn't help laughing: "And you in deepest mourning, too, and the old lady asleep right there. Although these two ladies are so young, they're your aunts after all. You really should have more respect for your mother. When your father gets back and we tell him you'll be slinking off like a dog that's been whipped."

Chia Jung let go his aunt in order to embrace and kiss the slaveys and said, "Oh, you darlings, you're so right. We'll let the two of them off."

The slaveys pushed him away and gave him a vigorous scolding. "Ill-fated little demon. You've got nursemaids and slaveys of your own but all you want to do is come messing about with us. People who really know the truth would say it's just naughtiness, but what about people who don't understand? And then there are all those dirty-minded tongue-waggers always meddling in things that don't concern them—they make a commotion that gets across to the Glory Mansion, wagging their tongues behind our backs and telling people what a corrupt set we are over here."

Chia Jung smiled. "Separate households, why can't they mind their own business? There's enough to keep them occupied anyway. All through history, even back in Han and T'ang times—haven't you heard the expressions 'filthy T'ang' and 'stinking Han?' So what do they expect with people like us? What family doesn't have a few romances? Don't ask me to tell you all about them. Even over there in the Glory Mansion where the family head Chia Cheng is so strict, Chia Lien still carried on with that little concubine of his. And Aunt Phoenix, who was so strong-willed that Uncle Chia Jui came to grief when he tried her out. Don't think that any of them got by me."

Talk gushed from Chia Jung like a river, once he had started he didn't care what he said, and in the middle of it all the old lady awoke. He paid his respects, and said, "We've put you to such trouble, Great-aunt. And we've been such a nuisance to Second Sister and Third Sister also, my father and I will always be grateful to you. But when everything is over with we'll bring the whole family to visit you and kowtow."

Dame Yu nodded her head. "Ah, my son, you always say such nice things. We're relatives after all, we're only doing what we should." Then she asked, "But how is your father? When did you hear the news and get back?"

"We just got back," answered Chia Jung with a smile. "I was sent here straight away to have a word with you and beg you whatever you do not to leave until everything's finished."

As he said this he winked at both his aunts. But Second Sister muttered under her breath, "Little monkey's brood, you can twist your tongue with the best of them. Why don't you leave us alone and go back and make trouble for your father?"

Chia Jung went on to Dame Yu, "You can set your mind at rest. My father spends every day worrying about Second Sister and Third Sister. He's on the lookout for a couple of handsome young men, nice and rich and from good families, that he can bring in as husbands for your daughters. He's been looking for years without success, but just now on the journey back we happened on one who will be just right."

Dame Yu was taking him perfectly seriously and asked at once, "What is his family?"

But the sisters put down their needlework and laughed as they beat Chia Jung with their fists: "Mother, you mustn't believe a word this wicked child says." Even the slaveys warned him: "The Lord of Heaven has eyes—watch out for thunderbolts!"

At this point servants came in to report: "Everything's ready. Please come out and check so that you can report to your father." And Chia Jung went giggling out of the room. As soon as he had seen to it that everything was satisfactorily prepared he hurried back to the monastery to report to Chia Chen. They spent that night distributing tasks among the various responsible servants, to make ready all the necessary banners and such things for the funeral procession into the city. This had been planned for dawn on the fourth day of the month, and messengers were sent to inform friends and relatives. When the day came the ceremonies were conducted with great glitter and brilliance and guests assembled like clouds in the sky. There were scores of thousands of people packing the sides of the road from the Iron Sill Monastery all the way to the Peace Mansion. Some sighed in sympathy, some gaped in awe, and there was the occasional educated person, a "half a jar of vinegar," who would complain that "Frugality, not ostentation, should be the rule for funerals"; but all of them endlessly discussed the details the entire length of the route. It was midafternoon by the time they arrived and set the coffin in position in the main hall. When the libations and formal expressions of grief were over the friends and relatives began to take their leave until there remained only the clan members, who busied themselves with entertaining the new arrivals and seeing off the departing guests. Of the closest relatives only Chia She remained to accompany the chief mourners. During this time Chia Chen and his son had been under the restraint imposed by the funeral rites. They had been obliged to sleep on straw mats with wooden pillows by the side of the coffin and to conduct themselves with all due funereal grief. Once the guests had left, however, they seized whatever opportunity offered to misbehave themselves with the womenfolk of the clan.

Pao-yü also had attended at the Peace Mansion each day, dressed in mourning and returning to his cottage in the garden only when the guests had gone in the evening. Phoenix was still not fully recovered and could not be present all the time. But she put herself out helping Madam Yu with the arrangements whenever there were services held and sutras read and friends and relatives offering sacrifices.

Several days passed and it was time for the departure of the coffin. The Matriarch's health was still not good and she kept Pao-yü at home to attend on her. Since Phoenix was still not feeling well she did not attend either. All the rest, including Chia She and his wife, Chia Lien and Madam Wang, escorted the procession to the Iron Sill Monastery accompanied by their household servants, both men and women. They returned home in the evening, but Chia Chen with his wife and son stayed on at the monastery to watch by the coffin. Not until the hundred days had passed did they accompany the coffin to the family burial ground. And all this time Dame Yu with her two daughters stayed to look after the house.

Now Chia Lien had long been aware of the beauty of the Yu sisters and bemoaned the cruel fate which denied him even a glimpse of them. In the recent days when the coffin of Chia Ching had been stationed in the mansion Chia Lien had got to know Second Sister and Third Sister very well through daily contact and of course he had begun to drool at the mouth. What was more, he knew that there had already been talk of their incestuous relationships with both Chia Chen and his son. So he let slip no opportunity to tease and provoke them in every way possible, flashing messages with glance and eyebrow. Third Sister responded only with cold reserve. Second Sister, on the other hand, had every inclination, but there were eyes and ears all about them and nothing could be done. Chia Lien was afraid, too, of the jealousy of Chia Chen, so he had to avoid any careless step. For the time being, then, he and Second Sister were obliged to content themselves with a communion of the mind. But now that his father's coffin had been removed to the monastery Chia Chen retained very few people in his home. Dame Yu with her two daughters stayed on in the principal rooms with a handful of slave-girls and serving women to do the rough work. The rest of the maids and the secondary wives were all in attendance at the monastery. The outdoor servants limited themselves to patrolling the grounds in the evenings and guarding the gates in the daytime and unless something unusual happened they never went indoors. This gave Chia Lien exactly the chance he had been waiting for. He stayed at the monastery under the pretext of keeping Chia Chen company, but he was all the time claiming the need to help out Chia Chen with various household matters so that he could get back to the Peace Mansion and his pursuit of Second Sister.

One day at this time Chia Chen received a report from Yü Lu, one of his bailiffs: "We spent a total of eleven hundred ounces of silver on tents, banners, mourning drapes, and wages for the attendants. We've actually paid five hundred, there are six hundred and ten ounces still owed. Two of the contractors sent their men over-yesterday pressing for payment and I need your instructions, sir."

"You could have got it from the storehouse already," said Chia Chen. "Why do you have to come bothering me?"

Yü Lu replied: "I went to the storehouse for it yesterday. But since the old gentleman passed away there have been all kinds of expenses, and with what's left they have to think of the hundred days' masses and the other costs at the monastery. They refuse to issue the money to me and that's why I've come to you now. I thought you might take it for the time being out of your private store or perhaps arrange a loan somewhere. If you can give me instructions I'll do what's necessary."

"You think this is the first time we've spent what we haven't got?" laughed Chia Chen. "Borrow it from somewhere and pay them. I don't care where."

Yü Lu laughed in return and said, "If it was just a hundred or two I could work it. But this is five or six hundred—there's nowhere I can go right now for such an amount."

Chia Chen thought for a moment and said to his son Jung, "Go ask your mother. Yesterday after the removal of the coffin we received five hundred ounces of silver as a funeral gift from the Chen family in Chiangnan. This hasn't been turned into the store yet. See if you can find it in the house and when you've scraped it together let him have it."

Chia Jung assented and went quickly across to discuss with Madam Yu. He returned to report to his father: "We've already spent two hundred ounces of that silver that came yesterday. The three hundred left over has been sent home and given into the old lady's keeping."

"In that case," said Chia Chen, "take Yü Lu back with you, ask the old lady for the money, and give it to him. While you're there you can make sure that everything's all right at home and pay your respects to your aunts. The rest of the money that's needed Yü Lu can borrow and add to what you give him."

Chia Jung and Yü Lu assented and were just on their way out when Chia Lien arrived. Yü Lu hastened forward to greet him. Chia Lien asked what was happening and Chia Chen gave him the details. Chia Lien said to himself, "A splendid opportunity to pay a call on Second Sister in the Peace Mansion." Aloud he said, "This isn't anything so important that you have to go borrowing from others. I got some silver yesterday that I haven't used. Why don't I let him have that to make up the amount and save trouble all round?"

"Excellent," said Chia Chen. "Tell Jung what he has to do and let him collect both sums."

"Oh, no," said Chia Lien hastily. "I shall have to go myself for this. Also it's several days since I was home, I ought to pay my respects to the Matriarch and my parents. Then I can go over to your house and make sure there's no trouble with the servants and I can pay my respects to Dame Yu at the same time."

"But I really feel embarrassed to put you to so much trouble," said Chia Chen with a smile.

Chia Lien smiled back. "We are as brothers. This is no trouble."

Then Chia Chen gave his instructions to his son. "Go with your uncle here and pay your respects and your mother's and mine to the Matriarch and to Chia She and the ladies. And inquire after the old lady's health, see if she is still having to take her medicine."

Point by point Chia Jung acknowledged his instructions, then left with Chia Lien. They mounted and rode into the city taking a few serving-boys with them. Uncle and nephew chatted as they rode. Chia Lien made a point of bringing the conversation round to Second Sister Yu. He praised her for her loveliness, what a delightful person she was, how easy and generous in her behavior, how soft spoken, how admirable and charming in every possible way. "Everyone praises my wife Phoenix, but the way I see it she can't hold a candle to your Second Aunt."

Chia Jung knew very well what he was after. He laughed and said, "Since you're so fond of her, why shouldn't I be your go-between and you can take her for your secondary wife. What do you think?"

Chia Lien laughed too: "Are you serious or are you just kidding?"

"I'm perfectly serious," said Chia Jung.

Chia Lien laughed again. "Fine, fine, only I'm afraid my wife would never agree. Your grandmother Dame Yu wouldn't go along with it either. In any case I've heard it said that Second Sister Yu is already betrothed."

"There's no problem there," said Chia Jung. "Second Sister and Third Sister Yu are my aunts, but they were Dame Yu's daughters by her first marriage. She brought them with her when she married my grandfather. As I understand it, when she was still with her first husband she promised Second Sister in marriage to a member of the Chang family who manage the Imperial Granary. This betrothal was arranged before they were born, when they were just on the way. Then later the Chang family got involved in a lawsuit and lost. Later my grandmother married again. It's been a dozen years or more since the two families were in any contact at all. My grandmother is always grumbling about it and wants to break off the betrothal. My father wants to make a new match for Second Sister also, he's just waiting till he can find the right person. All we have to do is send someone to find this Chang family, give them a dozen ounces of silver or so, and have a deed drawn up breaking off the engagement. These Chang people are very poor, I don't think they'll refuse to go along with it once they see the money. And they know what kind of people we are, too, there's no fear they won't come round. And to have someone like yourself take her as secondary wife, I'll guarantee both my grandmother and my father will be delighted. The only problem is your wife there."

By this stage Chia Lien's heart was in full bloom. He had nothing further to say and rode on with a vacant grin all over his face. Chia Jung pondered a little farther then said with a smile, "It will take some courage, but if you'll follow my advice I'll guarantee there will be no problem. Only, it's going to cost you a bit of money."

"Tell me what your advice is," said Chia Lien at once. "Whatever it is, just tell me."

"When you get home don't let a word of this get out," said Chia Jung. "Let me straighten things out with my father and get my grandmother's agreement. After that we'll buy a little house and the necessary furnishings somewhere behind the mansion, not far away. We'll send a few of the servants over there to look after your needs. Then you can choose a day and marry her without letting a mortal soul or the devils in Hell know about it. We will instruct the servants that they are not to let a whisper of this leak out. Your wife Phoenix lives in the inner quarters hidden away in a huge mansion—how is she ever going to find out? You can spend your time in both places alternately, and if it does come out in a year or so all you will get is a scolding from your father. Then all you'll need to say is that your wife has never given you a son, and that it's entirely for the sake of the continuance of the family line that you have made private arrangements of this kind outside the family. And then even Phoenix—when she sees that 'the rice has been cooked and served'—there will be nothing she can do about it. You can go get the Matriarch on your side and then there's nothing that can't be settled."

It is an ancient saying that "desire dims the luster of wisdom." Chia Lien was so obsessed by his longing for Second Sister's beauty that he took Chia Jung's words to represent the ultimate perfection of careful planning. He left completely out of his calculations all the many drawbacks: his own present mourning, the status of his first wife, his father's certain anger, and the jealousy of Phoenix. Nor did he realize that Chia Jung's motives were in no way disinterested. Chia Jung had had a craving for his aunt for some time past, but with his father at home he could hardly do as he liked. If Chia Lien now took her as his bride he would be forced to establish her somewhere on the outside and then there would be plenty of opportunities for deviltry when Chia Lien was not there. Chia Lien, of course, had no idea of this but expressed his gratitude to Jung: "What a wonderful nephew. If you can really pull this off I'll buy you a couple of the prettiest little slave-girls I can find as your reward."

By this time they had reached the gate of the Peace Mansion. "I'll go pay my respects to the Matriarch," said Chia Jung, "while you go in and get the money from my great aunt to hand over to Yü Lu."

"Don't let the Matriarch know that you and I came together," said Chia Lien with a smile and a nod.

"Of course not," said Chia Jung. Then he whispered into Chia Lien's ear: "If you happen to meet my Second Aunt today, don't get impatient. If anything comes out now things will be much harder to manage later on."

"Don't fuss. Off with you, I'll wait for you here," laughed Chia Lien.

And with that Chia Jung went off to pay his respects to the Matriarch.

As soon as Chia Lien entered the Peace Mansion he was greeted by the senior servants at the head of the rest. They surrounded him all the way to the main hall and he exchanged remarks with one after another of them simply as a formality. Then he dismissed the servants and entered the inner apartments alone. In fact, Chia Lien had long been on very close terms with Chia Chen, the master of the household. As they were members of the same generation there was no need for strict protocol between them and he had been used to entering without being announced. So he went straight to the principal sitting room where nursemaids waiting on the verandah parted the beaded drapes for him to enter.

On entering Chia Lien found only Second Sister Yu with two slaveys seated on the bed-platform in the southern half of the room pursuing their needlework. There was no sign of Third Sister or Dame Yu. He hastened forward to greet her. Second Sister with a smile offered him a seat then herself took one of the chairs in a row on the east side. Chia Lien insisted however that she take the seat of honor at the head of the row. After a few opening pleasantries he asked, smiling, "Where are your esteemed mother and Third Sister? How is it they're not with you?"

"They have some things to do in the back rooms," said Second Sister. "They'll be here in a moment."

By this time the attendant slave-girls had left to make tea and there was no one about. Chia Lien flashed glances time and again at Second Sister but she lowered her head and responded with no more than a slight smile. For his part Chia Lien dared make no rash or untoward move. But then he observed that Second Sister's hands were playing with a silk kerchief which served as the wrapping for a small package. So he made the pretense of fumbling at his own waist and said, "I've forgotten to bring my betel nut package. If you have some there won't you give me a piece?"

"I do have some," said Second Sister. "But I never let anyone else chew my betel nut."

Chia Lien laughed and made to come close to her and seize it. Afraid of the indecorous appearance if they were seen Second Sister tossed the package across to him with a giggle. Chia Lien caught it and poured out all the nuts. He picked out a piece which was half nibbled, stuck it in his mouth and began to chew it. Then he picked up the remainder and was just about to return the package in person when in came the two slaveys with the tea. While Chia Lien was taking the tea he managed at the same time surreptitiously to remove a "nine-dragon circlet" of Han jade which he carried at his waist. This he wrapped in a handkerchief and then seizing his moment when the slaveys weren't looking he threw it across to Second Sister. She made no move to pick it up but simply sat and drank her tea as though she had seen nothing.

There was a swish of the beaded drapes at the other side of the room and Dame Yu and Third Sister came in from the rear of the house with two more slaveys. Chia Lien signaled Second Sister with his eyes to pick up the circlet, but she still took no notice. Chia Lien had no idea what she was up to and began to panic. All he could do however was rise and greet the newcomers. Then when he looked behind him at Second Sister again he saw her smiling there completely unconcerned. But another glance showed him that the little package had disappeared and Chia Lien was able to breathe again.

All now took their seats and began to converse. Chia Lien said to Dame Yu, "According to your daughter, Madam Yu, there was a package of silver which she gave into your keeping just a little while ago. Now it is needed to repay a debt and your son-in-law has asked me to come to collect it and also to ask whether you are having any problems here."

Dame Yu responded by at once sending Second Sister with the key to get the silver. Meanwhile Chia Lien continued, "I also wanted to pay my respects to you, old lady, and have a look at my two cousins here. You are doing my family a great service, but I'm afraid we are imposing on the two young ladies very badly."

"Oh, there's no call for such concern," said Dame Yu with a smile. "We're all close relatives. It doesn't really make any difference whether we spend our time at home or over here. I can tell you, ever since my husband died we've had a hard time of it at home and we've been completely beholden to my son-in-law for his help. So now that there's such a sorrow in his household and there's nothing else we can do for him it isn't much just to look after the home for him. There's no question of putting on anyone."

As she was speaking Second Sister reappeared with the silver which she handed to her mother. Dame Yu passed it over to Chia Lien who had a slavey call in a nursemaid. "Give this to Yü Lu," he told this woman, "and tell him to take it over there and wait for me."

As the nursemaid assented and left they heard the voice of Chia Jung in the courtyard. A moment later he entered to greet his great-aunt and aunts and to say, smiling to Chia Lien, "Your father was just asking for you, I think there's something he wants you to do. He was going to send a messenger to the temple for you but I told him you'd be coming. Your father told me to hurry you along if I met you on the way."

Chia Lien rose at once and Chia Jung said to Dame Yu, "When I was telling you that my father was looking for a husband for Second Sister, he had in mind someone very similar in looks and station to Uncle Lien. What would you say to that?" And he stealthily pointed at Chia Lien and made a grimace at Second Sister.

Second Sister did not like to say anything but Third Sister scolded him, half jokingly but half in earnest. "You evil little monkey. What a shameless thing to say. Just wait, I'm going to tear your mouth."

Chia Jung had already run laughing out of the room and now Chia Lien in his turn laughingly took his leave. Reaching the main hall he warned the servants against gambling and drinking and so on. Then he whispered a plea to Chia Jung to hurry over to settle things with his father. Meanwhile Chia Lien took Yü Lu back to his own place where he gave him the silver to make up the sum he needed; then he went to see his father and pay his respects to the Matriarch.

Chia Jung, however, had nothing to do when Yü Lu had gone off with Chia Lien for the silver. So he went back to the inner apartments and teased his two aunts for a while before leaving. Returning to the monastery in the evening he reported to his father Chia Chen: "The silver has been given to Yü Lu. The Matriarch is much better and does not have to take her medicine any more."

Then while he was about it he described how Chia Lien during their journey back had developed the notion of taking Second Sister Yu as his secondary wife. He told how they were making ready a little house outside the mansion without letting Phoenix know about it. "It's all simply a matter of continuing the family line. And Second Sister Yu is someone we know, it's best to keep it in the family, much better than getting someone you don't know from an outside go-between. That's why Uncle Lien was so insistent that I talk to you about it"— only, he did not reveal that it had been his own idea in the first place.

Chia Chen thought for a while, then smiled and said, "Well, I suppose it will be all right, the only thing is that we don't know what Second Sister wants. Tomorrow you can go discuss it with your great-aunt and get her to sound out Second Sister before we make it definite."

He gave some further instructions to Chia Jung, then went across to tell his wife, Madam Yu, of the matter. Madam Yu realized that this was a bad business and made some effort to discourage it. But Chia Chen's mind was made up and Madam Yu had long been accustomed to submission. Moreover it was not for her to concern herself too deeply since they were only half-sisters. So all she could do was let the men go ahead with their nonsense.

As soon as daylight came the next morning Chia Jung went back into the city as planned. He reported to his great-aunt what his father had said together with a number of additions of his own devising. He told her what a fine man Chia Lien was and how Phoenix's sickness had already gone beyond hope of recovery. They were to prepare a cottage and live outside the mansion for the time being, but in a year or so with Phoenix dead Second Sister would enter the family as first wife of Chia Lien. He told her of the wedding gifts his father was planning and of the preparations Chia Lien was making to receive his bride; of how great-aunt herself would be taken in to spend her declin-

ing years with them and of how they would undertake also to secure a
husband for Third Sister in due course. All in all he talked the stars out
of the sky and left Dame Yu no room to refuse. Furthermore, the old
lady had long been dependent on Chia Chen for her maintenance and it
was Chia Chen himself who was supervising this present match. Nor
would she need to make any provisions herself for the dowry; and after
all Chia Lien was a youth of noble family far outranking the Changs.

And so the old lady hastened across to deliberate with Second Sister. Now Second Sister Yu had a nature no more stable than water. She
had already had an affair with her brother-in-law Chia Chen and she
heartily regretted her early and ill-advised betrothal to Chang Hua
which seemed to threaten to waste the rest of her life. Now that it was
Chia Lien whose passion she had stirred and Chia Chen who was supervising the match she had no possible reason to object and in fact she
nodded her head at once in assent. This was reported to Chia Jung who
relayed the news to his father.

The next day messengers were sent to summon Chia Lien to the
monastery where Chia Chen informed him of Dame Yu's agreement.
Naturally Chia Lien was overjoyed and his gratitude to Chia Chen and
his son knew no bounds. They proceeded to discuss the details of sending someone to search for a house and of ordering the head ornaments
and the clothes and furnishings Second Sister would need for her
dowry. Before many days had passed all was ready and a house of
moderate size (some twenty "beam-spaces") had been purchased in
Blossoming Sprig Alley, half a mile behind the street where the Glory
and Peace Mansions stood. They bought two little slave-girls also. They
were reluctant, however, to reassign any of the servants from the mansion. On the other hand, if they brought in outsiders they would be of
doubtful loyalty and rumors might easily get out. Then Chia Lien
thought of the family servant Pao Erh, the favors of whose wife he had
secretly enjoyed some years ago. Phoenix had found out and made a terrible fuss and the woman had hanged herself out of shame. Thereon
Chia Lien had given Pao Erh a hundred ounces of silver to find himself a
new wife. The man had for some time been hand in glove with Auntie
Tuo, the wife of Nitwit Tuo the cook. When Nitwit Tuo eventually
drank himself to death, Auntie Tuo observed that Pao Erh had amassed
a nice little pile, and married him. Furthermore, this Auntie Tuo herself
had been very accommodating to Chia Lien. At this time they were living somewhere outside the mansion. Once Chia Lien had bethought

himself of them he ordered the two of them into the new house where they could see to the needs of Second Sister. And Pao Erh and his wife were only too pleased to accept this stroke of good fortune.

The next task was to send messengers after Chang Hua and his father, who were to be forced to release Second Sister from her betrothal. The Chang family for generations had been in charge of the Imperial Granary. Death had taken one after another, but Chang Hua's father had still served in the same position. He had been a close friend of Dame Yu's former husband and that was why Chang Hua and Second Sister Yu had been betrothed from the womb. Years passed and the Changs got involved in an unfortunate lawsuit which robbed them of all their property. They had barely enough to provide food and clothing, let alone think of contracting a marriage. It had been ten years and more since Dame Yu had married again and in all that time not a word had passed between her and the Chang family. And now she had been summoned to enter the Chia household and was being forced to repudiate Second Sister's betrothal. She was not at all happy about this, but her fear of the power and influence of Chia Chen and his relatives forced her to go along with it. She wrote out a deed of cancellation. Old Mr. Yu handed over twenty ounces of silver and that was an end to the betrothal agreement between the two families.

Now that everything was in readiness Chia Lien selected the third of the month as an auspicious day to receive Second Sister as his bride.

Chia Lien and Chia Chen and his son made all their arrangements in concert and on the second of the month saw Dame Yu and Third Sister into the new house in advance. When Dame Yu looked it over she found it not quite up to Chia Jung's description, but still it was all very trim and comfortable and she and Third Sister were well satisfied. Pao Erh and his wife were all on fire with eagerness to please and every two minutes were calling Dame Yu "Mother-in-law" or "Old Lady." Third Sister they called "Auntie" or "Third Aunt."

At dawn the following day a palanquin, plain for the mourning period, brought Second Sister Yu to the house where every variety of incense and candles, paper horses and fancy quilts, wine to drink and things to eat had all been set out in readiness. Very shortly Chia Lien in his mourning garb arrived in a small palanquin. Bride and groom made obeisances to Heaven and Earth and the paper horses were burned. Dame Yu was proud indeed of Second Sister, who looked so different dressed from head to foot in her new finery. She was led into the bridal chamber where that night she and Chia Lien engaged in the "sporting of the phoenix," showering affection on each other in a hundred ways whose details need not concern us.

Chia Lien grew more and more deeply delighted and infatuated and could never think of enough to do to please Second Sister. He ordered Pao Erh and the rest to avoid any reference to her subordinate status but to call her madam, which was the term he used himself as though Phoenix had never existed. Whenever he had to go back home he simply claimed that he had been busy with matters in the Peace Mansion. Phoenix harbored no suspicions since she was well aware that he was very close to Chia Chen and would have much to discuss with him. Despite the great number of the servants none of them concerned themselves with what was happening. Even the telltales and rumormongers who specialized in ferreting out secrets made it their business to serve Chia Lien's interests. They were on the lookout for whatever advantage they might be able to gain and none of them was interested in letting out the secret.

And so Chia Lien continued to feel deeply grateful to Chia Chen. Each month Chia Lien brought five ounces of silver for the household expenses. When he was not there Dame Yu and her two daughters would eat their meals together; whenever Chia Lien came he would dine with his wife, and Dame Yu and Third Sister would eat in their own room. He brought over all the favorite little possessions that he had been accumulating for years and gave them into Second Sister's keeping. He discussed with her also every last detail of Phoenix's behavior, down to the most intimate secrets of the bedchamber. He assured Second Sister that she would become his first wife once Phoenix was dead. Second Sister naturally rejoiced at the prospect. And from this time forward the dozen or so members of the little household led a life of perfect ease and comfort.

[*The match proposed for Third Sister Yu was broken off when the young man concerned discovered the truth of the sisters' relations with Chia Lien and Chia Chen, and Third Sister's shame compelled her to take her own life. Not long after this Chia Lien was obliged to leave home for a while on official business. More and more members of the Chia household were becoming aware of the clandestine marriage, but they still managed to keep the secret from reaching the ears of Chia Lien's first wife, Phoenix.*]

One day at this time Pao-yü was returning from a chat with Black Jade in her cottage. He was oppressed by the sorrows Black Jade had to endure as an orphan, and wanted to share his thoughts with Pervading Fragrance. But when he reached his own rooms he found only Musk Moon and Autumn Ripple there. "Where is Pervading Fragrance?" he asked.

Musk Moon teased him: "Do you really think we've lost her? She's bound to be somewhere in the garden, in one cottage or another. So worked up when she isn't here the moment you call!"

"I wasn't worrying that she was lost," said Pao-yü smiling. "But I've just been to see Miss Black Jade, and she was very miserable. It turned out that Precious Clasp had sent her a present, a piece of local craftsmanship from her home district. The sight of it had brought on her homesickness, and I wanted to tell Pervading Fragrance about it and get her to go over there to cheer her up."

Bright Cloud came in just at this moment, and said, "You're back? Who is it needs cheering up this time?"

Pao-yü repeated what he had just told the others, and she said, "Pervading Fragrance has just gone out. She said she was going to visit Madam Phoenix, but she might go on to see Miss Black Jade after."

Pao-yü made no reply. Autumn Ripple brought tea, but after rinsing his mouth he handed the bowl to a slavey. He felt unsettled and could think of nothing better to do than lie sprawled across his bed.

Pervading Fragrance had got on with her needlework for a while during Pao-yü's absence. But then it had occurred to her that for some days past she had not been to see Phoenix, who was still unwell. Apparently Chia Lien had gone away, so this would be a good chance for a quiet talk. She told Bright Cloud: "Don't all of you go out at once, make sure there's someone here to attend to Master Pao-yü when he gets back."

"Well now," said Bright Cloud, "so you're the only one in this household who ever thinks of him, is that it? The rest of us just sit around doing nothing for our keep?"

Pervading Fragrance had laughed and taken her leave with no further word. Now she was on the path that led across the Blossom-

Drenched Bridge. Summer was just yielding place to autumn, and new lotus curled among the old in a dappling of pink and green across the garden pool. Pervading Fragrance lingered on the dike for a while relishing the sight. Then when she raised her head she caught sight of someone under the vine trellis swatting away at something with a whisk in her hand. Coming closer she found it was old Mother Chu.

The old dame came smirking up to greet her. "Have you managed to take a little break, miss, to enjoy the garden?"

"That's it," said Pervading Fragrance. "I'm just on my way to have a word with Madam Phoenix. But what is that you're doing?"

"Chasing off the bees," said the old woman. "It was so dry in the hot season this year, the insects have got to every one of our fruit trees. All the fruit are scarred and pitted all over, and a lot have fallen already. And you wouldn't believe these hornets, they're the worst of all. They get on a bunch of grapes, and who cares if they only take a bite at two or three of them, the juice from the ones they've attacked drips down on the rest and the whole bunch is ruined. Just look, miss, there's more fallen just while we've been talking here and I couldn't keep them off!"

"But even if you never stop you're not going to be able to chase them all away," said Pervading Fragrance. "Why don't you get one of the storekeepers to make you a whole lot of little bags out of window gauze. Put one over every bunch. It would let air through, and they wouldn't spoil."

The old woman gave a relieved smile: "Oh miss, that's just what I must do. This is the first year I've been looking after them, how am I to know a clever trick like that?" And she went on pleasantly, "But even though we've had so many spoiled this year, the taste is beautiful. I'll just pick one for you, you can taste it and see if I'm not right."

"What do you mean!" said Pervading Fragrance sternly. "They aren't ripe yet, but even if they were, it certainly wouldn't do for us to be eating them before the firstfruits have been presented to the mistress. You've been in service in the mansion here all your life, surely you know this is one of the rules?"

Old Mother Chu hastened to make amends: "Of course, miss. I only dared suggest it because I thought you'd enjoy one. And there I was going to break the rules! I'm just a silly old woman, I really am!"

"It's of no importance," said Pervading Fragrance. "Only, it's up to you older women to set an example, not to start things going wrong like this."

Pervading Fragrance left the garden now and made her way straight to Phoenix's house. From the courtyard she could already hear Phoenix's voice: "God in Heaven! Here I sit cooped up in this room, and they're making me feel like a thief in my own house!"

Obviously something was wrong, and Pervading Fragrance felt it would be awkward either to turn back or to go on in. So she deliberately made more noise with her feet as she approached. Then she called through the window, "Is Sister Equity at home?"

Equity responded to her call and came out to meet her. "Is Mistress Phoenix here also? I hope she is feeling better."—and with these words Pervading Fragrance entered the house.

Phoenix, fully dressed and wearing her ornaments, had been lying sprawled on the bed. She smiled and rose to her feet to greet Pervading Fragrance: "Well, that's better, you've remembered us. Why has it been so many days since you came over for a chat?"

"While you have been unwell I should really have come every day to ask after your health," said Pervading Fragrance. "I only thought you might be feeling tired and would welcome the chance to take things quietly. If we all came we should be a nuisance to you with our chatter."

"There's no question of being a nuisance," Phoenix laughed. "But of all the people Pao-yü has over there, it's only you he can rely on to look after him, and I suppose you can't leave him. Equity is always saying how often you think of me and ask after me. It just shows what a goodhearted person you are." And she had Equity set a stool by the bedside for Pervading Fragrance to sit down. Equity brought tea also, and Pervading Fragrance bowed and said, "Sister, please join us."

They had been chatting for a while when a slavey beckoned Equity into the outer room and whispered, "Wang-erh is here, he's waiting by the inner gate."

And Equity's whispered reply: "Very well, but tell him to go away and come back later. He mustn't hang around the gate."

Pervading Fragrance realized that something was the matter and very shortly stood up to take her leave. "Please come over for a chat whenever you are free," said Phoenix. "I shall really look forward to it." And she instructed Equity to see her out. Equity did so, past a little group of slaveys who stood there in a neat row scarcely daring to breathe. But Pervading Fragrance left without discovering what was wrong.

Now Equity came back to report: "Wang-erh has arrived, but I told him to go away and wait till Pervading Fragrance had left. Please tell me whether you want me to call him right away or wait a little longer."

"Bring him in!" said Phoenix, and Equity at once sent a slavey to call him. Meanwhile Phoenix asked Equity, "Now, just how was it you heard of this?"

"It was that little slavey just now," said Equity. "She said she was just passing by the gate when she overheard one of the serving-boys outside saying to another, 'The master's new wife is prettier than our old mistress, and she's good-natured, too. And then Wang-erh or some-body shouted at them and said, 'Stop all this about new mistresses and old mistresses! You'd better keep your mouths shut—if they hear about this inside there, you'll get your tongues cut out!'"

A slavey came in at this point: "Wang-erh is waiting outside."

"Call him i " said Phoenix with a harsh laugh.

"The mistress wants to see you," called the slavey, and Wang-erh hurried in.

After his greeting he stood waiting, hands drooping by his sides, in the far doorway of the outer room. But Phoenix said, "Over here! I've something to ask you." And now finally he came into the room, to stand just inside the door.

"Your master has got another woman somewhere," said Phoenix. "What do you know about it?"

Wang-erh went down with bent knee again and replied: "Madam, I'm at my station every day by the inner gate, I have no way of knowing what the master is doing outside."

"No, of course you know nothing about it," sneered Phoenix. "I suppose if you did, you wouldn't be stopping others from talking about it?"

Wang-erh realized that the gossip he had just overheard had got out and there was no hope of denying it. He knelt and said: "I really don't know what this is about, but just now I overheard some nonsense between Hsing-erh and Hsi-erh out there, and I choked them off. I have no idea what was behind it all, and I wouldn't dare invent anything to tell you. Please, Madam, ask Hsing-erh, he's the one who works for the master outside."

Phoenix spat at him in her fury, and raged: "You all dance when the same string is pulled, you rotten little turtles, not an ounce of decency between you! You think I don't know! Bring me that little turtle Hsing-erh! And don't you go away—I'll come back to you when I've got the truth out of him. All right, all right, now let's see what splendid servants I've got."

And Wang-erh could only offer a whole series of "Very goods," kowtow, and scramble to his feet again to go summon Hsing-erh.

Hsing-erh was idling with some of the serving-boys in the accounts office and was startled to receive Phoenix's summons. But still ho had no notion that the secret was out as he hurried after Wang-erh. Wang-erh entered first to report.

"Hsing-erh is here, Madam."

"Bring him in." Phoenix's voice was a screech.

Hsing-erh's nerve almost failed him at the sound, but he plucked up courage and entered.

"A fine lad we've got here," said Phoenix at once. "And fine things you've been up to with your master. Come on, let's have the truth now!"

Hsing-erh went weak at these words and at the sight of Phoenix's glare and the expressions on the faces of the slaveys on either side. Mechanically he fell to his knees and began to kowtow.

"Come to think of it, of course," said Phoenix, "I understand that this business has nothing to do with you really. Where you went wrong was in not letting me know about it before now. Tell the truth and I'll let you off; but one little falsehood, and you'd better start feeling how many stupid heads you've got on your shoulders!"

Shaking with fear and in the intervals of kowtowing, Hsing-erh said: "What is it you want to know about, Madam? Is it something I've mishandled for the master?"

Phoenix's rage flared at this, and she yelled, "Slap your mouth!" Wang-erh hurried across to slap him, but Phoenix shouted at him: "Not you, you damn fool, he's to slap his own face. Just wait, there'll be plenty of time for you both to slap your mouths."

Twisting himself from one side to the other Hsing-erh gave himself a dozen or more heavy slaps across the lips. "Enough!" shouted

Phoenix. Then: "I suppose you know nothing about this new bride your master's acquired outside the mansion, or his old wife inside the mansion either?"

Realizing that the story was out Hsing-erh panicked even further. He plucked off his cap and hammered away with his head until the tiled floor rang again. "Madam be merciful," he mumbled. "From now on I won't dare offer a false word!"

"Then out with it," said Phoenix.

Hsing-erh struggled up to a kneeling position and made his report: "I knew nothing about this affair to begin with. It seems it was one day when the funeral procession for the master of the Peace Mansion was going on. Yü Lu had gone to the monastery to get some silver from the master Chia Chen. Then your husband had to go back to the Peace Mansion with Chia Jung. On the way the two of them were talking about Second Sister Yu, Dame Yu's daughter that she brought with her, and the master was saying what a nice person she was. Master Jung started teasing him and saying he would be the go-between for the master with Second Mistress. . . ."

Phoenix spat in his face at this: "Ha! 'Second Mistress,' you shameless turtle's brood! And just how many mistresses do you think you've got?"

In haste Hsing-erh kowtowed again: "I deserve to die!"—And he peeped up at her, too scared to continue.

"Is that all?" said Phoenix. "Why don't you go on?"

Now Hsing-erh dared to speak again: "If Madam will excuse my slip, I'll go on with my report."

"What sort of farting nonsense is this!" Phoenix hissed. "What do you mean, 'excuse you!' It will be a lot better for you if you just tell me what happened next."

And so Hsing-erh continued: "The master was very pleased with this idea. And then, later, it all came about, but I don't know exactly how."

"Of course, of course," said Phoenix with the slightest sneer. "How would you know? After all, if you did know, you'd be in trouble now, wouldn't you?—Come on, the rest of it!"

"After that," said Hsing-erh, "young master Jung found a cottage for the master."

"Where?" asked Phoenix at once.

"It's just behind the mansion," said Hsing-erh.

"Oh!" said Phoenix. And she glanced at Equity: "You and I might just as well be dead. Listen to this!"

Equity dared make no sound. Hsing-erh continued: "Chia Chen gave some money to the Chang family, I don't know how much, but the Chang family stopped bothering."

"What's all this about the Chang family, or the Li family for that matter?" asked Phoenix. "How do they come into this?"

"You don't understand," said Hsing-erh. "Second Mistress . . ." But as he brought out this phrase he stopped to strike himself across the face again. Even Phoenix gave an exasperated laugh, and the attendant slaveys grimaced at each other. Hsing-erh thought for a moment, then offered: "That sister of Madam Yu's , , ,"

"Well, what?" Phoenix interrupted. "Get on with it."

"It seems that the sister of Madam Yu was betrothed when she was a child to someone called Chang, Chang Hua I think his name was, but now he's a poor man, practically a beggar. Master Chia Chen gave him some money and he's renounced his claim."

Phoenix nodded her head at this and turned to look at the slaveys: "Do you hear this? Little turtle's brood started off by saying he knew nothing about it."

Hsing-erh went on again: "Well, then the master had this cottage done up and took her in as his bride."

"Where was she married from?" asked Phoenix.

"Why, there at her mother's."

"Wonderful!" said Phoenix. Then, "Didn't anyone accompany the bridal procession?"

"Just young master Jung," said Hsing-erh, "together with a few slaveys and nursemaids. Nobody else."

"Wasn't Madam Yu there?"

"Only after a day or two," said Hsing-erh, "she went to call on them with a few things."

Phoenix chuckled at this and turned to Equity: "So that's why my husband was singing the praises of Madam Yu for a while!" Then her face grew stern again as she returned to Hsing-erh: "And who is looking after them? You, I suppose?"

Hsing-erh hastened to kowtow but said nothing. Phoenix went on: "That time you said you had something to see to over in the other mansion, I suppose it was this?"

"Sometimes I've had things to see to, sometimes I've been over to the cottage," said Hsing-erh.

"Who else is living there?" asked Phoenix.

"Her mother and her other sister. But a little while ago the sister went and cut her throat."

"And what was that about?"

Hsing-erh now told her of the affair between Third Sister and Liu Hsiang-lien. "Now there's a fortunate man," was Phoenix's comment. "No one is going to tag a cuckold's reputation onto him!" And she went on, "Haven't you anything else to tell me?"

"I don't know about anything else. But every word I've told you is true. If there's been one false word you can check on it and have me beaten to death and I won't complain."

Phoenix sat for a moment with lowered head. Then she pointed her finger at Hsing-erh: "Beat you to death is what I should do, you monkey's brood! Did you think you could keep me from knowing any of this? You were going to keep it from me just to please that stupid master of yours, and I'm sure your new mistress thought the world of you. If it weren't that you were too frightened to lie to me just now, don't think I wouldn't have your legs crushed!" And she shouted, "Now get out!"

Hsing-erh kowtowed yet again before scrambling to his feet and retreating as far as the outer doorway. But he did not dare leave immediately, and indeed Phoenix said, "Come back here. I've something else to say." He hastened to assume a pose of respectful attention, hands drooping, and she went on: "What's your hurry? Is your new mistress waiting to give you your reward?" He kept his gaze fixed on the floor. Now she said : "You're to go over there no more from now on. You're to be here whenever I want you. And just try being a second late! Now get out."

Hsing-erh got out a number of "Very good, Madams" and dodged through the doorway. But Phoenix called him once again, and back he came in a hurry.

"Just running to tell your master all about it, were you?" she asked.

"I wouldn't dare!" said Hsing-erh.

"One word of this when you get outside," said Phoenix, "and watch out for your skin!"

Nodding violently Hsing-erh finally managed to get out. "Is Wang-erh there?" called Phoenix. Wang-erh came hurrying up, and Phoenix glared at him for a full minute before addressing him. "Well, that's a fine piece of work, Wang-erh. Now off with you, and if one word of this gets out it will be you who pays."

Wang-erh nodded and slowly made his getaway. "Tea!" called Phoenix now, and the slaveys understood her intention and left the room.

Phoenix turned to Equity. "Did you hear all that? Wonderful, isn't it?" Equity could make no response beyond a sympathetic smile. Phoenix's anger mounted as she continued to think over what she had heard. She lay back on the bed, her mind working. All at once she gave a quick frown as a course of action presented itself. She called Equity, who hastened up to her. "I think this is the way we should handle this," said Phoenix. "There's no need to put off discussion of it till my husband gets back."

In fact when Chia Lien had reached P'ing-an-chou it so happened that the Treasurer was away at the border on an inspection tour which lasted for a month or so. Ignorant of his precise whereabouts Chia Lien could only wait where he was, and close on two months elapsed before Chia Lien could see the Treasurer, settle his affairs, and make his journey back.

When she learned of Chia Lien's delay Phoenix was certain her plan was the right one. First she called in workers of every trade to prepare a suite of three rooms in the eastern wing of her house. These rooms she decorated and furnished in exactly the style of her own principal apartments. Then on the fourteenth of the month she reported to the Matriarch and Madam Wang that at dawn on the following day she was going to offer incense in the convent. She chose Equity and three other maids to accompany her and told them of her plans before she entered her palanquin. She gave orders also that the menfolk accompanying the party should dress in mourning white. Hsing-erh led the little procession straight to the gate. Pao Erh's wife answered his knock, and Hsing-erh greeted her with a smile: "Please inform Second Mistress that First Mistress is here to visit her."

When Pao Erh's wife heard this announcement her soul shot straight out through the top of her head and she flew back inside to tell Second Sister Yu. Second Sister was startled in her turn, but since Phoenix was here the only possible course was to receive her with all due formality. She set her dress straight and hurried out to greet her. Phoenix descended from her palanquin at the gate and presented herself for Second Sister's inspection. Her head ornaments were of plain silver. Under a short jacket of satin white as moonlight she wore a robe of dark green satin with a raised pattern of silver thread, and her skirt was of plain white damask. Willow-leaf brows arching high, phoenix eyes bright with expression: elegant as the spring peach bough, austere as autumn aster. Two maidservants, the wives of Chou Jui and Wang-erh, supported her as she crossed the little courtyard. Second Sister hurried forward smiling to salute her, greeting her as "Elder Sister" and saying, "I had not expected the honor of this visit today and was unprepared to greet you outside the gate. Please excuse me!" And she made a deep obeisance.

Phoenix, smiling also, hastened to return her salutations, then at once took her hand and entered the cottage by her side. Seating Phoenix in the place of honor, Second Sister had a slavey bring a cushion for herself to kneel. "I am so young and ignorant, I have been obliged to rely on my mother and my sister for guidance in all things ever since my arrival here. Now that it has been my good fortune to meet you, I beg that you will not despise me as worthless but will instruct me in all I should do. My only goal is to exert my every effort in your service." And with this she began to make her bows before Phoenix.

But Phoenix at once left her seat and began to bow in return, saying as she did so: "But it is I, also, who am too young, and have been guided only by a mere woman's wisdom. I have been concerned only to urge our master to take care of himself and not to spend his nights outside among the 'flowers and willows,' to the distress of his parents. You and I have behaved like this out of our fond concern for him; but somehow he has misunderstood my motives. It would be different if he had just gone outside the family and commandeered someone else's women-folk, concealing everything from us. But here he has formally taken you as secondary wife, in perfectly correct fashion and with a perfectly proper wedding ceremony, and never said a word to me about it! I had already urged him to do this and not to delay, so that if a daughter should come of it, or with good fortune a son, I, too, should have support in my later years. How could he have taken me for one of those dreadful jealous wives, and arranged everything in secret like this?

"I truly don't know where to turn for the hurt he has done me. Only Heaven and Earth can truly know what is in my heart. For the last ten days I have been hearing whispers of what has happened. I said nothing for fear our master would misunderstand my feelings. But now that he is away for a while I have taken the opportunity to visit you like this. I want to beg you to put your trust in my deep concern for you, and come to live with me in my house. There we can be together day by day as sisters in all proper form and order, and with one accord we can assist our master in guarding his interests and protecting his health. How do you think I should feel if we were to remain like this, with myself at home and you here in another place? And then when other people get to hear of this it will be your reputation that suffers as well as my own. But the really important thing is our master's reputation—it's of little consequence if people gossip about you and me.

"Of course I know that there has been a lot of talk among the servants and underlings about how strict I have been in managing the household. It's a common thing for them to criticize behind one's back. But you know that old saying, 'a housewife is no better than a chamber pot.' If I had really been so intolerant, think of the elders in our husband's family, and all the cousins and the sisters-in-law—how do you suppose they would have tolerated *me* for so long? And here and now, when my husband has taken you as his secret bride and is living with you in this place: if I hadn't wanted this talk with you, how do you think I could have brought myself to visit you? Think of Equity—I have urged my husband time and again to take her as his secondary wife.

"It was Heaven and Earth and the Lord Buddha who let me discover what has happened, so that all these miserable people could be prevented from trampling on me. And now I want you to come into my home, to share everything I have—living quarters, servants, clothes, ornaments, everything will be the same for you as for me. With an intelligent woman like yourself, if you will really help me, I shall truly have a strong shoulder to lean on. Then we can stop the blabbing mouths of all those miserable people, and not only that, when our master returns and sees what has happened he will surely mend his ways. I am surely not one of those sour, jealous, devious wives: if you will join us, the three of us can live together in more perfect amity than ever before, and I shall really owe you a debt of gratitude. But if you will not come with me, then let me move out and come to live here with you. But I beg you, put in a good word for me with our master, leave me a little spot to stand on. Even if you want me to serve at your side, to comb your hair and assist in your toilet, that will be all I ask!"

And Phoenix began to sob and weep, and Second Sister wept with her.

The two of them now exchanged formal bows and seated themselves in proper order. Equity hurried forward to make obeisance in her turn. Second Sister guessed who she must be from the fineness of her dress and the superior grace of her bearing, and she rose in haste to help her to her feet. "Please don't do this," she said. "You and I should treat each other as equals."

But Phoenix rose also, smiling at this: "Sister, you must make her pay obeisance to you even if you have to break her arm. She was one of our little slave-girls, you must stop behaving like this towards her."

Now Phoenix had Chou Jui's wife unwrap the gifts she had brought: four rolls of finest quality silk, four sets of jeweled gold trinkets. Second Sister accepted them with a graceful bow. Tea was brought and they chatted over all that had taken place. Phoenix went on and on finding fault with her own behavior: "No one else is to blame. I can only ask you to take pity on me!"

Being a straightforward person herself, Second Sister was convinced of Phoenix's goodness, and thought, "It's a common thing for discontented underlings to slander their mistress." So she poured out everything that was in her heart, accepting Phoenix as an intimate. Moreover, there stood Chou Jui's wife and the other women at the side, singing the virtues of Phoenix's past management of the household: "It's just that she puts up with too much, and people take advantage of her and criticize," they said, and then, "The rooms are all prepared for you, please go and see for yourself."

Second Sister had always had the secret wish that she might move into the mansion to live, and she was certainly not inclined to object now. "I must surely go with you, Sister Phoenix. But what should be done about this place?"

"This is no problem," said Phoenix. "We'll have the boys carry Second Sister's chests and precious things across. You will not need these cheap things and we can have someone store them. Whoever Second Sister wants can stay here."

Second Sister responded at once: "Now that I have met you, sister, I shall place myself entirely in your hands for this move into your home. How should I act for myself when I have been here such a short time, and especially since I have never managed a household and am so ignorant? Let these boxes and chests be taken across. I really have nothing, these things are all our master's."

Phoenix thereupon ordered Chou Jui's wife to make careful notes and take good care of Second Sister's property in its transit to the suite in the eastern wing. She pressed Second Sister to make ready at once for the journey, and then the two of them went out hand in hand to enter the palanquin, where they sat together.

"Ours is a very strictly regulated family," Phoenix told her, keeping her voice low as they rode. "The Matriarch and Madam Wang know nothing about this matter. If they were to find out, our master would surely be beaten to death for taking you as his bride during this mourning period. So for the moment you had better avoid them. We have a vast garden where the cousins live, it's quite easy to get away from people there. It will be best if you stay there just for a day or two, until I can work something out. Then I shall let you know, and we can be together again."

"I am completely at your disposal," was Second Sister's reply.

The chair-bearers had been alerted in advance, and went trotting round to the back entrance rather than the main gate of the mansion. Leaving the palanquin and dismissing the attendants, Phoenix took Second Sister through the rear gate of the Grand View Garden to meet the widow Li Wan in her cottage.

By this time nine out of ten of the residents in the garden knew what was happening. Seeing Phoenix enter the garden with her guest by her side, they surged forward now, slaveys and nursemaids and all, to take a look at her, and Second Sister greeted them each in turn. Everyone began to sing the praises of her beauty and gentleness. One by one Phoenix instructed them: "Not a whisper of this must get out. I'll have your life if the Matriarch or Madam Wang finds out!"—But the nursemaids and slaveys in the garden without exception lived in terror of Phoenix, and realized the seriousness of what Chia Lien had done in a period of combined national and family mourning. Not one of them dared to meddle any further.

Quietly Phoenix asked Li Wan to take Second Sister in for a few days, "Then I will let you know and she can move across to my place." Li Wan knew that Phoenix had made rooms ready in her house, and it seemed reasonable to assent to this plan since it was the mourning period and all fuss should be avoided. Phoenix's next step was to dismiss the slaveys who had accompanied Second Sister thus far and replace them with just one of her own. She turned quietly to the women who watched over the garden and instructed them: "Take good care of her. If she runs away you will have me to reckon with!"

Phoenix left to further her private plans, but all the members of the household quietly marveled to each other: "Whatever has come over Phoenix, to cause her to behave so graciously?"

For her part Second Sister, when she saw where she was and how friendly all the girls in the garden were to her, began to feel completely at ease and very much at home. The strange thing was that only three days passed before the little slave-girl, Virtue, started to show signs of disobedience. Second Sister had said, "The hair oil is all used up. Go ask Mistress Phoenix to let you have some more."

But Virtue replied: "Second Mistress, remember where you are! How could you be so thoughtless? Our mistress has to see to the Matriarch's wants every day, and look after the wants of Madam This and Madam That and all the cousins and the sisters-in-law, not to speak of the servants, hundreds of them, men and women alike, looking to her for their orders day after day. Put it at the very least, she has ten or twenty major affairs to see to every day and forty or fifty little things. On the outside there are all the gifts and presents for everybody from the Empress herself down to the dukes and earls and counts and barons, and then all the family matters to attend to with relatives and friends. And money—thousands of ounces, millions of cash! All of it passing through her hands alone, in and out, day after day, everything that's to be done waiting on her word alone.

"Now how can you start bothering her with a little thing like this? I'd advise you to show a little patience. After all, we didn't come into the family in the proper way with a matchmaker and all, did we? It's only because she's a real saint such as you seldom come across that she's treating you so kindly. If it was someone just a little bit less tolerant she'd start a real row over this and throw you out! And there you'd be, no way to live or die, and what could you do about it?"

She went on half the night until Second Sister drooped her head. After a scolding like this she felt there was nothing she could do but adjust to things accordingly. But gradually Virtue began to be more and more remiss even in bringing her meals. She would come either too early or too late, and it was always leftovers. Second Sister reprimanded her a couple of times and she stared back and began to scream and shout. Second Sister did not like to have people think she was ungrateful, and put up with it for a week or so until she saw Phoenix again.

Phoenix came in all friendly and smiling, with "dear sister" forever on her lips. "If there is anything the servants are doing to displease you, and you can't control them," she said, "just let me know and I'll have them beaten." And she turned to the slavey and the nursemaid: "I know you inside out, you'll do anything to avoid a beating and you'll cheat anyone who's too soft with you. You fear no one as long as you think you can hide things from me! But if I hear one word from Second Mistress here, I'll have your heads!"

When she saw how concerned Phoenix was, Second Sister told herself, "With her on my side, what have I to worry about? It's a common thing for servants to forget their place. But if I accuse them to Phoenix they'll feel they have a grievance, and then everyone will say I am an intolerant mistress."—And she said nothing, but covered up for them.

Meanwhile Phoenix had sent Wang-erh out to check on Second Sister's history and had established that she had indeed been promised in marriage. Her betrothed was an eighteen-year-old boy whose only concern for his career was to gamble from morn till night. When his private fortune vanished his parents had thrown him out and now he lived on whatever he could make from his gambling. On receipt of old Dame Yu's twenty ounces of silver the father had agreed to cancel the betrothal, but the boy had not yet been told of this.

It seemed that the boy's name was Chang Hua. When Phoenix had learned all she needed to know she wrapped up twenty ounces of silver for Wang-erh, with secret orders to take care of Chang Hua and get him to make out an accusation. The plaint was to go to the authorities, and it would be against Chia Lien for abusing his wealth and power to force the cancellation of a marriage agreement so that he could put by his wife and remarry, and all this against the wishes and without the knowledge of his family, and in a time of national and family mourning.

But Chang Hua was too conscious of where his own advantage lay to be ready to rush into this. Phoenix fumed when Wang-erh brought back this news: "What a damn nuisance the fool is! The proverb is right, 'a mangy dog won't be helped over the wall.' But get it clear to him, I don't care if he accuses this family of plotting rebellion! All I want him to do is stir up a fuss so that everybody loses face. If it gets too bad he needn't worry, I can always quiet things down."

Wang-erh accordingly went back to Chang Hua with the whole story. He had received further instructions from Phoenix: "If Chang

Hua wants to lay plaint against you, too, you show him what he is to say, like this . . . I will look after you."

Assured that Phoenix would take the responsibility, Wang-erh allowed his own name to be entered on Chang Hua's writ of complaint. "You can accuse me of overstepping my position," he said, "and say that it was I who inveigled my master into all of this."

After this further discussion with Wang-erh, Chang Hua was able to bring himself to do it. He made out his writ of accusation and presented his case the following day at the censorate. The magistrate there in court saw that the accusation was against Chia Lien but that the name of Wang-erh, servant, appeared on the document. He therefore sent runners to summon Wang-erh to give evidence. Rather than take it upon themselves to invade the premises the runners thought of sending in a message, but Wang-erh was expecting them and didn't wait for the messenger. He was ready for them there on the street outside, and went up grinning to greet the runners: "I'm sorry to put you to all this trouble, it must be me you're after. You'd better tie me up right away."

They would not do this, but merely said, "Come on, brother, let's go, don't play around with us."

And so he was taken into court, where he knelt and was shown the writ of accusation. He read it slowly as though he had never seen it before, then kowtowed and said, "Your honor, I know all about this and it's true that my master did this. But this man Chang Hua has had a grievance against me for a long time and has dragged me into it on purpose to get his own back. There are others involved, too, and I beseech you to make further inquiries."

Now Chang Hua kowtowed in his turn: "I know there are others involved, but these are persons I wouldn't dare accuse, so I just made out my charges against their servant."

"You blockhead!" said Wang-erh, as planned in advance. "Why don't you get on with it! You're in the imperial court now, what does it matter if it's servant or master, you've got to tell the whole story!"

And so at this point Chang Hua spoke the name of Chia Jung.

The magistrate now had no recourse but to send for Chia Jung. Phoenix, when she received the confidential report of this new accusation from her agent Ch'ing-erh, at once summoned Wang Hsin and explained the situation to him. She instructed him to pass word to the magistrate that he should put on a good show of blustering, but content himself with giving these people a fright. And to reinforce this she gave Wang Hsin three hundred ounces of silver with which he managed to settle things at the magistrate's private residence that same night. Thoroughly aware of what was happening the magistrate pocketed the bribe and in court next day declared that the wastrel Chang Hua, fearful of defaulting on debts he owed to the Chia family, had invented a tissue of lies to slander innocent persons. The magistrate, after all, was an old friend of Wang Tzu-t'eng's, and Wang Hsin had taken the trouble to explain matters to him. Since it was a question of members of the Chia family, there was nothing to be done but wind up the case, set it aside and say no more about it beyond an order to Chia Jung to submit his own statement of evidence.

It was while Chia Jung and the others were just discussing this affair of Chia Lien's that the message came, "There's been an accusation brought against you, this is what it says. . . . You must deal with it at once."

The frightened Chia Jung ran at once to his father. "I was expecting this," said Chia Chen, "but I'm still surprised they have had the nerve." There and then he made a package of two hundred ounces of silver to be distributed at the censorate, and sent a servant to present the statement of evidence.

Just as this was going on the announcement came, "Mistress Phoenix from the Glory Mansion is here." Chia Chen jumped at this news, and both he and Chia Jung tried to get out of the way. But Phoenix was already upon them: "Well, cousin, this is a fine piece of work you have been engaged in!"

Chia Jung hastened forward to greet her, and Phoenix seized him by the arm and propelled him into the house with her. But Chia Chen smiled benevolently at the servants and said, "Now be sure you look after Mistress Phoenix properly. Have them slaughter some of the livestock and prepare a meal for her"—whereupon he had a horse saddled and made his getaway.

Still with Chia Jung in tow, Phoenix made her way through to the main reception room. Madam Yu now came out to welcome her, and asked anxiously, when she saw the forbidding expression on Phoenix's face, "What has happened to upset you like this?"

Phoenix spat straight in her face and cried, "No one else will take these wenches of your family, you have to come sneaking them into the Chia household! Is it only the Chia that have any worthwhile men left, have all the other men in the world died off? If you have to send them here, why can't it be done in proper style with go-betweens and witnesses and everybody in agreement? Your brains are all addled, or perhaps they're all clotted up with your powder and paint! Here you are in a time of national mourning and family mourning both, sending this woman into our family! And now there are accusations being brought against us, and even the courts are being told that I'm a jealous shrew! So now my name is brought up, and I face the prospect of being divorced! What mistakes have I made since I came here, what harm have I done you that has turned you against me like this? Or is it something the Matriarch and Madam Wang have told you that has set you to working up this scheme to squeeze me out? Now come on, let's you and I go to court, the two of us, let's state our case out there in the open, and then we'll come back and put it before the entire clan assembled, for all to see, and then I can be given my bill of divorcement and I'll go!"

Her tears flowed as she said all this, and she tugged at Madam Yu to drag her straight before the magistrate. In panic Chia Jung knelt to kowtow before her and to plead, "Aunt Phoenix, please calm yourself!"

Now Phoenix turned her rage on Chia Jung: "You, you evil-hearted wretch, may thunderbolts strike you dead and five devils carve up your corpse! What do you care how high the heavens are, how thick the earth, as long as you can go on from morn till night with your villainous hole-and-corner trade! No regard for face or decency, no regard for the imperial law, bringing the family's fame and fortune crashing down to ruin! Your dead wife there in the shades will never forgive you, the spirits of your ancestors will never forgive you—and you dare kneel there and tell me to 'calm myself!' "

She raised her hand to strike him, and frantically the terrified Chia Jung banged his head against the floor and cried, "Please don't be so angry against me, Aunt Phoenix! There's no need for you to slap me, I'll slap myself. Just don't be angry with me." With these words he started to twist his body from side to side and slap himself smartly across the face, at the same time engaging in self-interrogation: "Are you going to go on after this, doing as you like with no concern for the consequences? Are you going to go on just doing what Chia Lien tells you and taking no notice of Aunt Phoenix?"

The others in the room were torn between the desire to pacify him and the desire to laugh, but no one in fact dared to laugh.

Phoenix collapsed into the supporting embrace of Madam Yu.

Her cries of grief were enough to move heaven and earth, she wailed at the top of her voice: "It's not your seeking a new bride for my husband that I mind. But why did you have him break the rules and keep it all secret, so that I have to bear the reputation of a jealous shrew? Let's go to court right now rather than sit here waiting for the runners to fetch us! Or let's go over to the other mansion and have an open discussion with the Matriarch and Madam Wang and all the clan members. If I'm an intolerant woman and won't let my husband take a secondary wife, then hand me a bill of divorcement and I'll leave on the spot! I went in person to your Second Sister's to take her into my house. I didn't dare report this to the Matriarch and Madam Wang for fear of angering them. She's there in the garden now with all the best of things to eat and a crowd of servants looking after her. And meanwhile I'm having rooms prepared for her which will be exactly what I have for myself, so that she can move in as soon as the Matriarch has been informed. I had it all agreed with her that she should move in with me and we could all live together in perfect peace and harmony, and I would never say another word about what had happened—but then how was I to know she was already betrothed to someone else? I don't know what it is you're all up to, I was completely ignorant of this, you can imagine my fright yesterday when they came with an accusation against me! Even if I went to court it would be a bad loss of face for this Chia family of yours, and I had to sneak five hundred ounces of Madam Wang's silver to keep things quiet. They've even got my servant locked up at this minute!"

She wept and wailed, ranted and railed, and at last called loud and long on her ancestors and her mother and father, and sought to dash her head against the wall to kill herself. She had managed to knead and twist Madam Yu into a ball of noodles, soaking her clothing in tears and snivel. The only words Madam Yu could find were to her son Chia Jung: "You evil brat, conniving with your father in this dreadful thing! I said right at the start it was all wrong!"

At this Phoenix seized Madam Yu's face in her two hands and screamed at her: "Did you go out of your senses? Was your mouth all stuffed up with eggplant? Or did they stick a gag in it? Why didn't you come to tell me? If only you had told me, don't you see that everything would have been all right? Do you think it would ever have got to this stage, with the courts and the whole prefecture in an uproar? And now you blame them! It's always been said, 'with a virtuous wife a man will see little grief, better the core solid than the covering.' As long as you were doing as you should, they would never dare get up to these tricks. But you had neither the ability to do anything about it yourself nor the sense to tell anyone else! You, a gourd with its mouth sawn off, all you can do is pussyfoot around and hope for praise as a 'tolerant wife'! But since they're not afraid of you, they don't respect you either!"—And she spat on her over and over.

But Madam Yu wailed in her turn: "You think I didn't tell them? If you don't believe me, ask the servants how many times I urged them not to do it, begged them to listen to me. But what else could I do? You've every right to be angry and I can only sit here and acknowledge my fault."

The floor of the room was black with the kneeling bodies of secondary wives, serving-women, and little slave-girls who pleaded with Phoenix, smiling to soften their words: "Mistress Phoenix is so wise and enlightened. Of course our mistress was at fault, but she has been punished enough now. And she has always been so good to us servants and the other wives. Please leave her a little face now."

They offered Phoenix tea, but she shattered the cup.

In a little while Phoenix stopped crying, pushed her hair back and shouted at Chia Jung: "Go fetch your father! I've got something to ask him to his face: I want to know what the rites are that say you can get a new bride for your nephew when you're only just past the first month of mourning for your own father. I've never heard of this one and I'd like to study it so that I can better instruct you all in the days to come."

Chia Jung knelt and kowtowed again: "My father really wasn't involved in this. It was all my fault, I had my mouth full of crap and I talked Uncle Chia Lien into this affair. My father knew nothing about it. If you make trouble for me now I'm as good as dead. I can only beg you to punish me yourself and I'll abide by anything you say. And this lawsuit, I must beg you to deal with it, I couldn't manage anything as serious as that. Remember who you are—surely you know the saying, 'when your arm's broken, hide it in your sleeve.' I am the stupidest fool, and now that I've done this wicked thing I'm as helpless as any cat or dog in the household, but now you've shown me what's what, you're cleverer than I am—I have to come running to ask you to do whatever you can and keep things from getting out. Please think of me as your son, however wicked I've been and whatever terrible trouble I've caused, you've

still got to take pity on me even though I've done you such a wrong!"—
and he went on with his incessant kowtows.

With Chia Jung and his mother acting this way Phoenix found it
hard to press her attack any further. With a complete change of voice
and manner she made an abject obeisance before Madam Yu and said,
"You mustn't blame me, I'm too young to understand these things.
When I heard that we were being taken to court I was terrified, and
that's why I came rushing over with no thought for what was proper.
Jung is right, when your arm is broken you hide it in your sleeve.
Please don't blame me for what I've been saying. But you must take
my part with your husband, and plead with him to get this lawsuit out
of the way."

Both Madam Yu and Chia Jung hastened to reassure her. "Please
don't worry so much. Whatever happens there's no need to involve
your husband. You were just speaking of the five hundred ounces of
silver you had spent. We'll make it up out of our own funds and send it
across to you, it's out of the question that you should be made to pay,
and we should be even more ashamed. But there's one thing we must
ask you: please help us to smooth things over with the Matriarch and
the other ladies, it's best that they should never hear of this."

But this brought a fresh sneer to Phoenix's lips. "So now that
you've done all this behind my back you want to trick me into covering up for you with the others! I may be a simpleton, but I'm not as
simple as all that! You're concerned about your brother-in-law, but
that's my husband! If it worries you that there will be no children for
him, how do you think I feel about it? I've regarded your sister exactly
as though she were my own, when I first heard about her I was so
happy I couldn't sleep all night. I rushed to get the servants to prepare
rooms for her so that I could receive her then and there. But they are a
mean lot, and they said, 'You're too impetuous, madam, if you'll take
our advice you'll see what the Matriarch and Madam Wang say about
it, there'll be plenty of time to take her into the household after that.'
They made me want to scream and beat them—what could I say?
They wouldn't do as I wished, we were just in the middle of the argument, and then what happens?—Out of the blue comes this Chang
Hua and files an accusation against us! I was terrified, for two nights
running I never closed my eyes, yet I didn't dare make a sound. All I
could do was get someone to find out what sort of person this Chang
Hua was that he could afford such impudence. It took a couple of

days, and what did we find?—He's a beggar, a penniless scoundrel. I was so innocent, I asked, 'What's he charging us with?', but the servants said, 'It's true that Second Sister Yu was betrothed to him. But now he's desperate, it's just a question of whether he freezes to death or starves to death, one way or the other he's finished. So here comes this chance and he grabs at it. How can you blame him for going to court—even if it means death for him, at least it's better than dying of cold or starvation! Our master shouldn't have been in such a hurry. There are four faults he's committed: national mourning number one, family mourning number two, taking a wife without his parents' knowledge number three, putting aside his first wife number four. Like the proverb says, if you don't mind the executioner slicing you up you can pull the Emperor off his horse. Poverty has driven this Chang Hua crazy, he'll stop at nothing. And presented with a beautiful case like this, do you think he's going to wait to be invited to lay plaint against you?'

"Just think, sister: if I were one of the great strategists of history, a Han Hsin or a Chang Liang, I'd have been scared out of my wits and out of all my clever plans by a tale like this. With my husband away from home and no one to talk it over with, all I could do was pull out some money and try to patch things up. And imagine, the more I spend the more they come rattling their swords and trying to cheat me. I'm like the rat with a sore on its tail—it's a long one and it does a lot of bleeding! That's why I'm so upset and angry and had to come to you."

Madam Yu and Chia Jung broke in: "Don't distress yourself, of course we'll look after everything."

And Chia Jung added: "This Chang Hua is poor and desperate, and that's why he's willing to stake his life on a lawsuit against us. We can work it out. We'll pay him something and get him to confess that he's made false charges against us. Then we can settle that one for him, and when he comes out we'll give him a little bit more and that will be the end of it."

Phoenix grimaced. "Brilliant! Now I see how you do these things without regard for the consequences. If this is an example of your craft and cunning, I've been overestimating you for a long time past! If we do as you just described, he'll go along with it for the time being, get free of the court, take his money and that will of course be the end of it—for the moment. But people like this are shiftless scoundrels, they lay their hands on a bit of money and in three or four days there's nothing left. Then he'll be back again looking for an excuse to cheat us, spreading rumors about us, even if we've no reason to fear him he'll always be a nuisance. He'll always be able to say, if we claim to have done nothing wrong, why did we give him money in the first place?"

Chia Jung was bright enough to understand her meaning, and said with a smile, "I have another idea: 'if a troublemaker comes, get the troublemaker out.' You'll need me to settle this. I'll go to Chang Hua and ask him to make up his mind whether he really wants the girl, or whether he wants to be free of the whole thing, to take his money and go marry someone else. If he insists on the girl he's betrothed to, then I'll just have to go and urge Second Sister to leave us and become his wife; if it's the money he's after, then we'll just have to give it to him."

"That's all very well," said Phoenix at once, "but I refuse to give up Second Sister, I definitely refuse to send her away. No, nephew, if you've any regard for me you will simply have to give him a larger sum."

Chia Jung knew perfectly well that Phoenix was merely posing as the tolerant wife with these words and that her real desire was to send Second Sister off to marry her original betrothed. For the moment, however, he must simply go along with whatever she said.

Phoenix continued: "It was one thing when she was living outside, but how is it going to be if she stays on in the household with us? You had better come with me now and we'll report the situation to the Matriarch and Madam Wang."

Madam Yu fell into fresh panic at this, and clutched at Phoenix's sleeve begging to know what kind of story she could invent.

Phoenix replied with a sneer: "Who asked you to get involved in this when you completely lack the talent for it? I can't abide this kind of thing myself, but if you are so at a loss, well, I'm a softhearted person and fool enough to take it on even though I know you're taking advantage of me. What you must do is stay out of sight for the time being. I will take Second Sister to make her kowtows before the Matriarch and the other ladies. I shall say that this sister of yours caught my eye and pleased me very much, and since I still have not fully recovered my strength I had already been thinking of buying a couple of girls to help out. Once I had seen how pleasant your sister was, and since it would mean reinforcing a relationship which already existed, I wanted her to join my husband as secondary wife. But then there had been the deaths in the family, among the parents' generation and among the cousins, and we were finding it hard to meet our obligations in these days of mourning. If we had waited the requisite hundred days it would have been difficult for her, with no property to fall back on in her own family. So let's say that I took it upon myself to receive her into the household, and prepared one of the guest rooms for her for the time being, just until the mourning period is over and we can complete the formal marriage ceremonies. I've got a thick enough skin to brazen it out one way or the other—if there's any fault to be found, it won't end up at your door. Well, what do you think of it, the two of you? Will it do?"

Madam Yu and Chia Jung both spoke at once, smiles on their faces: "What breadth! What vision! It's you in the end we have to turn to for the wisest solution! And when all is settled, be assured we shall visit you to express our gratitude."

Madam Yu now instructed the slaveys to assist Madam Phoenix with her toilet, and she had wine and dishes set out which she served to Phoenix with her own hands. Phoenix then declined to stay longer and insisted on returning home.

Back once more in the garden Phoenix told Second Sister Yu all that had transpired, how concerned she had been, what she had found out, how they must act thus and thus to avoid disaster for all concerned, how she herself would be obliged to "open up this fishhead" to settle matters for everyone.

Second Sister could not thank her enough and agreed to accompany her on the visit to the Matriarch. Madam Yu also felt it impossible to stay away and came across to join them in the visit. "But just don't say anything," smiled Phoenix. "Let me do the talking."

"Of course, of course," said Madam Yu. "If any fault is found we shall have to put the blame on you."

They entered the Matriarch's apartments to find her surrounded by the young girl cousins from the garden who were chatting and joking to entertain her. The old lady gazed intently at this exquisite young lady in Phoenix's company, and asked, "From whose family does this child come? What a darling!"

Phoenix came forward: "Do you find her pleasing, Grandmother, when you take a careful look at her?" And she tugged at Second Sister's sleeve and said, "Make your kowtow at once, this is the Ancestress."

Second Sister kowtowed with the greatest formality. Phoenix pointed out the cousins to her each in turn so that she would know how to greet them after she had paid her respects to the older ladies. Second Sister carefully learned the name of each, after which she took up her position at one side, her head lowered.

The Matriarch looked her up and down, then smiled and asked, "What is your surname? And how old are you?"

"We'll leave this aside for the moment, Grandmother," Phoenix smiled back. "But tell me, is she prettier than I?"

The Matriarch put on her spectacles and gave orders to Mandarin Duck and Amber: "Bring her here so that I can look at her complexion."

Trying to hide their embarrassed smiles the slaveys pushed her forward. The Matriarch inspected her closely, then ordered Amber: "Hold out her hand for me to see." Mandarin Duck lifted up the girl's skirt as well.

The old lady took off her spectacles when the inspection was finished, and chuckled, "Very neat and trim! I would say she is prettier than you."

Phoenix smiled, then hastened to kneel before the Matriarch to deliver in careful detail, item by item, the speech she had composed in the presence of Madam Yu and Chia Jung. "We must ask you to look on her kindly, Grandmother, and give your consent to her entrance into the household before we complete the marriage ceremonies in a year's time."

"There's nothing amiss in this," said the Matriarch. "It's good that you should be so tolerant, but we must certainly wait for one year before completing the ceremonies."

Phoenix struck her head against the floor in response, then rose to ask, "May we have two of the servants take her to visit the older ladies, and say that this is your decision?"

The Matriarch assented and Second Sister was taken to pay her respects to Madam Hsing and the others. Madam Wang had been deeply concerned by rumors she had heard, and was naturally pleased by the arrangement that had now been made.

And so Second Sister Yu could at last feel that she had emerged into the light of day as she took up residence in the guest apartments.

Phoenix's next move was to send a messenger to incite Chang

Hua to claim back this girl who had originally been betrothed to him. In addition to various other gifts the messenger took a promise of money to enable Chang Hua to set up house.

Now Chang Hua from the start had had little stomach for bringing an accusation against the Chia family, and moreover Chia Jung had sent a man to put his own side of the case before the court: "Chang Hua had already repudiated the marriage agreement, and Second Sister Yu was already related to our family, it was a matter of receiving her into our household and not of abduction by force. The fact of the matter is that Chang Hua owed us money, and since he couldn't repay it when we pressed him he invented this slander against my master."

The magistrate's interests were closely intertwined with those of both the Chia and the Wang families, and furthermore he had been bribed. He ruled that Chang Hua was a wastrel driven by poverty into false pretences. He declined to accept the writ of accusation, but had Chang Hua beaten and thrown out.

Ch'ing-erh, however, had been busy arranging things so that Chang Hua was beaten only lightly, and now he worked Chang Hua round to resubmitting his accusation by saying, "This match of yours was formally established by your family: if you insist on demanding your bride, the court will have to rule in your favor."

Further instructions were carried to the magistrate through Wang Hsin, and so the ruling came down: "Chang Hua must repay his debt to the Chia family in full within the specified period. As to the match originally arranged, he must reclaim his bride when he has the ability to do so."

Word was sent to Chang Hua's father to appear in court to ratify this judgment. The father in turn had been primed by Ch'ing-erh, and now went off to the Chia household to claim his son's bride, delighted by the prospect of ending up with both the girl and the money.

Phoenix meanwhile, her face filled with alarm, reported these events to the Matriarch: "It's Madam Yu who has muddled things up this way. That Chang family had never repudiated the betrothal, and now they've been roused to bring this suit against us and look what the court has ruled!"

The Matriarch at once called in Madam Yu and accused her of mishandling the affair: "What do you call this? Your sister was betrothed from the womb and no repudiation ever made, and now we have a suit brought against us!"

The only reply Madam Yu could make was, "But he took our money, how can he pretend he didn't consent?"

Phoenix joined in at this point: "When Chang Hua gave evidence in court he said he had seen nothing of either money or the girl. And his father said, 'The girl's family once proposed breaking the match but we wouldn't consent; and then her father died and the Chia family took her for a secondary wife!'—We had no means of disproving this, we had to let him get away with his story. It's fortunate that my husband is away from home and we have not completed the marriage ceremonies, so that no great harm is done. But when the girl is here in our house how can we send her back—think of the loss of face!"

"Still there has been no completion of the marriage ceremonies," said the Matriarch, "so there is no question of our forcibly abducting a woman already betrothed. But we should let this man take her to avoid harm to our reputation. There'll be no difficulty in finding someone else perfectly suitable."

Second Sister Yu had been listening, and now submitted her appeal: "It is the truth that my mother gave him ten ounces of silver on such-and-such a date to withdraw his claim. It was his poverty drove him to make this accusation and deny what really happened. It is not true that my sister, Madam Yu, mishandled the matter."

"Obviously," said the Matriarch, "one should avoid stirring up these petty people. Well, we must leave it to Phoenix to settle all this."

Phoenix could only murmur her acknowledgment and withdraw. But she sent a messenger at once for Chia Jung. Chia Jung knew very well what was in Phoenix's mind: how would it look if Chang Hua were really to come for the girl? And so he discussed the situation with his father Chia Chen, and they sent a secret message to Chang Hua: "You have received a considerable amount of money by this time, why do you still insist on claiming your betrothed? Can't you see that if you persist in this obstinacy you'll make these gentlemen angry? And then they'll find some pretext or other, and you'll be a corpse no one is willing to bury! Go back home with the money you have, and you'll have no problem finding any wife you want. And if you will only leave now you shall have what funds you need for the journey."

"This sounds like the best plan!" Chang Hua told himself. When he talked it over with his father they discovered their total receipts amounted to a hundred pieces of gold. The following day, accordingly, the two of them rose at dawn and made their way back home.

Chia Jung checked the truth of this and reported to Phoenix and the Matriarch: "Chang Hua and his father made a false accusation and have fled in fear of discovery. The magistrate knows this but has decided not to have them pursued, and so the whole affair is over with."

Phoenix pondered this for a moment. If Chang Hua actually had taken Second Sister away with him, there would still have been the likelihood that Chia Lien on his return would retrieve her by offering the everwilling Chang yet another sum of cash. It was better all round that Second Sister should stay here, where Phoenix herself could hold the strings: that would give her the chance to see what could be done. But where was Chang Hua headed for now? Supposing he told others of all this, or at some future time tried once again to turn the tables on the Chia family? It seemed senseless to be bringing harm down on one's own head—to pass the sword hilt first into another's hands!

So Phoenix began to regret what had been done. But it was not long before she devised another plan. She passed secret instructions to Wang-erh to send a man after Chang Hua. This man was to make sure that Chang Hua met his death one way or another, either by execution after a fabricated charge of theft or by a carefully arranged disposal of some other kind. This was what must be done if the weed were to be got rid of roots and all and the family reputation protected.

Back in his own room with these instructions Wang-erh reflected: "What need for strong measures like these when the man is gone and the whole affair at an end? Murder is no child's game, it's for Heaven above to reckon with! Best to cook up a story for Mistress Phoenix and see how it all turns out."

Wang-erh therefore lay low for a few days away from the mansion, then returned to report to Phoenix: "Chang Hua had a few ounces of silver on him, and so when he reached Ching-k'ow, around dawn a couple of days after he left here, he was set upon by highwaymen and beaten to death. His old man is at the inn there, frightened out of his wits, running around verifying the corpse and arranging for the burial."

Phoenix did not believe him: "I shall send someone else to check, and if you're lying I'll have your teeth out!"—But in fact she did not take it any further. She renewed her cultivation of Second Sister's

friendship, and truly they were many times sweeter to each other than
any pair of genuine sisters.

When at last Chia Lien returned, his tasks completed, he went
first to the cottage. He found it locked and deserted but for an old
caretaker. When he asked what had happened the old man gave him the
whole story. Chia Lien's feet could barely find the stirrups, but round he
had to go to report to his parents the transactions he had just completed.
Chia She was very pleased, praised his efficiency and rewarded him with
a hundred ounces of silver and a concubine, a sixteen-year-old slavey
from his own household whose name was Autumn Violet.

Chia Lien kowtowed his thanks for these gifts, which delighted him
beyond measure. When he had paid his respects to the Matriarch and
the rest of the seniors he returned to his own quarters to greet Phoenix,
the misgivings he felt were all too evident in his looks. To his surprise,
however, Phoenix appeared quite different from her former self. She
came out to meet him with Second Sister Yu by her side, and the three of
them exchanged a few casual remarks. Then Chia Lien explained the
matter of Autumn Violet, and in doing so was quite unable to keep a certain amount of smug self-satisfaction out of his expression.

Phoenix at once ordered two serving-women to bring Violet over
in a carriage. Before the first thorn could be plucked from her heart,
here out of nowhere came another! But what could she do but swallow
her resentment and dissemble her true feelings beneath a gracious
manner? She had wine set out to welcome the newcomer, and went in
person to introduce Violet to the Matriarch, Madam Wang and the
others, while Chia Lien could only marvel to himself at the change in
her.

There is no need to describe Phoenix's various kindnesses to Second Sister Yu—while they were in public. But her real intentions were
very different, and when the others were not present she would say to
Second Sister, "I'm afraid you have got yourself a very bad reputation,
even with the Matriarch and the ladies of the family. There's talk of
misbehavior while you were still a maiden at home, and of how you
saw too much of Chia Chen. 'Nobody wanted her so you had to pick
her up and bring her here—why don't you send her packing and find
someone better?' You can imagine how angry I am when I hear things
like that! I've tried to find out who says these things, but I can't. And
as time goes on it gets worse, and how can we contradict these stories

in front of the servants? So here's another fishhead to be opened up!"

After an outburst or two of this kind Phoenix fell sick again of her own anger and could neither eat nor drink. With the exception of Equity, the slaveys and serving-women all began to whisper things and make broad hints to each other, ridiculing Second Sister behind her back.

Meanwhile Autumn Violet was telling herself that since she was the gift of Chia She she need take second place to no one. She had no regard even for Phoenix or Equity, let alone this woman whose adultery had preceded her marriage and who had no one to stand up for her. Phoenix listened to her with secret joy. Since sickness had obliged her to take to her bed again she no longer invited Second Sister to eat with her, but had food sent to the girl's room instead. None of the food she was given was really fit to eat. Equity could not countenance this treatment and took out money of her own to buy dishes for her, or at other times she would take Second Sister into the garden under the pretext of a stroll, and there in the garden kitchens would make soup for her. No one reported this to Phoenix until one day Violet chanced on them, whereupon she at once went prattling to Phoenix: "What Equity is doing is giving you a bad name. Perfectly good food here going to waste because she won't touch it, and then she has to go eating on the sly out in the garden."

This brought harsh words from Phoenix down on Equity's head: "Other people keep cats to catch mice, but my cat eats the chickens!"

Equity did not dare to remonstrate, but a coolness grew between herself and Phoenix and she began to detest Autumn Violet.

Several of the cousins in the garden, like Li Wan, Welcome Spring, and Compassion Spring, accepted the notion of Phoenix's kindness to Second Sister Yu. But Precious Clasp, Black Jade, and others worried about her in private. They did not wish to interfere, but taking pity on her they paid frequent visits with expressions of sympathy. Sometimes they would talk with her alone, and at these times her eyes would brim with tears and she would dash them away. Yet she dared issue no word of complaint against Phoenix, for there was no open sign of her enmity.

When Chia Lien had first come back he had been too impressed by Phoenix's new tolerance to worry further about Second Sister. Moreover, he had long been conscious of the large number of concubines and slave-girls in his father's establishment and had harbored secret longings without ever plucking up the courage to act. As for the girls themselves, Violet and the rest bitterly resented being the property of a blurry-eyed old man—"plenty of appetite but no teeth to chew with"— what use had he for them? Some had a sense of decorum and modesty, but the rest fell to flirting with the young scamps of the household. Some even made eyes at Chia Lien and tried for assignations with him, but fear of Chia She had so far kept them out of his hands. Even though Violet had plenty of interest in Chia Lien they had never managed to come together. And now a kindly fate had brought her to him as a gift! It was like hot flame meeting tinder, day after day they could no more be prised apart than glue from lacquer or swallows newly mated. The charms of Second Sister Yu paled as Violet became life itself in Chia Lien's eyes.

Though Phoenix hated Violet she was no less happy to have in her a means to be rid of Second Sister. This was "killing with a borrowed sword" or "watching the tigers fight from a seat up the hill": let Violet despatch Second Sister, then take her turn at Phoenix's own hands. With this in mind she would often spur Violet on when no one else was about: "You're too young to realize: Second Sister is Second Mistress now, there are times when even I have to yield place to her in our master's affections. If you openly quarrel with her you are seeking your own destruction."

Words like these made Violet madder than ever, and day after day she filled the air with imprecations: "First Mistress is too soft-hearted! You'd never find me as tolerant as that! What has happened to the dignity you used to be noted for? So generous, so magnanimous —but I'm not going to rub that piece of grit any further into my eye! Just let me have it out with that whore and she'll discover what's what!"

Phoenix pretended to be afraid to restrain her, and Second Sister wept with rage in her room, too angry to eat yet reluctant to speak to Chia Lien about it. Nor did she dare say a word to the Matriarch who asked next day why her eyes were swollen so red.

As a part of her scheming and maneuvering Violet went stealthily round to the Matriarch and Madam Wang to complain: "She's determined to make out she's dying, weeping and wailing there the whole day through. But what she's really doing is praying for *our* deaths, the mistress and me, so that she can have the master all to herself body and soul."

"She's been spoiled," was the Matriarch's comment, "and so it's not surprising she should turn out spiteful and envious. When Phoenix has treated her so kindly she must be a worthless baggage to squabble so jealously." And her liking for the girl gradually diminished.

The Matriarch's displeasure was the signal for the servants to trample on Second Sister in their efforts to curry favor with their superiors. She could have wished for death, so impossible had her life now become. And still it was to Equity's credit that behind the back of Phoenix she did what little things she could for the girl.

Now Second Sister was one of those people with "guts made of petals, flesh like snow"—she was in no way fitted to stand up to this kind of maltreatment, and after less than a month of such veiled malice exhaustion developed into sickness. Her limbs were overcome with lassitude, she could take neither food nor even tea, and gradually her features took on a pallid and wasted look.

Once Chia Lien chanced by, and since no one else was present she said to him, through her tears, "I shall not recover from this sickness. But I have been here six months now and I have a baby coming, though who is to tell whether it will be a son or a daughter? If Heaven will take pity on me there is a chance it can be born; if not, there is no hope for me, let alone the baby."

"Set your mind at ease," replied Chia Lien, weeping in his turn. "I shall send for the finest doctor to cure your sickness."

And with these words he went out at once to send for the doctor.

Unfortunately the celebrated Doctor Wang had gone off to serve as a medical officer with the army, in the hopes of securing an official title. Learning this Chia Lien's servants fell back on Hu Chün-jung, the doctor who years ago had treated the slave-girl Bright Cloud. Dr. Hu took the patient's pulse, diagnosed menstrual irregularity, and prescribed a general tonic.

"She has missed three periods now and has frequent attacks of nausea," said Chia Lien. "I believe she is pregnant."

Hu Chün-jung accordingly asked the old serving-woman to hold out the girl's hand once again for his inspection, and once again the bed-curtains opened. He stared at it for some time, then said, "There is some semblance of pregnancy, certainly, in the swelling of the hepatic vein. But this is a fiery condition produced by the hyperactivity of the wood element, just as the menstrual irregularity is the result of the dominance of wood in the liver. I shall have to make so bold as to ask the lady to permit me a brief glimpse of her precious countenance, so that I may see what aspect is there before daring to prescribe medicine for her."

Chia Lien had no recourse but to order the curtain raised at the corner, so that Second Sister's face was visible. Hu Chün-jung looked, but there was no "aspect" to be seen since her consciousness had already fled somewhere beyond the bounds of the sky. The curtain was dropped again. Chia Lien accompanied the doctor out of the room and asked his opinion. "This is not pregnancy," said Doctor Hu, "but rather coagulations restricting the flow of blood. The great need is to dissolve the blood clots to permit menstruation."

With this he wrote a prescription and took his leave. Chia Lien sent off for the herbs prescribed, measured out a dose and administered it to the patient. But by the middle of the night Second Sister was suffering agonizing pains in the belly, and before long there fell from her a male foetus already formed. The blood would not stop and Second Sister fainted away. When Chia Lien heard he railed against Hu Chün-jung and sent at once for another doctor to attend Second Sister while other servants tracked down Hu himself. But Dr. Hu was forewarned and had already packed and fled.

The new doctor gave his opinion: "She was far from strong in the first place, and it seems that certain vexations since the beginning of her pregnancy must have led to a melancholic congestion. The previous gentleman made the mistake of prescribing a remedy far too fierce in its effect. I am afraid the lady's vital forces are eight- or nine-tenths spent and at this moment it is hard to guarantee a cure. But there may be a hope of improvement if she takes both the brew and the pills together, and if she can be kept free of any discord which might tend to disturb her."

He left, while the frantic Chia Lien sought out the servant who had engaged Dr. Hu and had him beaten almost to death.

Phoenix was ten times more distracted than Chia Lien himself, and said, "It is our fate to be childless! When after all this time one comes we have to run into an ignorant quack like this!" Thereupon she burned incense and prostrated herself before the altars of Heaven and Earth, offering this prayer with deepest sincerity: "Let me gladly take the sickness upon myself so that Second Sister may be restored to health. Then if she can again conceive and bring forth a boy I shall take vows of fasting and praise to the Buddha."

Chia Lien and all who observed this were filled with praise. While Chia Lien stayed with Violet, Phoenix busied herself with preparing soups and drinks for Second Sister. She cursed Equity for being ill-fated, "like myself—but I have a recurring sickness, you don't and still you can't conceive. Second Sister has only got this way because you and I are ill-fated, or else because we've done something wrong and it has affected her."

And so she sent servants to consult fortunetellers, one of whom counseled that the harm to Second Sister had been caused by a female Cancer. All began to work this out, and finding that Violet was the only Cancer laid the blame at her door.

The vinegar of jealousy had already begun to collect in Violet's bosom as she watched Chia Lien sending for doctors and beating and cursing the servants in his concern for Second Sister. Now, when the blame was put on her and Phoenix herself came to urge her to go away for a few days, Violet burst out in tears and imprecations: "You've been listening to that pack of mangy mongrels flapping their vicious tongues! 'Both are water, but the wellspring doesn't interfere with the river'—how have I ever injured her? Such a darling creature—I suppose she had no contact with anyone outside, but as soon as she comes here somebody does something to 'injure' her! And what sort of little monster was it anyway—red eyes and white brows? She's only been trying to make a fool out of our master with his big, soft, cottony ears! Suppose there *is* a baby—who's to say whether its surname should be Chang or Wang or what? First Mistress may treasure a bastard brat of that sort, but not me! What's so special about a baby? Anyone can have one—takes a year or thereabouts, and there's no need for any hanky-panky to get it, either!"

Those who heard her had to fight the impulse to laugh. But then Madam Hsing chanced to visit, and Violet appealed to her: "The master and mistress are planning to send me back and I've nowhere to turn to. I throw myself on the great lady's mercy!"

Madam Hsing gave Phoenix a severe reprimand and turned to scold her son Chia Lien: "It's time you knew how to behave! No matter what she is like, she was your father's gift to you. What sort of regard can you have for your father if you will send her away in favor of someone you picked up from outside? Hadn't you better return her to your father first?"—And she left in a flush of indignation.

Violet now began to feel even surer of herself and took to yelling and cursing at Second Sister from directly outside her window. Naturally the poor girl's distress grew deeper still. That night Chia Lien spent in Violet's room, and when Phoenix had gone to sleep Equity went across to comfort Second Sister: "Just take care of yourself and get better, don't take any notice of that little beast."

Second Sister grasped at her and wept: "Equity, you have been the only one to care for me ever since I arrived in this house, and Heaven knows how much abuse you have had to bear with because of me. If I come through this alive I swear I shall repay your kindness; if I die as I fear I must, I shall repay you in our next incarnation."

Equity could not restrain her tears: "Thinking back, your troubles are all because of me. I was trying to act for the best; I've never kept anything from her, and I felt I had to tell her when I learned you were there with our master. This is what caused all the trouble."

Second Sister hastened to reassure her: "It isn't right to blame yourself. Even if you hadn't told her she would have been sure to find out somehow, you were simply the first to speak of it. And then, I was really anxious to enter this mansion to put things on a proper basis. It was not your fault at all."

They wept together and Equity said what she could to console her before she herself retired, the night already far advanced.

Now Second Sister searched her thoughts: "My sickness has taken full hold, I grow worse instead of better as the days pass. Surely there can be no recovery for me. And now I have lost my baby and have nothing to hope for—why should I put up with this rage against me? Better to die and have done! I've often heard that a person can suffocate by swallowing gold, and surely that's a cleaner way than hanging or cutting one's throat."

Her resolution made, she struggled to her feet and from one of her cases searched out a piece of gold of a certain weight. She placed the gold in her mouth and gritted her teeth to force it down her throat. She had to stretch her neck back several times before she could swallow it down. Then she hastened to dress herself and ornament her hair as neatly as she could before she lay down on the bed again. And neither man nor demon knew of this.

When next morning the slaveys and serving-women heard no calls from Second Sister they devoted themselves cheerfully to their own toilets. Phoenix and Violet went out to pay their morning calls. But Equity was indignant, and said, "What a callous lot you slaveys are!

You'll work if you're scolded and beaten, but if someone is lying sick you've no sympathy. Even if she were short with you, you should still behave properly and not like this. Your idea is, 'when the wall's collapsing, everybody gives it a shove!' "

At these words the slaveys hastened to push open the door and enter. Dressed and ornamented in her finest, Second Sister lay dead on the bed. And now all was panic and confusion as they screamed and shouted. Equity came and looked and cried aloud in her grief. Despite their long-ingrained fear of Phoenix the servants began to reflect on Second Sister's past gentleness and goodness to them and how different she had been from their mistress. Now that she lay dead each one of them wept for pity, though not one would have dared let Phoenix see her tears.

Soon all the household knew what had happened. Chia Lien came in, took the corpse in his embrace and wailed ceaselessly. Phoenix manufactured tears of her own and cried, "O cruel sister! How could you have turned your back on my love for you and left me alone in this way!"

Madam Yu, Chia Jung, and the rest all came to wail for a while and to console Chia Lien. Then Chia Lien sought permission from Madam Wang to rest the body of Second Sister in the Pear Fragrance Court for five days before removing her to the Iron Sill Monastery, and this was granted. Chia Lien gave prompt orders for the gate of the Pear Fragrance Court to be opened and the principal room prepared to receive the body. He felt it would be unseemly to have the body taken out via the gate in the rear, and so ordered a new gateway opened up specially for the occasion in the wall which gave on to the street across from the Pear Fragrance Court. Under awnings at each side altars were set up for Buddhist services. A soft couch was spread with cover and bolsters of embroidered satin, and Second Sister's body was laid on this and covered with a sheet. Eight serving-boys and a number of women formed the cortege as the body was transferred from within the house to the Pear Fragrance Court.

Meanwhile an astrologer was consulted, who, in order to make his predictions, lifted back the shroud. Second Sister's complexion seemed unchanged, and she looked even lovelier than in life. Chia Lien embraced the corpse and wailed: "You have died wronged, it was I who destroyed you."

Chia Jung hastened to console him: "Don't distress yourself, uncle, it was her own ill fate, that's all." And he pointed to the wall surrounding the Grand View Garden. Chia Lien took his meaning, and stealthily ground his foot muttering, "I've been so careless, but it will all come out in the end and I will avenge you."

The astrologer announced: "Since it was at six o'clock this morning the lady died, the third or the seventh days from now will be suitable for removal, but not the fifth. Tomorrow in the hour preceding dawn will be a most auspicious time for the encoffinment."

"Three days from now certainly will not do," said Chia Lien. "It will have to be seven. But my cousins are away, and I do not wish to delay the first funeral rites. When she has been taken out we will wait the requisite thirty-five days and then hold major services for closing the coffin. Then next year we will take her south for burial."

The astrologer gave his assent, wrote out a notice of death and took his leave. Pao-yü had already arrived to weep with them; the other members of the clan began to assemble, and Chia Lien hurried in search of Phoenix for money for the funeral expenses.

"What money?" asked Phoenix. "Have you no idea of the problems we've been having lately? Each month we fall further behind the month before, 'the chickens are eating the New Year's grain!' Yesterday I managed to pawn a pair of gold necklets for three hundred ounces of silver. And you dream of money—when I was through with what we needed there were twenty-odd ounces left. You can have that if you need it."

She had Equity bring out the silver and give it to Chia Lien. Then she left with the excuse that she must speak with the Matriarch. Chia Lien was too angry to find words. As a last resort he turned to Second Sister's private chests in search of the gifts he himself had made her in the past. But when he opened the chest he found it empty save for some tattered and broken ornaments and a few cast-off silk dresses. Second Sister had worn these things in the past, and now the sight of them brought tears to Chia Lien's eyes in a renewal of his grief. He made a bundle of her things and then without the help of serving-boy or slavey carried them out to burn.

Equity, at once grieving and ironically amused, surreptitiously brought out a packet containing two hundred ounces of silver in broken ingots. She lay in wait for Chia Lien in one of the siderooms and handed it to him: "Say nothing of this. And if you *must* weep for her, you have every opportunity to do it outside—don't come around here dabbing your eyes."

"You're right," said Chia Lien. He took the silver, and brought out a skirt for Equity in return: "She used to wear this when we were together. Won't you keep it for me as a memento?"

Equity accepted it and put it away with her own things.

Chia Lien rejoined the others and sent orders for a coffin-maker. A good coffin would be expensive, a cheaper one wouldn't do; so Chia Lien went off himself to supervise the work, and by evening brought back a set of good boards, bought on credit for five hundred ounces of silver, which overnight were fashioned into a coffin.

At the same time he set relays of servants to watch by the body. This was where he himself spent the nights also, rather than returning to his own rooms, while each day Buddhist monks and Taoist priests performed continuous services.

The Matriarch sent for Chia Lien to prohibit Second Sister's body from entering the family temple. This left him with no recourse but to get permission to reopen the grave of Third Sister Yu and bury Second Sister on top of her.

When the funeral took place it was attended only by Chia Lien and his cousin, Wang Hsin and his wife, and Madam Yu and her mother. Phoenix took no part in the matter but left Chia Lien to handle it entirely by himself.

TRANSLATED BY CYRIL BIRCH

The New Art of Autobiography

In strict terms, autobiography is far from a new art in China but goes back to Ssu-ma Ch'ien in the second century B.C. *Nor is Shen Fu's book an autobiography in the sense of an objective and reasonably chronological record. It has been suggested that "confession" might be a more appropriate label. The book's prime achievement is certainly its portrait of Yuen, the author's wife and "one of the loveliest women in Chinese literature" as Lin Yutang has called her. Yuen was born in 1763, the same year as Shen Fu. They were married at the age of seventeen and were together for twenty-three years before she died. Shen Fu's own death occurred some time after 1809.*

What is new about Six Chapters from a Floating Life *is its subjective quality. Shen Fu, an impecunious painter who now and then would find a job as yamen secretary, had genius in the invention and description of simple but elegant pleasures. But even the least of these involved Yuen and became part of the record of the love he shared with her.*

Shen Ts'ung-wen was born in 1902 and at the age of thirty wrote the account (Ts'ung-wen tzu chuan) of his own childhood and adolescence in a strangely medieval-seeming small garrison town in Hunan, among soldiers, aboriginals, and others who were later to people his stories and novels. The book offers macabre moments, such as the boy's search for his uncle's severed head among four hundred piled against the city wall in the aftermath of an abortive rebellion. Our present extract bears Shen Ts'ung-wen's hallmark of unsentimental but somehow whimsical pathos.

●

Shen Fu

From Six Chapters from a Floating Life

[*Fu sheng liu chi*]

For the Festival of Hungry Ghosts, on the fifteenth night of the seventh month, Yuen prepared a little feast in honor of those poor, unhappy spirits who have no living descendants to burn incense before their spirit-tablets. We were eating on the balcony of the pavilion and had invited the moon to drink with us, making a third at our celebration. Our cups were raised to drink the first toast, when suddenly, from nowhere it seemed, ominous clouds massed above our heads, darkening the clear sky and obscuring the face of our guest, the moon. Yuen shivered and turned pale.

"If the Gods mean that you and I are to grow white-headed together," she whispered, "the moon must come out again tonight!"

I, too, felt depressed and apprehensive, looking across the water to the darkness of the opposite shore, where fireflies, shining in the blackness like thousands of tiny, bright lanterns, wove in and out among the tangled willows. To dispel our fears and depression we began composing poetry, one of us starting a verse, the other finishing it; each composing a couplet in turn. Rhyming back and forth, we began to let our imagination run wild, indulging our most foolish fancies until we found ourselves laughing hysterically at the most ridiculous nonsense verses. Yuen choked and gasped, tears streaming down her cheeks. Breathless at last, she leant her head against my chest, filling the air with the fragrance of jasmine from her hair.

"I know that from ancient times jasmine has been the favorite ornament for women's hair," I said, patting her on the back to stop her choking, "but I had always thought that it was used because the flowers had the color and beauty of pearls. I had no idea that its fragrance was so enhanced when it blended with the perfumes of hair oil and face powder.

260

When jasmine smells like this, even the citron must take second place."

The choking had stopped now, and Yuen was resting, exhausted, in my arms.

"The citron is the aristocrat of perfumes," she said, "its fragrance is so subtle and elusive. But jasmine is a peasant, borrowing part of its personality from others; like a sycophant, it laughs and shrugs its shoulders while it insincerely curries favor."

"Why then," I asked her, "does my darling avoid the aristocrat and associate with the peasant?"

"The aristocrat pleases me, I suppose," she replied, "but I love the peasant."

As we talked, the third watch was drawing to a close, the wind was gradually sweeping away the clouds, and when the moon burst forth again in silver radiance, happiness once more filled our hearts. Standing by the window, we raised our cups in toasts to the moon and to each other. We were drinking the second toast when a commotion broke out under the bridge. Then we heard what sounded like a loud splash, as if someone had fallen into the water, but when we rushed to the window and looked down into the stream, there was nothing unusual to be seen. The water was as clear and smooth as a mirror. Not a sound now broke the stillness but the cry of a scurrying duck on the opposite bank. (I had always known that the gardens of the Ts'ang-lang Pavilion were haunted by the ghost of a man who had drowned in the canal, but because of Yuen's fear of the supernatural I had not dared to tell her about it.)

"Oh! That frightening noise!" Yuen cried, shuddering with terror. "What was it? Where did it come from?"

Horror-struck—our bodies trembling uncontrollably—we hastily closed the window and carried the wine into the room, where the gauze curtains hung motionless and the lamp-flame had shrunk to the size of a pea. Like the frightened man in the old story, "seeing the bow's reflection as a snake's shadow in the wine-cup," I nervously raised the lamp-wick and crept behind the curtains of the bed. There I found that Yuen was shivering and burning by turns. Before long, I, too, had developed a high fever.

For the next twenty days or so we lay in bed, exhausted and feverish, a prey to nameless fears.

How true is the ancient saying: "When happiness reaches its peak, calamity is sure to follow." The events of that terrible night seemed to be still another omen that we two should never grow old together.

East of the Gold Mother Bridge and north of Irrigation Channel Lane, an old woman lived in a house with a bamboo gate, a small cottage surrounded on all sides by orchards and vegetable gardens. Beyond the gate lay a pond about two hundred and fifty paces across, bordered by brilliant flowers, shade trees, and tangled masses of bamboo.

The place had formerly been the garden of Chang Shih-ch'eng of the Yüan dynasty, the famous rebel and salt-smuggler who built himself a palace on the site, after proclaiming himself a prince and capturing the city of Soochow, in the year 1356.

A short distance west of the cottage a mass of broken tile and rubble formed an artificial hill, from the top of which the surrounding country could be seen, a sparsely settled region of wild, uncultivated heath, broken here and there by clumps of tangled willows and bamboo.

After the old woman had once casually mentioned the place, Yuen could not put it out of her mind. Finally she spoke about it to me.

"Ever since leaving the Ts'ang-lang Pavilion," she said, "I have seen it every night in my dreams. But as we can't go back to live there, perhaps we should try to consider a second best. What would you think of this old woman's house?"

"As we are still facing the worst heat of the summer," I answered, "I have already thought of looking for a cool, refreshing place to spend the long, hot days. If this house really appeals to you, darling, I shall go and see if it is fit to live in. If it is, we can easily move our clothes and bedding over there and take a month's holiday. Would that please you?"

"I'm afraid your parents will never allow it," Yuen replied.

"In this case," I said, "I mean to ask them myself."

Next day, when I arrived at the house, I found that it was a small place of only two rooms, each divided down the center by a partition running from front to back. I could see at once that with paper windows and bamboo beds it would be a delightfully cool and quiet retreat; and when I told the old woman what I had in mind, she gladly vacated her bedroom and rented it to me.

By pasting white paper on the walls, I managed to change the appearance of the room completely and to make it look fresh and clean. Then I told my mother about the place and went to live there with Yuen.

Our only neighbors were an elderly couple who raised vegetables for the markets in the city. Learning that we were staying there to avoid the summer heat, and being anxious to see that we were comfortably settled, they came to pay us a visit, bringing as a present some fish from the pond and fresh vegetables from their garden. I tried to pay them for the vegetables, but they refused to take any money. When Yuen made them a pair of shoes in return for their kindness, however, they accepted them with gratitude.

We were in the seventh month, when the trees cast dense green shadows, breezes ruffled the surface of the pond, and the din of the cicadas was deafening.

Our neighbor had made us bamboo fishing-poles and Yuen and I used to go fishing every day, in a cool, shady place under the willows. Then, at twilight, we would climb to the top of the mound to watch the sunset's afterglow reflected on the gold and crimson clouds. If we felt inspired, we might begin composing poetry, reciting couplets like this one:

> Wild-beast clouds have swallowed the setting sun,
> And now the moon's bow shoots the falling stars.

After the moon had engraved her image on the surface of the pond and the crickets had started to chirp, I would carry out a bamboo couch and set it beside the hedge for us to sit on. When the old woman told us our wine was warmed and our supper cooked, we would sit there in the moonlight, laughing and drinking toast after toast until we were often not a little drunk before beginning to eat.

After dinner we would bathe, put on cool sandals, take our palm-leaf fans and go outside again. Lying on the couch, we waited until our two old neighbors arrived and began to while away the night with ancient tales of rewards and punishments, and deeds of bravery and steadfast devotion to duty. At midnight, feeling delightfully cool and refreshed, we went inside to bed, almost unable to believe that we were still living in the middle of the city.

I had asked our neighbor to buy us some chrysanthemums and plant them along the bamboo hedge. When the plants began to bloom, in the ninth month, Yuen and I decided to stay for another ten days or so to enjoy their beauty, and to send for my mother to come and see them also. The invitation pleased my mother and after she arrived we spent the whole day in front of the flowers, eating crab-legs and gossiping. This delighted Yuen.

"Some day we must build a house out here," she said. "We will have a diviner pick a lucky spot and then buy several acres of land for the house and gardens. We'll set our servant to planting vegetables and melons; then we can use the income for our living expenses. You can paint and I can do needlework to buy the wine for entertaining our friends. If we wear cheap cotton clothes and eat the vegetables from our own garden, we can spend our lives here together in perfect happiness. You would never have to travel to far places again, nor leave me at home alone."

How profoundly I wish that her dream had come true! But now, though the place is still in existence, the one who knew my innermost heart is dead. What a tragic and pitiful loss!

Half a *li* from my home, in Vinegar Storehouse Lane, stood a temple to the Goddess of Tung-t'ing Lake, the Temple of the Water-Fairy, commonly called the "Narcissus Temple." The temple itself, a maze of intricate corridors and winding verandas, was surrounded by a small, commonplace garden, with pavilions and arbors scattered here and there.

Every year, on the birthday of the goddess, each family in the neighborhood was given its own particular spot in the temple, which the members of the clan would decorate with hanging lanterns of a special kind having shelves in the center for holding vases of flowers. Under the lanterns, on the low tables at either side, they would arrange other vases, filling them with flowers that would later be judged in a floral competition.

Theatrical performances filled the day, and at night the place was brilliantly lighted by candles placed among the vases; a custom called "illumination of the flowers." The color and fragrance of the blossoms, the flickering shadows cast by the lanterns and candles, and the swirling smoke that floated above the bronze tripods of the incense-burners, all combined to create the impression of a feast by night in the Hall of the Dragon King.

The exhibiting families, to while away the hours, would play music and sing, drink tea and gossip, while the townspeople looked on, crowding like ants against the railings set up under the eaves. I was fortunate enough to be able to take an active part in the festival when some friends invited me to go with them to help arrange the candles and flowers. In the evening, when I came home to Yuen, I enthusiastically described the beauty of the scene.

"What a pity I am not a man," she sighed, "if I were, I could go with you and see it all for myself."

"If you wore one of my hats and gowns," I told her, "I think you could easily pass for a man." At once, she began to take down her long hair, quickly braiding it into a masculine queue. Then she thickened and darkened her beautiful moth-eyebrows with paint, before putting my hat on her head. The deception was quite successful in spite of the hair that still showed slightly around her temples. Finding, when she tried it on, that my gown was several inches too long for her, she stitched a tuck around the waist and covered it with a short jacket.

"But my feet," she wailed, "what can I do about them?"

Remembering that there were special shops selling "butterfly shoes," that can be worn with either bound or natural feet, I told her I would buy her a pair.

"And you can wear them afterwards for house slippers," I suggested.

Yuen was delighted. After supper she insisted on dressing up again, and once more braiding her queue. She strutted up and down, carefully imitating masculine gestures and trying to take long strides.

Suddenly, she changed her mind.

"I am not going," she decided. "What if someone should see through my disguise? And your parents—they would never allow me to go along with you." I urged her to change her mind and go with me.

"Everyone at the temple knows me," I persisted. "Even if anyone should recognize you, he would only laugh at you. As Mother is away visiting Ninth Sister and her husband, we could leave and come back in secret, with no one any the wiser."

Looking at her reflection in the mirror, Yuen shook with repressed laughter, until I took her by the arm and pulled her after me. In silence, then, we stole from the house without meeting a soul.

Arriving at the temple, we roamed around the grounds, causing no comment, no one recognizing Yuen nor guessing that she was not a man. When I introduced her to my friends as a visiting boy cousin, they only bowed politely and passed on. Late in the evening we reached a place where several ladies and young girls were sitting beside their floral display. Remembering them as members of the family of the exhibitor, Mr. Wang, Yuen hurried over to talk to them. They were very cordial to her until, in the course of the conversation, she leant over and thoughtlessly put her hand on the shoulder of one of the young ladies. This was a serious breach of good manners and angered the elderly servant who was sitting beside the girl.

"You young rascal," she shouted at the supposed young man, "how dare you take such a liberty!" Before I could step forward to explain and smooth things over, Yuen, realizing the seriousness of the situation, had pulled off her hat and raised her foot in its butterfly shoe.

"Look!" she cried, "I, too, am a woman!"

After the first few moments of surprise, their anger gave way to amusement and the whole family insisted on entertaining us with tea and cakes until I called a sedan chair to return home.

After the death of Mr. Ch'ien Shih-chu of Wu-chiang, I received a letter from my father asking me to go to his friend's funeral. Yuen took me aside and asked if she could go with me.

"You will be passing the T'ai Hu on your way to Wu-chiang," she said, "and I have always longed to see a wide expanse of water like the Great Lake."

"I am not looking forward to the loneliness of travelling without you," I answered. "It would be wonderful if you could go with me, darling, but I cannot think what excuse to give to my mother."

"I had better say that I want to go home to see my mother," Yuen said. "You go on ahead to the boat and I'll follow and meet you there later."

"If you do come," I said, "we should plan to anchor at the Bridge of Ten Thousand Years on the way home. We could wait to watch the moon rise, and perhaps finish the poems we began that night last year, when we were watching the moon at the Ts'ang-lang Pavilion."

Rising early the following morning, the eighteenth day of the sixth month, I went with a servant to the Distant River Ferry and boarded the boat to wait for Yuen, who arrived, before long, in a sedan chair. Shortly afterwards, the boat cast off; and after passing Roaring Tiger Bridge we began to see sailing boats, and sand birds, and water stretching to join the sky in one wide expanse of blue.

"So this is the Great Lake!" Yuen cried. "Now I can at last comprehend the immensity of the universe! My life has gained new meaning! But think of all the women who never leave their own courtyards, who must spend their whole lives without once enjoying a sight like this."

While we were talking, I saw the wind-swayed willows on the banks and knew that we had reached Wu-chiang. I lost no time, but climbed ashore at once, made my appearance at the funeral and returned to the boat again the moment I could do so. To my dismay I found the cabin dark and empty. Anxiously I asked the boatman what had become of Yuen.

"Don't you see someone down by the bridge?" he said, pointing to the shore. "Over there—in the shade of the willows—watching the cormorant fishers?"

Yuen had already climbed the bank with the boatman's daughter, and when I joined them, I saw that Yuen's face-powder was streaked and she was bathed in perspiration. Leaning on the girl, she stood there with a far-away look on her face, and seemed quite unaware of her surroundings.

"Darling, you are soaking wet," I said, touching her on the shoulder. Yuen turned her head.

"I was afraid someone from the Ch'ien family might come down to the boat," she said, "so I left to avoid any chance of a meeting. But why did you come back so soon?"

"To catch that philandering Ch'ien, of course!" I laughed, taking her hand and starting back to the boat.

When we reached the Bridge of Ten Thousand Years again, the sun was low in the sky. Dropping the cabin windows all the way to take advantage of the cool breeze, we sat there in our thin clothes fanning ourselves and eating slices of melon to distract our minds from the heat.

At one moment the bridge was a shining crimson in the reflected glow of the setting sun; the next, a mist had begun to hide the willows on the bank. Then, before the Silver Toad in the Moon had started to show his face, the flames of the fishermen's fires began to light up the whole river.

The boatman's daughter, Su-yin, was an old drinking companion of mine. She was quite an unusual girl, and, after I had sent my servant astern to have a drink with the boatman, I called her to come and sit with Yuen and me in the bow of the boat. I had not had the lanterns lit, preferring to sit there in darkness, waiting for the moon to rise, filling and refilling our wine cups as Yuen and I played a game of forfeits.

Su-yin listened intently for some time before she said: "I am quite good at wine games, but I confess I cannot follow this one. I have never heard it before. Would you explain it to me?"

Yuen tried to enlighten her, using all sorts of analogies and illustrative phrases, but Su-yin remained as ignorant as before.

"If Madame Professor will cease expounding," I laughed, "I will give Su-yin a simple illustration which will explain the matter clearly."

"Just how do you propose to illustrate it?" Yuen asked.

"The crane is an expert dancer," I replied, "but cannot plough. The ox knows how to plough, but cannot dance. That is the natural order of things. To reverse that order, to try and teach the ox to dance, would be a waste of time and trouble." Su-yin laughed.

"You mean to infer that I am stupid," she said, hitting me on the shoulder.

"After this," Yuen broke in sharply, "let us settle arguments with words, not blows; by using our mouths instead of our hands. Whoever disobeys this rule must drink a large cup of wine."

Su-yin, whose capacity for wine was heroic, poured herself a full cup and drank it in one breath.

"We should be permitted to use the hands for feeling and stroking, but not for hitting," I said jokingly.

Yuen playfully pushed Su-yin into my arms.

"Feel her and stroke her as much as you like," she said.

"What a silly girl you are, darling," I answered. "Love-making must be spontaneous, born of mutual desire. Lovers should be only semi-conscious; here and not-here. Love-making must come naturally or there is no pleasure in it. Only a boor grabs a woman and at once begins to caress her."

The fragrance of jasmine from the hair of the two girls suffused the air, combining with the odors of face powder, wine fumes, perspiration, and hair-oil to make a perfume both subtle and exciting.

"The smell of the peasant fills the bow of the boat," I said jokingly to Yuen. "It is so strong it disgusts me."

Su-yin sprang from my arms and started punching me with her closed fists.

"You profligate!" she screamed angrily. "Who told you to smell me?"

"You have broken the rule," Yuen called in a loud voice. "I fine you two large cups of wine."

"He insulted me by calling me a peasant," Su-yin raged. "Why shouldn't I punch him?"

"When he referred to 'the peasant,' " Yuen said quietly, "he was speaking of something you know nothing about. Drink the two forfeits and then I shall tell you the story."

After Su-yin had poured the two cups down, one right after the other, Yuen told her of our discussion about jasmine and citron, peasant and aristocrat, which had taken place the previous summer at the Ts'ang-lang Pavilion.

"In that case," Su-yin conceded, "I have blamed the wrong person. It was all my fault, I should be fined again."

A third time, she emptied a large cup of wine.

"For a long time, Miss Su," Yuen said now, "I have been hearing of your talent as a singer. Would you sing a song or two for us?"

For answer, the girl took up a pair of ivory chopsticks, commenced beating time on the edge of a bowl, and then started to sing.

Yuen sat drinking and listening until, without realizing it, she had become very drunk. I hired a sedan chair and sent her home without me, while I stayed a little longer in the pleasant company of Su-yin. Later on, I walked home alone in the moonlight.

At the time when this took place, we were staying with my friend, Lu Pan-fang, at his home, the Pavilion of the Tranquil Heart; and several days later, when Mrs. Lu heard a garbled version of the evening's events, she told Yuen about it in confidence.

"Your husband was drinking and making love with two sing-song girls a few nights ago, in a boat at the Bridge of Ten Thousand Years," she said. "Did you know about it?"

"I know that one of the sing-song girls bore a remarkable resemblance to me," Yuen laughed and began to tell Mrs. Lu the story from beginning to end. Mrs. Lu enjoyed it immensely and had a hearty laugh at herself and her ill-founded suspicions.

As a young man I was excessively fond of flowers and loved to prune and shape potted plants and trees. When I met Chang Lan-p'o he began to teach me the art of training branches and supporting joints, and after I had mastered these skills he showed me how to graft flowers. Later on, I also learned the placing of stones and designing of rock gardens.

The orchid we considered the peerless flower, selecting it as much for its subtle and delicate fragrance as for its beauty and grace. Fine varieties of orchids were very difficult to find, especially those worthy of being recorded in the Botanical Register. When Lan-p'o was dying he gave me a pot of spring orchids of the lotus type, with broad white centers, perfectly even "shoulders," and very slender stems. As the plant was a classic specimen of its type, I treasured its perfection like a piece of ancient jade. Yuen took care of it whenever my work as yamen secretary called me away from home. She always watered it herself and the plant flourished, producing a luxuriant growth of leaves and flowers.

One morning, about two years later, it suddenly withered and died. When I dug up the roots to inspect them, I saw that they were as white as jade, with many new shoots beginning to sprout. At first, I could not understand it. Was I just too unlucky, I wondered, to possess and enjoy such beauty? Sighing despondently, I dismissed the matter from my mind. But some time later I found out what had really happened. It seemed that a person who had asked for a cutting from the plant and had been refused, had then poured boiling water on it and killed it. After that, I vowed never to grow orchids again.

Azaleas were my second choice. Although the flowers had no fragrance they were very beautiful and lasted a long time. The plants were easy to trim and to train, but Yuen loved the green of the branches and leaves so much that she would not let me cut them back, and this made it difficult for me to train them to correct shapes. Unfortunately, Yuen felt this way about all the potted plants that she enjoyed.

Every year, in the autumn, I became completely devoted to the chrysanthemum. I loved to arrange the cut flowers in vases but did not like the potted plants. Not that I did not think the potted flowers beautiful, but our house having no garden, it was impossible for me to grow the plants myself, and those for sale at the market were overgrown and untrained; not at all what I would have chosen.

One day, as I was sweeping my ancestral graves in the hills, I found some very unusual stones with interesting streaks and lines running through them. I talked to Yuen about them when I went home.

"When Hsüan-chou stones are mixed with putty and arranged in white-stone dishes, the putty and stones blend well and the effect is very harmonious," I remarked. "These yellow stones from the hills are rugged and old-looking, but if we mix them with putty the yellow and white won't blend. All the seams and gaps will show up and the arrangement will look spotty. I wonder what else we could use instead of putty?"

"Why not pick out some of the poor, uninteresting stones and pound them to powder," Yuen said. "If we mix the powdered stones with the putty while it is still damp, the color will probably match when it dries."

After doing as she suggested, we took a rectangular Yi-hsing pottery dish and piled the stones and putty into a miniature mountain peak on the left side of it, with a rocky crag jutting out towards the right. On the surface of the mountain, we made criss-cross marks in the style of the rocks painted by Ni Tsan of the Yüan dynasty. This gave an effect of perspective and the finished arrangement looked very realistic—a precipitous cliff rising sharply from the rocks at the river's edge. Making a hollow in one corner of the dish, we filled it with river mud and planted it with duck-weed. Among the rocks we planted "clouds of the pine trees," bindweed. It was several days before the whole thing was finished.

Before the end of autumn the bindweed had spread all over the mountain and hung like wisteria from the rocky cliff. The flowers, when they bloomed, were a beautiful clear red. The duckweed, too, had sprouted luxuriantly from the mud and was now a mass of snowy white. Seeing the beauty of the contrasting red and white, we could easily imagine ourselves in fairyland.

Setting the dish under the eaves, we started discussing what should be done next, developing many themes: "Here there should be a lake with a pavilion—" "This spot calls for a thatched summer-house—" "This is the perfect place for the six-character inscription 'Place of Falling Flowers and Flowing Water'—" "Here we could build our house—here go fishing—here enjoy the view"; becoming, by this time, so much a part of the tiny landscape, with its hills and ravines, that it seemed to us as if we were really going to move there to live.

One night, a couple of misbegotten cats, fighting over food, fell off the eaves and hit the dish, knocking it off its stand and smashing it to fragments in an instant. Neither of us could help crying.

"Isn't it possible," I sighed, "to have even a little thing like this without incurring the envy of the gods?"

There were two places in Soochow, the South Garden and the North Garden, where the yellow rape flowers bloomed; but unfortunately neither place had a wine-seller from whom one could buy a drink. Supposing we carried a basket with us when we went there, what artistic pleasure could be gained from drinking cold wine among the flowers? Someone suggested that we try to find a wine-seller nearby; someone else argued that we should first look at the flowers and then go back to a wineshop; but neither of these alternatives would be as satisfying as drinking our warm wine in the company of the flowers.

We were undecided what to do, until Yuen said with a smile: "All you will have to do tomorrow is provide the wine money. I shall make myself responsible for providing a stove."

At this, the whole group started laughing and calling "Agreed." But after the others had gone I asked Yuen if she really meant to carry a stove along herself.

"Of course not," she answered. "But I have seen dumpling-sellers on the streets carrying their stoves, with their pans and all the necessities for preparing a meal; and I thought we could hire one of them to go with us. I could cook the food beforehand so that when we arrive we need only reheat it. Then we'll have everything we need, including tea and wine."

"It would be very pleasant to have both wine and tea," I agreed, "but we would need a pot to boil the water for the tea."

"We could take along an earthenware pot and an iron prong to slip through the handle. We could remove the dumpling-man's pan and suspend our pot over the stove on the iron prong. Add some extra fuel to boil the water—and we have our tea."

Clapping my hands in admiration, I declared it an excellent idea.

On the street I found a dumpling-seller called Pao, who gladly agreed, for a hundred cash, to go with us the following afternoon. When our friends arrived next day and I told them of the arrangement, they all thought it very clever.

We set off after lunch, carrying our mats and cushions. Arriving at the South Garden, we picked out a shady spot under some willows and

sat down on the ground in a circle. First we boiled the water and made
our tea. After we had drunk it, we began to warm the wine and heat
up the food that Yuen had prepared.

The day was now at its best, the breeze gentle, the sun glorious
above the golden fields of rape flowers. On the paths between the rice
paddies people in blue gowns with red sleeves crisscrossed back and
forth; butterflies and bees were circling and darting everywhere. This
alone was enough to intoxicate us, without the help of wine.

When the food was hot we sat down on the ground again, com-
mencing to eat with hearty appetites, and, as the dumpling-man was
not at all a vulgar person, insisting that he, too, join us in a drink. Sight-
seers who noticed us in passing must have thought our behavior very
strange. The wine cups were strewn in wild disorder among the dishes of
of half-eaten food and we were all now more than a little drunk; some
of us sitting, others lying stretched full-length; some of us singing, others whistling or shouting.

When the red sun was low in the sky, I began to want some rice-
gruel and sent the dumpling-man to buy some rice. After eating the
rice he cooked for us, we started off for home with our bellies comfortably full.

"Did you all enjoy the picnic?" Yuen asked us.

"We did," we all replied, "but without Madam and her clever
idea, the day would not have been nearly as much fun."

Smiling, then, we went our separate ways.

When it was time for the return of Yuen's spirit, my landlord who
lived in the same house went away to "avoid the spirit." The next-door
neighbors begged me to arrange the sacrificial dishes and leave, too,
but I gave them an evasive answer. I wanted to see Yuen's spirit if it
returned. A man from my own district, Chang Yu-men, pleaded with
me to go.

"If you allow yourself to come in contact with the spirit world,"
he warned me, "you may be entered and possessed by a demon. I really believe there are ghosts and I beg you not to make this experiment."

"I certainly believe they exist," I replied. "That is why I mean to
wait."

"Violating the taboo against a returning spirit," Chang persisted, "is bad luck for the living. Even if the spirit of your wife does come back to you, she is no longer a human being but has already become part of the nether world of Hades. If your beloved were really here you still would not see her without her human form, and you might risk arousing her powers of evil."

At the moment, I could not control the madness of love in my heart.

"Life and death are pre-ordained," I cried wildly. "If you are so concerned for my safety, why don't you keep me company yourself?"

"For your protection, I shall stay right outside the door," Chang replied. "If you see anything strange, call me and I shall come in."

Taking up a lamp, I went into Yuen's room, where everything seemed as it always had, except that the voice and face of my love were no longer there. Unable to help it, I broke into a flood of heart-broken tears.

Then, afraid that my sight might be blurred and I would miss what I so longed to see, I stopped crying and with wide-open eyes sat down on the bed to wait. Picking up my beloved's discarded dress which lay beside me, I held it in my arms and started stroking it. The cloth still held in its folds the fragrance of her body and I soon became so overcome with emotion that I lost consciousness for a moment.

"How could I have let myself fall asleep when I was waiting for her spirit to return!" I thought as I became aware of my surroundings again. Opening my eyes, I looked into all four corners of the room. I saw the two candles burning brightly on the table; but, even as I looked at them, their flames began shrinking slowly until they were no larger than beans.

I was horror-struck. My hair stood on end and my whole body was seized with an icy shiver. To stop my trembling, I rubbed my hands together and wiped my forehead, staring steadily at the candles all the time. Suddenly, both candle flames commenced to rise until they were more than a foot high and in danger of setting fire to the paper ceiling, and the light had become so bright that the whole room was lit up. Then, just as suddenly, the flames began shrinking and growing dimmer, until they were as tiny as before.

By this time my heart was pounding and my legs trembling. I wanted to call Chang to come in and look, but remembering Yuen's gentle spirit and retiring nature, I changed my mind, afraid that the presence in the room of a living stranger might distress her. Instead, I began calling her name, and implored her to appear to me. But nothing happened. I remained alone in the silence and dimness. Finally, the candle flames became bright again, but did not rise high as before. Then I went out and told Yu-men what I had seen. He thought me very strong and fearless, not knowing that mine was only the strength and bravery of love.

TRANSLATED BY SHIRLEY M. BLACK

Shen Ts'ung-wen

A Bandit Chief

[Ts'ung-wen tzu-chuan: Yi-ko ta-wang, extracts]

At that time a fellow from my hometown who was in the staff office said to me, "The unit's going to Szechwan and wants a dispatch clerk. Want to go?" He then told me that if I was willing to go I could earn nine dollars a month. If I agreed to go, he would discuss a transfer with the staff officer and later on if I wanted to return to West Hunan I could, it would be no trouble.

When I heard that I could go to Szechwan of course I was thoroughly delighted. It occurred to me that if I had gone with the other unit the last time, by now my corpse would have rotted. The last time I was lucky that I didn't get myself killed and since this life seemed to be an extra one, if a bullet should kill me this time, it wouldn't matter. The commander who was taking the unit to Eastern Szechwan this time was named Chang, and was the very same officer with whom I had failed to come to terms when I tried to join the army two years before in T'aoyüan. Ho Lung was the commander of the guard regiment and in addition there were battalion commanders Ku, Tseng, and Yang. Some of the people who went along may have thought that when they got to Szechwan they could pick up some loot, or take a wife. What I had in mind was neither money nor women. Of course, I was very poor then: a salary of six dollars, less two dollars for rations, left me with only four dollars in hand every month, but even if I had more I wouldn't know how to spend it. When I did get money I really had no way to use it except for playing the big spender and inviting my friends out to eat noodles. And as for women, well, the time for writing amatory poetry *à la* Wang Yen-hung's collection *It Might Rain* was already past, and I no longer felt that women were at all interesting. At the time what I needed seemed to be for my superiors to recognize some of my good points, for I always felt that I had some just waiting to be cultivated, developed, and matured. But there was another reason: I very much wanted to see the Wu Gorge. I had a couple of friends who had learned of the Wu Gorge from a book and then had hiked along the river from Ichang to Chungking. I had heard them talk about the size of the Wu Gorge, its height, its dangers and its marvels, and I was really enchanted. The thing a country fellow thinks about is staking his entire life on something extremely dangerous and then playing it to his heart's content. The garrison area that had been agreed upon with T'ang Tzu-mo, the Szechwan Army commander, was for the Kan Army to cover Yuyang, Lungtan, Pengshui, and Kungtan while the advance guard would go as far as Fuchou. I thought that when we got there it would be very easy to go on to the Wu Gorge.

I had already told the fellow from my hometown that I was willing to go without regard to money or rank, so three days later I set out behind the troops and horses. My duties were those of dispatch clerk. As usual, before we started out, everyone drew a month's pay from the Commissariat, and after I got my nine dollars, having nothing else to do, I bought a pair of dollar-and-twenty-cent silk socks and a half-catty of rock candy. The rest of the money I put in my belt. Since at that time of year the weather was very warm and there was no need for a quilt at night, I gave away my only two quilts in a show of generosity, put my little pack on my back and set out on the road. The possessions in my pack consisted of one old wadded jacket, one old lined jacket, one hand towel, one pair of lined pants, my pair of dollar-and-twenty-cent silk socks, one pair of navy blue wool shoes with leather soles and a pair of white unlined pants. In addition I had some collections of great calligraphy: a six-dollar edition of the *Inscription of the Yün-hui General,* a five-dollar edition of the *Prefaces to the Sages,* a two-dollar edition of the *Orchid Pavilion Preface,* and a five-dollar edition of Yü Shih-nan's *Confucian Temple Inscription.* In addition, I had a collection of Li Shang-yin's poetry. Stuck into the outside of my pack I had a pair of bamboo chopsticks, a toothbrush, and an enameled bowl suspended from a loop of fine metal chain run through a hole drilled in the rim. These were all my possessions. Even now I still find it touching to recall them. . . .

When we crossed the Kweichow-Hunan border we went up a rather steep hill called the Cotton Ridge, ten miles up and twelve down. That hill cost us an entire day, but when we had climbed such a height and looked down from beside a decrepit fortress at the cluster of little hills and the mist, the majestic natural prospect was truly a moving sight. The memory of these mountain peaks and the fortress still fascinates me even a dozen years later. When we were on the Szechwan border I remember we had to pass a rather large market-place: each market day, I was told, five thousand cattle and horses were traded there. We also passed an old temple with some pine trees so big around that even six men could not link hands around them. Within the temple, on the south side, was a White Bone Pagoda. It had an arched roof and was entirely built of stones carved with the Buddha's image and was some forty-five feet in diameter. Inside a round, well-like pit were scattered human bones, some of them wristbones still encased in braided silver bracelets. No one had taken them or even touched them. I heard a monk say that there had been an insurrection of "divinely-protected" rebels, and an entire city had been wiped out. The bones had been collected six months later, and must wait another three years for final cremation.

When our unit got to Eastern Szechwan, although we were still advancing, the command post had to stay in Lungtan temporarily. . . .

Since the place had a small river, naturally I liked to go to the river and sit alone on the high bank and watch the boats come upstream. The trackers with their tow ropes over their backs, bodies bent close to the rocks on the riverbank, the colors, the sounds, the atmosphere, made my heart pound. The scene was beautiful and always made me simultaneously joyful and melancholy. When the trackers had brought the boat to shore they would lie down on the river bank, take a long drink of the flowing water, and then get up and sit down on a rock and wipe the sweat from their arms and chests with their hands; it always touched me profoundly. . . .

When I went out, if I was alone I went to the Dragon Cave or to the river, but if there were more than two of us we often went across the river. Although the Szechwan Army had pulled out of the garrison area, they still had a captain and a small detachment stationed in a temple on the other side of the river. The higher echelons were on good terms, but the soldiers could not help but get into frequent fights and I was afraid to go alone for fear of getting the worst of it, but if there were two of us we could go anywhere without worrying.

All the time we were there I drew nine dollars a month, but if I didn't spend it eating noodles then it was used by my friends. Since I had not had any clothes made, I had only the clothes on my back. One day, since the weather was fine, I had washed my only shirt. Soon after it began to rain. The shirt was not yet dry and my other shirt was being worn by a friend. The messengers had all gone downstairs to eat and I could not walk barechested through the commander's quarters, so I nobly went hungry.

I've said that I knew all the messengers, haven't I? There were twelve of them, but I think the most interesting was a sergeant. This was a bandit, a great chief, a real man. He had killed about two hundred enemies with his two hands and had had seventeen wives. Physically, this great chief was rather small. He had a dark complexion and, except for his bright eyes, you could not tell from his appearance how strong and courageous he was. Years before, on the bank of the river at Chenchou in the dead of winter, someone had said, "Anyone who goes into this water doesn't care for his life." Without a word he stripped naked and splashed into the water just to show them. He swam around in the river, which was about a *li* wide, for almost an hour and when he came up on the shore he walked up to the fellow. "Is this bit of water going to take away a man's life?" Another time, someone said that a man had been playing poker and had his wallet cleaned out by another who had cheated. He said nothing, but soon after he went over and brought back the fellow's money, placed it beside him, and walked away without saying a word. This great chief had been saved once by the commander, so he was no longer playing bandit in the mountains but had become a confidant of the commander who had come up through the ranks. He enjoyed the salary and status of a captain but waited on the commander with the loyalty of a slave.

Since my quarters were right next to those of the great chief, if the two of us did not go out, he would come over to my room to chat. Whatever questions I asked him, he was always able to answer to my complete satisfaction. I studied a strange curriculum with him. From him I learned about such crimes as arson, murder, and rape, and from his rather frank explanations I was able to comprehend the hidden vital consciousness underlying such behavior. From him I learned what evil means and how such crimes, intolerable to society, still nurtured such a strong and violent soul. From his straightforward explanations I learned how strange and confusing are the phenomena produced by those mischances whose stuff is human life. This man before he became a bandit had been a good citizen, fearing trouble and timid before officials. Troops from the outside considered him a bandit who should be summarily executed but he simply fled and later really did become a great chief.

He could sing a little old-style opera, write a little, and could even paint flowers. Whenever he came to my room and grew tired of chatting, he would begin singing and leap up on my table and perform the opera pieces, "Taking the Three Passes" and "Destroying the Four Gates."

One day, seven of us were eating in the adjutant's quarters. Someone said he had heard that the Szechwan Army was holding a strange prisoner in a temple in the city, a famous beauty who had become a bandit chief at eighteen. After her capture the younger officers had all gone mad over her and two junior officers had even killed each other over her. After she was brought to the brigade headquarters, all the officers wanted to have her, but none of them had been able to get at her. On hearing this news I wanted to go and have a look at this girl bandit. Because of my curiosity it seemed that I constantly had to have such fresh scenes to nourish my soul, so as a joke I said that if anyone could take me to see her I would buy him a drink. In a few days, of course, I forgot all about it. One evening, just about twilight, I was alone cleaning my lamp chimney when the great chief suddenly came in and called to me, "Hey brother, let's go someplace and you can see something you've wanted to see."

Before I had a chance to ask him where we were going and what we were going to see, he had dragged me downstairs and out the camp gate.

We crossed the river to a temple where a platoon of Szechwan Army soldiers were stationed. He already seemed to be well acquainted with them for he hailed them and threw them a salute. We entered the temple and went straight to the rear hall and soon entered another courtyard. By a fence we saw a young woman.

The woman was sitting on a bright red rug with her back to us, sewing by a lamp. The great chief walked up to the fence, "Yao-mei, Yao-mei, I brought a little brother to see you!"

The woman turned around but since the lamplight was dim all I could see was a white face and a pair of very large eyes. She looked at me, then stood up, and walked over to us. As she drew near, I was looking at her through the fence, and her appearance really gave me a start! Her face was not what you would consider in any way that of a rare beauty, but her face and figure were in such well-proportioned harmony that she was truly not the ordinary sort. She was still wearing leg-irons, but they seemed to have been well wrapped with cloth so that when she walked there was no sound. After we had chatted through the fence I heard her ask the sergeant, "Brother Liu, what's wrong? Didn't you say something about a way out? Today's the sixteenth."

"I know it's already the sixteenth," the great chief said.

"If you know, that's fine."

"I'm worried. I went to the fortuneteller and he said that the time was not favorable. We can't do it."

The woman mumbled and spat out a "Pah!" then said nothing more. In her expression there seemed to be some resentment. Though I had my face turned aside admiring the lamplit scene, I was carefully attentive to the sergeant's behavior. I saw him face the woman and purse his lips at me and I understood that it would not do for me to stay here too long, so I said I would go back first. The woman wanted me to come back tomorrow so after I had agreed the sergeant saw me to the temple gate. At the temple gate he squeezed my hand as though there were a great many mysteries that he would let me know before long, then he went back inside.

At the time I was surprised that the woman did not seem like a bandit and thought that she must have come to this through some injustice. But I did not forget the other experiences at another time when we exterminated bandits in Huaihua, there are always a number of stupid things done in the army. . . . The night passed and the next morning while eating breakfast the others at the table all said I should buy them a drink, for the female bandit Wang Yao-mei had already been executed, and if I wanted to have a look when I got to the bridge I could see her. One of the men had seen it with his own eyes and said that when the woman was killed she said not a word but sat on her own big red rug with her normal expression and that when her head fell to the ground, her body did not fall over. The news shocked me. I had seen her just last evening and she had wanted me to come back today, how could she have been killed this morning? I finished breakfast and hurried to the bridge. Someone had already put the corpse in a plain wooden coffin and set it by the roadside. All that was left on the ground was a pool of blood and a pile of white ash from some paper money. Looking at the congealed blood on the ground I still did not quite believe it. My mind in a daze, I hurriedly walked back to the office to look for the sergeant. I found him lying on his bunk, but he did not speak. I did not dare question him but returned to my room and began to work. Before long I learned from another messenger the true reason for the incident.

The female bandit should have been decapitated long before, for although she was so elegant, she had a reputation for brutality. Although many of the officers ardently desired her, no one dared approach her and no one dared bail her out. It was all because she had seventy rifles buried somewhere and no one knew where the weapons were hidden. At the market prices then, this number of weapons was worth almost ten thousand dollars, which is no small sum, and for this reason they tried to find a way to trick her out of her guns, so they had detained her and treated her differently from the other prisoners. The sergeant knew of this matter and had got to know the Szechwan Army platoon leader and often went over there. After he got to know the woman he told her that he had sixty guns buried on the Hunan border and wanted to find a way to bail her out so that if together they dug up the guns and went into hiding in the hills they could live on fearlessly there as great chiefs. The woman trusted him and at night in the prison the two of them had been intimate. After this was discovered by the officers and because of it, early the next morning, the woman was dragged out by the soldiers and decapitated.

The soldiers stationed in the temple soon realized what the two of them had done that night in the prison. He had broken the soldier's taboo: it was unfair that what the other officers had been unable to get was in the end achieved by an outsider, for as the saying goes, "Good water does not flow into another's fields." So the platoon fixed bayonets and blocked the gate so that the sergeant couldn't go through. When someone called his name the sergeant understood his situation and, unruffled, he put on his belt and as he took up his two pistols he said, "Brothers, make up your minds. Birds fly everywhere and whoever catches them is the lucky one. If I've offended you today, I hope you'll excuse me. If you want to make a big thing of it and not raise your arms for me to slip under, then don't blame me, for my guns can't tell one man from the other." The soldiers knew that this was no fool and that if they did not let him pass it would cost them a couple of lives. And they were only a company of the Szechwan Army while there were four battalions of the Kan Army; an incident would not turn out well for them. So they cleared a path and let the sergeant pass, a pistol in each hand. He left and Wang Yao-mei was decapitated first thing the next morning.

After the woman was dead, the sergeant lay in his bunk almost a week without saying a word and without eating. No one dared bother him. At last he suddenly got up and carried on as active and unrestrained as before. He came into my room to see me. "Brother, my luck is really bad! Yao-mei died because of me so I wept for seven days, but now it's all right."

At the time he seemed both funny and pitiable. I couldn't very well say anything, but I squeezed his hand and smiled.

I stayed at Lungtan almost half a year.

At the time, since for various reasons the unit could not get to Fuchou, I still wanted to see the Wu Gorge but had not had a chance. Although I had made many good friends since I came here, except for a little calligraphy I had made no progress. Daily life was eating and drinking and watching executions, but the life did not seem capable of offering me sufficient satisfaction. Before long I had an opportunity to return to Hunan so I got a passport to take a small boat back. I figured that going by water I could pass through some famous and dangerous rapids and that I could see some new places. At the time the sergeant had become friends with a launderer and wanted to take the launderer's wife as his concubine. When the commander came out someone had handed him a complaint so there were complications. He told him that this would not do, saying that we were here as guests and such things were very bad for the army's reputation. The sergeant told others, "This is a matter of civilized freedom. If the commander will not permit it, I'll request a long-term leave, leave the army, and go back to my old job." Since he couldn't marry the launderer's wife, he actually did request a leave and the commander granted it immediately. The great chief wanted to travel on the same boat with me, so his name was added to mine on the passport. We checked out the boat and were ready to set out that afternoon. Just as we were finishing breakfast, he told me about what had happened before Wang Yao-mei was killed. Suddenly someone from the Commissariat came to ask him to clear his mess record and he ran downstairs quite happily. In less than a minute the assembly call was sounded downstairs and I heard the Officer of the Day call "Ready!" I was rather perplexed, thinking that it sounded as though someone was to be killed. But who? Were they shooting a deserter? Were they taking care of a local bully? As I heard people shouting, I pushed open the window and looked out. The sergeant was bound and standing in the courtyard. The guard had already assembled and formed in ranks ready to set out, and the Officer of the Day was waiting for instructions. As I watched, the great chief was pushed out.

The great chief's hands were tied behind his back. He hunched up his narrow shoulders and shouted out to the people in the two buildings, "Staff Officer, Adjutant, Chief Clerk, Judge Advocate, I demand justice, I beg the commander's mercy. Don't kill me! I've been with him for many years. I've done nothing wrong. My wife is working for the commander's wife in his home. Do me a good turn, say a kind word for me!"

Everyone looked at each other but did not speak. The commander, casually holding an ivory pipe in his hand, came out of the reception hall and quite genially and elegantly stood under the eaves. He smiled at the higher officers in the two buildings.

"Commander, have mercy. Don't kill me."

"Liu Yün-t'ing," the commander said, "don't say anything to make you lose more face. When a man docs something wrong and it's time for him to die he should die nobly. This is an army regulation. We're guests here. You went to a prison at night and raped a female prisoner. I remembered our good friendship over the years and was willing to overlook it, so I will not bring it up now. But now you are planning to return to your crimes, you are making ready to kidnap a woman of good family and go back home, deserting the army. I've been thinking that to let you go home to do bad things and lead an evil life would only make people hate you, it will be better to kill you and rid the area of an evil. Let's have no more talk. I'll take care of your woman and children. You be a man of more courage."

The great chief heard the commander's verdict and no longer called for justice, but smiled at the men in the two buildings and suddenly became more relaxed. "Fine, Commander. Thank you for looking after me for so many years. Goodbye, brothers." Then after a pause he said, "Commander, you're really a dreamer. Others have offered six thousand to get me to kill you, but I wouldn't do it." The commander seemed not to hear and turned away to order the adjutant to buy a good coffin.

Then the great chief was hustled out the main gate and I never saw him again. That afternoon I boarded the boat. My passport had originally had two names on it, but the great chief's name had been blotted out with red ink. The passport went through many bad rapids with me and five days later when I arrived at Paoching I handed it in to the adjutant for cancellation. As for the talented and uncommon Commander Chang, some three years later in Chenchou in Hunan, he and several orderlies were invited for a drink by a certain T'ien from divisional headquarters. As they entered the Kao-p'ing-erh Gate along with four sedan chair bearers, they were cut down by machine-gun fire even before the welcoming trumpets had stopped sounding. The bodies were casually dumped into a ditch and it was two months later before they were buried. As for the Captain T'ien of divisional headquarters who had assassinated him, it turned out that one year later, in the very same city, a unit commander sent by Yeh K'ai-hsin, the Hunan chairman, using the same ruse of inviting him as a guest, assassinated him in the narrow street in front of the Confucian temple.

TRANSLATED BY WILLIAM L. MACDONALD

Late Ch'ing Lyrics

The romantic mood prevails in the work of the first three poets in this selection: Chiang Shih-ch'üan (1725–85), leading playwright of his time and good friend of Yüan Mei; Tso Fu (1751–1833), who was a provincial governor; and the nineteenth-century lyricist Chiang Ch'un-lin (1818–68). Then the ex-censor Wang P'eng-yün (1848–1904) presages the revolutionaries by sounding the theme of decline of the dynasty and (in his second poem) of literature itself. Of the two poet-revolutionaries, Huang Hsing (1874–1916) was the chief planner of abortive uprisings in five Hunan cities in the year 1904. He became Sun Yatsen's lieutenant after the two met in Japan the following year. Mao Tse-tung was born in 1893 and schooled as a boy in the lyric tradition of Hunan province.

•

Chiang Shih-ch'üan

Tune: "Water Music Prelude"

[*Shui-tiao ko-t'ou*]

MEMORIES ON A JOURNEY BY BOAT

Lovebirds once sang in paradise
Who now like piteous bugs crawl each alone.
A tear for each star of the Milky Way
Trailing east across the sky:
Ten years we shared the bridal chamber,
Nine more your husband wandered far
So long, my hair forgets the feel of the comb.
Sorrow and sickness fill the years
Pains of parting all my thoughts.

In spring the silkworm spins its heartache
Summer the wildgoose longs to fly
Autumn the cricket grieves.
When shall I see you, laughing with your maids,
A stir of bright gems in the spring breeze?
News comes that you have grown so thin
Under the hardships I have brought you
—Yet never a change of heart.
Tonight across a thousand miles
For each alike the lamp glows red.

Tso Fu

Tune: "Wave-washed Sand"

[Lang-t'ao sha]

[Traveling in Szechuan, I picked a sprig of peach blossom by the Ts'ao Creek Posting-station. When the petals fell a few days later I carefully wrapped one and committed it to the Fu River to the accompaniment of this farewell song.]

Soft splash of oar in gentle waters
Sweet-smelling islets newly green
A flowering peach grove hides the painted lodge.
The soul of the spring hills is in this petal
Summoned to my lonely boat.

While dreams of home persist
Why cosset idle sorrows?
Chungchou once passed, Fuchou is still to come.
The Pa River will take you to the sea
—Just don't look back.

Tune: "South Bank"

[*Nan-p'u*]

NIGHT VISIT TO THE LUTE SONG PAVILION[1]

On Hsün-yang River
As the third watch sounds
The swelling tide brings frost and moon at once.
Across from me the line of the bank wavers,
Fishermen's lanterns flicker like stars
And somewhere music starts,
Chords of a lute
By the empty pavilion, relic of a thousand years.
Does another weary traveler,
Another trader's neglected wife
Come to evoke old ghosts?

I have my boat rowed nearer,
Prowl the rail
In search of those sad souls.
I, wanderer, homeless as old Chang Chien,
Threading a thousand miles of river towns,
Aging, sad like that bygone poet,
Moved like him
By these reed flowers and maple leaves.
But the notes of the lute break off
And fish and dragon lie silent, never roused.

---

[1] One of Po Chü-yi's most famous poems is a long ballad which describes his
encounter, on a moonlit river, with a trader's wife who sings to her lute a lament
for her bygone days of glory as a courtesan in the capital. The theme became
popular with Yüan and later dramatists.

Chiang Ch'un-lin

Tune: "Willow-tips Green

[*Liu-shao ch'ing*]

Garden of idleness:
The spring festival gone by
Wine fumes still hover over petaled earth,
The rowan flowers
As cherry-apple fades
Easing in the dusk.

With afterglow an east wind rises,
Lean where you may, the red rail never grows warm.
Specks of spring sadness
Like the clouds of spring
No sooner blow away than new ones form.

Tune: "The Beautiful Lady Yü"

[*Yü mei-jen*]

The crystal curtain of the mist rolls back,
A still night, cool breath of the trees.
Sickness has changed me: like the shedding *wu-t'ung*
In every stem of every leaf I fear the fall wind.

The Milky Way flows on: will wars never cease?
Swordpoints flourish and shatter like cold stars.
The Southern Dipper guides to the far capital
And gazing I forget the dew that soaks me here at the sky's
    edge.

Tune: "Wave-washed Sand"

[*Lang-t'ao sha*]

>Clouds press where the balustrade stands vacant,
>The new green fails among the far hills,
>Turn by turn come threads of rain, scraps of floss on the
>   wind.
>The festival of the graves is over
>But spring stays chill.
>
>If the blossom comes unbidden
>It can fade and fall the same.
>Time once again for hovering butterflies to pair.
>When she wakes tomorrow in her lacquered chamber
>Let her not raise the blind.

Tune: "Partridge Sky"

[*Che-ku t'ien*]

>The creek purls lightly past the willow fringe,
>By the lacquered window she wakes to the doves' calling.
>The screen's vision of emerald hills draws down her brows,
>The mirror ripples to her glance, but autumn waits at her
>   temples.
>
>Try the brush of jade,
>Sip the jasper cup,
>Wake to compose your griefs in verse, stop when the wine
>   takes hold.
>Tomorrow when the blossoms fall and the last wild goose flies
>Make your chamber fast against the chill spring rain.

Wang P'eng-yün

Tune: "The Charms of Nien-nu."

[*Nien-nu chiao*]

A VIEW OF THE MING TOMBS FROM THE TOPMOST
LEVEL OF THE YANG TERRACE

From this height the gaze wanders
Over the intricate embroidery
Of a garment seamed with rivers.
Trees shade the Ming Tombs, the Thirteen Emperors
On the Hill of Heaven's Span, a low mound from here.
An instant of cataclysm,
Gales from the circling ranges
Shred the last vestige of the royal aura.
The sea wave glints like golden corn
And ancient pines roar with the voice of dragons.

Only the wild-sown wastes spread for ever
And the White Wolf River thunders
Down the ages against the walls of cities.
Village elders see the world is changing
And urge their mountain spirits to stand guard.
Over the forest's flattened roof
Clouds jumble and shift.
I'd sprinkle wine, but none is left.
I look back, leaving the hills:
One peak still is lit by the setting sun.

Tune: "The Fish Poacher"

[*Mo yü tzu*]

IN REPLY TO A POEM FROM TZ'U-SHAN, THANKING ME FOR
THE GIFT OF SUNG AND YÜAN LYRICS I HAD HAD PRINTED

Now that the lyric voice wavers in wind-blown dust
Who is to speak the sorrows of his heart?
Ten years of carving, seeking from each new block
The truest music of the string unswept,
Only to sigh now
Finding my griefs in tune
With every beat that leaves the ivory fret!
I sigh for the men of old
Pour wine in honor of the noble dead:
Does any spirit rhymester
Understand my heartbreak?

The craft of letters
Furnishes kindling, covers jars:
True bell or tinkling cymbal, who can tell?
Tu Fu, who lifelong courted the perfect phrase
—Did his verse help him, though it made men marvel?
Take what you find here,
See if an odd page, a forgotten tune
Still has the power to engage your mind.
My toiling over
I'll drink myself merry, climb the Golden Terrace,
Thrash out a wild song from my lute
And let the storm rage at will.

Huang Hsing

Tune: "Mud by the Fourth Gate"

[*Ssu-men ni*]

To each true hero his hero's fame.
Why fear the makeshift's overreaching—
For him the shaft that pierces twice.
Brief, in our life span, the years of splendor:
Who shall disdain the youth full-grown?
Like steel a hundred times refined
Train up the sages of our day;
Our general with arrows three
Shall restore their rights and powers.
But dignify the beast, the serpent
And nought is won but a fresh striving for sway.

Tune: "The Oil-gourd"

[*Yu hu-lu*]

A hundred thousand razor-edged swords, a lightning flash
In one brief instant striking on Hopei.
When the sun has set
And the night breeze clears the mists
No beacon fires burn now in China
But the length of the Yellow River runs blood.
The felt tents scattered like foxes,
Dead leaves spinning in the west wind.
Before us the grand old country, peerless through the centu-
ries,
And we the first whip-crack, hot from our thousand-league
gallop.
This is no common deadlock of snipe and oyster
—Let no fisherman lick his lips.[2]

---

[2] Common metaphor for a struggle resulting in a stalemate which allows
a third party to reap the benefit.

Mao Tse-tung

Tune: "Spring Floods the Garden"

[*Ch'in yüan ch'un*]

SNOW

Northern grandeur:
Sealed with ice a thousand *li*,
Myriad more of swirling snow.
Within the Great Wall and beyond
Vast, vast the land.
The Yellow River, reach after reach
Stilled in its onward rush.
Silver snakes the writhing hills
Mammoths molded of wax the high plateaus
Striving to match the height of Heaven's lord.
And in clear sun
The whiteness binds a crimson gown
Ever more enchanting.

All these appealing charms of hill and stream
Made jealous suitors out of countless heroes.
But the First Emperor or Wu of the Han
Could boast of few refinements,
The founders of T'ang or Sung
Lacked elegance,
And one who lorded it across an age,
Genghis Khan,
Had no art but to draw his bow at eagles.
All went their way:
The search for true nobility
Waits on our time.

Tune: "Water Music Prelude"

[*Shui-tiao ko-t'ou*]

SWIMMING[1]

After a drink from Changsha
Taste the fish of Wuchang.
Rule a bar across river's length,
Stretch sight with skies of Ch'u,
Preferring beat of wind and wave
To aimless stroll in idle court.
This day a prize of leisure.
The Master's words at stream-side:
"Ever thus it flows."

Wind-sway of masts
Repose of Tortoise and Snake
And a great plan begun:
A single span to soar
North-south thoroughfare over nature's moat.
Then, west, erect new cliffs of stone
To block the rains of Witch's Range:
Calm lake born in gorge.
If still the goddess flourishes
What shocks from a changing world!

TRANSLATED BY CYRIL BIRCH

---

[1] Mao swam the Yangtze in the summer of 1956, at the age of sixty-three. In this poem commemorating the event he incorporated references to ancient legend, folk song, and classical poetry, to Confucius, to local landmarks (the hills "Tortoise" and "Snake"), and to the construction feats of his young regime, the Yangtze Bridge, and a new dam.

Republican Period

1911-

The Modern Short Story

The virtual apotheosis of Lu Hsün (Chou Shu-jen, 1881–1936) by Communist critics only underlines his status as the undoubted "father of modern Chinese literature." His story, "A Madman's Diary," when it appeared in 1918 marked a sharp break with the traditional tale. The language was refined from current speech and freed from the old clichés whether classical or colloquial. The form was a borrowing from the West, actually in this case from Gogol's story of the same title, though the content was totally original. Above all, the tone was that of bitter indictment of contemporary society.

Lu Hsün's longest work, "The True Story of Ah Q," does not reach novel length. His total output of stories was quite small; the second half of his creative career he devoted to the production of short essays, "random impressions." "Benediction" is characteristic in its scrupulously unsentimental clarity of observation of the world of peasant misery. Characteristic also (and reminiscent of the great nineteenth-century Russians) is the sense of futility which oppresses the author when as a member of the intelligentsia he contemplates the chasm between this peasant world and his own.

Mao Tun (Shen Yen-ping, b. 1896) has also won the high regard of Communist critics, and was made Minister of Culture in the People's Republic. He has been a much more prolific writer of fiction. His work records with documentary thoroughness the life of the student revolutionary, the plight of the native industrialist, the effects of the De-

pression (in "Spring Silkworms") on a silk-producing village near Shanghai, and similar social and economic themes from the world between the wars. Since 1949 he has limited himself to fiction criticism and the encouragement of young writers.

●

Lu Hsün

Benediction

[Chu fu]

I

The end of the year according to the lunar calendar is, after all, the right time for a year to end. A strange almost-new-year sort of atmosphere seems to overlay everything; pale grey clouds at evening, against which flash the hot little fires of crackers giving a thunderous boost to the kitchen god's ascent into Heaven. And as one draws into it the scene grows noisier, and scattered on the air is the sting of gunpowder.

On such a night I return to Luchen—my "home town" as I call it, but in reality I have no home there at all. I stay with Lu Ssu Lao-yeh, a relative one generation older than myself, a fellow who ought to be called "Fourth Uncle," according to the Chinese family way of reckoning. He holds the degree of *chien-sheng*, and talks all the time about the old virtues and the old ethics.

I find him not much changed; a little aged of course, but still without a whisker. We exchange salutations. After the "How are you?" he tells me I've grown fat. With that done, he at once commences a tirade against the "new party." But I know that the phrase to him still means poor old K'ang Yu-wei, and not myself. We have at any rate nothing in common, and before long I am left alone in the study.

Next day I get up very late, and after lunch go out to call on some relatives and friends. The day after is the same, and the day after that. None of them has changed much, each is a little older, and everywhere they are busily preparing for New Year prayers-of-blessing. It is a great thing in Luchen: every one exerts himself to show reverence, exhausts himself in performing rites, and falls down before the god of benediction to ask favors for the year ahead. There is much chicken-killing,

303

geese-slaughtering, and pork-buying; women go round with their arms raw and red from soaking in hot water, preparing such fowl. When they are thoroughly cooked they are placed on the altar, with chopsticks punched into them at all angles, and offered up as sacrifices at the sixth watch. Incense sticks and red candles are lighted, and the men (no women allowed) make obeisance and piously invite the blessing-spirits to eat away. And after this, of course, the firecrackers.

Every year it is that way, and the same in every home—except those of the miserable poor who cannot buy either sacrifices or candles or firecrackers—and this year is like any other. The sky is dark and gloomy, and in the afternoon snow falls—flakes like plum blossoms darting and dancing across a screen of smoke and bustle, and making everything more confused. By the time I return home the roof tiles are already washed white, and inside my room seems brighter. The reflection from the snow also touches up the large crimson character, "longevity," which hangs on a board against the wall. It is said to be the work of the legendary Ch'en T'uan. One of the scrolls has fallen down and is rolled up loosely and lying on the long table, but the other still admonishes me: "Understand deeply the reason of things, be moderate, and be gentle in heart and manner." On the desk under the window are incomplete volumes of the *K'ang Hsi Dictionary*, a set of *Recent Thoughts*, with collected commentaries, and the *Four Books*. How depressing!

I decide to return tomorrow, at the very latest, to the city.

The incident with Hsiang-lin Sao also has very much disturbed me. This afternoon I went to the eastern end of the town to visit a friend, and while returning I encountered her at the edge of the canal. The look in her staring eyes showed clearly enough that she was coming after me, so I waited. Although other folk I used to know in Luchen have apparently changed little, Hsiang-lin Sao was no longer the same. Her hair was all white, her face was alarmingly lean, hollow, and burnt a dark yellow. She looked completely exhausted, not at all like a woman not yet forty, but like a wooden thing with an expression of tragic sadness carved into it. Only the movement of her lusterless eyes showed that she still lived. In one hand she carried a bamboo basket: inside it was an empty broken bowl; and she held herself up by leaning on a bamboo pole. She had apparently become a beggar.

I stood waiting to be asked for money.

"So—you've come back?"

"Yes."

"That's good—and very timely. Tell me, you are a scholar, a man who has seen the world, a man of knowledge and experience"—her faded eyes very faintly glowed—"tell me, I just want to ask you one thing."

I could not, in ten thousand tries, have guessed what she would ask. I waited, saying nothing.

She moved nearer, lowered her voice, and spoke with great secrecy and earnestness.

"It is this: after a person dies is there indeed such a thing as the *soul*?"

Involuntarily I shuddered. Her eyes stuck into me like thorns. Here was a fine thing! I felt more embarrassed than a schoolboy given a surprise examination, with the teacher standing right beside him. Whether there was such a thing as the "soul" had never bothered me, and I had speculated little about it. How could I reply? In that brief moment I remembered that many people in Luchen believed in some kind of spirits, and probably she did, too. Perhaps I should say it was rather doubtful—but no, it was better to let her go on hoping. Why should I burden a person obviously on the "last road" with even more pain? Better for her sake to say yes.

"Perhaps," I stammered. "Yes, I suppose there is."

"Then there is also a *Hell*?"

"Ah—Hell?" She had trapped me, and I could only continue placatingly, "Hell? Well, to be logical, I dare say there ought to be. But, then, again—there may not be. What does it matter?"

"Then in this Hell do all the deceased members of a family come together again, face to face?"

"H'mm? Seeing face to face, eh?" I felt like a fool. Whatever knowledge I possessed, whatever mental dexterity, was utterly useless; here I had been confounded by three simple questions. I made up my mind to extricate myself from the mess, and wanted to repudiate everything I had said. But somehow I could not do so in the gaze of her intensely earnest and tragic eyes.

"That is to say . . . in fact, I cannot definitely say. Whether there is a soul or not in the end I am in no position to deny or affirm."

With that she did not persist, and taking advantage of her silence I strode away with long steps and hastened back to Fourth Uncle's home, feeling very depressed. I could not help thinking that perhaps my replies would have an evil effect on her. No doubt her loneliness and distress had become all the more unbearable at this time, when every one else seemed to be praying for benediction—but perhaps there was something else on her mind. Perhaps something that had recently happened to her. If so, then my answers might be responsible . . . for what? I soon laughed about the whole thing, and at my absurd habit of exaggerating the importance of casual happenings. Educators unquestionably would pronounce me mentally unbalanced. Hadn't I, after all, made it clear that all I could say was, "Cannot definitely say?" Even should all my replies be refuted, even if something happened to the woman, it could in no way concern me.

"Cannot definitely say" is a very convenient phrase. Bold and reckless youths often venture so far as to offer a positive opinion on critical questions for others, but responsible people, like officials and doctors, have to choose their words carefully, for if events belie their opinion then it becomes a serious affair. It is much more advisable to say, "Cannot definitely say"; obviously, it solves everything. This encounter with the woman mendicant impresses upon me the importance of that practice, for even in such cases the deepest wisdom lies in ambiguity.

Nevertheless, I continue to feel troubled, and when the night is gone I wake up with the incident still on my mind. It is like an unlucky presentiment of a movement of fate. Outside the day is still gloomy, with flurrying snow, and in the dull study my uneasiness gradually increases. Certainly I must go back to the city tomorrow. . . . To be sure, there is still unsampled the celebrated pure-cooked fish-fins at Fu Hsing Lou—excellent eating and very cheap at only a dollar a big plate. Has the price by now increased? Although many of my boyhood friends have melted away like clouds in the sky, there must remain, at least, the incomparable fish-fins of Luchen, and these I must eat, even though I eat alone. . . . All the same, I am returning tomorrow. . . .

Because I have so often seen things happen exactly as I predicted —but hoped against, and tried to believe improbable—so I am not unprepared for this occasion to provide no exception. Towards evening some of the family gather in an inner room, and from fragments of their talk I gather they are discussing some event with no little annoyance. Presently all the voices cease except one, that of Fourth

Uncle, who thunders out above the thud of his own pacing feet: "Not a day earlier nor a day later, but just at this season she decides upon it. From this alone we can see that she belongs to a species utterly devoid of human sense!"

My curiosity is soon followed by a vague discomfort, as if these words have some special meaning for me. I go out and look into the room, but every one has vanished. Suppressing my increasing impatience, I wait till the servant comes to fill my teapot with hot water. Not until then am I able to confirm my suspicions.

"Who was it Fourth Uncle was blowing up about a while ago?"

"Who but Hsiang-lin Sao?" he replies in the brief and positive manner of our language.

"What has happened to her?" I demand in an anxious voice.

"Aged."

"Dead?" My heart twinges and seems to jump back; my face burns. But he doesn't notice my emotion at all, doesn't even lift his head, so that I control myself to the end of further questioning.

"When did she die, then?"

"When? Last night—or possibly today. I cannot definitely say."

"What did she die of?"

"What did she die of? Could it indeed be anything else but poverty?" His words are absolutely colorless, and without even looking at me he goes out.

My terror at first is great, but I reason that this is a thing which was bound to happen very soon, and it is merely an accident that I even know about it. I further reassure my conscience by recalling my noncommittal "Cannot definitely say," and the servant's report that it was simply a case of "death by poverty." Still, now and then I feel a prick of guilt, I don't know exactly why, and when I sit down beside dignified old Fourth Uncle I am continually thinking of opening a discussion about Hsiang-lin Sao. But how to do it? He still lives in a world of religious interdicts, and at this time of year these are like an impenetrable forest. You cannot, of course, mention anything connected with death, illness, crime, and so on, unless it is absolutely imperative. Even then, such references must be disguised in a queer riddle-language in order not to offend the hovering ancestral spirits. I torture my brain to remember the necessary formula, but, alas, I cannot recall the right phrases, and at length have to give it up.

Fourth Uncle throughout the meal wears an austere look on his

face. At last I suspect that he regards me also as "belonging to a species utterly devoid of human sense," since "neither a day earlier, nor a
day later, but just at this season" I have put in an appearance. To
loosen his heart and save him further anxiety I tell him that I have determined to return tomorrow. He doesn't urge me to stay very enthusiastically, and I conclude that my surmise was correct. And thus in a
cheerless mood I finish my meal.

The short day is ended, the curtain of snow dropping over it earlier than usual even in this month, and the black night falls like a
shroud over the whole town. People still busy themselves under the
lamplight, but just beyond my window there is the quiet of death.
Snow lies like a down mattress over the earth, and the still falling
flakes make a faint *suh-suh* sound that adds to the intense loneliness
and the unbearable melancholy. Sitting alone under the yellow rays of
the rape-oil lamp, my mind goes back again to that blown-out flicker,
Hsiang-lin Sao.

This woman, who once stood among us in this house, thrown now,
like an old toy discarded by a child, on to the dust heap. For those who
find the world amusing, for the kind for whom she is created, no doubt
if they think about her at all, it is simply to wonder why the devil she
should so long have had the effrontery to continue to exist. Well, she
has obliged them by disappearing at last, swept away thoroughly by
the demon Wu-ch'ang, and a very tidy job. I don't know whether
there is such a thing as the "soul" that lives on after death, but it
would be a great improvement if people like Hsiang-lin Sao were
never born, would it not? Then nobody would be troubled, neither the
despised nor those who despise them.

Listening to the *suh-suh* of the leafy autumnal snow I go on mus-
ing, and gradually find some comfort in my reflections. It is like
putting together an intricate puzzle, but in the end the incidents of her
life fit together into a single whole.

II

Hsiang-lin Sao was not a native of Luchen. She arrived in early winter
one year with Old Woman Wei, who bargained in the labor of others.
Fourth Uncle had decided to hire a new servant, and Hsiang-lin Sao
was Old Woman Wei's candidate for the job.

She wore a white scarf wrapped round her head, a blue jacket, a pale green vest, and a black skirt. She was perhaps twenty-six or twenty-seven, still quite young and rather pretty, with ruddy cheeks and a bronzed face. Old Woman Wei said that she was a neighbor of her mother's. Her husband had died, she explained, and so she had to seek work outside.

Fourth Uncle wrinkled up his brow, and his wife, looking at him, knew what he meant. He didn't like hiring a widow. But Fourth Aunt scrutinized her carefully, noting that her hands and feet looked strong and capable, and that she had honest, direct eyes. She impressed her as a woman who would be content with her lot, and not likely to complain about hard work; and so in spite of her husband's wrinkled brow Fourth Aunt agreed to give her a trial. For three days she worked as if leisure of any kind bored her; she proved very energetic and as strong as a man. Fourth Aunt then definitely hired her, the wage being five hundred cash per month.

Everybody called her simply Hsiang-lin Sao, without asking for her surname. Old Woman Wei was, however, a native of Wei Family Mountain, and since she claimed that Hsiang-lin Sao came from that village no doubt her surname also was Wei. Like most mountaineers, she talked little, and only answered others' questions in monosyllables, and so it took more than ten days to pry out of her the bare facts that there was still a severe mother-in-law in her home; that her young brother-in-law cut wood for a living; that she had lost her husband, ten years her junior, the previous spring; and that he also had lived by cutting firewood. This was about all people could get out of her.

Day followed day, and Hsiang-lin Sao's work was just as regular. She never slackened, she never complained about the food, she never seemed to tire. People agreed that Old Lord Lu Ssu had found a worthy worker, quick and diligent, more so in fact than a man. Even at New Year she did all the sweeping, dusting, washing, and other household duties, besides preparing geese and chickens and all the sacrifices, without any other help. She seemed to thrive on it. Her skin became whiter, and she fattened a little.

New Year had just passed when one day she came hurrying up from the canal, where she had been washing rice. She was much agitated. She said she had seen, on the opposite bank, a man who looked very much like her late husband's first cousin, and she was afraid he had come to take her away. Fourth Aunt was alarmed and suspicious. Why should he be coming for her? Asked for details, Hsiang-lin Sao could give none. Fourth Uncle, when he heard the story, wrinkled his brow and announced: "This is very bad. It looks as though she has run away, instead of being ordered."

And, as it turned out, he was correct. She was a runaway widow.

Some ten days later, when everybody was gradually forgetting the incident, Old Woman Wei suddenly appeared, accompanied by a woman who, she claimed, was Hsiang-lin Sao's mother-in-law. The latter seemed not at all like a tongue-bound mountaineer, but knew how to talk, and after a few courtesy words got to the subject of her business at once. She said she had come to take her daughter-in-law back home. It was spring, there was much to be done at home, and in the house at present were none but the very old and the very young. Hsiang-lin Sao was needed.

"Since it is her own mother-in-law who requests it, how can we deny the justice of it?" said Fourth Uncle.

Hsiang-lin Sao's wage, therefore, was figured out. It was discovered that altogether one thousand seven hundred and fifty cash were due. She had let the sum accumulate with her master, not taking out even a single cash for use. Without any more words, this amount was handed over to the mother-in-law, although Hsiang-lin Sao was not present. The woman also took Hsiang-lin Sao's clothes, thanked Fourth Uncle and left. It was then past noon. . . .

"*Ai-ya!* The rice? Didn't Hsiang-lin Sao go out to scour the rice?"

Fourth Aunt, some time later, cried out this question in a startled way. She had forgotten all about Hsiang-lin Sao until her hunger reminded her of rice, and the rice reminded her of the former servant.

Everybody scattered and began searching for the rice basket. Fourth Aunt herself went first to the kitchen, next to the front hall, and then into the bedroom, but she didn't see a shadow of the object of her search. Fourth Uncle wandered outside, but he saw nothing of it either till he came near the canal. There, upright on the bank, with a cabbage near by, lay the missing basket.

Apparently not until then had anyone thought to inquire in what manner Hsiang-lin Sao had departed with her mother-in-law. Now eyewitnesses appeared who reported that early in the morning a white-canopied boat anchored in the canal, and lay there idly for some time. The awning hid the occupants, and no one knew who was in it. Presently Hsiang-lin Sao came to the bank, and just as she was about to kneel down for water two men quickly jumped out, grabbed her,

and forcibly put her inside the boat. They seemed to be mountain people, but they certainly took her against her will; she cried and shouted
for help several times. Afterwards she was hushed up, evidently with
some kind of gag. Nothing more happened until the arrival of two
women, one of whom was Old Woman Wei. Nobody saw very clearly
what had happened to Hsiang-lin Sao, but those who peered in declared that she seemed to have been bound and thrown on the deck of
the cabin.

"Outrageous!" exclaimed Fourth Uncle. On reflection, however,
he simply ended impotently, "But after all. . . ."

Fourth Aunt herself had to prepare the food that day, and her son
Ah Niu made the fire.

In the afternoon Old Woman Wei reappeared.

"Outrageous!" Fourth Uncle greeted her.

"What is this? How wonderful! You have honored us once more
with your presence!" Fourth Aunt, washing dishes, angrily shouted at
the old bargain-maker. "You yourself recommend her to us, then you
come with companions to abduct her from the household. This affair is
a veritable volcanic eruption. How do you suppose it will look to outsiders? Are you playing a joke at our expense, or what is it?"

"*Ai-ya! Ai-ya!* I have surely been fooled and tricked. I came here
to explain to you. Now how was I to know she was a rebel? She came
to me, begged me to get her work, and I took her for genuine. Who
would have known that she was doing it behind her mother-in-law's
back, without in fact even asking for permission? I'm unable to look in
your face, my lord and my lady. It's all my fault, the fault of a careless
old fool. I can't look you in the face.

". . . Fortunately, your home is generous and forgiving, and will
not punish insignificant people like myself too strictly, eh? And next
time the person I recommend must be doubly good to make up for this
sin. . . ."

"But—" interjected Fourth Uncle, who, however, could get no
further.

And so the affair of Hsiang-lin Sao came to an end, and indeed she
herself would have been entirely forgotten were it not that Fourth
Aunt had such difficulty with subsequent servants. They were too lazy,
or they were gluttonous, and in extreme cases they were both lazy and
gluttonous, and in truth were totally undesirable. In her distress,
Fourth Aunt always mentioned the exemplary Hsiang-lin Sao. "I won-

der how she is living," she would say, inwardly wishing that some misfortune would oblige her to return to work. By the time the next New Year rolled round, however, she had given up hope of ever seeing her again.

Towards the end of the holidays Old Woman Wei called one day to kowtow and offer felicitations. She had already drunk herself into semi-intoxication, and was in a garrulous mood. She explained that because of a visit to her mother's home in Wei Village, where she had stayed for several days, she was late this year in paying her courtesy calls. During the course of the conversation their talk naturally touched upon Hsiang-lin Sao.

"Her?" the old woman cried shrilly and with alcoholic enthusiasm. "There's a lucky woman! You know, when her mother-in-law came after her here she had at that time already been promised to a certain Ho Lao-liu, of Ho Village. After staying in her home only a few days she was loaded again into the Flowery Sedan Chair and borne away!"

"*Ai-ya*, what a mother!" Fourth Aunt exclaimed.

"*Ai-ya*, my lady! You speak from behind a lofty door. We mountaineers, of the small-doored families, for us what does it matter? You see, she had a young brother-in-law, and he had to be married. If Hsiang-lin Sao was not married off first, where would the family get money enough for the brother-in-law's presents to his betrothed? So you understand the mother-in-law is by no means a stupid woman, but keen and calculating. Moreover, she married the daughter-in-law to an inner mountain dweller. Why? Don't you see? Marrying her to a local man, she would have got only a small betrothal gift, but, since few women want to marry deep into the mountains, the price is higher. Hence the husband actually paid eighty thousand cash for Hsiang-lin Sao! Now the son of the family has also been married, and he gave his bride presents costing but five thousand cash. After deducting the cost of the wedding there still remained over ten thousand cash profit. Is she clever or not? Good figuring, eh?"

"And Hsiang-lin Sao—she obeyed all right?"

"Well, it wasn't a question of obedience. Anybody in such a situation has to make a protest, of course. They simply tie her up, lift her into the Flowery Sedan Chair, bear her away to the groom's home, forcibly put the Flowery Hat on her head, forcibly make her kowtow in the ancestral hall, forcibly 'lock her up' with the man—and the thing is done."

"*Ai-ya!*"

"But Hsiang-lin Sao was unusually rebellious. I heard people say that she made a terrific struggle. In fact, it was said that she was different from most women, probably because she had worked in your home—the home of a scholar. My lady, I have seen much in these years. Among widows who remarry I have seen the kind who cry and shout. I have seen those who threaten suicide. There is even the kind who, after being taken to the groom's home, refuse to make the kowtow to Heaven and Earth, and even go so far as to smash the Flowery Candles used to light the bridal chamber! But Hsiang-lin Sao was like none of those.

"From the beginning she fought like a tigress. She screamed and she cursed, and by the time she reached Ho Village her throat was so raw that she had almost lost her voice. She had to be dragged out of the sedan chair. It took two men to get her into the ancestral hall, and still she would not kowtow. Only for one moment they carelessly loosened their grip on her, and *ai-ya!* by Buddha's name! she knocked her head a sound whack on the incense altar, and cut a deep gash from which blood spurted out thickly! They used two handfuls of incense ash on the wound, and bound it up with two thicknesses of red cloth, and still it bled. Actually, she struggled till the very last, when they locked her with her husband in the bridal room, and even then she cursed! This was indeed a *protest. Ai-ya*, it really was!"

She shook her gnarled head, bent her gaze on the floor, and was silent.

"How was it afterwards?"

"They say she did not get up the first day, nor the second."

"Afterwards?"

"After that? Oh, she finally got up. At the end of the year she bore him a child, a boy. While I was at my mother's home I saw some people who had returned from Ho Village, and they said they had seen her. Mother and son were both fat. Above their heads was fortunately no mother-in-law. Her husband, it seems, is strong and a good worker. He owns his own house. *Ai-ya*, she is a lucky one indeed."

From that time on Fourth Aunt gave up any thought of Hsiang-lin Sao's excellent work, or at any rate she ceased to mention her name.

III

In the autumn, two years after Old Woman Wei had brought news of Hsiang-lin Sao's extraordinary good luck, our old servant stood once more in person before the hall of Fourth Uncle's home. On the table she laid a round chestnut-shaped basket and a small bedding-roll. She still wore a white scarf on her head, black skirt, blue jacket, and "moon-white" vest. Her complexion was about the same, except that her cheeks had lost all their color. Traces of tears lay at the corners of her eyes, from which all the old brightness and luster seemed washed away. Moreover, with her once more appeared Old Woman Wei, wearing on her face an expression of commiseration. She babbled to Fourth Aunt: "So it is truly said, 'Heaven holds many an unpredictable wind and cloud.' Her husband was a strong and healthy man. Who would have guessed that at a green age he would be cut down by fever? He had actually recovered from the illness, but ate a bowl of cold rice, and it attacked him again. Fortunately she had the son. By cutting wood, plucking tea-leaves, raising silkworms—and she is skilled at each of these jobs—she could make a living. Could anyone have predicted that the child itself would be carried off by a wolf? A fact! By a wolf!

"It was already late spring, long after the time when anyone fears a wolf. Who could have anticipated this one's boldness? *Ai-ya!* And now she is left only her own bare body. Her late husband's elder brother-in-law took possession of the house, and everything in it, and he drove her out without a penny. She is, in fact, in the 'no-road no-destination' predicament, and can but return to beg you to take her in once more. She no longer has any connections whatever. Knowing you want to change servants, I brought her along. Since she already knows your ways, it's certain she'll be more satisfactory than a raw hand."

"I was truly stupid, truly," said Hsiang-lin Sao in a piteous voice, and lifting up her faded eyes for a moment. "I only knew that when the snow lies on the mountains the wild animals will sometimes venture into the valleys and will even come into the villages in search of food. I did not know that they could be so fierce long after the coming of spring. I got up early one morning, took a small basket of beans, and told little Ah Mao to sit in the doorway and string the beans. He was very bright, and he was obedient. He always listened to every word, and this morning he did so, and I left him in the doorway. I myself went behind the house to chop kindling and to scour rice. I had just put the rice in the boiler and was ready to cook the beans, so I called to Ah Mao. He didn't answer. I went round to the door, but there was no Ah Mao; only beans scattered on the ground. He never wandered to play, but I hurried to each door to ask for him. Nobody had seen him. I was terror-stricken! I begged people to help me hunt for him. All the morning and into the afternoon we moved back and forth, looking into every corner. Finally we found one of his little shoes hanging on a thorn bush. From that moment every one said that he had been seized by a wolf, but I would not believe it. After a little while, going farther into the mountains, we . . . found . . . him. Lying in a grassy lair was his body, with the five organs missing. But the bean basket was still tightly clutched in his little hand." Here she broke down, and could only make incoherent sounds, without stringing a sentence together.

Fourth Aunt had at first hesitated, but after hearing this story her eyes reddened, and she instantly told the widow to take her things to the servants' quarters. Old Woman Wei sighed with relief, as if she had just put down a heavy bundle. Hsiang-lin Sao quieted somewhat, and without waiting for a second invitation she took her bedding-roll into the familiar room.

Thus she once more became a worker in Luchen, and everybody still called her Hsiang-lin Sao, after her first husband.

But she was no longer the same woman. After a few days her mistress and master noticed that she was heavy of hand and foot, that she was listless at her work, that her memory was bad, and over her corpselike face all day there never crossed the shadow of a smile. One could tell by Fourth Aunt's tone of voice that she was already dissatisfied, and with Fourth Uncle it was the same. He had, as usual, wrinkled his brow in disapproval when she had first arrived, but since they had been having endless difficulties with servants he had raised no serious objection to the reemployment of Hsiang-lin Sao. Now, however, he informed Fourth Aunt, that, though the woman's case seemed indeed very lamentable, and it was permissible because of that to give her work, still she was obviously out of tune with Heaven and Earth. She must not, therefore, be allowed to pollute precious vessels with her soiled hands, and especially on ceremonial occasions Fourth Aunt herself must prepare all food. Otherwise the ancestral spirits would be offended and, likely as not, refuse to touch a crumb.

These ancestral sacrifices were, in fact, the most important affairs in Fourth Uncle's home, for he still rigidly adhered to the old beliefs. Formerly they had been busy times for Hsiang-lin Sao also, and so the next time the altar was placed in the center of the hall and covered with a fine cloth she began to arrange the wine cups and bowls and chopsticks on it exactly as before.

"Hsiang-lin Sao," Fourth Aunt cried, rushing in, "never mind that. I'll fix the things."

Puzzled, she withdrew and proceeded to take out the candlesticks.

"Never mind that, either. I'll get the candlesticks," Fourth Aunt said again.

Hsiang-lin Sao walked about several times in a rather dazed manner, and ended up by finding nothing to do, for Fourth Aunt was always ahead of her. She went away filled with suspicion. She found the only use they had for her that day was to sit in the kitchen and keep the fire burning.

People in Luchen continued to call her Hsiang-lin Sao, but there was a different tone in their voices. They still talked with her, but smiled in a cool way, and with faint contempt. She did not seem to notice, or perhaps did not care. She only stared beyond them, and talked always about the thing that day and night clung to her mind.

"I was truly stupid," she would repeat. "I only knew that when the snow lies on the mountains the wild animals will sometimes venture into the valleys and will even come into the villages in search of food. I did not know that they could be so fierce long after the coming of spring. . . ."

Retelling her story in the same words, she would end up sobbing and striking her breast.

Every one who heard it was moved, and even the sneering men, listening, would loosen their smiles and go off in depressed spirits. The women not only forgot all their contempt for her, but at the moment forgave her entirely for her black sins—remarrying and causing the death not only of a second husband but also of his child—and in many cases ended by joining with her in weeping at the end of the tragic narrative. She talked of nothing else, only this incident that had become the central fact of her life, and she told it again and again.

Before long, however, the entire population of Luchen had heard her story not once but several times, and the most generous old women, even the Buddha-chanters, could not muster up a tear when she spoke of it. Nearly everybody in the town could recite the story word for word, and it bored them excessively to hear it repeated.

"I was truly stupid, truly," she would begin.

"Yes, you only knew that when the snow lies on the mountains the wild animals will sometimes venture into the valleys and will even come into the villages in search of food. . . ." Her audience would recite the next lines, cruelly cutting her short, and walk away.

With her mouth hanging open, Hsiang-lin Sao would stand stupefied for a while, stare as if seeing someone for the first time, and then drag away slowly as if weary of her continued existence. But her obsession gave her no rest, and she ingenuously tried to interest others in it by indirect approaches. Seeing a bean, a small basket, or other people's children, she would innocently lead up to the tragedy of Ah Mao. Looking at a child three or four years old, for instance, she would say: "If Ah Mao were still here, he would be just about that size."

Frightened by the wild light in Hsiang-lin Sao's eyes, the children signaled for a retreat by pulling on their mother's skirts. She would therefore soon find herself alone again, and falter off until the next time. Pretty soon everyone understood these tactics, too, and made fun of her. When they saw her staring morosely at an infant they would look at her mockingly.

"Hsiang-lin Sao, if your Ah Mao were still here, wouldn't he be just about that big?"

Probably she had not suspected that her misery had long since ceased to afford any vicarious enjoyment for anyone, and that the whole episode had now become loathsome to her former sympathizers, but the meaning of this kind of mockery pierced her armor of preoccupation at last, and she understood. She glanced at the jester, but did not utter a word of response.

IV

Luchen never loses its enthusiasm for the celebration of New Year. Promptly after the twentieth of the Twelfth Moon the festivities begin.

Next year at this time Fourth Uncle hired an extra male worker, and in addition a certain Liu Ma, to prepare the chickens and geese. This Liu Ma was a "good woman," a Buddhist vegetarian who really kept her vow not to kill living creatures. Hsiang-lin Sao, whose hands

were polluted, could only feed the fire and sit watching Liu Ma working over the sacred vessels. Outside a fine snow was matting the earth.

"*Ai-ya*, I was truly stupid," said Hsiang-lin Sao, staring despondently at the sky.

"Hsiang-lin Sao, you are back on the same trail!" Liu Ma interrupted, with some exasperation. "Listen to me, is it true you got the
scar by knocking your forehead against the altar in protest?"

"Um-huh."

"I ask you this: If you hated it that much, how was it that later on
you actually submitted?"

"I?"

"Ah, you! It seems to me you must have been half-willing otherwise—"

"Ha, ha! You don't understand how great were his muscles."

"No, I don't. I don't believe that strength such as your own was
not enough to resist him. It is clear to me that you must have been
ready for it yourself."

"Ah—*you!* I'd like to see you try it yourself, and see how long you
could struggle."

Liu Ma's old face crinkled into a laugh, so that it looked like a
polished walnut. Her dry eyes rested on Hsiang-lin Sao's scar for a moment, and then sought out her eyes. She spoke again.

"You are really not very clever. One more effort that time really
to kill yourself would have been better for you. As it is, you lived with
your second man less than two years, and that is all you got for your
great crime. Just think about it: when you go into the next world you
will be held in dispute between the spirits of your two husbands. How
can the matter be settled? Only one way: Yama, the Emperor of Hell,
can do nothing else but saw you in half and divide you equally between the two men. That, I think, is a fact."

An expression of mingled fear and astonishment crept over
Hsiang-lin Sao's face. This was something she had not considered before, had never even heard in her mountain village.

"My advice is that you'd better make amends before it is too late.
Go to the Temple of the Earth Spirit and contribute money for a
threshold. This threshold, stepped on by a thousand, stepped over by
ten thousand, can suffer for you and perhaps atone for the crime. Thus
you may avoid suffering after death."

Hsiang-lin Sao did not say a word, but felt intolerably crushed with pain. Next day dark shadows encircled her eyes. Right after breakfast she went off to the temple to beg the priest to let her buy a new threshold. He stubbornly refused at first, and only when she released a flood of tears would he consider it. Then, unwillingly, he admitted that it might be arranged for twelve thousand cash.

She had long since stopped talking with the villagers, who shunned her and the tiresome narrative of Ah Mao's death, but news soon spread that there was a development in her case. Many people came now and inquisitively referred to the scar on her forehead.

"Hsiang-lin Sao, I ask you this: Why was it that you submitted to the man?"

"Regrettable, regrettable," sighed another, "that the knock was not deep enough."

She understood well enough the mockery and irony of their words, and she did not reply. She simply continued to perform her duties in silence. Near the end of next year's service she drew the money due to her from Fourth Aunt, exchanged it for twelve silver dollars, and asked permission to visit in the west end of the town. Before the next meal she returned, much altered. Her face no longer seemed troubled, her eyes held some life in them for the first time in months, and she was in a cheerful mood. She told Fourth Aunt that she had bought a threshold for the temple.

During the Coming-on-Winter Festival she worked tirelessly, and on the day of making sacrifices she was simply bursting with energy. Fourth Aunt brought out the holy utensils, and Ah Niu carried the altar to the center of the room. Hsiang-lin Sao promptly went over to bring out the wine cups and chopsticks.

"Never mind," Fourth Aunt cried out. "Don't touch them."

She withdrew her hand as if it had been burned, her face turned ashen, and she did not move, but stood as if transfixed. She remained standing there, in fact, until Fourth Uncle came in to light the offertory incense and ordered her away.

From that day she declined rapidly. It was not merely a physical impoverishment that ensued, but the spark of life in her was dimmed almost to extinction. She became extremely nervous, and developed a morbid fear of darkness or the sight of anyone, even her master or mistress. She became altogether as timid and frightened as a little mouse that has wandered from its hole to blink for a moment in the glaring light of day. In half a year her hair lost all its color. Her memory became so clouded that she sometimes forgot even to scour the rice.

"What has got into her? How has she become like that? It's better not to have her around," Fourth Aunt began saying in her presence.

But "become like that" she had, and there did not seem to be any possibility of improving her. They talked of sending her away, or of returning her to the management of Old Woman Wei. Nothing came of it while I was still in Luchen, but the plan was soon afterwards carried out. Whether Old Woman Wei actually took charge of her for a while after she left Fourth Uncle's home or whether she at once became a beggar I never learned.

I am awakened by giant firecrackers, and see yellow tongues of flame, and then immediately afterwards hear the sharp *pipipopo* of exploding gunpowder. It is near the fifth watch, and time for the prayers and blessings. Still only drowsily aware of the world, I hear far away the steady explosive notes, one after another, and then more rapidly and thickly, until the whole sky is echoing, and the whirling snowflakes, eddying out of little white balls themselves like something shot from above, hover everywhere. Within the compass of the medley of sound and gentle storm I feel somehow a nostalgic contentment, and all the brooding of the dead day and the early night is forgotten in the stir around me, lost in the air of expectancy that pervades these homes about to receive benediction. What a satisfaction it is to understand that the Holy Spirits of Heaven and Earth, having bountifully inhaled their fill of offertory meat and wine and incense, now limp about drunkenly in the wide air. In such a mood they are certain to dispense boundless prosperity on the good people of Luchen!

TRANSLATED BY EDGAR SNOW AND YAO HSIN-NUNG

Mao Tun

Spring Silkworms

[Ch'un ts'an]

I

Old T'ung-pao sat on a rock on the towpath with his back to the sun, his long-stemmed pipe leaning against his side. The Tomb Festival over, the sun was already strong and felt as warm as a brazier of fire. It made him hotter than ever to see the Shaohsing trackers pulling hard at their lines, large drops of sweat falling from their brows in spite of their open cotton shirts. T'ung-pao was still wearing his winter coat; he had not foreseen the sudden warm spell and had not thought of redeeming his lighter garment from the pawnshop.

"Even the weather is not what it used to be!" muttered T'ung-pao, spitting into the canal.

There were not many passing boats, and the occasional ripples and eddies that broke the mirrorlike surface of the greenish water and blurred the placid reflections of the mud banks and neat rows of mulberry trees never lasted long. Presently one could make out the trees again, swaying from side to side at first like drunken men and then becoming motionless and clear and distinct as before, their fistlike buds already giving forth tiny, tender leaves. The fields were still cracked and dry, but the mulberry trees had already come into their own. There seemed to be no end to the rows along the banks and there was another extensive grove back of T'ung-pao. They seemed to thrive on the sunlit warmth, their tender leaves growing visibly each second.

Not far from where he sat there was a grey white building beside the towpath. This was the cocoon shed. A couple of weeks previously it had housed troops, and a few short trenches still scarred the fields. The Japanese were said to be approaching and the rich had fled the town, but now the troops had left in their turn and the shed would stay deserted until the spring cocoon sales. Squire Ch'en's oldest son was saying that the buyers would not come at all this year because the Shanghai factories had been made idle by the war, but T'ung-pao would not believe this. He had lived sixty years and had yet to see the time when mulberry leaves would be allowed to wither on the trees or be used for fodder, unless of course if the eggs should fail to hatch, as has sometimes happened according to the unpredictable whims of Heaven.

"How warm it is for this time of year!" T'ung-pao thought again, hopefully, because it was just after a warm spring like this almost two score years ago that there occurred one of the best silk crops ever known. He remembered it well: it was also the year of his marriage. His family fortune was then on the upward swing. His father worked like a faithful old ox, knew and could do everything; his grandfather, who had been a Taiping captive in his time, was still vigorous in spite of his great age. At that time, too, the house of Ch'en had not yet begun its decline, for though the old squire had already died the young squire had not yet taken to opium smoking. T'ung-pao had a vague feeling that the fortunes of the Ch'ens were somehow intertwined with those of his own family, though one was about the richest family in the town while his was only well-to-do as peasants went.

Both his grandfather and the old squire had been captives of the Taiping rebels and both had escaped before the rebellion was suppressed. Local legend had it that the old squire had made off with a considerable sum in Taiping gold and that it was this gold which enabled him to go into the silk business and amass a huge fortune. During that time T'ung-pao's family flourished too. Year after year the silk crops had been good and in ten years his family had been able to acquire twenty *mou* of rice land and more than ten *mou* of mulberry trees. They were the most prosperous family in the village, just as the Ch'ens were the richest in the town.

But gradually both families had declined. T'ung-pao no longer had any rice land left and was more than three hundred dollars in debt besides. As for the Ch'en family, it was long ago "finished." It was said that the reason for their rapid decline was that the ghosts of the Taiping rebels had sued in the courts of the nether world and had been warranted by King Yama to collect. T'ung-pao was inclined to think there was something to this notion, otherwise why should the young squire suddenly acquire the opium habit? He could not, however, figure out why the fortunes of his own family should decline at the same time. He was certain that his grandfather did not make off with any Taiping gold. It was true that his grandfather had to kill a Taiping sentinel in making his escape, but had not his family atoned for this by holding services for the dead rebel as long as he could remember? The man's soul must surely have found its reincarnation long ago. He did not know much about his grandfather, but he knew his father as an honest and hard-working man and could not think of anything he himself had done that should merit the misfortunes that had befallen him. His older son, Ah Ssu, and his wife were both industrious and thrifty, and his younger son, Ah Tuo, was not a bad sort, though he was flighty at times as all young people were inclined to be.

T'ung-pao sadly lifted his brown, wrinkled face and surveyed the scene before him. The canal, the boats, the mulberry groves on either bank—everything was much the same as it had been two score years ago. But the world had changed: often they lived on nothing but pumpkins, and he was more than three hundred dollars in debt.

Several blasts from a steam whistle suddenly came from around a bend in the canal. Soon a tug swept majestically into view with a string of three boats in tow. The smaller craft on the canal scurried out of the way of the puffing monster, but soon they were engulfed in the wake of the tug and its train and seesawed up and down as the air became filled with the sound of the engine and the odor of oil. T'ung-pao watched the tug with hatred in his eyes as it disappeared around the next bend. He had always entertained a deep enmity against such foreign deviltry as steam boats and the like. He had never seen a foreigner himself, but his father told him that the old squire had seen some, that they had red hair and green eyes and walked with straight knees. The old squire had no use for foreigners either and used to say that it was they that had made off with all the money and left everyone poor. T'ung-pao was only eight when he last saw the old squire, everything he knew of him was what he had been told; but when he thought of these words, "It's the foreigners who've made off with all the money," he seemed to be able to picture the old man stroking his beard, shaking his head.

T'ung-pao had no doubt that the old squire was right. He knew from his own experience that since foreign yarn and cloth and kerosene appeared in town and the steamer in the river, he got less and less for the things that he produced with his own labor and had to pay more and more for the things he had to buy. It was thus that he became poorer and poorer until now he had none of the rice land that his father had left him and was in debt besides. He did not hate the foreigners without reason! Even among the villagers he was remarkable for the vehemence of his antiforeign sentiments.

Five years back someone told him that there had been another change in government and that it was the aim of the new Nationalist government to rescue the people from foreign oppression. T'ung-pao did not believe it, for he had noticed on his trips to town that the youngsters who shouted "Down with the foreigners" all wore foreign clothes. He had a suspicion that these youths were secretly in league with the foreigners and only pretended to be their enemies in order to fool honest people like himself. He was even more convinced that he was right when the slogan "Down with the foreigners" was dropped and things became dearer and dearer and the taxes heavier and heavier. T'ung-pao was sure that the foreigner had a hand in these things.

The last straw for T'ung-pao was that cocoons hatched from foreign eggs should actually sell for ten dollars more a *picul*. He had always been on friendly terms with his daughter-in-law, but they quarreled on this score. She had wanted to use foreign eggs the year before. His younger son Ah Tuo sided with her, and her husband was of the same mind though he did not say much about it. Unable to withstand their pressure, T'ung-pao had to compromise at last and allow them to use one sheet of foreign eggs out of the five that they decided to hatch this year.

"The world is becoming worse and worse," he said to himself. "After a few years even the mulberry leaves will have to be foreign! I am sick of it all!"

T'ung-pao picked up his long pipe and knocked it out violently on the ground at his feet. Under the vertical sun his shadow was just a lump of charcoal on the ground, and he boiled in his tattered jacket. He loosened the neck, fanned himself, and stood up to go back.

Paddy fields lay behind the mulberry grove, their half-turned soil dry and cracking. Here and there were planted patches and a scent came strong from the golden rape flowers. In the distance was the cluster of cottages where T'ung-pao's family had lived for three generations now. White smoke curled above the roofs.

T'ung-pao walked through the mulberries, along the dike between the paddies, and looked back again at the tender bursting buds. As he did so a boy in his early teens came skipping up and calling, "Grandpa! It's dinnertime, Mum's waiting for you."

"Uh-huh." It was his grandson Little Pao. The Tomb Festival only just past and the buds opening like little fingers—he had seen this only twice in his lifetime. It would be a fine crop: how many cocoons from five sheets of eggs? As long as it wasn't like last year they could get rid of some of their debts.

Little Pao had come up and was looking like himself at the green velvet on the gnarled branches. He jumped up and down and clapped his little hands:

"Bursting buds at the Tomb Feast,
The silk girls clap their hands!"

A smile came to old T'ung-pao's wrinkled face: it was a good omen. He rested his hand on the boy's head, cleanshaven as a monk's, and new hopes stirred in his careworn, old heart.

II

The weather continued warm and the fingerlike tender leaves were now the size of small hands. The trees around the village itself seemed to be better than ever, like a cover of green brocade spreading into the distance over a low, grey-white fence. As the trees grew so did the hope in the hearts of the peasants. The entire village was mobilized in preparation for the silkworms. The utensils used in the rearing were taken out from the fuel sheds to be washed and repaired, and the women and children engaged in these tasks lined the brook that passed through the village.

None of the women and children was very healthy looking. From the beginning of spring they had had to cut down on their meager food, and their garments were all old and worn. They looked little better than beggars. They were not, however, dispirited; they were sustained by their great endurance and their great hope. In their simple minds they felt sure that so long as nothing happened to their silkworms everything would come out all right. When they thought how in a month's time the glossy green leaves would turn into jingling silver dollars, their hearts were filled with laughter though their stomachs gurgled with hunger.

Among the women was T'ung-pao's daughter-in-law Fourth Sister with Little Pao by her side. They had finished washing the feeding trays and the hatching baskets and were wiping their brows with the flap of their coats.

"Fourth Sister, are you using foreign eggs this year?" The voice of a young woman of twenty or so came across the creek. It was Liu-pao, sister of their neighbor Lu Fu-ch'ing.

"Don't ask me!" Fourth Sister answered with passion, as if ready for a quarrel. "Pa is the one who decides. Little Pao's dad did what he could to persuade the old man, but in the end we are hatching only one sheet of foreign eggs. The doddering old fool hates everything foreign as if it were his sworn foe, yet he doesn't seem to mind foreign-style silver dollars!"

The gibe provoked a gale of laughter.

A man walked across the husking field on the other side of the brook. As he stepped on the log bridge Fourth Sister called to him: "Brother Tuo, come and help me take these things home. These trays are as heavy as dead dogs when they are wet."

Ah Tuo lifted the pile of trays and carried them on his head and walked off swinging his hands like oars. He was a good-natured young fellow and was always willing to lend the women a hand when they had anything heavy to be moved or to be rescued from the brook. The trays looked like an oversized bamboo hat on him. There was another gale of laughter when he wiggled his waist in the manner of city women.

"Ah Tuo! Come back here and carry something home for me, too," said Lotus, wife of Li Keng-sheng, T'ung-pao's immediate neighbor, laughing with the rest.

"Call me something nicer if you want me to carry your things for you," answered Ah Tuo without stopping. He soon reached his own porch, where he set down the trays.

"Then let me call you godson!" Lotus said with a loud laugh. She was unlike the rest of the women because of her unusually white complexion, but her face was very flat and her eyes were mere slits. She had been a slave girl in some family in town and was already notorious for her habit of flirting with the menfolk though she had been married to the taciturn Li Keng-sheng only half a year.

"The shameless thing!" someone muttered on the other side of the brook. Thereupon Lotus's piglike eyes popped open as she shouted: "Who are you speaking of? Come out and say it in the open if you dare!"

"It's none of your business! She who is without shame knows best who I'm speaking of, for 'even the dead man knows who's kicked his coffin.' Why should you care?" It was Liu-pao, another of the lively ones.

They splashed water at each other. Some of the women joined in the exchange of words, while the children laughed and hooted. Fourth Sister, not wishing to be involved, picked up the remaining baskets and went home with Little Pao. Ah Tuo stood on the porch watching the fun.

T'ung-pao came out of the room with the tray stands that he had to repair. His face darkened when he caught Ah Tuo idly standing there watching the women. He never approved of Ah Tuo's banter with the women of the village, particularly with Lotus, whom he regarded as an evil creature: "That bitch is under the White Tiger star, get going with her and you'll ruin us all."

"Are you enjoying the scenery, Ah Tuo?" he shouted at his son. "Ah Ssu is making cocoon trees in the back; go and help him!" He did not take his disapproving eyes off his son until the latter had gone. Then he set to work examining the worm holes on the stands and repairing them wherever necessary. He had done a great deal of carpentering in his time, but his fingers now were stiff with age. After a while he had to rest his aching fingers and as he did so he looked up at the five sheets of eggs hanging from a bamboo pole in the room.

Fourth Sister sat under the eaves pasting paper over the hatching baskets. To save a few coppers they had used old newspapers the year before. The silkworms had not been healthy, and T'ung-pao had said it was because it was sacrilegious to use paper with characters on it. In order to buy regular paper for the purpose this year they had all gone without a meal. Fourth Sister spread out evenly the gosling yellow paper and pasted it down, then stuck on the three tiny patterns bought at the same time, the "jewel casket" and the two "Silkworm Princes," tiny figures on horseback carrying pennants.

"Fourth Sister, the twenty loads of leaves we bought have used up all the thirty dollars we borrowed through your father. What are we going to do after our rice is gone? What we have will last only another two days." T'ung-pao raised his head from his work, breathing hard as he spoke to his daughter-in-law. The money was borrowed at two-and-a-half percent monthly interest. This was considered low, and it was only because Fourth Sister's father was an old tenant of the creditor that they had been able to get such a favorable rate. It was conditional on full repayment after the harvest.

"It was not such a good idea to put all the money in leaves," complained Fourth Sister as she set out the baskets to dry. "We may not be able to use all of them—we didn't last year."

"What are you talking about! You'll bring ill luck on us before we even get started. Do you expect it to be like last year always? We can only gather a little over ten loads from our own trees. How can that be enough for five sheets of eggs?"

"Yes, yes, you are always right. All I know is that you can cook rice only when there is some to cook and when there isn't you have to go hungry!"

Fourth Sister answered with some passion, for she had not yet forgiven her father-in-law for their argument over the relative merits of foreign and domestic eggs. T'ung-pao's face darkened and he said no more.

As the hatching days approached, the entire village of some thirty families became tense with hope and anxiety, forgetting it seemed even their gnawing hunger. They borrowed and sought credit wherever they could and ate whatever they could get, often nothing but pumpkins and potatoes. None of them had more than a handful of rice stored away. The harvest had been good the year before but what with the landlord, creditors, regular taxes, and special assessments, they had long ago exhausted their store. Their only hope now lay in the silkworms; all their loans were secured by the promise that they would be paid after the harvest.

As the period of Germinating Rains drew near, the "cloth" in every household began to take on a green hue. This became the only topic of conversation wherever women met.

"Liu-pao's are going to start warming!"

"Lotus says they will be warming the cloth tomorrow. I don't see how it can be so soon."

"Taoist Huang got a fortune that says leaves will reach four dollars a *picul* this year!"

Fourth Sister was worried because she could not detect any green on their own five sheets of eggs. Ah Ssu could not find any either when he took the sheets to the light and examined them carefully. He tried to reassure his wife: "Warm them anyway. They're always slower, these Hangchow eggs." She pursed her lips and said nothing; old T'ung-pao's wrinkled face grew long, he felt things were wrong but he, too, would say nothing. Fortunately their anxiety did not last long, for spots of green began to show the following day. Fourth Sister told her husband at once, then old T'ung-pao, Ah Tuo, even her son Little Pao. Then immediately she put the precious things against her breast to warm, sitting quietly as if feeding an infant. At night she slept with them, hardly daring to stir though the tiny eggs against her flesh made her itch. She was as happy, and as fearful, as before the birth of her first child!

The room for the silkworms had been made ready some days before. On the second day of warming T'ung-pao smeared a head of garlic with mud and put it in a corner of the room. It was believed that the more leaves there were on the garlic on the day the silkworms hatched, the better would be the harvest. The entire village was now engaged in this warming of the cloths. There were few signs of women along the brook or on the husking grounds. An undeclared state of emergency seemed to exist: even the best of friends and the most intimate of neighbors refrained from visiting one another, for it was no joking matter to disturb the shy and sensitive goddess who protected the silkworms. They talked briefly in whispers when they met outside. It was a sacred season.

The atmosphere was even tenser when the "black ladies" began to emerge from the eggs. This generally happened perilously close to the day that ushered in the period of Germinating Rains and it was imperative to time the hatching so that it would not be necessary to gather them on that particular day. In T'ung-pao's house the first grubs appeared just before the tabooed day, but they were able to avoid disaster by transferring the cloths from the warm breast of Fourth Sister to the silkworms' room. T'ung-pao stole a glance at the garlic and his heart almost stopped beating, for only one or two cloves had sprouted. He did not dare to take another look but only prayed for the best.

The day for harvesting the "black ladies" finally came. Fourth Sister was restless and excited, continually watching the rising steam from the pot, for the right moment to start operations was when the steam rose straight up in the air. T'ung-pao lit the incense and candles and reverently set them before the kitchen god. Ah Ssu and Ah Tuo went out to the fields to gather wild flowers, while Little Pao cut up lampwick grass into fine shreds for the mixture used in gathering the newly hatched worms. Toward noon everything was ready for the big moment. When the pot began to boil vigorously and steam to rise straight up into the air, Fourth Sister jumped up, stuck in her hair a paper flower dedicated to the silkworms and a pair of goose feathers, and went into the room, accompanied by old T'ung-pao with a steel-yard beam and her husband with the prepared mixture of wild flowers and lampwick grass. Fourth Sister separated the two layers of cloth and sprinkled the mixture on them. Then taking the beam from T'ung-pao she laid the cloths across it, took a goose feather and began to brush the "black ladies" off gently into the papered baskets. The same procedure was followed with the other sheets, but the last, which contained the foreign eggs, was brushed off into a separate basket. When all was done Fourth Sister took the paper flower and the feathers and stuck them on the edge of one of the baskets.

It was a solemn ceremony, one that had been observed for hundreds and hundreds of years. It was as solemn an occasion as the sacrifice before a military campaign, for it was to inaugurate a month of relentless struggle against bad weather and ill luck during which there would be no rest day or night. The "black ladies" looked healthy as they crawled about in the small baskets; their color was as it should be. T'ung-pao and Fourth Sister both breathed sighs of relief, though the former's face clouded whenever he stole a glance at the head of garlic, for the sprouts had not grown noticeably. Could it be that it was going to be like last year again?

III

Fortunately the prognostications of the garlic did not prove very accurate this time. Though it was rainy during the first and second molting and the weather colder than around the Tomb Festival, the "precious things" were all very healthy. It was the same with the "precious things" all over the village. An atmosphere of happiness prevailed, even the brook seemed to gurgle with laughter. The only exception was the household of Lotus, for the worms weighed only twenty pounds at their third "sleep," and just before the fourth Lotus's husband was seen in the act of emptying three baskets into the brook. This circumstance made the villagers redouble their vigilance against the contamination of the unfortunate woman. They would not even pass by her house and went out of their way to avoid her and her taciturn husband. They did not want to catch a single glance of her or exchange a single word with her for fear that they might be infected by her family's misfortune. T'ung-pao warned Ah Tuo not to be seen with Lotus. "I'll lay a charge against you before the magistrate if I catch you talking to that woman," he shouted at his son loud enough for Lotus to hear. Little Pao also was strictly prohibited from playing in front of Lotus's house or talking to anyone there. Ah Tuo said nothing; he alone did not take much notice of these superstitions. Besides, he was too busy to talk to anyone.

T'ung pao's silkworms weighed three hundred pounds after the "great sleep." For two days and two nights no one, not even Little Pao, had a chance to close his eyes. The worms were in rare condition; only twice in T'ung-pao's memory had there been anything to equal it, once when he was married and the other time when Ah Ssu was born. They consumed seven loads of leaves the first day. Every one of the worms was fat and glossy, while every member of T'ung-pao's household looked thinner and had red streaks round his sleepless eyes. It did not take much calculation to know how much more leaf would be needed before the worms were ready to "climb up the mountain."

"The squire has nothing to lend," T'ung-pao said to Ah Ssu. "We'll have to ask your father-in-law to try his employers again."

"We still have about ten loads on our own trees, enough for another day," Ah Ssu said, hardly able to keep his eyes open.

"What nonsense," T'ung-pao said impatiently. "It was only two days ago they started eating. They'll be eating for another three days after tomorrow. We need another thirty loads, thirty loads."

Their conversation was interrupted by shouts from the husking ground: Ah Tuo had brought another five loads, and they went out to help strip the leaves. Fourth Sister rushed out from the silkworms' room to join in, and so did Liu-pao, who had time to spare because she was raising fewer worms this year. Stars dotted the sky and a light breeze blew, sounds of happy labor came from all over the village, and a raucous voice called, "Leaf prices are soaring! Up to four dollars a load in town this afternoon!"

It would cost T'ung-pao one hundred and twenty dollars to buy enough leaves to see them through. He took some comfort in the thought that he would harvest at least five hundred pounds of cocoons and that at fifty dollars a hundred pounds he would get more than enough to pay his debts.

A quiet voice came from where they were stripping the leaves: "They say things aren't going well over on the east side. Probably the price of leaves won't go up much more."

It was Liu-pao: old T'ung-pao relaxed. She was standing with Ah Tuo beside a basket stripping leaves. They were close together in the faint starlight, and they were hidden by the branches. All at once she felt a hand on her thigh, and a pinch. She knew very well who it was and managed not to giggle or call out. But when the hand was cupping her breast, she jumped and yelled *"Ai-ya!"*

"What's up?" Fourth Sister lifted her head from her work.

Liu-pao's face burned; she glanced at Ah Tuo, then stripped away furiously at the leaves with her head down: "Nothing. Must have been a caterpillar bit me."

Ah Tuo bit his lip to keep from laughing. For two weeks he had had neither enough food nor enough sleep, but loss of weight hadn't affected his spirits. He had none of T'ung-pao's worrying disposition. He didn't believe they could wipe out their debts and get their own land back with a single good cocoon crop or rice harvest; he knew they would stay poor however hard they worked, however they broke their backs. Still he worked with a will: it was something he enjoyed, just like flirting with Liu-pao.

Next morning old T'ung-pao went off to town in search of a loan to buy more leaves. He agreed with Fourth Sister before he left that they would have to mortgage their last bit of property, the mulberry grove that produced fifteen loads of leaves a year.

They bought the extra thirty loads. When the first consignment of leaves arrived, the "precious things" had already been without food for more than half an hour and it was heartbreaking to see them raise their heads and swing them hither and yon in search of leaves. A crunching sound filled the room as soon as the leaves were spread on the beds, so loud that those in the room had difficulty in hearing one another. Almost in no time the leaves had disappeared and the beds were again white with the voracious worms. It took the whole family to keep the beds covered with leaves. But this was the last five minutes of the battle; in two more days the "precious things" would be ready to "climb up the mountain" and perform their appointed task.

One night Ah Tuo was alone on watch in the room, so that T'ung-pao and Ah Ssu could have a little rest. It was a moonlit night and there was a small fire in the room for the silkworms. Around the second watch he spread a new layer of leaves on the beds and then squatted by the fire to wait for the next round. His eyes grew heavy and he gradually dozed off. He was awakened by what he thought was a noise at the door, but he was too sleepy to investigate and dozed off again, though subconsciously he detected an unusual rustling sound amidst the familiar crunching of leaves. Suddenly he awoke with a jerk of his drooping head just in time to catch the swishing of the reed screen against the door and a glimpse of someone gliding away. Ah Tuo jumped up and ran out. Through the open gate he could see the intruder walking rapidly towards the brook. Ah Tuo flew after the thief and in another moment had flung his quarry to the ground.

"Ah Tuo, kill me if you want to but don't tell anyone!"

It was Lotus's voice, and it made Ah Tuo shudder. Her piggish eyes were fixed on his but he could not detect any trace of fear in them.

"What have you stolen?" Ah Tuo asked.

"Some of your 'precious things!' "

"Where have you put them?"

"I have thrown them in the brook!"

Ah Tuo's face grew harsh as he realized her wicked intention.

"How wicked you are! What have we ever done to you?"

"What have you done? Plenty! It was not my fault that our precious things did not live. Since I did you no harm and your precious things have flourished, why should you look upon me as the star of evil and avoid me like the plague? You have all treated me as if I were not human!"

Lotus had got up as she spoke, her face distorted with hatred. Ah Tuo looked at her for a moment and then said, "I am not going to hurt you; you can go now."

Ah Tuo went back to the room, no longer sleepy in the least. The "precious things" were unharmed. He felt neither pity nor hatred for Lotus, but her words came back to him. He felt there was something between them that could never be straightened out, but couldn't have said what it was or what caused it. Soon he forgot the whole thing.

The "precious things" kept on devouring leaves as if possessed. At dawn T'ung-pao and Fourth Sister came to relieve Ah Tuo. They picked up the silkworms that had gradually turned from white to pink and held them against the light to see if they had become translucent. Their hearts overflowed with happiness. When Fourth Sister went to the brook to draw water, however, Liu-pao approached her and said in a low voice, "Last night between the second and third watch I saw that woman come out of your house, followed by Ah Tuo. They stood close together and talked a long time. Fourth Sister, how can you let such things go on in your house?"

Fourth Sister rushed home and told her husband and then T'ung-pao what she had heard. Ah Tuo, when summoned, denied everything and said that Liu-pao must have been dreaming. T'ung-pao took some consolation in the fact that so far there had been no sign of the curse on the silkworms themselves, but there was Liu-pao's unshakable evidence and she could not have made up the whole story. He only hoped that the unlucky woman did not actually step into the room but had only met Ah Tuo outside.

T'ung-pao became full of misgivings about the future. He knew well that it was possible for everything to go fine all along the way only to have the worms die on the trees. But he did not dare to think of that possibility, for just to think of it was enough to bring ill luck.

IV

The silkworms had at last mounted the trees but the anxieties of the growers were by no means over, for there was as yet no assurance that their labor and investment would be rewarded. They did not however let these doubts stop them from their work. Fires were placed under the "mountains" in order to force the silkworms up. The whole family squatted round the trees and listened to the rustling of the straws as the silkworms crawled among them, each trying to find a corner to spin its chamber of silk. They would smile broadly or their hearts would sink according to whether they could hear the reassuring sound or not. If they happened to look up and catch a drop of water from above, they did not mind at all, for that meant there was at least one silkworm ready to get to work at that moment.

Ah Tuo had already parted the reed mats several times to peep inside. When Little Pao saw him do this he grabbed him to ask if the precious things had started their cocoons yet. Ah Tuo stuck his tongue out and made a devil-face in reply.

Three days later the fires were withdrawn. No longer able to endure the suspense, Fourth Sister drew aside one corner of the screens and took a peep. Her heart leaped for joy, for the entire "mountain" was covered with a snowy mass of cocoons! She had never seen a crop like this in all her life! Joy and laughter filled the household. Their anxieties were over at last. The "precious things" had played fair and had not devoured leaves at four dollars a load without doing something to show for it, and they themselves had not gone without food and sleep for nothing: Heaven had rewarded them.

The same sound of joy and laughter rose everywhere in the village. The Goddess of Silkworms had been good to them. Every one of the twenty or thirty families would gather at least a seventy or eighty percent capacity crop. As for T'ung-pao's family, they expected a hundred and twenty or even hundred and thirty percent crop.

Women and children were again seen on the husking field and along the brook. They were thinner than a month ago, their eyes more sunken and their voices hoarser, but they were in high spirits. They talked about their struggles and dreamed of piles of bright silver dollars; some of them looked forward to redeeming their summer garments from the pawnshop, while others felt their mouths water in anticipation of the fish they might treat themselves to at the Dragon Boat Festival.

That night there was gossip about the affair between Lotus and Ah Tuo. Liu-pao spread it around, how Lotus was "so shameless, presented herself right at his door!" The men leered, the women called on the Buddha, scolded, said T'ung-pao's household had done well to avoid the curse, the Bodhisattvas and their own ancestors must be protecting them.

The actual harvesting of the cocoons followed the next day, attended by visits from friends and relatives bringing gifts and good wishes. Chang Ts'ai-fa, Fourth Sister's father, came to congratulate T'ung-pao and brought cakes, fruits, and salted fish. Little Pao was as happy as a pup frolicking in the snow.

"T'ung-pao, are you going to sell your cocoons or reel them yourself?" Chang asked, as the two sat under a willow tree by the brook. The old man was a connoisseur of the pleasures of life and had a head full of all kinds of marvels he had learned from the storytellers before the Temple of the City God. He had by heart the *Tales of Sui and T'ang* with their rebels and battles, salt-smugglers, and bandit lairs. He was a great talker of nonsense, and T'ung-pao contented himself with a short answer, "I'll sell them, of course."

But old Chang smote his thigh and sighed. He stood up and pointed in the direction of the building used by the buyers, behind the rows of stripped mulberries: "T'ung-pao! Your cocoons are gathered, but the doors are still shut tight! They're not going to buy this year! The rebels are everywhere and no new emperor appears, the world is in turmoil! There'll be no trade this year!"

T'ung-pao smiled to himself—how could you believe such a thing? All those cocoon sheds all over the countryside—how could they all just sit there with closed doors? And there had been a deal with the Japanese, there would be no more fighting, the troops had been withdrawn from the cocoon sheds.

Old man Chang changed the subject to the latest town gossip, which coming from him inevitably was full of references to the tales he had heard from the storytellers. He ended up by pressing, as middleman, for repayment of the loan he had arranged for T'ung-pao, the thirty silver dollars.

He left T'ung-pao uneasy in mind and anxious to see for himself. The buyers' sheds were indeed still closed. For the moment T'ung-pao was panic-stricken, but when he went home and saw the basket upon basket of fine, firm cocoons that he had harvested he forgot his worries. He could not believe such fine cocoons would find no market.

Gradually, however, the atmosphere of the village changed from one of joy and laughter to one of despair, as news began to arrive that none of the factories in the region was going to open for the season. Instead of the scouts for the cocoon buyers who in other years would march up and down the village during this season, the village was now crowded with creditors and tax collectors. And none of them would accept cocoons in payment.

Curses and sighs of despair echoed throughout the entire village. It never occurred to the villagers even in their dreams that the extraordinarily fine crop of cocoons would increase their difficulties. But it did not help to complain and say that the world had changed. The cocoons would not keep and it was necessary to reel them at home if they could not sell them to the factories. Already some of the families had brought out their long neglected spinning wheels.

"We'll reel the silk ourselves," T'ung-pao said to his daughter-in-law. "We always did that anyway until the foreigners started this factory business."

"But we have over five hundred pounds of cocoons! How many spinning wheels do you plan to use?"

Fourth Sister was right. It was impossible for them to reel all the cocoons themselves and they could not afford to hire help. Ah Ssu agreed with his wife and bitterly reproached his father: "If you had only listened to us and hatched only one sheet of eggs, we would have had enough leaves from our own land."

T'ung-pao had nothing to say to this.

Presently a ray of hope came to them. Taoist Huang had learned from somewhere that the factories at Wusih were buying cocoons as usual. Taoist Huang was not really a priest at all, just an ordinary peasant; he and old T'ung-pao had always got along very well. T'ung-pao asked him all about it, then agreed with Ah Ssu that they should take the cocoons for sale in Wusih.

"Nearly three hundred *li* by boat, six days for the return trip," the old man said to his son in a quarrelsome voice. "Dammit, it's like going off to war! But what else can we do? We can't eat the cocoons, and we can't hold off on our debt payments much longer!"

Ah Ssu did not argue. They borrowed a small boat and bought strips of matting to protect the cocoons. It was fine weather as it happened, and with Ah Tuo along as well the little "expeditionary force" set out to sell their cocoons.

Five days later they returned with one basket of cocoons still unsold. The Wusih factory had been unusually severe in their selection and paid only thirty dollars a hundred pounds for the cocoons from foreign eggs, only twelve dollars for the native variety. Though T'ung-pao's cocoons were of the finest quality they rejected almost a hundred pounds of the lot. T'ung-pao got one hundred and eleven dollars in all and had only an even hundred left after the expenses of the journey, not enough to pay off the debts they had contracted in order to buy leaves. T'ung-pao was so mortified that he fell sick on the way back and had to be carried home.

Fourth Sister borrowed a spinning wheel from Liu-pao's house and set to work reeling the rejected cocoons. It took her six days to finish the work. As they were again without rice, she sent Ah Ssu to town to sell the silk. There was no market for it at all and even the pawnshop would not loan anything against it. After a great deal of begging and wheedling he was allowed to use it to redeem the *picul* of rice that they had pawned before the Tomb Festival.

And so it happened that everyone in T'ung-pao's village got deeper into debt because of their spring silkworm crop. Because T'ung-pao had hatched five sheets of eggs and reaped an exceptional harvest, he lost as a consequence a piece of land that produced fifteen loads of mulberry leaves, and thirty dollars besides, to say nothing of a whole month of short rations and loss of sleep.

TRANSLATION BY CHI-CHEN WANG (SUPPLEMENTED)

The New Verse

In the nineteen-twenties a new generation of talented poets responded vigorously to the challenge of the "new verse." Two leading figures were Hsü Chih-mo (1895–1931) and Wen Yi-to (1899–1946). They were associated in the establishment of the Crescent Moon school, which of all the numerous literary associations of the time was the most fertile training ground for poets and the most productive of good poetry. Both men had studied abroad; Hsü in particular found himself as a poet in Cambridge, where he lived a romantic idyll. He has been said to be a better essayist than poet, and a section from his celebrated essay "The Cambridge I Knew" opens our selection from his work. Both men, though they experimented with many possibilities, committed themselves largely to the use of rhyme and regular meters. Their excesses, readily apparent, lie in uncontrolled sensibility; their successes are no less real as they draw on the rich vocabulary and imagery of the Chinese lyrical tradition to express their imaginative new perceptions. Hsü was a singer, using the modern idiom with grace and charm; Wen was a painter with words, somber but vibrant. Both men died violently, Hsü in an airplane accident, Wen the victim of assassination for his progressive sympathies.

Ai Ch'ing (Chiang Hai-ch'eng, b. 1910) belongs to the next generation of poets, who came to maturity in the thirties. He worked and studied in France and on his return to China (where he was quickly jailed) he soon established his characteristic poetic style. He writes a spare, rhymeless verse, sometimes prosaic-seeming, but studded with powerful images and capable of deeply moving effects.

Feng Chih (b. 1905) studied and taught German literature and had a lasting admiration for Rilke. He made his debut as a poet in the mid-twenties, but the sonnets of which seven appear below were written in 1941. A Feng Chih sonnet represents one of the most successful realizations in modern Chinese of a form taken over from the West.

•

Hsü Chih-mo

From "The Cambridge I Knew"

[*Wo so chih-tao-ti K'ang-ch'iao*]

On both banks of the river Cam are lush meadows which retain their verdure the four seasons round. Looking out from the upper story of the Fellows' Hall one may see in the fields across the river, morning or evening, always a dozen or so dun cows and white horses, hoof and fetlock lost in the rioting grasses, chewing away at their ease, while the buttercups that star the meadows sway in the breeze to the measure of their swishing tails. Each end of the bridge receives shade from weeping willows and oaks, and the water is clear to the bottom, not four feet in depth, and evenly set with long-stemmed water plants. These riverside meadows were another of my delights. In the early morning or towards evening I would often go to seat myself on this natural brocade, sometimes to read, sometimes to look at the water; sometimes to lie back and watch the clouds cross the sky, sometimes turning over to embrace the yielding earth.

But the romance of the river is not limited to the elegance of its banks. You must rent a boat for your pleasure. There is more than one kind. there is the usual double-sculled rowboat, and the light, swift canoe, and then, most characteristic of all, the long punt. This last is something seldom found elsewhere. It is about twenty feet in length and three feet broad, and you stand erect on the stern and propel it along with a great pole. This poling is an art. I am too clumsy a person, and from first to last was never able to master the technique. When you first start off to experiment, you are likely to swing the boat sideways across the stream, all ends up and stuck like a cork in a bunghole. The English are not a people given to open laughter, but be on guard for the eyebrow raised in silence! I cannot guess how many times the erstwhile orderly calm of the river was shattered by my novice blundering. From first to last I truly never learnt; and each time I trotted up indomitable to rent a punt for yet another attempt, one white bearded boatman would always comment with some sarcasm, "Heavy work, these punts, sir, and tiring on a hot day like this. Wouldn't you be better with a paddle in a nice canoe?" I would of course reject his advice, and with a touch of the long pole would move my punt out into the stream; but the result, inevitably, would be the truncation of the river one section after another.

To stand on the bridge and watch others punt, how effortless it seemed, and how graceful! Especially on a Sunday there would be a number of girl experts, all in white, their full skirts blowing gently in the breeze, each wearing on her head a wide-brimmed straw hat whose reflection trembled among the water plants. To observe the stance of one of these girls as she emerged from the arch of the bridge: the long pole resting in her fingers would seem to have no weight at all, yet when she lightly, casually touched it into the ripples and dipped ever so slightly at the knees, the punt would swing out from the shadow of the bridge and go gliding forward like a long green fish. The agile skill, the ease, the delicate grace of these girls truly are themes for song.

As summer begins and the sun's warmth gradually grows you rent a little boat and row out to the shade of the bridge to lie reading your book or dreaming your dreams, while the scent of the flowering chestnuts wafts across the water and the sound of the fishes' nibbling teases your ear. Or in a dusk of early autumn, to be close to the cold gleam of the new moon, you seek out a secluded spot far upstream. Fun-loving youngsters take their girl-friends along, decorate the sides of the boat with pair after pair of gay oriental paper lanterns, take a gramophone and pile soft cushions inside the boat. They, too, make for the lonely places to enjoy their outdoor pleasures—and who is there but would delight to hear that music borne up from the water below as it traces dreamscapes and bright hopes of spring across the quiet river!

For people who have grown used to city life it is not easy to recognize the changing seasons. When we see the leaves fall we know it is autumn, when we see them come green we know it is spring. When it gets cold fill the stove, when it gets hot, let it out, change your cotton gown for a padded one, change your padded gown for a thin one: that is all there is to it. What is happening among the stars in the sky, what is happening in the soil underground, what is happening in the windy air, these things are no concern of ours. Let's get busy, one way and another there are so many things to be done, who has the patience to bother about the stars in their courses, the plants as they grow and wither, the transfigurations of the wind-blown clouds? And at the same time we complain of our way of life: in suffering, irritation, frustration, deadly boredom, who will claim it a joy to be alive? Who is there who does not, to some degree or another, heap curses on this life?

Yet an unsatisfactory life is mostly of our own choosing. I am one who has faith in life. I believe that life is not in the least as dismal as most of us, from our personal experience alone, tend to infer. The root of our ills is that we forget our origins. Man is the child of nature just as the petal or bird on the branch is the child of nature; but we, alas, are men of enlightenment, we enter daily deeper into society and remove ourselves daily further from nature. A plant that has left the soil, or a fish that has left the water—can it be happy? Can it survive? From nature we draw our life; from nature it is our lot to draw our continued sustenance. What great, rustling tree is there whose tangled twisting roots do not penetrate down into endless depths of earth? We can never be independent. Happy the child who never must leave the maternal embrace; wholesome the man who stays ever close to nature. It does not mean that we have to go roaming with the deer and wild boar, or to seek out the caves of the immortals; for the treatment of the depression our lives present to us, we need only the mild prescription, "not to leave nature entirely ignored"—and there is hope that our symptoms will find relief. Roll in the green grass a time or two, go for a few dips in the sea, climb to a high place to watch a few dawns and sunsets and you will find the burden eased from your shoulders.

This is a most superficial doctrine, of course. But if I had not passed those days in Cambridge I could never have had this conviction. That spring—alone in all my life, though I grieve to say this—was not spent in vain. For that spring alone my life was natural, was truly joyful!—Even though it so chanced that that was also the time when I experienced most deeply the agony of life. What I did have then was leisure, liberty, the chance to be absolutely alone. However strange it may sound, it seemed for the first time then that I distinguished the light of stars and moon, the green of grass, the scents of flowers, the energy of flowing water. Shall I ever be able to forget that search for the coming of spring? How many dawns did I brave the chill to walk alone in woods where hoarfrost covered the ground—to hear the speech of birds, to glimpse the rising sun, to seek the gradual resurrection of the flowers and grasses from the soil, to comprehend to the full the subtlest, most mysterious hints of spring. Ah, that's the cuckoo, just arrived, there on that dark branch to which a few withered leaves still cling, rehearsing his new set of calls! Ah, here's the first snowdrop thrusting through the half-frozen soil, and ah, isn't this a new wash of verdure over the silent willows?

Utterly still, this highroad gleaming with the damp of dawn, only the bell of a milkman's cart in the distance to touch in the surrounding silence with sound. Walk on along this road, and at the end of it turn off on a narrow path into the woods. Go on where the mists hang thicker, where the dawn filters palely through the interlaced shade of elms above your head; and still farther, right through the woods, until before you lie broad, level meadows and you can make out cottages, and the new green of wheat fields, and beyond these two or three low hills, dumpling-shaped, through which a road winds half-concealed. The sky's edge blurs in mist, and that sharp silhouette is the church of a nearby village. This region is the plain of the English Midlands, its topography a noiseless rise and fall like the swell of a calm sea; no mountains are in sight, only meadows constantly green and fertile farmlands. If you look back from that hillock there, you see Cambridge as nothing but a verdant swathe of woods close-set at one part and another with slender spires. Of the graceful Cam no trace is to be seen, but as your eye follows that brocade sash of trees you may imagine the course of its leisurely waters. Cottages and copses lie like checkers on this board; where there is a cottage there will be a patch of welcome shade, where there is a patch of shade there will be a cottage. This rising at dawn is the time to see the smoke from kitchen chimneys: as the dawn mists gradually rise and draw back the grey white curtain from the sky (best of all, after a light shower of rain), then the smoke from chimneys far and near, in threads, in strands, in coils, airily or sluggishly, thick grey or pale blue or white, gradually ascends through the tranquil dawn air and gradually disappears, as though dawn prayers of men were fading raggedly into the halls of Heaven. Only rarely is the rising sun visible on these days of early spring. But when it does break through, the early riser knows no greater delight. In an instant the color of the fields deepens, a gold powder like a film of gauze dusts the grass, the trees, the roads, the farms. In an instant the land all about is tenderly suffused with the opulence of morning. In an instant your own heart drinks in its portion of the glory of the dayspring. "Spring!" the victorious air seems to whisper by your ear. "Spring!" your joyful soul seems to echo back.

As you wait attendance on the river in her splendor, each day brings its own report of the progress of spring. Give heed to the moss-traces on the stones, give heed to flowers blooming among the dead grasses, give heed to variations in the water's flow, give heed to the sunshot clouds, give heed to the new-found voices of the birds. To the seeker of news of the spring the timid little snowdrop is a messenger boy. The bluebell and the sweet smelling grass are the first cries of happiness. The shrinking violet, the finely-etched iris, the fun-loving crocus, the resilient daisy—by this time the world is dazzled by the radiance of spring, there is no further need to bestir yourself in search of it.

Fresh brilliance of the spring: this is your time for roaming. Admirable transport authorities—here, unlike China, where does one fail to find a broad, level-faced highway? Walking is a joy, but an even greater joy is to ride a bicycle. Bicycling is a universal skill in Cambridge: women, small children, old men alike relish the pleasure of the two-wheeled dance. (In Cambridge they say there is no fear of the theft of a bicycle: no one cares to steal one, for the simple reason that everyone has his own.) Pick any direction you like, take any road you like, go along with the gentle grass-flavored breeze, let your wheels bear you far away, and I will guarantee you a tonic for the soul from your few hours' drifting. Pleasant shade and sweet grasses are what the road will offer you for your rest at any point you choose. If flowers are your delight, here at hand are meadows rich as brocade. If birds are your delight, here at hand are songsters of subtlest variety. If children are your delight, guileless youngsters are everywhere in this countryside. If friendship is your delight, here at hand are country folk who cast no suspicious eye on the stranger from afar, wherever you go you can "present yourself" like a wandering monk at the temple gate and find lodging for the night, with fresh milk and tasty new potatoes for supper and eye-appealing fruits for your delectation. If drinking is your delight, every inn in this countryside has laid in for your benefit a stock of the finest new brews, and if the dark ale is too strong, there is cider or ginger ale to slake your thirst and refresh you. To take along a book, walk three or four miles, select a peaceful spot, watch the sky, listen to the birds, read, and when you grow tired to lie back in the long tangles of grass and pursue your dreams—can you imagine a pastime more congenial, more the natural thing to do?

There is a couplet of Lu Fang-weng's,

> Send the call for a swift horse to greet the crescent moon,
> Or mount a light carriage to take the cool air of dusk,

which describes the stylish pleasures of a district magistrate. Though in my time at Cambridge I had no horse to ride nor palanquin to carry me, I had nonetheless a style of my own: often as evening flamed in the west I would ride in pursuit, straight into the great flat disc of the sun at the sky's edge. There is no catching the sun, despite the boasts of Father Braggart, but by this means I was able to enjoy a good deal more than my fair share of the lingering beauty of the twilight. Two or three experiences linger to this day vividly as paintings in my mind. To speak only of sunset gazing: our only idea, usually, is to climb a mountain or to be by the coast, but in fact all that is needed is a wide expanse of horizon, and the sunset glow over a flat landscape can be equally wonderful. I sought once a place where, resting my arms on a farmer's fence at the edge of a great field of waving wheat, I could watch the transfigurations of the western sky. Another time, just as I came out on to a broad high road, a large flock of sheep came by on their way back from being let out to grass. The oversized sun struck their backs into a myriad strands of shining gold, yet the sky's blue was darkling; all that remained in the scarcely bearable brilliance was an open road, a flock of beasts. I felt a sudden mysterious weight press on my heart, and I actually knelt down before that trembling, fading golden glow. On yet another occasion, a sight even harder to forget: I stood by a meadow so broad that its farther edge was lost to view, where scarlet poppies bloomed everywhere upright in the green grass like a myriad golden lamps. The sun's rays, slanting from the edge of brown clouds, created by some magic a weird purple, transparent-seeming, a light hardly to be borne, and in an instant before my dazzled vision the meadow was transformed into—but better not say, for you would not believe it even if I told you!

It is two years and more, Cambridge, since I left you, yet who shall tell the hidden ache of my homesickness? If there is one thing of all others that I long for, it is to lie propped alone on the soft grass as the dusk, throbbing with the chimes of vespers, covers the spreading fields, and to watch the first great star shine out at the edge of the sky!

Second Farewell to Cambridge

[*Tsai pieh K'ang-ch'iao*]

Lightly let me leave now,
  Lightly as first I came;
Lightly wave farewell
  To the western sky aflame.

Golden willow on river path,
  A bride in the setting sun:
Her splendor on the stream
  In my heart makes ripples run.

Green fronds upon the mud
  Below surface lazily sway:
Could I only live as a water plant
  Where Cam winds her gentle way!

That pool in the elm tree's shade,
  No spring, but a rainbow it seems,
Shattered among the rushes,
  Steeped in a rainbow dream.

A dream? To pole with a long pole
  Where the green grass greener springs
A punt loaded with starlight,
  And in dapple of starlight to sing.

But I have no voice to sing,
  Silent the farewell pipe,
The very insects for me are still
  And still is Cambridge tonight.

Silently I leave now,
Silent as that first day,
With shake of sleeve, to carry
Not a wisp of cloud away.

Seven, Stone Tiger Lane

[*Shih-hu hu-t'ung ch'i hao*]

There are times when our little courtyard
ripples with infinite tenderness:
Winsome wisteria, bosom bared,
invites the caress of persimmon leaves,
From his hundred-foot height the sophora
stoops in the breeze to embrace the wild apple,
The yellow dog by the fence watches over
his little friend Amber, fast asleep,
The birds sing their latest mating songs,
trilling on without cease—
There are times when our little courtyard
ripples with infinite tenderness.

There are times when our little courtyard
shades in the setting of a dream:
Across the green shadows the haze after rain
weaves a sealed and silent darkness,
Facing my fading orchids, a single squatting frog
listens out for the cry of a worm in the next garden.
A weary raincloud, still unspent,
stretches above the sophora's top,
That circling flutter before the eaves—
is it a bat or a dragonfly?
There are times when our little courtyard
shades in the setting of a dream.

There are times when our little courtyard
can only respond with a sigh:
A sigh for the times of storm,
when countless red blossoms are pounded and pulped
by the rain,

A sigh for the early autumn,
    when leaves still green fret free with regret from the
      branch,
A sigh for the still of night,
    when the moon has boarded her cloud-bark, over the
      west wall now,
And the wind carries a dirge for a passing,
    cold gusts from a distant lane—
There are times when our little courtyard
    can only respond with a sigh.

There are times when our little courtyard
    is inundated with joy:
In the dusk, after rain, the garden
    is shaded, fragrant, and cool,
Old Pegleg, the toper, clutches his great jar,
    his bad leg pointing to the sky,
And drains his cup, a pint, a quart,
    till warmth of wine fills heart and cheeks,
A mythical Bacchus-figure,
    swept along on the bubbling of laughter—
There are times when our little courtyard
    is inundated with joy.

Joy of the Snowflake

[*Hsüeh-hua-ti k'uai-lo*]

If I could be a single snowflake
Fluttering free in the currents of air
    My destination would still be clear
    Drifting, drifting, drifting—
Here on earth my place would be clear.

No forsaken lonely valley
No wooded hillside cold and still
    Nor to the empty alley's chill
    Drifting, drifting, drifting—
I'd have my destination still!

In my graceful airborne swirling
I'd spy the sweet place of her abode
    Wait till she walked in garden glade—
    Drifting, drifting, drifting—
Ah, hers the fragrance of plum-blossom shade!

At last in the liberty of my lightness
Gently I'd lodge in the bosom of her dress
    And seek, seek the soft surge of her breast—
    Melting, melting, melting—
Melt in the soft surge of her breast!

A Song of Dead Leaves

[*Lo yeh hsiao ch'ang*]

A rustling against the balustrade
    (As I drift ever nearer the realm of dreams)
I tell myself, these are her footsteps at last—
    In this still night.

The sound of tapping here at my window
    (I press ever closer the frontier of sleep)
She must be here to plague me again—and see,
    I remain calm!

The sound of breathing draws near my bed
    And (half-dreaming, half in a daze) I cry,
"You will never understand me—what good then
    To hurt me more!"

The sound of a sigh falls by my pillow
    (I cling now to the dream I am dreaming)
"I wronged you" you say—now your hot tears
    Scalding my cheek!

These noises trouble my dream-locked spirit
    (In the garden the dead leaves dance, flurries before
        the breeze)
My dream ends, sleep clears, I find my tormentor
    Is only the voice of autumn!

P'i-pa in Midnight Alley

[*Pan-yeh shen-hsiang p'i-pa*]

Startled again from dreams by this *p'i-pa* in depth of night!
　　Whose is the sorrowing
　　Whose the fingers
That like a chill breeze, a dismal rain, an eddy of falling
　　　petals
　　Through the stillness of night
　　Through the shades of slumber
Quiver the taut strings, plucking at random note after note
　　To blend into still night, empty street,
　　Willow hung with waning moon
—Ah, dying moon's half-circle, image of fading hope—
　　　while he
　　Of the cap bursting its seams
　　Of the body iron-chained
Leaps and laughs like a maniac along the path of time.
　　"It's over," he says, "blow out your lamp."
　　She waits beyond the grave
Waits for your kiss, waits for your kiss, waits for your kiss.

Sea Rhyme

[*Hai yün*]

I

　　"Maiden, solitary maiden:
　　　Why do you linger here
　　　On the dusk-darkened shore?
　　Maiden, maiden, turn back!"
　　　"Ah no, I do not please,

For love of the evening breeze."—
On the sand of the shore, against sunset clouds
A girl with wind-tossed hair
   Wanders at ease.

II

"Maiden with streaming hair:
   Why do you roam at will
   Here by the ocean chill?
Maiden, maiden, turn back!"
   "Ah no, first hear me sing,
   Sea wave accompanying."—
In the light of the stars, the cool wind carries
The high clear voice of a girl
   Rising, falling.

III

"Maiden, maiden so daring:
   A black curtain rips at edge of sky,
   Storm tides threaten, rearing high—
Maiden, maiden, turn back!"
   "Ah no, see me dance free as air,
   As gulls in the spray disappear."—
In the fall of night, on sand of shore
Tenuously a shadow whirls
   Forsaken there.

IV

"Hear now the raging ocean's roar,
   Maiden, maiden, turn back!
   See the waves spring like beasts at the shore,
Maiden, maiden, turn back!"
   "Ah no, the waves turn not for me,
   I love the haul and plunge of the sea!"
In chant of the tide, in glow of wave
Through spume and spray in panic she turns
   Stumblingly.

V

"Maiden, where are you, maiden?
　Where now your song's pellucid trace,
　Your dancing limbs of slender grace,
Where are you, maiden so daring?"
Black night swallows the starglow,
　At sea's edge all light is hidden,
Tides abolish shore,
　On shore, no sign of maiden—
　No sign of maiden.

On Hearing the Chant of Intercession at the Temple of Heaven's Stillness at Ch'angchou

[*Ch'ang-chou T'ien-ning-ssu wen li-ch'an sheng*]

Like hearing, couched on one's back amid long-stemmed rioting grasses in the sunlight welcome as fire's warmth, the first summer call of the partridge which sounds from sky's edge up to the clouds and echoes from clouds back to the edge of sky;

like hearing, through the tropic air eiderdown-soft of a desert night when the moonlight's tender fingertips stroke lightly one by one the scorched fragments of rock, hauntingly, hauntingly borne from afar the sound of a camel bell which nears, nears, and again moves away . . . ;

like hearing, in a sequestered valley of the hills where the bold stars of dusk alone illumine a world bereft of sunlight and the grasses and the trees are bowed in silent prayer, an old fortuneteller, blind man led by a young boy, the clanging of whose gong reverberates through this realm of lowering dark;

like hearing, on some ocean rock savagely struck by breakers tiger-fierce while a black cloudwrack bandages tight the sky, the sea in low and gentle tones confessing its every crime before the storm's menace;

like hearing, among Himalayan peaks, echoing through innumerable ravines of shining snow the rush of clouds from beyond the sky driven by winds from beyond the sky;

like hearing, from behind the scenes in the theater of life, the onstage symphony which blends laughter of vanity with screams of pain and despair, wild yell of rapine and massacre with shrill song of death wish and suicide;

I have heard the chant of intercession in the Temple of Heaven's Stillness!

Whence comes this godhead? Earth has no second realm such as this!

Sound of drum, sound of bell, sound of stone chime, sound of wood block, sound of the Buddha's name . . . as this music rolls and flows in stately measure through the great hall, stilled are the eddies of numberless conflicts, toned are the clashes of numberless bright tints, dissolved are the numberless hierarchies of men. . . .

This sound of Buddha's name, this sound of bell, sound of drum, sound of wood block, sound of stone chime (swelling in harmony filling the universe, loosing a speck of the dust of time) brings to fulfillment an endless number of *karma* centuries long;

whence comes this great harmony?—cessation of all movement, cessation of all disturbance in the radiant sea of the stars, in the pipe-song of the Thousand Earths, in the flood of Destiny;

to the limits of Heaven and Earth, in among the hall's lacquered pillars, on the brow of the Buddha image, in the wide sleeves of my robe, in my ears and at my temples, in the pit of my stomach, in my heart, in my dream. . . .

In my dream, this moment's revelation, blue sky, white water, warm soft maternal bosom of green grass, is this my birthplace, this the land of my belonging?

Shining of wings in infinity soaring!

Flow of joy from the source of Enlightenment, manifest now in this great, solemn calm, this calm of Release, harmonious, limitless calm!

O hymn Nirvana! Extol Nirvana!

Wen Yi-to

Dead Water

[*Ssu shui*]

Here is a ditch of hopeless dead water,
The breeze can raise no ripple on this surface,
Here's where you dump old brass and rusty iron,
Or cheerfully waste your leftover soup.

But scraps of brass may hue to turquoise,
Peach blossoms flower from rusting cans,
The greasy scum weave a texture of gauze
And a tinted haze steam up from the germs.

Let this dead water ferment into green wine
Frothing with pearly beads of foam:
Tiny beads chuckle, turn into big beads,
Burst at the onslaught of raiding gnats.

So this ditch of hopeless dead water
May well boast a certain splendor;
Then if the frogs can't bear the silence
Out of dead water a song will rise.

Here is a ditch of hopeless dead water,
Here is no place for beauty to dwell.
Let ugliness take over and develop it,
See what kind of a world will emerge.

Tranquil Night

[*Ching yeh*]

Lamplight, and these four walls bleached white by its
gleam,
Table and chair, old faithfuls, friends who share my room,
Now and then from old books their good, musty smell,
My teacup waits to serve me, pale and virginal.
The little one in his mother's arms feeds at the breast,
A steady breathing tells me my elder son sleeps fast.
For the sacred still of night, for peace absolute
A full hymn of thankfulness trembles in my throat.
But suddenly a change, and the song is a hymn of hate—
I cannot take your bribe, O still and tranquil night!
A peace enclosed and measured—what is this to covet?
Wider are the bounds of the world I must inhabit.
No four walls can block the ear from battle's surge and
shout—
How then will you try to still the pounding of my heart?

Oh, rather let this mouth be stopped with mud or sand
If one man's joys and sorrows are all it finds to sing;
Rather that moles should burrow their way through this my
skull
And the corpse-worms be welcome from my own their flesh
to fill
If for "a Flask of Wine, a Book of Verse, and Thou"
—For calm borne on the pace of the clock the still night
through—
I should be deaf to moans of neighbors all about,
Blind to the trembling shadow of orphan or widowed mate,
To the soldier convulsed in his trench, the lunatic gnawing
his rail,
To all the tragic dramas that grind beneath life's mill.
Ah happiness! No longer can I take the bribe you offer,
No more is my world for these four walls to enclose and
measure.

Listen!—Again the cannon, and the howling of Yama's
    horde.
Tranquil night—can you still the pounding of my heart?

TRANSLATED BY CYRIL BIRCH

Red Candle

[*Hung chu*]

> *"When the candle turns to ashes the tears begin to dry"*
> —LI SHANG-YIN.

Oh red candle!
So red a candle!
Oh poet!
Spit out your heart and compare,
Can it be the same color?

Oh red candle!
Who made the wax—gave you your body?
Who lit the flame—lit your soul?
And why must you burn to ashes,
Before you release the light?
Mistake on mistake;
Paradox, contradiction.

Oh red candle,
There is no mistake, no mistake!
It was to burn out your light—
This was nature's method.

Oh red candle!
Since you have been made, then burn,
Burn, burn,
Burn up the dream of men,—
Burn up the blood of men—
And save from it their soul
And break down their prison.

Oh red candle! When your heart's fire gives light,
Then it is the day for tears to flow.

Oh red candle!
The craftsman made you,
Intentionally to burn.
Now you are burning,
Why break your heart in tears.
Oh I know
It is the cruel wind come to invade your light,
When you burn unsteadily,
Then in agitation you weep.

Oh red candle!
Flow! Why do you not shed tears?
Will you let your flesh ceaselessly flow towards men,
To cultivate comfort-bringing flowers
And ripen into happy fruit.

Oh red candle!
When you weep one tear, part of your heart turns to dust.
Heart turned to ashes, tears wept are your fate,
To create light is your destiny.

Oh red candle!
"Ask not about the harvest, ask about the ploughing."

You Swear by the Sun

[*Ni chih-cho t'ai-yang ch'i shih*]

You swear by the sun, and call on the horizon's cold wild
geese
To bear witness to your constancy. Very well, I believe you
completely,
And even those tears of passion don't surprise me,
But if you were to talk of the constancy of seas and moun-
tains . . .
Then I should die of laughter. Isn't this instant
Enough to make me drunk with happiness? Why talk of "for-
ever"?
Love? You know I have no more than one breath of desire,
Hurry and grip my heart! Hurry! But you are going, you're
going . . .

I've long anticipated that trick—it isn't any changefulness—
"Forever" was long ago given to someone else, only the
chaff is my share,
Your youth is what the others have received—your imperish-
able spring.
You don't believe me? If one day Death were to show you
his warrant
Would you go? Go, go to his embrace,
And talk to him about your constancy like the seas and the
mountains.

The Last Day

[*Mo jih*]

The water from the dew gurgles in the pipe,
The green tongue of banana leaf licks the window pane,
The whitewashed walls on all four sides are retreating,
Alone I cannot fill such a large room.

In my heart burns a bowl of fire,
Quietly I wait for the arrival of a distant guest,
I feed the fire with cobwebs and mice droppings,
And use the armor of mottled snakes for firewood.

The cockcrow is pressing; in the bowl is a heap of cinders,
A gust of dank wind steals to touch my mouth,
So the guest is standing before my eyes:
I clear my throat and follow the guest.

Ai Ch'ing

Setting Out

[*Ch'u fa*]

Like a canoe scattering sweet scents
Leaving a small deserted island,
A passionate and thoughtful young man
Was leaving his little village. . . .

I did not like the village—
It seemed as commonplace as a willow
As obtuse as a water buffalo;
I passed my boyhood there,

And those more ignorant than myself had ridiculed me,
I said not a word but had a hidden wish in my heart,
I wanted to go outside and get more experience than they,
I wanted to go very far—to places not even seen in dreams;

Places much better than here, much better,
Where people would pass their days like immortals,
And not hear the sound of husking grain that makes one
    dizzy,
And not see the tiresome faces of the priest and medicine
    woman.

Father counted out five pieces, five pieces of new dollars,
Wrapped in red paper he handed them to me with a sermon!
But I was thinking of something entirely different,
I was thinking of the burning brightness of the sea in a
    bay. . . .

You scolding sparrows, why make such a row—
Don't you know that I am about to go?
And you, honest farm laborers at home,
Why are your faces always full of worries?

The morning sunshine lay on the stone-paved road,
My heart pitied the village
Like a decrepit old man
Standing at the foot of a forked hill. . . .

Goodbye my poverty-stricken village
My old dog, you had better go back!
Let the forked hill protect your peace and safety
Wait till I'm old, too, I shall come back to be with you again.

The Wheelbarrows

[*Shou-t'ui-ch'e*]

In the areas watered by the Yellow River
In the countless dry riverbeds
Wheelbarrows
With their single wheel
Give out squeaks that make the cloudy sky contract
Pass through the cold and the silence
From the foot of this hill
To the foot of that hill
Crying aloud
The gloom of the people of the North.

In ice- and snow-locked days
Between small poverty-stricken villages
The wheelbarrow
With its single wheel
Carves a deep furrow in the layer of ash-yellow earth
Across plains and deserts
From this road
To that road
Weaving
The gloom of the people of the North.

The North

[*Pei-fang*]

> *One day*
> *The poet from the Mongolian plain*
> *Said to me,*
> *"The North is sad."*

Yes,
The North is sad.
From beyond the frontier blow
The desert winds
Which have already scraped away the green color of life
And the brightness of sunlight
—The expanse of ash-yellow murk
Is covered with an unpeelable layer of sand—
The storm screams that rush from the horizon
Bring with them terror
Madly
Sweeping over the wide earth;
The desert wilderness
Is frozen in the cold wind of December,
The villages, the hillsides, the river banks,
The dilapidated walls and deserted graves,
All wear the melancholy of the color of the earth. . . .
A lone traveler
Body bent forward
Shading his face with his hand
In the wind and sand
Breathes with difficulty
Step by step
Struggles forward. . . .
A few mules
—Beasts with sad eyes and tired ears—
Carry the earth's

Painful burden,
Their weary steps
Gently tread
The North country's
Long and lonely roads. . . .
The streams have long since dried up
The river beds are full of the traces of wheels,
The earth and the people of the North
Thirstily look for
The flowing springs that nourish life.
Withered trees
And squat houses
Isolated, gloomy
Are scattered below the grey dark sky.
In the sky,
The sun cannot be seen,
Only flocks of geese gathered into droves
Confused geese
Flapping their black wings calling out their restlessness and
      grief
Fleeing from this desolate place
Fleeing to
The green shaded sky of the South. . . .

The North is sad
And the endless Yellow River
Churning turbulent waves
Has poured down upon the broad North
Disasters and misfortunes,
And the frost of years
Has carved into the broad North
Poverty and hunger.

And I
—This traveler from the South—
Actually love this gloomy North.
The face-assaulting wind and sand
And bone-penetrating cold

Have never made me curse;
I love this sad land of my country,
The expanse of boundless desert
Arouses my respect
—I see
Our ancestors
Leading flocks of sheep
Blowing on their pipes
Sink into the dusk of this big desert;
We are treading
In the layers of ancient loose earth
Entrusted with our ancestors' bones—
It was this land they pioneered,
Several thousand years ago
They were here
And battled with the nature that struck at them,
To protect their land
They never once bowed to shame,
They have died
And left the land to us—
I love this sad land,
Its huge but lean space
Giving us simplicity of speech
And expansiveness of manner,
I believe that this speech and this manner
Will live on in the big land with strength
Never to be destroyed,
I love this sad land,
      This ancient land
—This soil
Has nourished what I love
The most hard-up
The most ancient of races on Earth.

The Gamblers

[*Tu-po-ti jen-men*]

At the foot of the dark, dank walls of the city
In the corners between pitch black houses
Numerous gamblers squat in a circle
Tensely watching the outcome, lose or win

Dirty, ragged, obtuse yet passionate
Wriggling their bodies, craning their necks
Victorious shouting, and disappointed cursing
Follow the sound of each coin falling to the ground

The women carrying children stand to one side
Hair wild, fixing their stare on the ground
With children hungry, tearful, and struggling
Yet mesmerized by their husbands' loss or win

Squatting then standing up, standing up then squatting again
And thumping their thighs to give a surprised happy shout
Faces red, mouths open, in excitement
Thinking at one go to wrench around their poverty-stricken
    fate

The losers win, the winners lose
What doesn't change is the dirt, the rags, and the stupidity
At dusk in disappointment they scatter
Each one returning to his pitch black house

TRANSLATED BY TAO TAO SANDERS

Old Man

[*Lao-jen*]

To the right of that perpendicular
A black uniform, part of, in tatters,
Three brass buttons in line with the vertical
Glow with the pale yellow flame of lamps.
—But the oil is almost dry.
Copper colored cheeks with antique gleam,
A few withered hairs coil against
The wrinkled palms of unstraightening hands.
He grips life's tail as it jerks away
—An eel wriggling into the mud.
He shakes his ancient coppery head,
Curses flower from the foam of his spittle;
And all his words
Are dyed with the tint of hunger.

TRANSLATED BY CYRIL BIRCH

Feng Chih

Seven Sonnets

I

We stand prepared deeply to partake
Of unimaginable wonders.
In the onflowing months and years, suddenly
A comet bursts through, a wind gusts forth:

Our life in this instant
Seems suddenly to place all pain and joy
In a first embrace before our eyes,
Frozen into an imposing, immovable form.

We praise those small insects
Which, on copulating once
Or once withstanding danger,

Bind up their wondrous lives.
The whole of our life is to receive
The wind's sudden gust, the comet's bursting through.

II

Often in the rustic plains I see
A village lad or a farmer's wife
Weeping toward the silent crystal sky.
Is it because of a scolding, or

The loss of a toy?
Is it because of a husband's death
Or a son's sickness?
Such ceaseless weeping makes it seem

That all of life is fit into
A frame, and outside that frame
There is no human life, no world.

I think they must have
Shed their tears from ages past
For a despairing universe.

III

TO THE POET TU FU

You suffered hunger in barren villages,
You often thought of the dead in the ditches,
And you never ceased to sing laments
For the loss of strength and beauty among men:

On the battlefield there were heroes dead and wounded,
In the heavens falling stars,
Ten thousand horses faded away with the floating
    clouds. . . .
Your whole life was an offering to them.

Your poverty glistened and shone
Like a sage's tattered robe.
Even a single thread or strand remaining in this world

Has an inexhaustible sacred strength.
All the official caps and carriages in the world
Reflect but pitiful forms before its light.

IV

TO VAN GOGH

Your passion bursts everywhere into flame,
You take a bunch of yellow sunflowers
And burn them, dark dense cypresses
And burn them. And then there are people walking

Under the blazing sun, and they, too, are
Flames shouting pleas toward the heights.
But one small, withered, lonely tree
In early spring, a small prison garden,

And people in a murky room, with lowered heads,
Peeling potatoes: these all
Are like blocks of ice which will never melt.

Among these, however, you painted a drawbridge,
Painted a comely little boat: did you want to
Welcome across these unfortunate ones?

V

You say you love most of all to see those fields where
Pathways one after another fill with life—
How many steps of nameless travelers
Trod out these lively roads!

In the fields of our souls
Are also twisting roads, one after another,
But most of the travelers who have walked these roads
Knew not where they were going:

Lonely lads, white-haired men and wives,
And also youthful men and women,
And also friends already dead, they all

Trod out these roads for us;
We remember their footsteps
And will not let these paths overgrow with weeds.

VI

TO A LITTER OF PUPS

For half a month rain continued to fall.
Ever since you were born
You had known only damp and melancholy.
Then one day the rain clouds suddenly dispersed,

Sunrays illumined the walls,
And I saw your mother
Carry you into the sunlight
And let you submit your bodies

For the first time to the sunrays' warmth,
Until the sun sank, and she
Carried you back again. You don't have

A memory, but this experience
Will fuse into the sound of barking,
And you, deep at night, will bark forth the light.

VII

Here, several thousand years ago,
Every place already seemed
To contain our lives;
Before we were born

A singing sound
From illusory skies,
From green grass and blue cypresses
Already sang our fate.

We are burdened with grief,
How can we ever hope
To hear those songs now?

See that small flying insect—
In its hovering
Every moment is eternal life.

TRANSLATED BY JEANNETTE FAUROT

Spoken Drama
on a Historical Theme

Much of the modern "spoken" drama has drawn its material from contemporary life, following such models as Ibsen's later plays. Or again like Eugene O'Neill, such a leading playwright as Ts'ao Yü has worked out themes from classical Greek tragedy in terms of the society of his own time. Yet several modern dramatists, like their predecessors working in operatic modes, have taken their themes from China's past: Kuo Mo-jo for example, or most recently Wu Han whose play Hai Jui Dismissed from Office (Hai Jui pa kuan) *was tinder for the sparks of the Cultural Revolution.*

Yao Hsin-nung was born in 1905; since 1948 he has been resident in Hong Kong and Hawaii. He completed his most celebrated play, The Malice of Empire (Ch'ing kung yüan), *in 1941. Memories were still alive of that most formidable and unscrupulous despot, the Empress Dowager Tz'u-hsi, and of the abortive struggle of the young Kuang-hsü Emperor to bring some measure of reform to the dynasty which barely survived the old termagant herself. Yao Hsin-nung's play closely observes historical authenticity, convincingly recreates the claustrophobic atmosphere of the Ch'ing palace, but most importantly offers a penetrating analysis of the psychology of tyranny. For this last reason it has been a thorn in the flesh of those in authority. The play was banned under the Japanese occupation, and in its film version became a* cause célèbre *in the People's Republic where it was reinterpreted as a "revisionist" polemic.*

From the first scene of act one, here reprinted, we can already anticipate the climax of the play in the forced suicide of Lady Chen, the

young emperor's favorite consort, after the defeat of both the Reform
Movement and the Boxer reaction. The central irony is that this per-
sonal triumph of the backward-looking Empress Dowager spells the cer-
tain doom of the dynasty she has so relentlessly struggled to perpet-
uate.

●

Yao Hsin-nung

The Malice of Empire, Act I, Scene 1

[*Ch'ing kung yüan*]

THE CONSORT HUMILIATED

TIME: Early summer, 1894, late afternoon.

PLACE: Main courtyard of the South Lake Mutual Pleasure Pavilion.

(*Near the left wall of the courtyard a bamboo clump rises above a pile of stones overgrown with ferns. A moon gate within the wall on the right [upstage] carries on its upper beam the inscription "Welcome Kingfisher"—symbolically, "Abode of Pleasure." Downstage right and near the wall a rock suggests, by its shape, a thick bamboo trunk. It is flanked by several plantains. Above the rear wall, far upstage, branches of a bamboo grove and roofs of the Mutual Pleasure Pavilion are visible. An entryway through this rear wall, with low steps visible, provides immediate access to the pavilion itself. Downstage, right of center, stands a marble-topped chess table. On either side stand drum-shaped porcelain stools ornamented in the traditional five colors [black, white, blue, red, and yellow].*

As the curtain rises, LADY CHIN [*the older sister of the* EMPEROR'S *favorite,* LADY CHEN] *is strolling in the courtyard and watching, with mingled amusement and concern, two palace girls,* CH'UN-YEN *and* CH'UN-SHOU, *who are playing with a large box camera set on a tripod. At a gesture from* CH'UN-YEN, LADY CHIN, *holding a fan, takes up a rigid, facing-the-camera pose in front of the moon gate.* CH'UN-YEN *dives in under the black cloth of this late-nineteenth-century box camera.*)

CH'UN-YEN (*her head emerging again from under the black cloth*):

377

Looking through a camera is certainly very odd, isn't it! Everything is upside down! Even Lady Chin's shadow.

CH'UN-SHOU: Now let me look.

CH'UN-YEN: Well, just let me look first, just once more.

CH'UN-SHOU: You've been looking and looking. Let me look now. (CH'UN-YEN *concedes.*) Everything really is upside down, really! But still I can tell that Lady Chin is holding her fan.

CHIN: But now you two had better stop playing around. You might ruin the machine. (*She turns towards the rear entryway and calls.*) Come on, hurry up, little sister. If you're going to take my picture, why don't you come and do it?

CHEN (*offstage rear, as within the pavilion*): I'm coming. I'm changing my clothes.

CHIN: Well, hurry up. It's hot out here. Why should I stand around all this time? If you don't come right now, I'm leaving.

(LADY CHEN *enters. She is imitating, with deliberate exaggeration, a young man's hasty stride. She wears black trousers, a long, pale yellow overshirt, a short blue vest, and a black gauze skullcap topped with a red coral button and ornamented, at the forehead, with a huge pearl.*)

CHEN (*also imitating a boy's voice and offhand manner*): Here I am. Here I am. Come on now. Greet your Emperor properly.

CHIN (*startled, and reproving*): What a way to behave! And dressing up like a boy again!

CHEN: But just look. Now! Don't I look like him?

(*She emphasizes* "him," *implying that she resembles the* EMPEROR.)

CHIN: All right, you give a good imitation. But I hope you don't start thinking you are the Emperor.

CHEN: Come on now. Everybody! Kowtow!

CHIN: Shame on you!

CHEN: Well, all right. Then let's pretend I'm Old Buddha. Now watch me. (*She points to* CH'UN-YEN.) You be Li Lien-ying. I am Old Buddha.

(*Assuming the heavy, slow tread of the dowager,* LADY CHEN *advances as if addressing Li Lien-ying and points abruptly at* LADY CHIN.)

CHEN: This one here. Shameless slave-wench. Haul her out! Give her forty heavy strokes!

CHIN: You've lost your mind!

CHEN: I have not! Oh, well. Let's take the picture.

(*Abruptly resuming her own natural pace and voice, she walks over to the camera.* LADY CHIN *resumes her pose, as before, standing by the moon gate.*)

CHEN (*about to put her head under the camera cloth*): Don't hold your neck so stiff. You look like some silly girl trying to impress a boy. The whole point in taking pictures is to have people looking natural.

(*As* LADY CHEN *thrusts her head under the cloth,* CH'UN-YEN *and* CH'UN-SHOU *run up and peer into the lens.*)

CHEN: Get away from there. (*She points towards* LADY CHIN.) Don't move. (*She shoves in the film plate and quickly drops the lens cover.*) There. Now you take me.

CHIN: I'm tired.

CHEN: Well, let's go in and you can rest.

CHIN: And you'd better take off that outfit and put on your regular clothes. If the Empress comes over, she'll have plenty of tales about you to take to Old Buddha.

CHEN: Oh, let her talk. She doesn't scare me.

CHIN: But all the same, she is the Empress.

CHEN: Hmph! Empress! Just because she's Old Buddha's niece. She's a usurper, that kind of an Empress. Nothing very impressive about that.

CHIN: Must you keep on talking right out like this?

CHEN: Why not? Just what can the empress do about it? Do you think she can eat us alive?

CHIN: That's as may be, but I say you'd better change into your own clothes. Just suppose Old Buddha herself comes by and catches you like this. Then we'll see some fun!

CH'UN-SHOU (*kneeling before* LADY CHEN): May I report, we've heard that Old Buddha is coming out to view the lotus flowers. She may come through here. We can't be sure she won't.

CHEN: Nonsense. It's too early for lotus flowers.

CH'UN-YEN (*approaching and kneeling beside her companion*): Your slave would be glad to agree with you. But our eunuch reported a single blossom already opened over here on South Lake. Since this is a good omen, Old Buddha is coming over on purpose to see it.

CHIN: Are you sure?

CH'UN-YEN: Your slave would not dare tell a lie.

(CH'UN-SHOU *and* CH'UN-YEN *now stand up again.*)

CHIN: We'd better find that eunuch and ask him for sure.

CHEN: But you can't. I've already sent him out to the Tung-hua Gate, to the camera shop.

CHIN: Speaking of that camera shop, this reminds me— (*She speaks to* CH'UN-YEN *and* CH'UN-SHOU.) You two go inside.

CH'UN-YEN *and* CH'UN-SHOU (*as they withdraw through the rear doorway*): Your servant obeys.

CHEN: What's wrong now?

CHIN: Just last night, less than half an hour after the Emperor had summoned you to the Ying-t'ai, Nieh Pa-shih came over to speak with me. He said someone had told Old Buddha that it was you who set up that camera shop outside the Tung-hua Gate and put the eunuch in charge of it.

CHEN (*expressing concern and dismay*): Oh-oh. And what is Old Buddha saying about it?

CHIN: Old Buddha is not pleased. She says maybe it is all right to take pictures here inside the palace grounds, but that camera shop just outside the palace gates cannot be permitted—because if people in general find out who really owns the shop, it won't look good.

CHEN (*after a moment's reflection*): The only one who would go running to her to tell her about this is the Empress. And still our Empress has the impudence to ask me to see to it that the Emperor finds a job for the son of her wet nurse.

CHIN: But what's the use of getting into a wrangle with her?

CHEN: But then why doesn't she behave like an Empress? Can't she be anything more than a spy working for Old Buddha? She picks up some piece of slander or other about the Emperor to pass on to Old Buddha every day. And now she's started carrying tales about us, too.

CHIN: Enough. Enough of this. Don't talk any more of this nonsense. If anyone overhears you, the worse for us. Come on now, I'll take your picture.

CHEN: People outside think we have such a fine life in here, happy as the Immortals. Nobody knows we're worse off than the poorest little housewives. And every day, what are we doing? Bending our necks, docilely taking orders from those who won't give up one little inch of power. Instead they hate us! They hate us! They are deliberately burying us alive! This is no life at all. It's just misery!

(*Rushing into* LADY CHIN's *arms,* LADY CHEN *rests her head on her sister's shoulder and sobs violently.*)

CHIN: Now, now, don't cry any more. What's the use?

CHEN (*raising her head*): Here we've been, inside the palace, for six whole years. They won't even let us go visit our own parents. Big sister, how can I help feeling miserable?

CHIN (*with a wry smile*): Don't cry any more. You're not a child. Come take another picture. (*Turning her head,* LADY CHIN *flicks away her own tears with her sleeve.*) You were gay and giddy enough to go in for all this dressing up like a boy emperor. So now! Shall I take your picture?

CHEN: Now my eyes are all swollen.

CHIN: That won't matter. (*She calls towards the pavilion.*) Ch'un-yen! Bring Lady Chen's dressing case! Hurry!

CH'UN-YEN (*from beyond the courtyard wall*): Coming!

CHEN (*with childlike petulance*): Big sister, I don't want you to take my picture now.

(CH'UN-YEN *and* CH'UN-SHOU *enter, carrying respectively a dressing case and a mirror. They kneel before* LADY CHEN.)

CHIN: No more of this. Stop acting like a child.

(LADY CHIN *busily powders* LADY CHEN'*s face.* LADY CHEN *grudgingly removes the skullcap and smooths her hair before the mirror.*)

CHIN: See? See what happens when you cry like that?

CHEN (*to* CH'UN-YEN *and* CH'UN-SHOU): That's all.

(*The palace girls, carrying the case and mirror, make a slow and obviously reluctant exit.* LADY CHEN *and* LADY CHIN *go over to the camera.*)

CHIN: But you know I don't know how to take pictures. You'll have to show me.

CHEN: It's very simple. All we need to do is change the film plate. (*She puts in a new plate.*) There you are. Just wait till I'm ready, then take off the lens cover, and then put it back on, just the way I did. That's all there is to it.

(LADY CHIN *puts her head under the camera cloth.* LADY CHEN *takes up a position exactly where* LADY CHIN *was standing for the earlier picture, a few paces in front of the moon gate. Just as* LADY CHIN'*s hand is groping to reach and remove the camera lens cover, the moon gate opens wide enough to admit the* EMPRESS, *who slides in behind* LADY CHEN. LADY CHIN, *who has seen this in the camera just as she removed the lens cover, at once abandons the camera and salutes, with bowed head, bent knee, and half-lifted hand, palm upwards.*)

CHIN: May your fortune be kind, Empress.

(*The* EMPRESS *makes acknowledgment with an abrupt nod.* LADY CHEN, *clearly trapped and a little apprehensive, makes the ceremonial bow.*)

CHEN: May your fortune be kind, Empress.

EMPRESS (*ignoring* LADY CHEN): You two certainly do find ways of amusing yourselves. Even taking pictures of each other! I've already told Old Buddha, and I'll be right here with her when she comes to see for herself. She says she is delighted and that one of these days she'll have you make a picture of her.

CHIN: Empress, wouldn't you like to come inside with us and sit down awhile?

EMPRESS: Not at all necessary. It's cool enough now. We can sit down out here.

(*The* EMPRESS *seats herself on one of the porcelain stools. The sisters remain standing.* CH'UN-YEN *and* CH'UN-SHOU *emerge from the pavilion gate. They carry trays of tea and fruit. Kneeling, they present them. The* EMPRESS *takes a cup of tea and a piece of fruit, sets them on the table, and then ignores them.* LADY CHIN *waves the girls away and again, reluctantly, they withdraw.*)

EMPRESS (*ostentatiously surveying* LADY CHEN): In that boy's outfit you are even more fetching.

CHEN: I put it on just for fun, to make a picture. If it annoys you, your slave will withdraw and change into her more usual clothes.

EMPRESS: Not at all necessary. But tell me, has he been here recently?

CHEN (*suavely*): Empress, to whom do you refer?

EMPRESS (*irked, but bland*): Has the Emperor been here recently?

CHEN: These last few days, because of the trouble with those reactionary Tung-hsüeh in Korea, the Emperor has been conferring with his advisers. Perhaps he is still over at Inner Strength Hall.

EMPRESS: When I was with Old Buddha this morning I heard her mention this Korea matter, but I don't understand much about such affairs.

CHIN: This particular affair is a worry to the Emperor. It's been three days since he was here.

EMPRESS (*ignoring* LADY CHIN *and continuing to address* LADY CHEN): Last night did he summon you to the Ying-t'ai?

CHEN: Yes.

EMPRESS (*with a slightly insistent smile*): Well? Then you've discussed the other matter with him?

CHEN: Because of the Korean troubles, the Emperor is preoccupied. He doesn't eat or even drink his tea. Consequently, your slave has not yet mentioned that other matter to His Majesty.

EMPRESS (*her tone is icy*): Very well. If you have not mentioned it. . . . Of course mine is a very minor matter.

(LADY CHIN, *who has been standing somewhat apart during this colloquy, quietly advances a step or two so that she can momentarily catch* LADY CHEN'S *eye. By her expression* LADY CHIN *is warning* LADY CHEN *even more firmly than her words suggest.*)

CHIN (*directly to* LADY CHEN): Next time you really should mention this matter to the Emperor.

EMPRESS (*ignoring* LADY CHIN *and continuing to address* LADY CHEN): I must trouble you about something else also. I don't know whether you are willing to undertake it.

CHEN: Whatever service your slave can render, you are welcome to command.

EMPRESS: This may need a few words of explanation. For several years past my second maternal uncle has been finding it very difficult to meet his expenses. It's true he has a comfortable post in one of the ministries, but there are many demands, including of course his social obligations. He really doesn't earn enough to support his family. Every year he goes more deeply into debt. As the saying goes, a great person has great difficulties, the little people have little difficulties.

CHEN: The situation for your slave is not to be compared with that of even the little people.

EMPRESS: Recently my uncle asked Hsiao-te Chang to mention to me that there is currently a vacancy at Foochow for a general of the armed forces. My uncle would like me to ask the Emperor to appoint him to this post. If you would beg the Emperor, rather soon, to grant my uncle this appointment, I should be grateful. Would you be willing?

CHEN: If you, the Empress, chose to say just a word to Old Buddha, wouldn't this be more effective?

EMPRESS: But in recent weeks I have already had to ask the Venerable Lady to grant two other appointments. I dare not open my mouth again just now on matters of this sort.

CHEN: If you were to drop a word to Li, the chief eunuch, this would be equally effective. Except for the power of Old Buddha, his is second to none.

EMPRESS: Please don't joke. Serious matters should be discussed seriously. Now, may I trouble you to put in a word with the Emperor? I know you are very close to him.

CHEN: In your slave's opinion, her influence cannot compare with that of others.

EMPRESS (*with open sarcasm*): Is there anyone who doesn't know that you are the only person the Emperor pays any attention to?

CHEN (*maintaining a polite smile*): Whoever begs a favor of the Emperor can persuade him. Kindly excuse your slave for being so forthright. But she always says to those present exactly what she would say in their absence.

EMPRESS (*now thoroughly angry*): If you don't want to put in a word for me, that's that. Just because you think you have the protection of the emperor, you needn't suppose you'll get away with all this impudence.

CHIN (*promptly, to the* EMPRESS): Please don't be upset. She's still too young to know how to handle words properly. Please don't hold it against her.

EMPRESS: So you want me to excuse her! I only expect her not to hate me and to put in a good word for me with the Emperor. That's the most I can hope for.

(*While the* EMPRESS *is speaking, the eunuch* HSIAO-TE CHANG *has come in through the moon gate. He catches her eye before the others observe him.*)

EMPRESS: Hsiao-te Chang!

HSIAO-TE (*bowing*): My lady. . . .

EMPRESS: Summon the sedan chair.

HSIAO-TE: Your slave hears. (*He shouts.*) The Empress summons the sedan chair.

CHIN: Empress, won't you please delay just one moment? Let your slave beg her younger sister to make her apologies to you. If your health should suffer because she has upset you, this would be most unfortunate.

EMPRESS (*rising, and ignoring both sisters*): An apology! To me? How should I dare expect such an honor? (*She proceeds towards the moon gate.*)

CHIN (*urgently*): Little sister! Little sister!

(LADY CHEN, *standing by the chess table, makes no move.* LADY CHIN *hastily turns and bows as the* EMPRESS *exits, followed by* HSIAO-TE CHANG. LADY CHIN, *now thoroughly impatient, returns to* LADY CHEN.)

CHIN: Now look what you've done, you've let her go away angry.

CHEN: What of that?

CHIN: Won't you just go out now, before they start off, and say a few words to calm her down and avoid more trouble?

CHEN: I can't put on an act just to get along with people like her, and besides, why should I flatter her?

CHIN: I'm not saying you should flatter her. I'm saying that you haven't learnt to control yourself and that you're just headstrong and stubborn. If she carries off too many more ugly reports to Old Buddha, there'll be more than trouble. There'll be catastrophe.

CHEN: What are you so afraid of? Even with them all working together to make me miserable, the worst they can do is put me to death.

CHIN (*putting her hand over* LADY CHEN's *mouth*): The more you talk, the worse you get. You must know the whole vast Ch'ing empire is controlled by the *Yehonala*, by the Empress Dowager and her relatives. There's no use trying to fight them.

CHEN (*pushing aside* LADY CHIN's *hand but holding it gently*): Do you still imagine that the *Yehonala* crowd will remain in power here for ever? Do you think the Emperor is still a helpless child? There'll come a day when we shall take over the power here.

CHIN: As to that. . . . Well, perhaps you are right. There is the saying, a person of worth does not accept insults. And I do admit, little sister, you're brilliant—really clever. But cleverness should include keeping a clear head. Think before you speak!

CHEN (*hanging her head, but then looking up*): It's not that I haven't a clear head, it's just that, even when I know what is involved, having her insult me just makes me explode. You know, big sister, I always have had a quick temper.

CHIN: If as you say you do recognize what is involved, then take my advice and go make your apologies to the Empress. There's still time to forestall trouble.

CHEN (*petulant again*): I'll risk death rather than apologize.

CHIN: Just a moment ago you were claiming to have a clear head. So why do you have to act like an addlepate again?

CHEN: I was deliberately rude to her just now. How could I have enough face to apologize?

CHIN: There is another saying, "the truly great know when to bend and when to keep a straight back." Will you for this once take my advice?

CHEN (*pleading*): You are a dear, good big sister, but don't force me into this. Let me wait until tomorrow.

CHIN: Tomorrow may be too late.

CHEN: Well then, how if I wait a little and go over later this evening?

CHIN: This is no matter to be dawdling about. Once she tattles to Old Buddha, it's already too late.

CHEN: Well. . . .

CHIN (*firmly*): Go! Now!

CHEN (*tearfully, and pulling* LADY CHIN's *arm about her own waist*): Dear big sister, please try to understand.

CHIN: (*taking* LADY CHEN's *hand and speaking softly*): Please listen to your big sister and just go apologize, now, without any more fuss.

CHEN (*brushing tears from her eyes*): Well, will you also be a dear, big sister and go with me?

CHIN (*seizing* LADY CHEN's *hand and pulling her towards the moon gate*): All right, I'll go with you, but let's go!

(*At this moment the old eunuch,* NIEH PA-SHIH, *comes through the gate.*)

NIEH (*bowing*): May fortune be kind, Lady Chen. May fortune be kind, Lady Chin.

CHEN: What's happened, Nieh Pa-shih?

NIEH: Permit me, my ladies. I come to tell you that Old Buddha is very angry with you.

(*The two sisters exchange glances.*)

CHEN: What is she angry about?

NIEH: When Old Buddha came over here to view that lotus blossom, we noticed she was already upset about something. And because just these past several days there's been that rebellion in Korea, the Venerable Lady announced that this one lotus blossom is a bad omen.

CHEN: But what has this to do with me?

NIEH: Now she has turned on you. When Old Buddha was tired and some of the slaves carried her over by the bubbling spring for a rest, the Empress came up.

CHIN: What was the Empress saying?

NIEH: I was posted outside. I couldn't hear much. But I could hear Old Buddha was in a temper and she kept shouting about "Lady Chen!" and the Empress kept on mumbling something or other. Old Buddha is getting more and more furious.

CHIN (*to* LADY CHEN): Now you're really in for it, just as I said. The Empress is not going to be easy to handle now.

(*At this moment the head of* LI LIEN-YING *is visible through the opening in the moon gate.*)

CHEN (*to* NIEH): Anything more?

NIEH: Nothing more.

CHIN: Very well then. Go back at once wherever Old Buddha assigned you. If you let her find out you've been over here, you're in for a terrible beating.

NIEH: No matter. You saved me once and I still owe you many, many thanks.

(*As* NIEH *turns to leave, the* EMPRESS DOWAGER, *leaning on the arm of* LI LIEN-YING *and followed by the* EMPRESS *and several attendants* [LADIES-IN-WAITING, PALACE GIRLS, EUNUCHS], *advances slowly through the gate. Her face exhibits barely controlled fury.* NIEH *attempts to fade back behind the bamboos upstage left and he is, in fact, partly hidden by the incoming entourage, but the* DOWAGER *has already seen him.*)

DOWAGER: Where are you off to? You! You think I don't see you, you scum of the earth? Nieh!

NIEH (*advancing and kneeling*): Your slave deserves death.

DOWAGER: So! Your legs can carry you fast enough, the moment I turn my head. Perhaps they carried you here ahead of me—with some news?

NIEH: Your slave would not dare.

DOWAGER: Well, what brought you here?

NIEH (*uneasily*): Your slave saw that these ladies were not accompanying Old Buddha. Old Buddha was alone, viewing the lotus.

Your slave thought you would not enjoy the viewing, being alone. He came to ask the ladies to join you.

DOWAGER (*with a frozen smile, and permitting* LI *to assist in settling her on one of the porcelain stools*): This is indeed wonderful, your showing such concern for me. (*The frozen smile turns off and her eyes flash.*) But you do have your wits about you. You tell a lie admirably. Why aren't you slapping your own mouth? (NIEH *slaps his mouth.*) So you're trying to trick me! You're a spy perhaps? The truth now. What are you trying to cover up? Let's have the truth this time.

NIEH: Your slave dares not play tricks.

LI: Well then, who ordered you to come here?

(LI *is fanning the* DOWAGER *with a short-handled, round banana-leaf fan.*)

NIEH: The Emperor.

DOWAGER: The Emperor!

NIEH: The Emperor commanded your slave to. . . .

DOWAGER: What did he command?

NIEH: The palace domains are so vast, the Emperor says the ladies might not be aware every time Old Buddha perhaps wishes to have them in attendance. He commanded your slave to be alert in reminding the ladies when Old Buddha may wish them to accompany her.

DOWAGER (*scornfully*): A good and devoted Emperor! (*Portentously.*) Tell me, are you in the service of the Emperor or are you serving me?

NIEH: Your slave serves Old Buddha.

DOWAGER: So, slippery tongue! In my service, but here you are prying into my private business, spying!

NIEH: Your slave is not a spy.

DOWAGER: You dare argue with me? (*She addresses* LI LIEN-YING.) Have him hauled out. Forty heavy strokes.

(*Two* EUNUCHS *enter and hustle* NIEH *along. Just as he is yanked through the gate,* NIEH *manages to call out towards* LADY CHEN *and* LADY CHIN.)

NIEH: You ladies will try to help this slave?

(LADY CHEN, *who throughout this episode has been conspicuously miserable and angry, at once kneels before the* DOWAGER.)

CHEN: I beg the grace of Old Buddha. Pardon this slave.

DOWAGER (*exchanging with* LI LIEN-YING *a malicious smile*): If anyone else tried to beg such a favor, I certainly would not grant it. But look who is here, begging! Lady Chen! Should I dare disobey her? So! Let her see what she gets for her begging. Li, order the eunuchs to give Nieh eighty heavy strokes. Then have them haul him back in here so that he can thank Lady Chen, before we ship him off to the work gangs on the Amur River.

LI: Aye! (*Calling beyond the gate.*) Listen, you out there. Let him have eighty! Heavy strokes! Then shoo him in here again. To thank Lady Chen for her great kindness.

EUNUCHS (*outside*): Aye!

(*The thud of the bamboo rod and the cries of* NIEH PA-SHIH *punctuate the following interchange.*)

DOWAGER (*with a mocking smile, to* LADY CHEN): When I am having someone beaten you beg me to pardon him. No wonder, my lady, all the eunuchs say you are so tenderhearted and generous.

(LADY CHEN *stands silent, her face without expression.*)

LI: Does the Emperor affirm that Lady Chen is loyal and honest?

DOWAGER (*bitterly*): To the Emperor's mind this old woman no longer exists. He hates me, and he hates the Empress. He would be happy if we were both dead. And this is your doing! (*She is addressing* LADY CHEN, *who bends her head slightly, as though both agreeing and avoiding further encounter.*) But Heaven is against you. Look at me! I'm alive and healthier than ever. A few months from now we'll celebrate my sixtieth birthday!

(*For a moment everyone stands motionless. The only sound is the thud of the bamboo, upstage beyond the wall, a low groan from* NIEH, *and the voice of a* EUNUCH, *counting.*)

EUNUCH (*offstage*): Seventy-eight! Seventy-nine! Eighty! Done!

DOWAGER (*to* LADY CHEN): You hear? Now he is well beaten. Now your devoted slave will thank you.

(LADY CHEN *continues to stare into space, avoiding the* DOWAGER's *eyes. Two* EUNUCHS *drag* NIEH *in through the moon gate and fling him on his knees in front of the* DOWAGER.)

NIEH (*faintly*): I beseech Old Buddha, let this old slave die.

(LADY CHEN *buries her face in her hands.*)

DOWAGER (*with her malicious smile*): You ought not to beg for death until you have first expressed your thanks to Lady Chen. Get over there!

(NIEH *turns his head towards* LADY CHEN *but otherwise does not move.*)

DOWAGER: Get over there!

NIEH: Your slave cannot walk.

LI: If you can't walk, crawl!

(*On his hands and knees* NIEH *crawls towards* LADY CHEN, *who is sobbing silently, her face still buried in her hands.*)

NIEH (*softly*): Your slave gives thanks to his lady.

CHEN: Nieh Pa-shih! It is all my fault.

NIEH: Your slave does not think you are to blame.

DOWAGER: Who wants to hear such nonsense! (*She addresses* LI.) Go slap his mouth!

(LI *slaps him. Blood oozes from* NIEH's *mouth.*)

LI: So you've really made up your mind to die! Say thanks to Lady Chen and get this over with.

NIEH (*almost inaudibly*): Thank you, my lady.

LI (*to* EUNUCHS): Now get him out of here.

(*Exeunt* EUNUCHS, *dragging* NIEH, *who is already breathing his last. They throw him outside the gate but themselves return to stand just inside the gate once more. The* DOWAGER, *meanwhile, has risen to her feet and is pointing at the camera.*)

DOWAGER (*to* LI): What's that three-legged thing over there?

LI: That? (*He goes to the camera, lifts the cloth, makes a play of careful investigation.*) I wonder what this can be? Ah, now I know! It is called a camera.

DOWAGER (*taking a step towards* LADY CHEN): For some time I have been hearing that you know how to take pictures. Really, there is no doubt you are the cleverest among all my people here in the palace. You also have some literary ability. I understand that you have been composing poems. You are something of a painter, too. And now you are even able to work this foreign devils' machine.

CHEN (*remotely*): It simply helps me to pass the time when I am melancholy and depressed.

DOWAGER (*coolly*): Melancholy and depressed? (*Now she attacks directly.*) Tell me, who opened that photographer's shop outside the Tung-hua Gate?

CHIN: That was. . . .

CHEN (*interrupting* LADY CHIN's *attempt to divert the attack*): I, your slave, opened it.

DOWAGER: And you even have the impudence to admit it! It isn't enough with all the mischief you've already been up to, here in the palace. Now you're out to make trouble for the Emperor by opening a shop outside the palace and setting yourself up in business. (*She now addresses* LI LIEN-YING.) Have that foreign devils' machine taken outside and burned.

LI: Aye! (*He summons two* BOY EUNUCHS.) Take it outside and burn it.

BOY EUNUCHS: Aye!

(*Exeunt, carrying camera and tripod.*)

DOWAGER: Send someone to seal up that shop outside the Tung-hua Gate.

LI: Aye! (LI *bows, appears to be about to transmit the order to one of the* BOY EUNUCHS, *but then suddenly kneels before the* DOWAGER.) May I report to Old Buddha, the business at that photography shop seems to be flourishing. Wouldn't it be a pity to shut it down?

DOWAGER (*thoughtfully*): Well—let me reward you. I give that shop to you. (*She sits down.*)

LI: Thank you, Old Buddha. (*He touches his forehead to the ground, then rises.*)

DOWAGER: You should also thank Lady Chen. Though I have generously given you the shop, it was she after all who established it.

LI: As Old Buddha commands. (*He bows towards* LADY CHEN.) Thank you, my lady. (LADY CHEN *ignores him.* LI, *stepping behind the* DOWAGER, *begins to fan her. At the same time he blatantly sticks out his tongue at* LADY CHEN *and, addressing the* DOWAGER, *observes loudly—*) Quite an impossible creature!

DOWAGER: Since she even overlooks me, how could you expect her to take any notice of you?

LI: Exactly, Old Buddha.

DOWAGER: She even carries herself like an Emperor. Aren't those even the Emperor's clothes she's wearing?

CHEN: These clothes are not the emperor's. Your slave made them with her own hands.

DOWAGER: Your wardrobe is already more lavish than anyone else's. You have red dresses, green dresses, every day something new. And now you even have boy's clothes.

CHEN: We have no household law against wearing such clothes.

DOWAGER (*rapping the table and standing up brusquely*): What do you mean, household law! My word is the household law! (*She addresses* LI.) Take those clothes off her. Rip them off and tear them up! (*The* DOWAGER *sits down again.*)

LI (*bowing*): Aye! (*Approaching* LADY CHEN, *he bows to her.*) Wouldn't it be preferable for my lady to obey the order herself? (LADY CHEN *stands rigid.*) Well then (*he raises his hand as if about to remove her blue vest*), don't blame this slave if he removes these clothes with his own hands.

CHEN: How dare you! (*She slaps him on the mouth.*)

LI: Ow! (*He retreats, rubbing his jaw.*)

CHIN (*appalled*): Little sister!

DOWAGER (*rising and shouting*): Kneel down! Kneel, I tell you! Kneel!

(*Seeing* LADY CHEN *still stubborn,* LADY CHIN *places herself between her sister and the* DOWAGER.)

CHIN (*urgently*): Little sister! Little sister! You'd better. . . . You'd better . . . kneel down!

(*Reluctantly, under the pressure of* LADY CHIN'*s hand on her shoulder,* LADY CHEN *finally kneels.*)

DOWAGER (*now standing directly over* LADY CHEN *and glaring down at her*): Impudence! Even those who might want to kick a dog keep an eye out for its master! But you! Daring to slap one of my own men!

LI (*spitting*): This is too much! She's even jarred my teeth loose!

DOWAGER: Look what you've done to my poor man!

LI (*promptly kneeling and sniveling, like a spoilt child*): Your poor slave suffers all this, all for you, Old Buddha. Never in all his life has he ever been treated like this. Let Old Buddha send him home. Your slave is not able to serve Old Buddha now.

(*He knocks his forehead on the ground.*)

DOWAGER: Get up! I'll take care of this!

LI: Thank you, Old Buddha.

DOWAGER (*to* LADY CHEN): To strike him is to strike me. (*The* DOWAGER'*s voice now rises to a shriek.*) Are you defying me? Will you now slap your own mouth? (LADY CHEN, *though still kneeling, looks up at her calmly and steadily. The* DOWAGER *now screams towards* LI.) Come here!

LI (*rising and bowing*): Old Buddha!

DOWAGER: Slap her face!

LI: Aye! (*As he approaches* LADY CHEN, *she gets to her feet and looks him full in the eyes.* LI *cringes, retreats, and again kneels before the* DOWAGER.) Old Buddha, I can no longer be of use to you.

DOWAGER: What are you afraid of?

LI (*still kneeling, but with a gesture summoning the two* EUNUCHS *who previously handled* NIEH): Bring her over here!

(*With tiger swiftness the two* EUNUCHS *pounce on* LADY CHEN. *They twist her arms and block her knees. She struggles.*)

CHEN: Let go! Let go of me!

LI (*rising and bowing*): My Lady Chen, you understand this is an order from Old Buddha.

DOWAGER: Slap her mouth for me! Slap it hard!

LI (*bowing*): Aye!

(*Ostentatiously rolling up his sleeve,* LI *raises his arm and is about to lunge at* LADY CHEN *when the* EMPEROR *appears in the gateway.*)

EMPEROR: Stop this!

(*At his voice the two* EUNUCHS *release* LADY CHEN, *and* LI's *slap fans empty air. Her arms thrown up over her face,* LADY CHEN *plunges past the* EMPEROR *and flees through the rear exit into the pavilion. The company stands terrorstruck, all except the* DOWAGER, *and* LI, *who scuttles to the* DOWAGER's *side.*)

EMPEROR: Scoundrel!

DOWAGER (*addressing both the* EMPEROR *and* LI): Stand where you are!

EMPEROR (*his voice vibrating with fury*): Scoundrel! Are you defying me?

DOWAGER: I gave him the order to strike her.

EMPEROR (*taken aback*): What is going on here?

(*Through the rear gate the palace girl* CH'UN-YEN *rushes in panting and sobbing.*)

CH'UN-YEN: Lady Chen! Our poor Lady Chen! She ran her head right into the wall of her room, and she's lying there unconscious! She doesn't move. What shall we do?

EMPRESS: Well, what shall we do? I'll go see what's happening. (*She starts towards the pavilion.*)

EMPEROR: Stay here. No need for you. (*He starts towards the pavilion.*)

DOWAGER: Stop there, right where you are. (*He turns and faces her.*) Here you are looking straight at me and you haven't even bowed to me. Your mind's on nothing but coddling that little bitch. (*She snaps at* LADY CHIN.) Go look after that sister of yours. If she dies, no doubt people will be ready to talk and say I killed her.

CHIN: As you command. (*She bolts into the pavilion.*)

EMPEROR (*bitterly*): If she's dead, perhaps that's just as well. Perhaps it would be better if we were both dead.

DOWAGER: What's this? Are you conniving with her against me?

EMPEROR: Your minister would not dare.

(*The* DOWAGER *stands up, strides about, flings her arms violently, shrieks.*)

DOWAGER: Every one of you is against me! You are all trying to drive me into my grave! (*She shakes her fist at the* EMPEROR.) So you think because now you're in charge of state affairs you can defy me! Just let me remind you! You and I (*her voice now steadies*) are figures behind the screen in a shadow play. (*Now her voice is very even.*) Whatever happens that screen mustn't get torn. (*She turns abruptly to* LI.) Come! We're leaving! (*She strides towards the moon gate, the entourage turning to follow her.*)

LI (*bowing*): Aye! (*He leaps forward and takes the* DOWAGER's *arm, meanwhile also shouting towards offstage right.*) Bring up the sedan chair!

VOICES (*offstage*): Aye! Aye! (*Sounds of flurried activity.*)

DOWAGER (*at the gate, to* LI): No, we are going to stroll a while.

(*Exeunt all, except the* EMPEROR. *He now takes a deep breath and starts to enter the gate to the pavilion. But at this moment* WANG SHANG, *his eunuch, rushes in through the moon gate and hurries after him.* WANG SHANG *bows.*)

EMPEROR: You're still waiting for me! I'd nearly forgotten about you.

(*The* EMPEROR *and* WANG SHANG *now move downstage right, approaching the chess table.*)

WANG SHANG: Over at Inner Strength Hall the princes and ministers are still waiting, waiting for your final decision.

EMPEROR: I came over here to sound out Old Buddha's opinion. I wasn't expecting to run into domestic troubles worse than what's going on in Korea.

WANG: That's as may be, but still it is the Emperor who must decide whether we negotiate a peace or declare war.

EMPEROR (*slapping the chess table*): Order them to open the attack!

WANG: But in Li Hung-chang's report to the throne, doesn't he point out that the Japanese navy is stronger than ours, and doesn't he advise Your Majesty to negotiate for peace?

EMPEROR: But what can we do? Half the funds allotted for ships and cannon Old Buddha makes off with, to build the Summer Palace, and the rest of the funds disappear into the pockets of Li Lien-ying. It will be our own fault if we are defeated.

WANG: The Emperor is understandably upset just now. He would be wise to reconsider carefully.

EMPEROR (*sharply*): Suppose the Japanese come here and occupy the capital, wipe out the dynasty, kill us all. What of it? This is the worst that can happen—and it might be the best, for everyone. (*He pauses.*) Go back now. Tell the princes and ministers to draft the imperial decree. I'll come as soon as I can.

WANG: Aye!

(WANG SHANG *departs through the moon gate. The* EMPEROR, *in overt despair, pounds his fist against his forehead. He enters the pavilion. It is growing dark.*)

(*The curtain closes slowly.*)

TRANSLATED BY JEREMY INGALLS

The Creation of a
"People's Literature"

The nineteen forties and fifties saw a great outpouring of stories in re
sponse to governmental insistence on the need for a new "mass" literature. Every now and then appeared a tale whose vividness of observation and warm humanity transcended the level of propaganda.

"The Smashing of the Dragon King" is such a tale. It could be
classified as just another contribution to the "resist superstition" movement, and seen, as an overt exercise on such a theme, to be so much
less effective than for example Lu Hsün's earlier portrait of the terrified
peasant woman in "Benediction." But a judgment of this kind would
do no justice to the fine comic creations of Zodiac Mah and Inky-nob
the Sorceress, the compassionate portrayal of Uncle Boils or the exuber-
ant evocation of the procession and its terminal donnybrook.

"Wang T'ieh" is probably a pseudonym: no other writings by this
man have come to prominence.

●

Wang T'ieh

The Smashing of the Dragon King

[Shuai Lung Wang]

I

"SAVE THE SEEDLINGS!"

Mahs' Bend is a little village in a valley. This particular village is even more cramped than its neighbors, and if you stood at the head of the valley and looked in you wouldn't believe there could be anyone living there.

Everyone in the village has the name Mah. As soon as a child is old enough to understand, it hears the story of the founding of the village: "When the ancestors of the Mah clan moved into this valley there were only the two of them, man and wife, who had split off from the family back in Shansi, under the old pagoda tree in Hung-tung County. When they left their kinfolk they broke up a great pot and brought a piece with them, so that afterwards they could prove their kinship by this fragment of the pot. That's why the people of Mahs' Bend are sometimes called the 'Broken Pot Mahs'." By now the sons and grandsons of Mr. and Mrs. Mah have multiplied to forty or fifty families, all of them still living huddled together here. For the land there is, the population is quite dense enough.

From the valley bottom you can see neither the fields nor the sun. If you want to see the fields you must climb to the top of the hill. From there you can make out the scattered terraces, a square here, a patch there, a strip or two at the foot of a cliff, a strip or two more on top of a mound. They grow mostly castor-oil plant, seedling grain, pumpkins, and sprouts.

This year on the fifteenth of the fourth month there was a heavy fall of rain, and everyone in the village got his seedlings in early. But then the rain thinned off a bit. The people of Mahs' Bend watched the blue sky, hoping for rain. The farmers watched them pass, the fortnight periods they call by name, "grain fills," "grain in ear," "summer solstice." They counted the days from the fifth of the fifth month to the sixth of the sixth. Every time a patch of cloud appeared the people scrambled up the ridge in their joy, to watch the sky. But just as the clouds began to cover the sun a wind would blow up and sweep every last shred of cloud from view. Time and again their hopes had been disappointed. And by the double sixth the spring seedlings were several inches above the soil.

It was terrible dry weather, the seedlings were like babies robbed of their milk. First they grew listless and couldn't stand upright, then half a leaf would turn yellow, then the whole leaf, then the stalk, until one by one they died. The pumpkin vines had been spread out and the first flowers were opening when the leaves went dry. It was time to bed down the vines—but who could find the stomach for this work when the soil was rock hard?

The first dog days passed and the granite cliffs still shone out naked from the hillside, the shooting grain still hadn't covered up the surface of the ground. It had looked as though the persimmons might hang on, but now for lack of rain they were dropping unripe, layering the ground. Elms, pagoda trees, privets had been stripped bare of their leaves, and now the bellies of the cattle and the bellies of the people grew emptier every day. The villagers found their faces swelling, their stomachs distending, and every kind of disease began to spread.

"Lord of Heaven, save the seedlings!" But they had cried out too often, even the children were sick of repeating it.

How to save the seedlings? Everyone demanded a solution.

It's true that two miles or so from the village, on Green Spring Hill, there was a spring of clear water, and with men with carrying-poles or beasts of burden to fetch the water you could save something at any rate. But the people of Mahs' Bend didn't hold with this idea. When the government sent a cadre to mobilize teams they said it was too far and, what was more, nobody had ever done that since the ancestors first came to the valley. Things being so, they soon ate up the government's relief grain, and still no one could think of a way out. "Eat it up! Eat it and fill your belly if it's only this once!" Many of them fully intended to go on like this.

But what ways did they think of to save the seedlings? They felt the only way was to ask the help of the spirits.

"Lord of Heaven, save our seedlings for us!" Some of the villagers turned their faces in prayer to Heaven, but the heavens still shone bright and clear and rainless.

"Save our little seedlings for us, Lord of our Kitchen!" The men knelt with their wives and children before the kitchen gods, but the heavens still shone bright and clear.

"Save our little seedlings for us, O Jade Emperor!" Little groups of people knelt in prayer in front of the temple to the supreme divinity of the Taoists, but still the rain did not come.

The people of the village prayed in every temple they had. And each day more of the seedlings died.

It was just at this point that someone or other trumped up a plausible story: "The fact is that the first ancestor of our clan was related to the Dragon King. They lived together here in Mahs' Bend, and in those days the harvests were always plentiful enough. Then when the Dragon King moved off, thousands of miles away to far Yünnan, he said to our ancestor just before he left, "If ever any great disaster befalls your descendants," he said, "just you send for me and I'll see them through.""

The story didn't take long to get around. One told ten and ten told a hundred, and before long the whole village had heard it. It sprouted leaves and blossoms in the telling, too, and someone added the information that the Dragon King had actually manifested himself in Mahs' Bend, and had even been seen, in the great drought of 1901.

Old San-mao was reckoned the oldest inhabitant, but he was a bit pigheaded when they first asked him about it, and "Rubbish!" he said. They cursed him for an old fool, so he changed his mind to "Don't remember," but at last he grew more obliging still and settled the matter to everyone's satisfaction by admitting, fair and square, "Yes, it happened all right." With this the rumor that had been spread turned into gospel truth.

"The Dragon King can save our seedlings." Everybody believed this.

But there are only three temples in Mahs' Bend, one to the Jade Emperor, one to the Goddess of Mercy, and one to the Earth Spirit. There is none at all to the Dragon King.

II

MR. ZODIAC MAH

Useless to speak of Mahs' Bend without first introducing Mr. Zodiac Mah, for he is its prize exhibit.

His real name is Mah Shang-hsien, and his age about fifty. In his thirties he sprouted a couple of wisps of mustache, so some call him "Mustache Mah." As a boy he studied for six years with a tutor, the graduate Chang from the village of Changs' End. He read the *Great Learning*, the *Doctrine of the Mean*, the *Mencius*, the *Analects* first half and second half, though unfortunately the tutor never got round to explaining what they meant. Everyone said that Mahs' Bend was going to produce a graduate, but he was very unlucky, for the government abolished the examinations without waiting for Mr. Mah to sit for them.

Poor Mr. Mah, for whom the times were so sadly out of joint, had no choice but to sit at home and attend to his own affairs. He was by no means prepared to make farm work his life, however, and so in the less busy days of winter and spring he devoted himself to learning the signs of the zodiac and to more advanced studies of the *yin* and the *yang*. In less than two years he had developed the capacity to choose a site for a grave that would ensure undisturbed rest for its occupant, to cast horoscopes from the hour, day, month, and year of birth, to determine the mutual compatibility or otherwise of those planning to marry. Gradually the whole village learned to invite the assistance of Mr. Mah whenever there was to be a wedding or a funeral.

But it was the siting of Hu Lien's father's grave that really made his name. Three miles from the village lay Hus' Hollow, and when one of the Hu clan, a trader, wanted to bury his father he engaged Mr. Mah to determine the site. Later on this Hu Lien made some lucky deals in secondhand clothing and found himself with quite a pile of money. He pushed and prospered and within eight years owned ten acres of land and had opened a secondhand clothes store. You don't see such a sudden fortune in the valley villages more than once in several generations, and the guess was that the influence of his ancestral tombs was at the bottom of it. Mr. Mah saw his opening, and made it known that into the selection of Hu Lien's grave-site had gone "seven sevens forty-nine days," with a testing of the topographical emanations night after night in the middle watches: no wonder the family had flourished! When this got about it convinced all and sundry of Mr. Mah's genius and mastery of the *yin* and *yang* and the zodiac. Before long his personal name was forgotten and he became simply Mr. Zodiac Mah.

As his fame spread daily it was not long before a procession of people was coming from two miles, five miles, a score of miles away to ask Mr. Mah to cast horoscopes or compare for marital compatibility, or to ask him to prognosticate or to check the "wind and water"—to determine whether a site for house or tomb was in a location favorable to the spirits. There was a constant commotion of visitors at his gate. And nobody who troubled Mr. Mah in this way cared to let him go empty-handed. Some gave presents and some gave rice—either gave him rice directly or did an odd job of work for him. Mr. Mah's situation began to improve. He not only fed and clothed himself more handsomely than anyone else, but bought up five acres of land, a herd of goats, a team of oxen.

There were few who could read and write in Mahs' Bend, and so of course Mr. Mah with his flourishing fortune and his manifest erudition began to be revered as a genuine sage. Advice from him was mandatory in anything related to the communal welfare, he was touted as the man to preside at the Tomb Feast, the prayers for rain, the lantern festivals for the spirits, the blessing of the seedlings.

I suppose this golden age must have lasted for ten full years before shame and disaster finally fell on Zodiac Mah's head.

It was a fellow villager, Mah San-hsiang, who was behind it all. Mah San-hsiang was building a new cottage, and from choosing the site to deciding the time most suitable for starting to dig, fitting the windows, placing the rafters and making the offerings to the God of Building, the whole kit and caboodle was Mr. Mah's to handle. But before the house had been up three days Mah San-hsiang's wife died of a sudden illness. Then as it happened they were a little careless while the funeral was going on: the house caught fire, and half of this brand-new edifice burnt to a crisp. Mah San-hsiang threw a fit and went crazy; the story got to him that the site was governed by the devil-star, whose sign is corpses, and Mah San-hsiang grabbed a knife and ran screaming imprecations up to Zodiac Mah's front door. Mr. Mah jumped the garden wall and ran off in terror, but by the end of the affair his reputation had dropped a mile. He himself however explained that the whole thing had been predetermined by the horoscopes.

From this time the crowd at his door started thinning out, and Mr. Mah began to confine his activities to various communal concerns. Unless it was personal friends who asked him to cast or compare horoscopes or tell their fortunes, he would flatly refuse to take things on.

There was something of a revival of his fame after the start of the Japanese War. He was felt to be very effective in organizing the community to deal with the troops who passed through now and again in their flight from the front. Then the Communists' Eighth Route Army came through and the Japanese mounted a sweep against them. Mr. Mah consulted the trigrams which predicted that the Japanese would not harm the village. As it happened, the Nips came over the hill in front of the village, straight into an Eighth Route Army ambush, which proved to one and all the accuracy of Mr. Mah's calculations.

When they set up Farmers' Relief Committees in the surrounding villages, two or three youths of Mahs' Bend joined the movement as well and spread it about that they were to "deal with" the communal affairs. Mr. Mah at this very cleverly gave up all the work he had been doing for the community. But when he had thus retired the village discovered that it didn't possess anyone else who could read and write and keep accounts, and so it appointed Mah San-chu as temporary caretaker. But this Mah San-chu was the very same man who had always handled the community matters, the one who had always done the legwork for Zodiac Mah, and in fact it was still Mr. Zodiac Mah who was the brains behind all that went on.

So now Zodiac Mah's empire was more firmly secured than ever. Mah San-chu was proposed and accepted as chairman of the "Help Resistance—Speed Production Committee"; his son "Tiger" became head of the activist team, and Zodiac himself remained the village's prize exhibit.

III

INKY-NOB THE SORCERESS

"The Dragon King can save the seedlings, and he was related to the founders of the Mah clan": since this story was setting everyone by the ear, we must surely make it our business to find out what wind blew it into the village.

Don't despair, dear reader: as they say, "Where there're ripples you'll find a breeze, where there're maggots you'll find flies." To get to the root of this matter we shall need a word or two about the spirit world of Mahs' Bend.

There are other people in Mahs' Bend, besides the famous and eminent Mr. Zodiac Mah, who understand the inner secrets of the cosmos and have frequent intercourse with the spirit world, and the next on the list is Inky-nob the Sorceress.

As a matter of fact, it's hard to think of Mr. Zodiac Mah without at the same time thinking of Inky-nob, for she is Zodiac's closest friend, she is in fact his girl. They say "fancy lovers never last long," but these two have been going together for fully twenty years now. Inky-nob will be over forty by this time, and she is a favorite topic of conversation among the older men with mustaches. To the middle-aged of the village she has been known in course of time by three different nicknames. At fourteen or fifteen she was a front-rank beauty, she used to wear tiny red shoes embroidered with flowers, and usually a tassel at the point of the toes; and it was this that led to her first nickname, "Radish-whiskers." After she became friendly with Mr. Mah, and without waiting to be promised in marriage, she had a couple of babies. She got herself a very bad name, and people said her father had "no chance of posterity." They tried frantically to find a husband for her, but no one dared take her on and there was nothing they could do about it. So then, at Mr. Mah's suggestion, she took to herself the name of sorceress, and began to play about with magic, peddling holy water and magic pills, and letting it be known, moreover, that she intended to "guard her chastity and never marry," and to cultivate herself in preparation for becoming an Immortal. That's why all through her twenties she was known as "The Immortal."

I forget which year it was when Inky-nob suddenly up and married a haberdashery peddler from Seven Mile Inn; but within four years she was a widow. So what then? She brought her belongings back to Mahs' Bend, back to her parents' home, where she continued to associate with Zodiac Mah and resumed her search for immortality. Then in an ill-starred year she contracted a disease of the scalp, and all her hair fell out. Proud of her looks for thirty years and more, naturally, it didn't take her long to think of a bright idea for a makeshift. This was to rub black ink from time to time into her bald scalp; and that's how her nickname changed to "Inky-nob." All of Mahs' Bend from now on called her "Inky-nob the Sorceress," or just "Inky-nob" for short.

Inky-nob's parents died, and she had no brothers or sisters but just lived on all by herself. With Mr. Mah's frequent visits there was plenty going on in the house. As they say, "The hero's home has a magic of its own," and soon enough Inky-nob's became the gathering-place for all who took a hand in the communal concerns. This was where the affairs of the community were deliberated; this was where much of the communal property found its way; this was where the community leaders ate and drank, for Inky-nob was a smart cook and produced a tasty dish. The whole yield from the couple of acres of communal field worked by Mr. Mah used to find its way year by year into Inky-nob's larder. When times were good there was always plenty to eat at Inky-nob's; but this was a year of famine and starvation, and Mr. Mah was very cautious—it was not till after dark with the village in bed that a good smell began to come from Inky-nob's kitchen.

One evening Zodiac Mah made his way as usual to Inky-nob's house, a tobacco pipe in his hand a good three feet long. Inky-nob had half a pan of noodle soup ready for him, with some dried delicacies to go with it. Mr. Mah happening to have room in his belly, he heaped up a big bowl, and holding his mustaches clear with his fingers began to drink. Inky-nob kept him company, both hands stroking her little brin-dled cat. Clandestine lovers of long standing, they behaved every whit the same as a properly married couple. They chatted about odds and ends of housekeeping, and then got on to the terrible lack of rain. Zo-diac Mah said, "The Heavens have their stars and the Earth has its pulse. If the river of the Milky Way isn't full the water can't flow, and if the Earth's pulse is blocked the springs can't get through. . . ." Inky-nob was listening, half-comprehending, when all at once Mr. Mah looked up to the sky and sighed, deeply and at length, towards the brilliant starlit heavens.

Before his sigh had died away there came a sudden voice in re-sponse from the doorway: "Strange times! What are you distressing yourself about, Mr. Mah? Here's another government ordinance ar-rived, come on, read it out to us!" Mr. Mah gave a start, but when he fixed his eyes on the speaker it was none other than Mah San-chu, the community's "caretaker," chairman of the "Help Resistance—Speed Production Committee." Mr. Mah at once dragged him to a seat, nor did Inky-nob dawdle but passed him a bowl of noodle soup neither too thin nor too stiff. Mah San-chu, dispensing with the demands of etiquette, began to gulp it down in great sucking mouthfuls.

Mr. Mah took over the ordinance and held it to the lamp to read, scratching at his skullcap the while and forgetting even to finish his noodles. Every word of the ordinance had to do with confiscating the villagers' food stocks and the produce of the communal land, for the temporary relief of famine victims. Mr. Mah reflected that this would mean enquiries about the two acres of communal land that he farmed, and about his own stores of grain—you couldn't guarantee there wouldn't be a few malcontents coming to borrow. But what could you do about it?

With these thoughts he pushed his bowl aside and looked up with another long-drawn sigh. His companion couldn't figure out what was the matter, and gaped in alarm.

Mr. Mah read out the ordinance, after which the three of them sat mute for a while. Then there was some discussion and they all agreed on suppressing the ordinance and keeping quiet about relieving famine victims until after they had prayed for rain. In this way the poor of the village would be fully occupied with the Dragon King, and wouldn't go bothering their heads about where the produce of the communal land had gone to. Their policy settled, Mr. Mah made sure there was no stranger about and then said this and that and the other to his two faithful supporters. These two nodded their heads in agreement, and that was how the rumor was born about the Dragon King being a relative of the Mahs' first ancestor.

Mah San-chu trotted out of Inky-nob's house and found that a number of the villagers were still out in the street, not yet gone to bed. He gathered them together, and to the burning of dried sagebrush torches they smoked and chatted. There was much coughing and sighing, and many a despairing remark of the type of "When Heaven wants to destroy men it doesn't need a sword." It was clear to Mah San-chu that panic was in all their minds, and he took the occasion to roll out the rumor they had just fabricated. He volunteered also the information that Mr. Mah had seen it written, "clear as daylight in the clan genealogy." All who heard this nonsense felt they had found the road to salvation, and they all agreed, "Yes, it will be a good deed, we're all willing."

A word from you, a word from me, it was quicker than the radio and the whole village knew of it in a twinkling.

IV

THE DRAGON KING SENDS A DREAM

Early the next morning Uncle Boils (he had a tumor on the back of his neck) came in from the fields. He was the jumpiest man in the village, and came running through the streets to Inky-nob's house looking for Mr. Mah without ever thinking to put down his manure fork. The second he entered the gate he bumped into Mr. Mah standing in the yard with an almanac in his hand. Uncle Boils asked him about this business of the Dragon King and expressed his eagerness to go praying for rain, and delivered as well the views of his neighbors on the matter. Zodiac Mah realized that the story was in fact believed by all, and thereupon he began sonorously to read out: "Under Jupiter the wood element reigns in the East, under Mars the fire element reigns in the South. Fire indicates burning. . . . Today, tomorrow . . . the day after tomorrow." After a minute or two of careful counting on his fingertips he announced in a loud voice: "But the day after tomorrow is a day of fire, and the Dragon King is subdued by fire." At this point Mr. Mah stopped again, only to resume his directions after stealing a glance at Uncle Boils' face and noting its expression of concentration and satisfaction: "The whole village must join in the prayers, nor must they delay beyond today or tomorrow, for the Dragon King is an awful spirit and swift in his wrath."

The more Uncle Boils heard, the more he was impressed by the strength and aptness of Mr. Mah's reasoning. He was quick to agree: "As I see it, we must ask you gentlemen to take it on, for the younger men would only bungle a ceremony of this kind. Don't you think you had better lead us, Mr. Mah?"

"Ai! I'm past it! I'm an old lion who's lost his teeth and can't bite any more!" Mr. Mah's reply was deliberately intended to fan the flames by blowing cold. It left Uncle Boils with eyes staring wide and not a word to say.

By this time Mr. Mah had guessed nine-tenths of what was in the other man's mind. He pointed his pipe at the ground: "Uncle Boils, you must go find Mah San-chu. He's the 'Help Resistance—Speed Production' chairman, he's the best one to decide."

Brimming with enthusiasm Uncle Boils wheeled round, picked up his manure fork and went off in search of Mah San-chu.

The matter of praying for rain brought many others seeking Mr. Mah even before breakfast: Second Dog, Mah Ch'ing-t'ai, Mah Ch'ing-ho. . . . And every one of them in his own way agreed that the Dragon King should be appealed to. Mr. Mah gave each of them an on-the-spot disquisition on the principles of *yin* and *yang*.

After breakfast was over, not only were there more and more men coming for Mr. Mah, the women were there as well to consult Inky-nob. The most zealous of all were the wife of Little Happy, second-in-command of the militia platoon, and Old Red-eyes, the wife of Mah San-chu. These two were known through the village as "novices"; whenever the spirit descended on Inky-nob they would be there to fill her pipe, fetch water, light incense sticks, burn the sacrificial paper ingots; if people didn't understand one of Inky-nob's mystic prophecies they would be there to interpret. These two "novices" arrived at Inky-nob's house giggling and nudging each other and wanting her to take the spirit upon herself at once. Inky-nob had the same idea, but unfortunately wasn't quite ready for them and could only make a vague sort of reply. When everyone had gone she talked things over with Zodiac Mah, and the upshot was that that same afternoon, on the hillside west of the village of Mahs' Bend, Inky-nob the Sorceress would give a great display of her arts.

On this western slope of Mahs' Bend is a pagoda tree of great age, and near its roots a little cave in the rocks. Long ago a wooden board was erected here with the inscription "In Sincerity Lies Magic," and it was spread about that this was the abode of a fairy fox. The tree and the cave had become even more sacrosanct since Inky-nob's graduation as a sorceress, and now she had built a small temple beneath the pagoda tree. She had set up two or three clay idols, and on the altar had placed a gaily enameled vase containing a large number of flowers made of red and green paper. No matter how they had to scrape and save for it, the peasants never missed burning a few sticks of incense at this temple on the first and fifteenth of every month. And on this particular afternoon there was more going on at the temple than ever before in its history.

You could see them from the edge of the village, a big semicircle of women and another semicircle of men kneeling in front of the temple. Inky-nob was there, looking more spiritual than ever. She clapped her eyelids shut and made a series of passes with a pink silk handkerchief. Then her neck began to jerk like a hen eating corn and she started muttering something. Before long the faithful of both sexes who were closest to her began to promulgate her message: "She had a dream last night. She got instructions from the Dragon King. The Dragon King is willing to save the people of Mahs' Bend. We have to wait till midnight and then carry an image of the Dragon King to the east of the village one mile. We have to burn incense and kowtow, and then shout three times in succession for the Dragon King. She guarantees the ground will be soaked within three days."

Everyone was thrilled with this prognostication, and kowtowed and gave thanks to Inky-nob. The two "novices," Old Red-eyes and Little Happy's wife, knelt close by her and fanned unceasingly—Inky-nob had put a lot of energy into her performance, and it was the dog days, the beads of sweat from her scalp rolled down and carried with them the ink she had rubbed on, so that her face was streaked with black all over.

Inky-nob's trance lasted in the end from just after the midday meal until the sun was declining in the west. More and more people came in, and Mah San-chu thoughtfully set up a long table in front of the temple with a couple of incense stoves on it so that people could have somewhere to burn their incense.

Although they had a hard time of it, the tenants of Mah's Bend, none of them was averse to spending money when anything to do with the spirits came along. The old sesame-candy vendor from Three Mile Bend alone sold three baskets of candy during the day, all for people to give as offerings. And one man who was sick obtained some magic medicine, and in the evening sent Inky-nob a couple of pounds of white noodles as a gift.

v

THE STEALING OF THE DRAGON KING

From long ago there has been handed down, in the villages within a thirty-mile radius of Mahs' Bend, the custom of "stealing the Dragon King": in time of drought the people of one village will go to another and steal that village's Dragon King. They say a stolen Dragon King is more than usually efficacious, and the village from which it has been stolen will have a poorer harvest that year. The farmers all believed that when you stole a Dragon King you stole that year's "abundance." So when you went to steal one you had to go at the time least expected, the middle of the night for example.

Now that Inky-nob's trance had pointed out the way to pray for rain, the faithful of Mahs' Bend set their hopes on stealing a Dragon King from some other village. Zodiac Mah and Mah San-chu were also occupied with planning this matter. They considered carefully all the villages for three miles round: only Seven Mile Inn had a temple to the Dragon King. In this temple were altogether twenty-four portable idols, and the one with the blue face was the Dragon King himself. But when it came to going along to Seven Mile Inn and stealing it, both Zodiac and Mah San-chu felt no little trepidation: Seven Mile Inn was a big village of over two hundred families, with a militia of twenty or thirty men. Furthermore, the principal clan there was the Yangs, and the Mahs and the Yangs had been feuding ever since Inky-nob returned to Mahs' Bend with her property years ago. If they now went and stole the thing they might stir up trouble of some sort, and so they deliberated from dawn to dusk without coming to any decision.

When dusk fell people had time to spare, and little groups of twos and threes gathered to discuss the affair of stealing the Dragon King. As a natural thing they drifted towards Inky-nob's to find out what was happening; the din grew louder and louder, and before long her courtyard was one black mass of people. Zodiac and his colleagues were really feeling quite embarrassed by this time, until Tiger Mah, the leader of the activist squad, seeing that his father Mah San-chu was finding it hard to get out of doing what was expected of him, stuck his chest out and elbowed his way to the front. He rolled up his sleeves and spat on his palms, clenched his fists, and said, "It's easy. Scared? Scared of what? Scared of getting kicked by a canary? I'll go! And if I don't bring it back I'm a babe in arms!"

Tiger Mah, leader of the activist squad, a real wild one: the squabbling died away at once when he came out with this remark. Tiger is the sort who blazes up when he sees a fire, and in no time he got together a handful of like-minded youngsters who weren't too bothered about the rights and wrongs of the business. Nor did they bother to wait until people were in bed before they set out for Seven Mile Inn.

Just when dawn was breaking the next morning, the sky still blotched with black, the wife of the peasant Mah Ch'ang-shun got up and prepared to mill some grain. On opening the door she made out dimly in the black shadows by the doorpost the squatting figure of a man. "Who is it?" she yelled half-a-dozen times, but whoever it was just went on sitting there solidly without a sound. She ran back into the house in terror, roused her husband, called the alarm: "There's a demon!" Now this Mah Ch'ang-shun was one of the more sensible people of the village, but although he wasn't fully convinced, his wife's panting fright set up a few doubts in his mind; he hurriedly lit a lamp and picked up an axe and went out to have a look. And there he was, the last person you'd have thought of: blue face, red beard, clay head, clay feet, the Dragon King himself. Furious, Mah Ch'ang-shun ripped a couple of tufts out of the idol's beard, then took it up on his back and dropped it down again beside the well.

And why had they dumped the Dragon King by Mah Ch'ang-shun's door? It was all a subtle scheme of Zodiac Mah's. One of the rules of the game of stealing the Dragon King is that if you set down the stolen image by somebody's door, that person has to fork out for the ceremonies. Mah Ch'ang-shun was only a hired hand, but the previous year he had been to Farmers' Council meetings in another village, and had come back with the idea of setting up a Council in Mahs' Bend, and what was more, of getting things straightened out in their community association. Zodiac Mah had had no love for this man for a long time, and time and again he had sought an opportunity to get at him. This was a golden one, and Zodiac Mah it was who had deliberately dumped the Dragon King on his doorstep. The beauty of it was that Mah Ch'ang-shun himself was perfectly aware of the reason for it.

By the time the sun was well up everyone knew that the theft of the Dragon King had been accomplished, and great rejoicings began. Mah San-chu had a matting shed erected, Tiger brought along a big drum, Uncle Boils dug up a gong from somewhere, *kaboom kaboom!* they banged away, the heavens reechoed, it was a glorious din.

That day the whole village mobilized. The young men got busy making a carrying-platform; Mah Ch'ing-t'ai, Mah Ch'ing-ho, and other elders rushed off to the shops and the market to buy incense and paper ingots and yellow streamers; the children picked willow twigs from the bottoms and plaited them into little caps to wear; Inky-nob and her two "novices" led a gang of women with new brooms sweeping the street clean. Inky-nob had plastered her scalp with glistening black ink, and with a red paper flower stuck into her few remaining strands of hair she coquetted all over the street. Fun? It was better than New Year's.

Mahs' Bend had woken up again, Mahs' Bend had come back to life. Everyone seemed to have forgotten his hunger, and the cry was raised in the neighboring villages: "The one true Dragon King has manifested himself in Mahs' Bend!"

VI

PRAYING FOR RAIN

The one true Dragon King had manifested himself in Mahs' Bend, and there was so much excitement that none of the villagers had time to concern himself with the work in the fields. They had all brought in their incense, paper ingots, yellow streamers, all the rest of the offerings, and they had got hold of two yards of red calico to make the Dragon King a new robe. Every street and every alley was filled with children wearing caps plaited from willow twigs, yelling and chanting:

> Days of rain,
> Rain every day.
> Look at the soil, is it black or grey?
> If it's dry, let it rain,
> If it's not bring clouds again.

Inky-nob led the van of a band of women, those in front sweeping all along the street with bright new brooms, those behind scattering drops of water all over the ground out of the washbowls they carried. Behind these again, gongs and drums clanging and thumping; and four lads carrying the Dragon King in a red lacquer chair, perambulating all over the place, circling every well and weaving up and down every ditch they could find. They grew weary with it, panting and sweating, and the sun of the dog days scorched their heads till they looked like nothing more than steamed dumplings; yet not one of them dared breathe a word of complaint. And all the time not a shred of cloud in the sky, yet the people walked up and down behind Mah San-chu crying, "It's raining! It's raining!" Praying for rain had turned them into idiots, bewitched, their brains had leaked out through their earholes, they'd gone mad. If anyone just then had dared to say "But there isn't any rain!" the crowd would have set on him and broken every bone in his body.

Each household was preparing its offering to the Dragon King. The better-off people made noodles out of white wheat flour and cooked them up with some dried chrysanthemum flowers; the middling peasants did their best to find some white flour for noodles, and mixed in a bit of bean flour; all the poor peasants could do was fry up some bean-flour noodles in vegetable oil, and add a piece of sesame candy for the god . . . but one thing was certain, each one of them brought forth what he could for the sacrifice. For all normal purposes they were down to tightening their belts and picking their teeth for dinner, but when it came to offerings for the god they went crazy, nothing was too precious, nothing grudged.

While the peasants were thus absorbed in burning their incense and making their offerings, Mr. Zodiac Mah busied himself with certain private calculations. The red calico he had bought for the community had cost ten dollars a foot; it went down in the accounts at eleven and a half. He added seventy cents to the incense and paper things. He made no record of the contributions people had made of money for incense, and whenever he came across a new banknote he put it quietly by. As for Mah San-chu and Inky-nob, their standard of living had risen considerably. Three bowls of noodles a day, and sesame candy and dried chrysanthemum flowers to go with them—their bellies grew taut as drumskins, and in fact Mah San-chu developed indigestion from the very first day. He had a sweet tooth for the candy and flowers and put away three pounds of the noodles at every sitting, which left him no room in his belly for soup. What with this and the hot weather he got constipated, and whenever he could snatch a minute he would be squatting in the hemp patch straining away. . . .

And in this fashion the one true Dragon King manifested himself for three whole days.

On the evening of the fourth day they decided to follow the directions of Inky-nob's "spirit." When it got to eight or nine in the evening Zodiac Mah quietly drew Tiger aside. He gave him his instructions, thus and so, and then Tiger set out well in advance.

With nightfall, but before the first watch, the masters of ceremonies gathered the people together, and with gongs and drums and lighted torches, and men carrying incense and ingots and yellow streamers, and still the Dragon King on his throne with four lads carrying him, a long and noisy procession moved off east from the village. When they reached a gully where the road forked, just about a mile from the village, the invokers of rain came to a halt. They set the torches up and burned the incense and ingots and streamers, and then they knelt in rows and made a whole string of bows and obeisances. Mr. Zodiac Mah knelt in the very front row, and read out in a loud voice the prayer for rain he had prepared beforehand:

"Whereas in this year of great drought, in this month of perilous famine, the descendants of the clan of Mah do reverently and in full sincerity turn their gaze to the south, to Yünnan, to the mighty spirit the great Dragon King, with burning of incense and with obeisances we do implore Your Majesty to take cognizance of your relationship with the first ancestor of our clan, to look down in pity on your descendants, to send clouds in dense array, rain in copious flow. . . ."

As Mr. Mah read on, every soul present listened with concentration and with humble respect, though no one had much idea what a dense array or a copious flow was, let alone a cognizance. When he had finished there was another round of head-knocking before Mr. Zodiac Mah finally raised his voice and called, "O Dragon King!" All listened carefully: not a sound; and then after a short interval the second call. Again all listened carefully: and this time from a great distance came an answering *Boom*. . . . When the third call ended they heard, from a hilltop a few hundred yards away, a noise as of great boulders crashing one after another down the hillside. Poor devils, praying for rain, not one of them by this time but felt his courage wavering, a tingling in the roots of his hair, cold shivers all down his back; there they knelt in unanimous accord, without a flicker of a movement, thinking, "The Dragon King has power indeed! He's really come. . . ."

They went on with this tomfoolery till the fifth watch, it was nearly dawn before they split up and went home to get some sleep. Tiger Mah came running up to Zodiac Mah and said with a vacuous grin, "Well! I forgot to make a noise when you called the first time, it was not till the second time that I remembered to stick a handkerchief over my mouth and start calling back . . . and then I stumbled and sent three huge rocks rolling down."

Mr. Mah did not find this at all amusing, but contented himself with a solemn word of warning: "You must make sure the villagers don't find out about this. If by any chance they do, it will mean a severe loss of face for us all."

TWO UNFORESEEN EVENTS

Mr. Mah had led the faithful of both sexes thrice to hail the Dragon King in the depths of night, and had been rewarded by a *Boom boom!* in response. On their return all felt that nothing now could delay the rain.

But it was most unfortunate: there still wasn't the slightest wisp of cloud in the sky, and to crown everything a wind blew up. In the early morning a howling wind began to sweep down from the higher mountains to the northwest. Dust covered earth and sky, the sun darkened, from the surrounding hills rose up a dark brown fog of dust.

The one sandstorm was as bad as ten days of drought. Before, there had been a little yellow mist above the soil, but now after this wind it was like husks pressed dry of their oil, the last drop of moisture was blown away. And the seedlings? Already like babies robbed of their milk, half-dying, they were in no state to stand up to this wind. It dried the last moisture from the veins of the seedlings; the creeping vines and the flowers of the pumpkins were whipped by the fierce wind until the petals dropped one after another from the receptacles. And then the persimmons: people were frantic. "Bake persimmons in a bun, beats a stewpot when it's done"—flour milled from dried persimmons mixed in with grain husks was the lifeline of the peasants. No wonder they panicked—the storm had brought down the little half-formed persimmons, had broken the peasants' lifeline.

The wind howled, and the howling of wolves could not have chilled their hearts more. . . .

The farmers were really desperate now. They hadn't the heart to make any more offerings or burn any more incense, but went again to beg Mr. Mah and Inky-nob the Sorceress for their advice.

"The Dragon King has come, but why has he brought wind instead of rain?"

"The Dragon King was a water spirit, surely there shouldn't be this dry wind?"

"We've no way out now. The seedlings, the persimmons . . . it's all over."

Moans and groans and all the lamentations of despair filled Mr. Mah's ears. Mr. Mah at this juncture was beside himself with anxiety.

Streams of cold perspiration flowed past his temples, there was a burning along his spine, something kept thudding in his chest, his mustaches quivered and trembled and shook. . . .

It was just then that Mah Ch'ing-t'ai and Uncle Boils came running up, in a state of panic, their faces white, obviously something dreadful had happened. They took no notice of the clamor of voices, but shouted out at once, "Trouble! We're in a mess now! There's real trouble!" Neither of them could get his words out properly.

People stopped talking when they saw how things were, and transferred all their attention to these two. "What is it?" they asked, "What's happened?"

Now they were honest, simple fellows, the two of them, as soon as they got into a fright it was as though they had hot turnips in their mouths, all they could do was nod their heads and make burbling noises, and nobody knew what they were driving at.

"Go and have a look! You'll soon know!" The others left off interrogating them and moved off like a swarm of bees to the Dragon King's shed. There they saw what had happened: Tiger Mah and two or three other lads had hold of a man from Seven Mile Inn and were beating him up. Blood flowed from his burst nose, bits of clay stuck to his hair, the ground all round was littered with peanuts and dried pumpkin seeds. . . .

They always say, "a real hero will take on a village," "a feud goes on from father to son," "corner a dog and he'll bite". . . . This fellow had had a bad time at the hands of the Mah clan. Zodiac Mah could see the trouble in store and got people to break it up with a good deal of tugging and jostling; the peddler already had two black eyes, and he didn't stop to ask about his peanut tray but went running off, wild with rage, back to Seven Mile Inn.

A string of questions elicited what had happened: the peddler had seen that it was the Dragon King from Seven Mile Inn that Mahs' Bend had stolen, and of course in great indignation he had made several very rude remarks and started a row with Tiger Mah.

But there was too much happening to pay any further attention to him now. The hot wind kept up all day, it was dusk before there was the least abatement. In the face of such uncooperative weather Mr. Mah could do no more than put out a statement: "There are still some in Mahs' Bend whose hearts are not sincere, and so the Dragon King at his first coming brought with him a drying wind." Inky-nob had another visit from the spirits, and gave out: "When the Dragon King reached Mahs' Bend he was offended by the insincerity and meagerness of the offerings, but still it will be first the wind and then the rain."

These were very reasonable interpretations, and people saw no cause for disbelief. It was at this point that Mah Ch'ing-t'ai and Uncle Boils put forward a suggestion: "Let's give the Dragon King a magistrate's procession."

"Let's have a magistrate's procession!" The faithful of both sexes joined in a chorus of assent. "There's sure to be rain then."

"It's the only way, a procession. If we don't, it's an insult to the Dragon King!"

VIII

THE SMASHING OF THE DRAGON KING

The drying wind had dropped. The hopes of rain had revived with the clearing weather, and today there was to be a magistrate's procession.

A magistrate's procession is a marvelous affair. At the instigation of Mah San-chu people raked out from their storing-places the old official insignia, the flagpoles, the sedan chair screens which they recovered with red and green cloth. Then there were the gilt lacquer orbs, halberds, lances, steel-handled whips, lanterns shaped like open bowls held up high. All these things were laid out around the Dragon King's shed, and then the placards for clearing the way, and the flying tiger banners, and all the rest were dished out among the people who would carry them.

Zodiac Mah wrote out the itinerary in advance. the procession would set out from Mahs' Bend and take a circular route via Three Mile Bend, Hus' Hollow and Shihs' Gulch, passing round behind Seven Mile Inn. It should really have followed the main street of Seven Mile Inn, but the idea was to avoid any possible awkwardness by extending the route a mile or so and going round behind the village . . . this part of the plan was of course the fruit of Mr. Mah's years and experience.

Three salvos were fired from the small local defense cannon. The peasants assembled before the Dragon King's shed, all of them convinced that nothing could be smarter or more worthwhile than a magistrate's procession. Most of the men wore their New Year's clothes, and the women had wrapped new headscarves round their hair. While they waited for orders to start from the chairman of the community association, Mah San-chu, a number of them squeezed into the shed to have another look at the offerings they had made to the Dragon King. Offerings covered also the three tables in front of the shed, and blue smoke curled up from the incense stoves to wreathe the shed in fragrant clouds. Inky-nob squatted before the image, fanned with reed fans by her two assistant novices.

After the whole company of the faithful had burned incense and performed kowtows and the cannon had let off three more salvos, the great mob taking part in the procession set out from the village with Mah San-chu at their head. The music struck up at once. There were far more musicians this time; in addition to the original gongs and drums there were cymbals and trumpets, pipes and flutes, *tara-tara* making the earth tremble, you could hear them from miles away. . . . When Zodiac Mah had watched them out of sight he turned and went back with the womenfolk.

The Dragon King sat aloft on his portable throne in splendid majesty as they carried him along paths that wound like a sheep's guts across the parched hillsides. The dust flew up from the shuffling feet, rising high in the air. Dust stuck to their sweating temples, dust clung to their sweat-soaked jackets, dust bleared the Dragon King's eyes. . . . They passed through Three Mile Bend, Hus' Hollow, Shihs' Gulch, and every time they came to a village they blew and they banged, startling the innumerable onlookers who had gathered to watch the fun. So slow was their progress that it was afternoon before they reached the back of Seven Mile Inn. They were hot and parched, their bellies empty and their legs aching, their feet stumbled, and they were very weary.

Just at this juncture a bunch of people came bursting out of the village. Even from this distance it was clear they were in a terrible hurry. As they drew nearer it grew more and more apparent that something was wrong; and their leader was none other than the little peddler who had had the beating two days previously. They all had sticks in their hands and a nasty, threatening look about them; and they came running right up in front of the throne, blocking the way, asking, "What call have you to come stealing our Dragon King and beating people up? Who do you think you are?" Although Mah San-chu tried to calm things down and avoid a fuss and mumbled a few apologetic phrases, as soon as they caught sight of Tiger Mah and the other lads their tempers flared up. "Eyes go bloodshot when rivals meet," as they say, and they wasted no more breath but started to lay about them.

"No one can stand clear when a fight starts." The second they laid hands on each other they stopped bothering about subtle distinctions between black and white. Soon there was a heaving mass of bodies, the dust flying, sticks and staves humming through the air; the Dragon King's litter got smashed and the carrying-poles came in as temporary weapons; the lacquer flagpoles, the sedan-chair poles, the gilt lacquer orbs and halberds all joined the arsenal. When the sticks snapped they used fists and feet, twisting and tugging and hitting, they were in no mood to bother about any Dragon King. His litter was torn apart and wielded furiously, and the Dragon King himself was tossed over and broken into pieces, until finally his clay corpse was nothing but a trampled mass of smithereens.

The injured lay writhing and yelling on the ground, where before long they looked like clods of soil with bits of blood and skin sticking to them. Some had their clothes torn to shreds and the naked flesh stared out; some had all the fight knocked out of them and crawled to one side to recover; by the time the headman of Seven Mile Inn hurried to the scene they had fought themselves to a standstill, and it became possible with force and persuasion to separate the two sides.

In the end there were seven or eight seriously injured on each side. Tiger Mah was the worst, both legs were near broken and blood poured from a cruel cut from a cudgel across his forehead; he was in a daze, barely conscious. Mah San-chu had been hurt as well, and lay amongst a heap of broken rain-prayer paraphernalia.

All for the sake of the Dragon King the two villages had brought down on themselves a terrible disaster, they had joined in a bloody tragedy the like of which hadn't been seen for many years.

IX

THE ARREST OF ZODIAC MAH

A vicious brawl, a dozen or more injured: from the less serious, with gashed heads and bloody noses, to those who lay moaning semiconscious. And who was to take the responsibility for this near-fatal up-heaval? The headman of Seven Mile Inn lost not a second in com-posing a detailed account of the happenings for the district authority, and at the same time had stretchers made to carry the casualties to his village, where for the time being they could be cared for and treated.

God works in a mysterious way, and although Zodiac Mah was re-puted to have the key to the secrets of the universe, he was oddly un-able to foresee that he would stir up this calamity. He was compla-cently awaiting the return of the magistrate's procession, reflecting that once again a good part of the expenses had stuck to his own fingers, and in the interval he busied himself with his reckonings as he cooked the communal accounts. The beads of his abacus rattled across the frame as he carefully distributed the costs among all the villagers involved on the basis of acreage of land owned. Mr. Mah made his esti-mates with the utmost precision: "Thirty-four dollars and a quarter; seventy-six thirty—no, it's a big sum, they'll never work it out, we'll call it eighty."

Uncle Boils and Mah Ch'ing-t'ai were among those who had taken part in the procession, but soon after the brawl with the villagers of Seven Mile Inn began they saw that the prospects weren't too good and tried quietly to make off. Unhappily they were not young men, they couldn't move smartly enough, and moreover Mah Ch'ing-t'ai wore his hair in a half-pigtail at the back of his head; before they could get away someone had grabbed hold of Mah Ch'ing-t'ai's pigtail. But they were just a couple of ordinary decent farmers, and so they were only given a few light taps and then let go. They arrived back at Mahs' Bend frightened and flustered and downcast, and without bothering to go home they made straight for Inky-nob's in search of Mr. Mah. He was not there, but Inky-nob chanced just at that moment to have the spirit upon her. The room was filled with women listening to Inky-nob moaning with eyes closed. They were startled to see Uncle Boils cov-ered head to foot in dust, and Mah Ch'ing-t'ai with the front of his jacket torn off and one shoe missing. When they had told their story and refused to guarantee that Mah San-chu and his son were still alive even, San-chu's wife, Red-eyes, couldn't restrain herself from wailing and shrieking, and all the women whose menfolk were in the proces-sion started crying aloud in their fright. The room resounded to the weeping and wailing, and Inky-nob's spirit visitors were soon scared off. Inky-nob was alarmed and ashamed, her cheeks paled and flushed by turns, she didn't know where to put herself, nor what to say for herself. Paying no attention this time to the world of the spirits she went skulking off to find Mr. Mah.

Mr. Mah came rushing into Inky-nob's to find Uncle Boils and Mah Ch'ing-t'ai in this distressed plight, chorusing, "The sky's falling, the sky's falling! There's terrible trouble, there'll be lives lost!" Zodiac Mah was scared stiff, for a while he was speechless, then when he heard that Mah San-chu and his son were being beaten up he fell to trembling all over like a poisoned rat, he simply didn't know what to do about it.

What to do? What to do? Mr. Mah wrung his hands and shuffled his feet and thought and thought, but "of the thirty-six stratagems, the best is to run away," and with all the speed he could muster he picked up his feet to run. . . .

But just as Mr. Mah was on his way out he bumped into Mah San-chu's wife and half a dozen other wailing women who held him back, pestering him to betake himself to Seven Mile Inn and see what was happening. Mr. Mah met this unfavorable situation with hemming and hawing, but by the time he had fobbed them off with vague promises the sun was already sinking behind the hills.

Mr. Mah had no further chance to get away: two armed men from the district office came straight for him. They wasted no time on words but were for tying him up straight away. Mr. Mah was still dreaming of a plan to save himself, so he put on an air of great serenity and faked up a smile: "I am sorry indeed to have given you this trouble, my friends. Whatever it is you want we can talk it over, but why not come along to my home first for a bowl of soup?" He searched in his pockets for a few banknotes while he was speaking, but before he could get them out the two armed comrades had hold of him on either side and were trussing him up with very little ceremony.

Zodiac Mah was sent off under escort to the district. It was already dusk when little groups of the only slightly injured and those who had got off scot-free came drifting back to the village. All wore a forlorn and dejected air, straggling back with their broken paraphernalia, their gongs and drums. . . . As for the Dragon King, there wasn't the faintest sign of him, and people weren't even interested enough to ask after him; the only comments to be heard were, "Is anybody badly hurt? What about Mah San-chu and Tiger? Will they come through? Lot of ruddy nonsense, the whole business!"

And of course there was a good deal of coughing and sniffing as people looked at each other and then at the deserted shed of the Dragon King.

During the evening it got about that a government worker had arrived and was staying at Mah Ch'ang-shun's house.

X

WATERING THE SEEDLINGS

Stealing a Dragon King, praying for rain, a magistrate's procession—what was the result of it all? Getting on for twenty people had been badly hurt, everyone in the village had lost a fortnight's work, huge sums of money had been squandered on incense and offerings: this sort of thing was the result of it all.

Had the rain responded to the prayers? Look at the sky. It was the end of the third week of the dog days now, and not once had the sky so much as clouded over. Famine and distress continued, and grew more serious all the time.

Well then, what *did* they do about it in the end?

What Liu, the worker sent down from district, said was: fetch water for the seedlings. The peasants who didn't own beasts of burden must organize themselves with buckets slung on carrying-poles; those who did must drive their beasts to fetch water. Water the seedlings, save them, if it has to be one plant at a time, one patch at a time. The women and children must go up on the hillsides and pick leaves, elm leaves, peach, almond, pagoda tree, or whatever, and boil them down and pickle them any way they could. From the moment the work of production began not one person must be allowed to die of starvation.

But nobody had much faith in any of these ideas.

Uncle Boils came back from the magistrate's procession full of forebodings that the shattering to pieces of the Dragon King would be counted a major sin, and if they didn't have dragons come to seize them they would at least be scourged with thunderbolts. It would never rain again, and death by starvation was the only thing they could look forward to. So he preferred to lie starving on his bed rather than fetch water for the seedlings; and the rest of the peasants were no different, when they came across the government worker they would say, "We've nothing to eat, we can hardly stand up let alone fetch water." They sank deeper and deeper into their despair.

Then one afternoon the gongs started clanging again. Uncle Boils was out of all patience and started grumbling, "We can't even stay alive, what are the gongs for?"

"Mah Ch'ang-shun has been made chairman of the Farmers' Council," replied his son Baldy. "He's going to distribute grain today!"

Dubious but curious, Uncle Boils dragged himself out on the street, where in fact he found a good number of the peasants making their way to the community offices with empty sacks in their hands. From the distance it looked like a marketplace, there was already such a commotion up there. The first thing he noticed when he got there was Mah Ch'ang-shun and Liu, the government worker, standing by the altar to the Spirit of the Earth. A table beside them was loaded with old, thick, account books. A rectangular poster had been newly pasted on the wall. It was full of tightly packed black characters, and a number of young men who were learning to read were trying to make them out.

In a little while Liu made a speech. Uncle Boils wasn't quite sure whether he understood much of it, but then Mah Ch'ang-shun spoke and he understood nearly all of that. "Mr. Mah has been punished . . . for dishonesty . . . community accounts." All sorts of doubts and suspicions started going through Uncle Boils' mind. What annoyed him most of all was that here was this Mah Ch'ang-shun, who had started off tending sheep when he was a child, who had worked as a hired lad and didn't know a single character—what right had he to start managing the community affairs? He turned his back and was making off, when his wife behind him grabbed his arm and said, pointing, "Look, they're bringing the grain out." He looked and there they were, coming out of Inky-nob's house carrying two big sacks of grain.

They proceeded to read out the names and distribute grain. Uncle Boils never dreamt it would ever get round to his turn, and his name had to be read out two or three times before he recognized it. Then he said, still hesitating, " 'A man born to be poor will never get rich from windfalls.' Besides—how could I ever face Mr. Mah?" His wife, furious, stuck her hand over his mouth, and in the end he went back home with more than ten pounds of yellow millet.

It was different now when he got back home, everyone had something to eat and cheered up. His son Baldy recited the details of the money Zodiac Mah had twisted the villagers out of. He would have to give up three acres of communal land, and there was to be an investigation into the yields of previous years. . . . Uncle Boils could only say, half sympathetically, " 'When the prince does wrong his subjects share his guilt.' Zodiac Mah has been a very unfortunate man."

But from then on Uncle Boils' whole family started fetching water for their seedlings.

After this combined "settling of accounts," anticorruption drive and famine relief, the villagers of Mahs' Bend learned for the first time the way of "self-help through production."

In the work of carrying water the newly established Farmers' Council assumed the function of providing a model. All the villagers who had received relief soon came to understand what it was all about. The shoots so long deprived of rain, the yellow soil that was smoking dry, the half-dead pumpkins, all got their drink of water and began to show new spirit. The influence of this new spirit spread over the whole village, and all began to realize the advantages of transporting water for irrigation. In the end every draft animal in the village was out carrying loads of water, and before long all the seedlings began to come back to life.

XI

THE SEEDLINGS FLOURISH

By the end of the dog days every slope within half a mile of Mahs' Bend had had one watering. From the point of death the seedlings had been brought back to life, even the plants which had withered down to the second leaf-fork slowly regained their strength. And there wasn't a peasant in the village but was frantically at work.

The heavy rains came before the dog days were out. The massed black clouds came up from the southeast till they covered the sky, and the hilltops were enveloped in mist; there wasn't a breath of wind. The raindrops fell steadily and evenly, as big as pennies, making a noise as they fell. It was like water poured down from somewhere up in midair. It rained for five full days and nights, and when the sky finally cleared the ditches were full to overflowing, the fields three inches under water, and the water still flowing down off the dykes. Everywhere frogs were croaking.

The rain soaked every inch of soil and put new heart into every man. The newly formed Farmers' Relief Council mobilized the whole village to sow grain and vegetables to fill in the gaps; the government issued all sorts of seed, turnip, rape-turnip, greens, buckwheat. The peasants were busy day and night, all of them hurrying to get the seeds in, till there wasn't an empty inch of soil.

After a time the village of Mahs' Bend took on a different aspect: the grain shot up from the soil, although the length of stalk varied a lot if you compared the places that had been watered with the places that hadn't. The vegetables were growing, too, the pumpkins sent out new vines and some of them already had tiny fruits forming on them. The hills all round were glossy green with tender young grass and the cows and sheep were no longer crying out mournfully.

Everyone said, "The government's an improvement over the Dragon King."

People soon stopped asking about Mr. Zodiac Mah. The story got round that he was still in a government prison and had been sentenced to penal servitude. As for Inky-nob, she had lost any reputation she ever had in all this process. Soon after the government worker first arrived he invited her to make a public admission of her faults and failings, and after this people were too busy fetching water for their seedlings to bother about her and her spirits; and she herself had lost too much face to be anxious about seeing friends very often. Not long ago I heard that she's finding life hard, and is even thinking of getting herself another husband.

TRANSLATED BY CYRIL BIRCH

A Novelist in Exile

*Eileen Chang (Chang Ai-ling) was born in Shanghai, and it was in that
city during the later years of the Second World War that she emerged
as an original writer of great evocative power. She left the mainland in
1952, and three years later took up residence in the United States
where she is currently engaged in writing and literary research.*

*She has written many short stories and several novels including
Rice-sprout Song (Yang-ko), a bitterly disillusioning story of village life
under the Chinese Communists. One of her most incisive works, however, is The Golden Cangue (Chin so chi), which traces the degenera-
tion of a woman—with the society about her—from the last days of
the Manchu empire to the eve of the war against Japan. Eileen Chang
wrote The Rouge of the North in English (though she informs us that
the dialogue was "conceived in Chinese"). The title refers to the expression "the face powder of southern dynasties, the rouge of northern
lands," a traditional metonymy for beautiful women. It is the story of
Yindi, the "Ch'i-ch'iao" of The Golden Cangue, but considerably ex-
tended and revised from the earlier novella. The title of the new Chinese version of Rouge of the North is Yüan nü.*

•

Eileen Chang

From The Rouge of the North

The Betrothal of Yindi

[*Chapters 1 and 2*]

Shanghai slept early in those days, already settling down at eight o'clock, the blue-green evening sky clearing as the sediments of darkness and hubbub slowly sank to the bottom. Electric lights were as yet uncommon in the Old City. The pebble-paved side street was almost pitch dark with all the little shops boarded up for the night. The man had it entirely to himself. He weaved happily from one side of the street to the other, humming Peking opera with an occasional *Ti guh lung di dung* to simulate the musical accompaniment. For coolness he had his pigtail piled on top of his head and his shirt open all the way down baring the chest. He fanned himself noisily in the back under the shirt with a palm-leaf fan.

He passed a shop where the large peephole was kept open to let in some air. There were voices inside but all one could see was a palm-leaf fan busily waving in the yellow lamplit square. It made him dizzy watching it. He walked on keeping close to the wall for support. There in the darkness he suddenly felt something cool and long slither down his back with a kind of swimming motion. He leaped high into the air and jumped again trying to shake it off. He turned around thinking that he would brush it off with his fan. It was only his pigtail that had come loose.

"Lay its mother!" he swore half laughing. To cover up his confusion in front of invisible spectators he flapped his fan loudly against his buttocks and swung into the slow measured "square step," walking with feet wide apart, toes pointing outwards in the manner of mandarins in Peking opera, and sang,

432

"I, the king, drunk in the Peach Blossom Palace,
With Han Su-ngo of beauty matchless."

That reminded him. Turning around he looked about him and re-traced his steps peering at all the familiar shopfronts until he came to the right one. He pounded loudly on the boards and shouted, "Miss! Miss!"

"Who is it?" a man called out from upstairs. "What for?"

"Miss! Miss! I buy sesame oil," he called out.

"We're closed, come tomorrow," the girl snapped.

"Old customer, Miss!"

He kept pounding the boards. She finally came downstairs grumbling. Through the chinks between the boards he could see the light grow as she carried the lamp into the room. The wooden shutter over the peephole was pushed up with a clatter and he smelled a whiff of the pungent sticky juice of wood shavings that women put on their hair. Her face appeared and pulled back at once. The lamp shining up from under the chin had made the lips stand out bright pink and sculpted. It looked unreal at this close range looming out of a hole in the darkness and disappearing. But he knew it so well, the neat gold mask, a short face on top of the long neck and sloping shoulders. Bangs cut into a pointed arch swept down winglike over wide cheeks, joined with the wisp in front of the ears that was plastered down to shape the face. A small purplish red mark stood like a spindle between the brows where she had pinched herself over and over again to pinch the heat sickness out of the system. She probably knew it was becoming as she was seldom without it all through summer.

"Hurry, pass me the bottle." She stuck a hand out and he seized it.

"Let's hold hands," he giggled. "Let's hold hands, Miss."

"Dead man," she screamed, "die from a thousand sword cuts!"

He giggled, muttering to himself with quiet satisfaction, "Sesame Oil Beauty." They called her that in the neighborhood.

She twisted her wrist about, knocking the silver-trimmed black rattan bangle on the edges of the peephole. He tried to pull out the trailing silk handkerchief tucked in the bracelet, which fitted so tightly he had trouble getting it out. She jerked back but his other hand held on.

"Take pity on me, Miss," he whispered. "I die from thinking of you, Miss."

"Will you let go or not, dead man?" She stamped her feet and brought the flame of the lamp to his hand. The blackened dish of oil stood on a tall unpainted wooden stand. He almost upset it snatching his hand away.

"*Ai-yo, ai-yo,*" he cried. "Miss, how can you be so cruel?"

"What's all this yelling?" her brother shouted from upstairs.

"The dead man grabbed my hand. Rotten corpse afloat! Corpse on the roadside. What do you take me for? Open your eyes and look, dead man."

Her brother's wife poked her head out of the window. "Gone. Who was it?"

"Who else but that dead carpenter? It would be my luck to run into a ghost today. Pig! Tramp! Why don't you go and pass water and look into the puddle, see your ugly face."

"All right now," her brother called out, "after all we're neighbors."

"That's just it," she shouted back, "doesn't it embarrass him to come and make a row in the middle of the night as if he doesn't know what sort of people we are? Next time he comes see if I don't hit him with the bolt. This time the tramp got off lightly. Born without eyes, dead man? May your mother be laid. Lay your ancestors eight generations back."

She had got into the spirit of it. Her voice carried down the block. At last her brother spoke up again, "All right, all right, don't yell, as if you're afraid people don't know. It's nothing that will give us face."

"You want face?" she turned on him. "You want face? You think people don't know what you do behind my back? Can you wonder people look down on me?"

"Still yelling? How is it a young girl has no shame?" Bingfa had already lowered his voice but Yindi raised hers another notch. The very mention of their quarrel had brought up all her anger.

"And you have shame? You've lost all of Father and Mother's face. So I'm shouting—if I didn't make enough of a row you'd have sold your own sister even. If I had known I'd never have shown myself. I felt so cheap and all your doing and you call me shameless?"

Bingfa leaned forward so suddenly his bare back sucked at the wicker chair with a light smack. But he was washing his feet, standing his long legs in a red-painted wooden basin with three feet.

"All right, all right," his wife said, "let her. After all a girl is a guest in the house. She'll soon be married and gone." She dropped her voice. "Marry her off quick. As the old saying goes, 'A grown daughter is not worth keeping. Keep her, keep her and she turns into an enemy.' And the way people talk, they'd say we want her to sit at the counter and draw crowds. A living signboard."

He did not say anything as he wiped his feet with a shredded towel, grey with use.

"I tell you I'm really worried. There's bound to be trouble one of these days with all these men hanging around."

He was alarmed. "Why, have you noticed anything?"

"Well, like tonight. I have no time to keep an eye on her, so many children to take care of, otherwise I'd watch the shop myself, less worries all round."

"Actually she would have done all right if she'd been given to the Wongs. They've just opened a branch at the Bridge of the Eight Immortals." He jerked his head slightly in that direction.

"It's your fault really, it's for you to decide. How can you let her pick and choose? Without parents it's you, the brother, who gets the blame if she's not married. Next time you just have to be firm."

He fell silent again. He would just as soon let it slide from year to year, there never was enough money for the trousseau, as if she didn't know. She looked at him. So did the red goose, all neck, which served as a handle to the basin. Carved in the flat on both sides, the profile reared up tall and straight in front of him, fixing him with a concentric eye. He stepped into his cloth shoes, heels trodden down to make do as slippers. Feet planted far apart he turned away and spat. As if she had got her answer she picked up the basin by its neck and clumped downstairs on her bound feet to empty the water on the street outside.

She met Yindi coming up. Without a word Yindi backed down to let her pass on the narrow stairs. The little frame house was giving out all the heat absorbed during the day in fiery puffs. Yindi went back to her stifling room with a headache. She pushed back her wet bangs and opened her high collar, highest in front just under the cheekbones for a hollow-cheeked effect, with a broad black trimming greasy and frayed around the edges. The side-fastened overblouse came down to the knees, as tight as the trousers of the same blue glass cloth, all wrinkled. She felt under the pillow for a copper coin. Dipping it in a bowl of water she sat down in front of the mirror and scraped her neck with it, to scratch out the heat sickness. The square hole in the middle of the large coin gave her a nice grip. She scraped hard in long expert strokes, dipping it back in water from time to time. Three wide stripes of mottled purple and red appeared running alongside her throat. The bruised skin burned but she felt slightly eased around the heart. The nape of the neck should also be scraped but she could not do that herself and would not want to ask her sister-in-law.

The matchmaker was a friend of her sister-in-law's, an Aunt Wu. Bingfa's wife got to know her from clubbing together to raise funds once a month, each taking the pot in turn. Aunt Wu was good at getting people to join. She also sold lotteries, peddled enameled trinkets and embroidered trimmings to rich families she knew, and made matches and delivered babies on the side. She had once worked as a maid. She got the Chais some business. A lady praying for a sick child had promised the god twenty catties of sesame oil a month for the eternal lamp. She had arranged for Bingfa to send the oil to the temple every month, as he still did in two jars slung from a shoulder pole.

This time she came to see Bingfa's wife one night and turned up again a couple of days later with two women in dark clothes with a northern accent. Yindi had thought it was strange the way they stared at her as they filed past the counter. Bingfa's wife gave them tea inside the shop but they did not stay long. When they were leaving she insisted on getting rickshaws for them and called out to Yindi, "Give me some change." Yindi had no choice but to get money from the cashbox and come out from behind the counter. Everybody was standing in the street protesting. In the act of pushing back the money one of the women held her hands and looked at them, turning them over.

"Here, be careful, Miss, don't step into the puddle." Aunt Wu bent down and lifted her trouser legs a little showing the feet.

She didn't like it. According to Bingfa's wife these were amahs of the lady who donated the oil to the temple. Aunt Wu had happened to bring them along. But Aunt Wu came again. Afterwards her brother's wife spoke to her for the first time about the blind son of a high mandarin's family. They were going to get him a concubine because of the difficulty of making a suitable match for him, so this one would be just like a wife. She realized that those two women must have been trusted amahs of the Yaos sent here to look her over, carefully inspecting her hands and feet as people did in shopping for concubines to see if there was skin disease and if the bound feet were small and well-shaped. She quarreled with Bingfa and his wife for subjecting her to this. People were sure to think that she had been examined with her consent.

When nothing came of it it would seem as if she did not pass the test.

It was true that her brother and sister-in-law had never thought of making money out of her before. She was the goods you lose money on, what they call daughters. At least concubines did not have to bring a trousseau. Even now it seemed to her that they did not think of her as a source of wealth but rather as an obstacle to their coming into a small fortune. Her position at home was getting to be impossible.

The men in the neighborhood talked and joked about her behind her back but when they actually came face to face with her they seldom had anything to say. Sometimes they were bold like this carpenter who made trouble tonight. He would lean across the counter with a slight smile staring at her with eyes like two wet mouths. Filling his bottle she would set it down with a bang.

"Twenty coins."

"*Tch, tch!* Why so fierce?"

Gazing into the air, her golden face impassive with the red mark between the brows, she suddenly spat out the words "Dead man!" and turned her head aside, giggling.

He went away vastly tickled.

This kind of thing would get her nothing but a bad name. She was already known as a flirt which was perhaps why matchmakers did not wear out her doorstep as one might expect, being called the Sesame Oil Beauty. Eighteen and not even engaged. With her own brother and sister-in-law plotting against her she felt like a fugitive carrying a jewel that endangered her life and was not marketable.

Tiny green insects flew around the lamp in droves, falling dead on the table with a dry rustle. Perhaps it would be cooler if she blew out the lamp. She sat in the dark fanning herself. Men are all alike. There was one who seemed a bit different though, Young Liu at the pharmacy across the street, tall, pale, and as pretty as a girl in his long dark gown, not a speck of dust on his white cloth socks. It was a wonder how well-groomed he was, living in the shop with nobody to look after his things. She had often caught him looking across at her. Actually if he were not so timid he could have contrived to pay the Chais an occasional visit since he came from the same village as her mother on the outskirts of Shanghai. Her maternal grandparents were still alive. When they came for visits they often dropped in at the pharmacy to bring him some message. He seldom had a chance to go home.

She went with her brother's family to see her grandparents during the New Year. They should have gone on the first of the first moon or the second or third at the latest, the days reserved for close relatives. But her grandparents were poor and partly dependent on Bingfa, so they did not have time for them until the fifth. They spent the afternoon at the village. Her grandmother mentioned that Young Liu was back for the New Year but had already returned to the shop. While she had not exactly expected to meet him there it disappointed her all the same. She felt bitter about her brother and his wife putting off the visit until the fifth. They are so snobbish, she said to herself. She made it out as if she were indignant purely on her grandparents' behalf. It would not be like this if Mother was alive, she thought, and tears welled up in her eyes.

She had always liked the smell of a pharmacy, the acrid sweetness of preserved herbs chilled in the stone-paved large dark interiors. She went to buy medicine for her sister-in-law during her last confinement. Young Liu came forward with a smile and nod as if they had met and waited on her with lowered eyes, not saying much. She liked to watch him turn to the rows of little black drawers with set-in brass rings curled like a stylized cloud. He pulled them out one after the other, the householder in some fantastic home. The tiny scales stick and brass weights were like toys. When she got home she found wrapped with the other herbs a big package of dried white chrysanthemums that was not in the prescription. Several of these flowers soaked in a cup of hot water make a cooling summer drink. She was not too fond of the grassy fragrance but she enjoyed making it every day watching the small white chrysanthemums plump out under water. She never had a chance to thank him. He would not want others to know that he had made free with the shop's goods.

That was all there was to it. She got up from her chair and stood at the window. A small illumined red square on the door differentiated the pharmacy from the other stores. They had kept their peephole open with a piece of red paper pasted over it and an oil lamp behind, illuminating the written words, *In emergency cases please enter by back door.* Somehow as she looked at the clear red square that would be kept aglow throughout the night, a vague sadness came over her that quieted the heart.

The boy selling oil puffs at a stall slept half-naked on the board where the dough was kneaded. The wire cage for holding the foot-long oil puffs stood empty near his head. The breakfast rush was over. The street barber sat nodding on his stool. Aside from plaiting men's pigtails and shaving their front hair to get a domed forehead he also rented his towel and enamel basin to passers-by who wanted to wash their faces. With no business and with the afternoon heat upon him, he gradually sank forward in sleep, burying his face in the basin.

A hawker came with a flat pole on his shoulder loaded with bamboo chairs stacked mountain-high. He parked his wares on the shady side of the street, conveniently sat on one of those stumpy pale green chairs, and went to sleep.

Yindi sat behind the counter under the vertical signboard that said in big gilt characters, *Children and old men not cheated*. Farther out to her left stood another black-and-gold signboard, one of a pair that flanked the shopfront reaching down to the pavement, *Sesame oil from small grindstone, peanut oil, and sesame butter*. She was edging a slipper with the kind of cross-stitch called "mistaken to the end." It had a nice tragic ring and the pattern of thin broken lines was more delicate than the usual dogtooth. Her needle grew rusty from perspiration. Her eyes also felt gritty. The sun had got to the two big white enamel jars beside her with big yellow tongues of peanut butter hanging out. The buzz of the flies made her still drowsier.

She looked up and saw her grandparents coming, holding palm-leaf fans overhead for shade. They must be in bad straits or they wouldn't choose such a scorching day to walk all the way here from the country. She was sorry to have to tell them that Bingfa and his wife were not at home, gone for the day with the children to the wife's family.

It always depressed her to see the red-cheeked, timidly smiling old couple in their faded and patched blue garments. Without asking them whether they had had lunch she wiped the table, set out two pairs of chopsticks, and went into the kitchen to warm the rice and the leftover dishes although it was already midafternoon. There was cabbage, melon, and bean curd. The tall wooden rice bucket was painted bright red with the ubiquitous goose handle rearing its flat head straight up, a round eye on each side. As she filled their rice bowls she patted down the rice so that it stood out of the bowl in a high mound round at the top. There were actually two bowls in one. Still her grandmother said, "Press it, Miss, press harder."

Husband and wife sat down facing each other and ate quietly. The blinding sunlight shone right into their faces but they seemed not to notice it in their heavy dreamlike calm. Now and then their bowls and chopsticks tinkled faintly. Watching them she felt a little dazed and forlorn, like waking up dry-mouthed in the setting sun after a long nap.

They each finished three hard-packed bowls of rice. The old woman helped her to clear away the dishes while the old man napped in a chair, his fan over his face.

As they returned to the front of the shop after washing up they heard in the distance the thin flat twang of three-strings, the instrument played by blind fortunetellers. The blind man was a long time in coming. The desultory music of the three-strings threaded in and out of the streets and alleys lined with black-roofed white houses, the little tune repeating itself winding in and out in a connected swastika design. For Yindi it called up a vision of her future set out like the plan of a town. Her hand went inside her blouse counting the copper coins in the pocket.

Her grandmother was also digging into her pocket. "Let's call in the fortuneteller," she said with a guilty little giggle.

"You want your fortune told, Grandmother?" She decided that she would wait and see if the man got the facts right in her grandmother's past.

They waited at the door. The little street was mostly frame houses with open fronts, the worn brownish-red paint quite hidden by all the big lacquered signboards. The upper-story windows seemed to bulge out with glass like dirty soap bubbles, yellow at the edges.

"Mr. Fortuneteller!"

She hoped that their shouts would attract Young Liu's attention so he would know her grandmother was here. Maybe he could manage to slip over for a while and ask for news of home. But he seemed occupied at the pharmacy.

Ever since this talk of making her a blind man's concubine she had felt a kind of constraint, not unmixed with disgust, at the sight of the blind fortunetellers in the street. She hung back a little as the man approached with his stick. The old woman took him by the elbow and helped him over the doorstep. He did not have a little boy to guide him around, probably because he was familiar with the neighborhood. He was middle-aged, his sallow face was leonine with down-slanting ridges. Genteel and cautious, he looked like a tailor in his wrinkled long gown. And like tailors and all men whose professions subjected them to women's whims, he wore the sour smile of patience taxed to the limit.

The old woman got him a chair. "Sit down, sir."

"*Ao, ao!*" he answered, affecting the falsetto of the singing story-tellers of Soochow. First placing a hand on the back of the chair, he lowered himself into the seat.

The old woman drew up a chair and sat opposite him, close enough to rub knees with him so she would not miss a word. After she had told him her date and hour of birth he mumbled to himself making some calculations. Then tuning up the three-strings he readily sang of her life, naming all the important events.

> ". . . I figure in your fourteenth spring
> You lost your kind parent first thing.
> I figure in your fifteenth spring
> The red *luan* bird star was moving."

Standing behind her grandmother's chair she tried to catch the lines rattling on with great rapidity. The kind parent means mother, the opposite of the severe parent, father. She understood that much and the star of the red *luan* bird is the marriage star. She did not know when her great-grandmother died but she seemed to have heard that her grandmother had been engaged before birth, what was called "pointing at the belly to make a marriage." But she was not married early, so nothing could have happened at the age of fifteen. So this fortuneteller was no good. She was glad she had not wasted her own money on him. She thought it strange that the old woman did not seem aware of any mistakes. And she could not have missed anything; being an old hand at this she must be thoroughly familiar with the phraseology. She kept nodding her head encouragingly saying "*Um, um,*" acknowledging the various events with a smugly satisfied air as if everything had turned out just as he said.

Her two sons were both shiftless. He said she could lean on one of her sons and could look forward to ten years of "old luck."

"And then? What else?" she pressed, placidly insatiable. "How am I going to end up?"

Yindi realizes with some astonishment that at sixty-five she still thinks she will end up different from what she is now.

He sighed. "It's a happy ending even if it's late in coming." He sang another couple of lines repeating his promises.

"And what else? What else?"

Yindi felt ashamed for her when he said with an embarrassed little laugh, "There isn't anything else, though, Old Mistress."

She paid him reluctantly and led him out of the shop. This time Yindi knew that Young Liu definitely saw them but he showed no sign of recognition. She was upset, wondering if he had heard anything about her, about those people looking her over as a prospective concubine. It couldn't be about the row with the carpenter that night?

"Your side gets all the sun," said her grandmother. Was she comparing this side with the pharmacy across the street? Then she had also seen Young Liu. She did not greet him either.

"I wonder when your brother and sister-in-law are coming home," she said. "I want to speak to them about something," she added importantly. She was so proud to have come to them on some business apart from borrowing money, she couldn't go away leaving it unsaid. There had been a struggle, she was not supposed to tell Yindi who was not to be told at all if the others were against it.

"Young Mr. Liu's mother came to see us yesterday," she finally said and Yindi understood at once. "Young Mr. Liu is so nice, so quiet and good-natured," she said half to herself. "He's got a good job. Although they're not rich they'll always have rice to eat. They have very few people in the family, nice and quiet. His elder sister is married already and the younger one will be before long. The mother is easy to get along with."

Yindi reached up to rub the needle on her hair and went on sewing.

"You are the only granddaughter we have, Miss. It would be nice to have you living near us. No use being shy. Poor child, you have no mother but you can tell Grandmother. It's all right to tell Grandmother."

"Tell you what, Grandmother?"

"You don't have to be shy with Grandmother."

"What's the matter with Grandmother today? I don't understand a word you say."

The old woman cackled and was content to let the matter drop. She was clearly willing.

The fortuneteller was coming back after making his round. At the sound of the three-strings strumming far off she felt a strange sense of loss in the midst of her happiness. She need not wonder any more about the future. Her fate was sealed.

Somehow she had never thought of it from that angle, that she would be living with his mother in the country raising cabbages, in a yellow mud house smelling of nightsoil with here and there a tree misted by pink blossoms for a short while in spring. He would be home only for a few days out of the whole year. All year long she would be alone with the old woman and time, whose one idea was to make her an old woman.

Young Liu was not the pushing kind. He would probably remain a shop assistant to the end of his days. They had clerks with whiskers in the same store, much respected. They wore long gowns while her brother with his messier job wore jacket and trousers like a laborer, but he owned his business. People would say it was a pity, she could have done better. Perhaps it was only natural qualms when it actually came to making an irrevocable decision, the more so because of the possibilities that all beautiful girls seemed to have, something incalculable about them. No matter how restricted, they may yet end up as empress or courtesan. She did not know exactly what it was that made her say, when her grandmother asked again what time Bingfa would be home, "They won't be back for dinner." The old couple could not wait that long. They decided to go home and come again the next day.

Bingfa and his wife returned with the children soon after his parents left and were none too pleased to hear that they had been here. Bingfa's wife remarked that they had come for money not long before. Throughout dinner she criticized the way they handled their money and let themselves be imposed upon by their no-good sons.

Yindi said nothing. She was heavy-hearted wondering how her brother and sister-in-law would take the Lius' proposal. What to do if they disapproved? It was one thing to put up a fight against a match and another thing to insist on marrying somebody. Of course there must be something between them. How far had it gone? Her sister-in-law was sure to make the most of it behind her back.

After dinner somebody banged on the door calling hoarsely for "Sister-in-law Bingfa." It sounded like that Wu woman. Coming just now it filled her with dread. Why is it tonight of all nights? Whatever it is this time, it's going to make things that much more difficult.

Bingfa's wife hurried down to open the door. She sounded a little embarrassed and apologetic because of what had happened before, but Aunt Wu was loud and hearty. As they came upstairs she even asked, "Where's Miss? Gone to bed already? I'm getting to be famous as a matchmaker. All the girls run and hide wherever I go."

She was dark and squat, freckled even on the arms, or were those "longevity spots," the brown marks of age? Nobody knew how old she was. In her profession it was not so good to grow old. People began to wonder about your faculties and judgment. Her popeyes stared seriously out of the round open face. The starch on her blue glass-cloth blouse smelled sour with sweat. When she came into the room where the light was brighter, Bingfa's wife saw she was wearing all her gold rings and earrings and at the back of her head a gold ear-spoon tucked into the little bun and a small red plush bat with a gold paper cutout of the character *fu* stuck between its wings. *Bien-fu*, bat which puns with *fu*, blessings.

"You went to a wedding?"

"No, I've just been to the Yaos to wish their Old Mistress a happy birthday."

"We've been out, too, only just came back," Bingfa's wife said.

"I came straight here after the birthday feast. Running around in this hot weather—I wouldn't do this for just anybody, to tell you the truth."

"Yes, isn't it hot today?"

Aunt Wu demanded attention with a downward movement of her palm-leaf fan and raised her voice so that it could be heard in the next room; she did not trust them to repeat it correctly. "It just happened when I was there today their young masters and mistresses came up to kowtow to Old Mistress, and she saw that they all came in pairs. All except Second Master. So afterwards Old Mistress said, the second branch should have a wife too, otherwise it won't look right on such occasions. It doesn't matter if the family is not well off as long as the girl is nice. So I said, in that case the Chai girl is just right." She stuck her fan into the back of her collar and leaned forward to whisper, "Old Mistress was not pleased. She said, Old Wu, you've been snubbed once already, do you want to be snubbed twice? After all, there are plenty of girls in the world."

The Chais could only smile.

She scratched the back of her neck with the fan handle. "So I risked losing my old face; I said, Old Mistress, it just shows that the girl has character. She doesn't want to be a concubine no matter how rich and great the family is. As Confucius said, choose a wife for her virtues, choose a concubine for her looks. Not that this girl has no looks, I needn't boast, your own people have seen for themselves. And Old Mistress laughed saying, 'Confucius never said any such thing. But there is something in what you said.' "

When she saw that the husband and wife still smiled saying nothing she leaned closer and dropped her voice, letting it rise again as she went on, "Now I say a sentence only when there is such a sentence. This may offend you: Old Mistress said a shop in the interior is all right, in the same city it's too near, embarrassing in front of relatives. I said *hey-yee*! Old Mistress, you don't know these old business families in the Old City; they keep to themselves, ordinarily they'd never give their daughters to outsiders—isn't that so?"

Bingfa's wife said uncertainly, "Of course nothing could be better if she's to go over there as the big one."

"I don't blame you for being uneasy, but go outside and ask around: Does a family like theirs have to cheat to get a concubine? It was all because of what Old Mistress said before, as the second branch has no wife the concubine will have to run the house, so she has to be from a respectable family and can read and write and calculate, on top of being pretty. That made it difficult, otherwise they wouldn't have put it off for so long—lucky for your young miss. You wait and see: the three teas, the six gifts, the red lamps, the flowered sedan chair, all the usual marriage trimmings, if there's one thing missing, just collar Old Wu and slap her face. Really when good luck comes, even the city wall can't hold it back. I don't know what good deeds your ancestors must have done. You can't find such a match even if you go looking for it with a lantern."

Bingfa cleared his throat. "Aunt Wu is no outsider, it's all right to tell you, we'd want to ask my sister first—"

"After all a brother and sister-in-law are not the same thing as parents," his wife put in. "This is a matter of a lifetime. Best to ask her."

"Sure, ask her. Your young miss is no fool. Their two young mistresses, one is a daughter of the Mas of Kaifeng, the other is Premier Wu's granddaughter, and both beauties, the pick of the pick. Their Second Master is just three years older than your young lady. His eyes are inconvenient but everybody says he's the best of the brothers. So learned and as gentle as a girl. In case your young lady goes over there and finds any one thing I said to be untrue, if she tells me to die standing up I won't dare die sitting down."

They all laughed. She left saying she would come for the answer tomorrow. After a whispered consultation Bingfa's wife went into Yindi's room. She was sewing with her back to the door.

"Miss, you must have heard what Aunt Wu said." But she sat down and told her everything all over again. "What do you think, Miss?" she asked several times without getting an answer but no tears either, which emboldened her to snatch the sewing away. "Talk, Miss."

Yindi kept her head down and started to pluck ribs off her palm-leaf fan.

"Speak, Miss."

Finally, with a violent twist of her body that sent the long pigtail flying into the air, she turned around in her chair to face the other way. "Such a nuisance!"

"At last Miss has opened her golden mouth."

Bingfa's wife got up and did obeisance half-laughing, placing one hand on top of the other over her right ribs and moving the hands up and down a bit. "So then, congratulations, Miss."

She was gone. The room seemed changed and the lamplight had taken on a reddish tint. Yindi sat plucking ribs off her fan. So the man she married would never see what she looked like. Part of her died at this. All the blind men she knew told fortunes. Some had horrible-looking eyes. What kind did he have? You must not believe matchmakers. What else was wrong? It must be something very bad. But amidst the sense of danger and treachery she already saw him as the young Peking opera actor in a night scene sitting with an elbow on the table, eyes closed on the handsome face painted pink and white. It was as if she were to live out the rest of her life on a lighted stage with music accompanying her every movement. Or on a lighted lantern like the painted figures on it, their red sleeves turned a pale orange against the light.

She thought of Young Liu. It was all his own fault for not sending the matchmaker earlier. That was just like him. People like that would never amount to much in the world. For all you know he had hesitated because people talked about her. She felt sorry about it all the same. But wasn't it fate that he should wait until the same day as the Yaos?

The sound of the neighbors' babies crying, the angry voices and loud spitting, the scuffling of a slipper sole rubbing out the spit on the floorboards, these familiar night noises seemed to be already receding into the distance. How tired she was of being poor. Every little thing could become a sin or sacrifice and turn people against each other. She had known that ever since her mother died. When her father died she was still little and her brother was not yet married. If only her mother was here to hear the news.

Her straw mat rustled and crunched all night with her turning and tossing. The cocks were crowing when she went to sleep. Soon she was wakened by the nightsoil carts coming from afar in the moist grey dawn, the wooden wheels rattling over the cobblestones. Every now and then one of the men pushing and pulling it gave a yell to wake up everybody to come out and empty their chamber pots. The cry heard in half-sleep sounded even louder and more terrifying, a short gruff bark with no words to it, curiously uncertain as if he were the only man in the world and no longer knew how to speak, ecstatic, too, because it was all his, all the desolation.

Her sister-in-law was up. It was not a girl's place to go out groping in the dark. The thumps of the bound feet on the stairs were as heavy and well-spaced as a gang of laborers beating down piling. After a while a board rattled as it was forced down from the shopfront. She dozed off again in these everyday noises, reassuringly close.

ORIGINAL ENGLISH BY EILEEN CHANG

New Poets of Taiwan

A poetic renaissance began in Taiwan rather more than a decade ago which continues with a vitality and a wealth of talent reminiscent of an age one full generation earlier. Of the six poets represented below Chou Meng-tieh is the oldest, born in 1920. Lo Fu (Mo Lo-fu, b. 1927), Shang Ch'in (Lo Yen, b. 1931), and Ya Hsien (Wang Ch'ing-lin, b. 1932), all like Chou Meng-tieh, came to Taiwan from the mainland; so did Yip Wai-lim (b. 1937), who himself made these translations. Only the youngest of the group, Yeh Shan (Wang Ching-hsien) was actually born in Taiwan (in 1940). Two men (Lo Fu and Ya Hsien) are military officers; two more (Yip Wai-lim and Yeh Shan) currently teach comparative literature in American universities.

Their poetry is seldom "easy." Often it reflects only too clearly their situation as Yip Wai-lim himself describes it: "crushed by the traumatic breakup of the Chinese world-view, and a nightmarish, mutilated reality, as well as by the fearful existential absurdity around them." Again, in Lo Fu's words: "What we see in the mirror is not the image of modern men, but their merciless destinies against which writing poetry is a form of revenge."

Yip Wai-lim makes a penetrating analysis of the process of their writing: "Ya Hsien and Lo Fu seek to beat life and rhythm into each fragment *of experience, action, and situation, and* let *these energized* fragments *work out their own scheme."*

Obviously these poets have taken much from modern Western writers. Yet, even in translation, they leave no doubt of their identity as Chinese poets. The depth and breadth, the bitterness and the glory of their cultural heritage come out overtly in images of dusty plains, sunflowers, and burning cities, and in their preoccupation with ancient myth (cf. Ya Hsien's "On Streets of China"; Yeh Shan has a recent long poem, not translated here, on the Taiwanese aboriginal goddess of the hunt). Though their language is wholly contemporary, their meters may echo ancient forms: the overlapping tropes of Shang Ch'in's "Escaping Sky," for example, recall the song-pattern "Plum-blossom Wine" used in Yüan plays (see Donald Keene's translation of such a song from Autumn in the Palace of Han, Anthology of Chinese Literature, Vol. 1, p. 442). *In their agony, and in the beauty born of their agony, these poets carry the rich flow of the Chinese lyric into the mainstream of world literature.*

●

Chou Meng-tieh

At the End of the Watercourse

[*Hsing tao shui ch'iung ch'u*]

At the end of the watercourse
There is no end, there is no water,
But a stretch of floating scent
Cold in the eyes, in the ears, and on the clothes.

You are the fountainhead;
I am ripples in the fountain.
We met
    in the beginning of the cold, the end of the cold
Like the winds and the eyes of the winds

Waking up suddenly, transported to look into each other,
To see you in me, me in you,
To see you above, behind, before, and around;
But a smile, and a thousand years gone forever!
You have a flower to bloom in your heart,
Blooming before the first petal swells.
Who is the first petal?
The first cold? the unfading ripples?

At the end of the watercourse
There is no end, there is no water,
But a stretch of floating scent
Cold in the eyes, in the ears, and on the clothes.

The Passer-through-the-walls

[*Ch'uan ch'iang jen*]

Scorching and yet chilling,
Your traces are winds—
All the walls, though cast in bronze,
Prick up their ears,
And as if attracted by curses
They move in great multitudes toward you.

Every corner of darkness is pasted with your eyes.
Your eyes are nets,
Netting directions—directions toward you
And directions leading away from you.

The Hunter lights up your window every night.
Your window, sometimes widely open,
Sometimes closed tightly;
Sometimes it is darker when it is open than closed.
Your eyes are filled with fluorescence, with yellow dust-
        mist. . . .

The Hunter says that only he has your key.
The Hunter says if you happen to leave the window open
He will gently close it for you. . . .

Lo Fu

From Death in the Stone Cell

[*Shih-shih-chi ssu-wang*]

Merely lifting my head toward a neighboring lane, I am stu-
  pefied—
In the morning, a man rebels against death with his naked
  body
And allows a black tributary to roar in his veins
I am stupefied: my eyesight sweeps past a stone wall
And chisels on it two troughs of blood.

My face spreads like a tree; the tree grows in the fire.
All quiet but pupils move behind the eyes,
Toward directions people dare not talk about:
I am indeed a sawed-off bitter pear tree
On whose annual rings you can still hear clearly winds and
  cicadas.

Matches, a blast of flame, embrace the entire world.
Before city is burnt, a desperado is born in hurrahs.
Snow season: sunflower twists its neck for echoes of the sun.
I again see, corridor's shadow flashes in from door's crevice
To pursue and kill a pot of fire.

Light centered: bats eat up rings and rings of streetlamps.
Our hearts totally crushed by a vainly emptied house.
Some clothes glimmer, some faces rot from within,
So much coughing, so many dried palms
Cannot hold the slightest warmth.

You are an unwakened lotus, a flat fish running from summer,

A nameless finger straying across the lyre,
The first acquaintance of two white hands between rose
   and rattlesnake.
In an afternoon after the autumn has deserted the thresh-
   ing yard,
You insist that you are an urn of bone ashes, knowing no sadness.

No one will bargain with you, now locked in the cell, for
   love in the body:
Death is a broken flower vase that needs no striking to be
   smashed,
And after the sun sets you will see blood crying in history—
   Why didn't you recognize the change of complexion before the city was burnt?
Why do you want the Cross to nail the turning light of the
   nuns' eyes?

If indeed there were a wheat seed weeping among rocks,
Kneaded to pieces by a certain action or gesture,
I would have the experience of being chewed,
I would cry out coldly, like an iceberg:
"O Food, you are being murdered by the plentiful barn!"

The anxiety of summer still crawls slowly on the forehead of
   winter,
Slowly passing through the eyesight between two walls, eyesight and tendrils
Hanging on the entire room. When diverse colors come silently over,
The trifles to be forgotten are not forgotten and, dejected the
   whole day,
I have since been called something meaningless and tired.

And so you divide the feast of your own body in the dugouts,
Like doctors who write their theses with plasma exchanging
   reputations for eyeballs,
When guests leave the session one by one,
There will be no more discussion why the sun doesn't come
   out from the gun barrel
So as to let war write biographies for generals.

Finding complaisance in a lizard's eyesight and obstinacy in its
    skin complexion,
At noon, I thought you could be the same sort of animal,
And thought of war—war is a black skirt that forever defies
    folding.
When death kicks in two the rainbow above my roof,
I suddenly remember you had a pair of eyes eaten once by the
    cuttlefish.

And morning is a beetle that walks on its back,
Chewing as it goes on. I am the leftover night,
Barely hearing stars crying among the joints of teeth.
I write my dying commands on the wind and on the sun about
    to rise,
And only by sneezing can I remember what eats me is myself.
On the forehead there is propped up a black tent, like a tear
    lodging on the cheek.
I walk into the sun and come out of the sunflower,
Not knowing whether wearing green clothes would look like
    clouds,
Which being single, grow lean from sickness in a valley.
After I finish carving death on the tombstone, I break the knife
    in two.

The Firstborn Blackness

[*Ch'u-sheng-chih hei*]

Unable to tell yet whose hand it is—your door opening
    slowly,
I flash into your pupils and drink the blackness in them.
You are the root and fruit, holding a thousand years in one
    core.
We make a circle and dance and get fire from it,
And thus I am burnt by the blackness of your pupils.

You pave a road from your eyebrows leading to morning
Morning, receiving the fall of another star, wakes up.

To prove pain is the echo of your coming or the footprint
of your going,
You close your eyes to carve your own silence
So quiet that we cannot open our eyes.

To be naked: is this the reason you have for your arrival?
Daughter, before I knew you I had tasted the salt in your
eyes
Inside your mother's womb you had learned how to wake
up
And how with your fingers to knead time into sound on
your little bed
And thrust with your palms to push day back into night.

We have been clothed with light, with the clearness of a
lotus.
We have been dazzled by death and the moving stillness of
a nave.
And you are the road of yesterday, one rut among the thou-
sands,
When the dinner tray is holding your future,
You are greedily eating our present.

Structured from some gestures of sleep and a whole black
night,
You are an oyster, whose two shells draw in the roaring
sea.
O Crying! I live to swallow what gives voice.
Let me, steadily, walk out of your pupils
And announce to all the hair: *I am this blackness.*

The world is an armless sleeve: your arrival is wanting in
everything.
You stretch two palms, stretching to grasp a tomorrow.
You are the firstborn blackness; one flash is a swank ban-
quet.
All the guests look at you with prickly eyes—
To grow a Bo tree in your pupils.

Shang Ch'in

Gradient of the Milky Way

[*T'ien-ho-ti hsieh-tu*]

> In the north-northwest of the empyrean
> The sheepflocks are muteness in file,
> One fashion of longing
> In another fashion.
> The pasture lies in the east of the Milky Way while
> The pond in the deep of the heart,
> The heart at the corpulent loins of the guitar.
>
> But in one night the Milky Way
> With its gradient
> Seems to have twisted silence
> And lowered its very elemental leaf
> To the water
> To receive those stars.
>
> The Milky Way lowers itself to the water.
> Stars cry out silently.
> Many simple limbs and forms
> Are moved by their own shadows.
> The guitar sails on the sound-wave and
>   the meadow
> Drifts under the cordage;
> Sheds tears
>   and becomes the sister of the pond.
>
> Between the high-tension wire and the grape trellis
> The Milky Way stoops toward itself,

That is, straight toward my southeast.
The dead sound of the motor is bound
By two lines of eucalyptus.

                              The mildewed
Sighing becomes a sound-blast at midnight.
My friend asks the way with a cube of sugar
And gets lost in the jungle under the eaves.
No one knows how at sea you were, seeing her wash her hair,
Meanwhile the Milky Way is beneath the pasture;
No one knows how at sea I was, seeing you dry your hair in
      the sun.
God of the Earth, how boring it is to die!
Time leaks away in the market basket
To become beehives
To make
Honey that tastes sweet only to the blind.

Ever since the Milky Way moved its gradient
To the flat, flat corner of my forehead
In the north-northwest of the empyrean
There is day and night—
      Night gone never returns
      Day come never goes again—
March jolts on our shoulders,
Skirts are burnt by our gaze, pretty bodies
Dissolve in a lane of sunshine,
Leaving the gradient of the Milky Way
In the empty drinking glass.

The Queue Being Unbraided

[*Pu pei pien-chieh shih-ti ta-pien*]

Whirled up, the dust is as convulsed as the cordage being stranded
Coiled together, the ropes are as confused as the queue being braided
            (This is false)

The queue being unbraided   Early spring dusk   Lying lazy in bed
even after 10 A.M.   On the terrace a clog with a broken lace   The
queue being unbraided   Under it a slender white neck

    A beggar cooling himself at the gate of drainage   A policeman
back from night duties   Tinkling of earrings in a hot-spring bath   A
disused bomb and a deserted ship

And the hawser on the deserted ship; and the queue being unbraided;
and lazy in bed, yawning; and a tear from the right eye flows to the
left: "I thought the water in your lake was sweet!" and the tear from
the left eye has already passed the ear's door—telling her how slack
the evening winds are in the suburbs—and is flowing into the unbraided hair.

The Maguey

[*Lung-she-lan*]

       Since you plucked your feet out of the pond
           densely grown with the watercress,
       Your wrist watch indicates half-past three,
           pointing to the weed-webbed heart;
       And the yew trees are darkly still beneath the floating ash
          leaves.
          Moon sees weeds
          Ghosts see moon
          Water and moon invisible
          Water and moon immobile

       The Goddess Star is a spring on a soldier's rifle, holding
       The hazardous Milky Way, my heart's direction.
       And eyelashes projected from early spring
       Are rainbows above your fictional death.

       Thereupon, what remains in my heart is the maguey.
       Doctor, why does the oleander bloom incessantly? and
       Blooming is sickness, doctor.
                  This is no desert.

This is the zone for dozing and you are an electric fan;
You are the windshield wipers still working after the car
   stops.
Only you are the stillness, because you are the only sound.

The Escaping Sky

[*T'ao-wang-ti t'ien-k'ung*]

The deadman's face is a swamp unseen by men;
A swamp in the wasteland is the escape of part of the sky.
The fugitive sky is the brimming of roses;
The brimming of roses is the snow that has never fallen.
The fallen snow is a string being twanged;
A string being twanged is a tear in the veins.
The rising tears are burning hearts;
And burning hearts are swamps, their wastelands.

Ya Hsien

Salt

[*Yen*]

Our old woman had never met Dostoevsky after all. In the spring she only cried: Salt! Give me a peck of salt! The angels were singing in the elms. That year the garden peas scarcely blossomed.

Seven hundred miles away the camel caravans led by the Minister of Salt were passing along the seaside. No blade of seaweed ever showed up in our old woman's pupils. She only cried: Salt! Salt! Give me a peck of salt! The laughing angels covered her up with a shower of snow.

In 1911 the partymen arrived in Wuchang. Our old woman left her foot-binding cloth up on the elms and went off into the breath of wild dogs and under the wings of the baldheaded vulture. Many voices whined in the winds: Salt! Salt! Give me a peck of salt! Almost all the garden peas blossomed with white flowers that year. After all Dostoevsky had never met our old woman.

On Streets of China

[*Tsai Chung-kuo chieh-shang*]

> The blotting paper of dreams and moons.
> Poets put on suits of corduroy.
> The public telephones cannot be connected to the celestial
> Nü Wo.[1]

---

[1] Nü Wo, creator-goddess who repaired cracks in the firmament with stone slabs.

Thoughts walk on roads like scripts on oracle bones.
To feast on cooked wheat in an immense cauldron with the
  Muse.
Sandwiches and beefsteaks are thus left unattended.
Poets put on suits of corduroy.

In the dust, Huangti, our first Emperor, shouts.
The trolley buses have left our Queen's phaeton rusted.
Since they have gaslights and neonlights,
We will not lend them our old old sun.
Recall, the greatest battle with Tzu-yu, Huangti's enemy.
Recall, the Song of Reeling Silk sung by Lei-chu, Huangti's
  queen.
Recall, that poets did not put on suits of corduroy.

No congress meetings and nothing had ever really happened.
Confucius had never imposed royalties on books by Lao Tzu.
Airplanes roar and pass by a row of smoke-shrouded willows.
The tides of students' strikes dash on the eroded palace
  walls.
Without coffee without ever initiating a revolution, Li Po
  wrote his poetry,
Not to mention his not having to put on suits of corduroy.

Unexpectedly Whitman's collection did not come from Tun-
  huang.[2]
Oceanliners say: Beyond the four seas there are another
  four seas.
A beggar in the subway stretches out his black bowl.
Sailors flirt with girls scantily dressed.
And toward the left: red lights, and toward the right: red
  lights.
And poets put on suits of corduroy.

The advertisement for quinine is pasted on the face of our
  Husbandry Master.[3]

---

[2] As did Buddhist scriptures, secular texts and mural paintings, walled up
in the temple caves at Tun-huang in the tenth century and rediscovered only
in the twentieth.
[3] Shen Nung, legendary emperor, discoverer of medicinal herbs.

When spring comes, everyone is busy talking about inter-
   planetary trips.
Steam whistles strangle the workmen. Pamphlets on democ-
   racy.
Bus stops. Lawyers and electric chairs.
On the gates of the city you will see no more heads hang-
   ing up as deterrents.
Fu Hsi's[4] Eight Trigrams cannot catch up with the Nobel
   prizes.
The cypress in Confucius' hometown is made into railway ties.
If you want to put on anything, put on suits of corduroy.

The blotting paper of dreams and moons.
Poets put on suits of corduroy.
People say there has never been such a creature as the dragon.
So feast on cooked wheat in an immense cauldron with the
   Muse.
So thoughts walk on roads like scripts on oracle bones.
And wait for the people coming out at the end of sexy movies.
And put on suits of corduroy.

---

[4] Legendary emperor, inventor of writing, the Eight Trigrams being the
prototype.

Yip Wai-lim

Are Such the Voices . . .

[*Hsü-ch'ü (Chi)*]

> Are such the voices we never heard, O you dumbfounded
>   season
> Voices of falling, voices of shining and blooming?
> Are you the rising that doubles the sea and the sky
> And lets the yearlong hair of clouds stir
> The conflagration of the ancient hoofs
> From the white erosive flood?
> Where, one may ask, does the song end?
> Among the blue, blue hills?
> And where, the yellow birds' way?
> Where, the sea gulls' flight?
> When all colors are now governed by one
> When all voices stay in your face
> The cities in the horizon disperse and cliffs sink
> The tremendous flapping now strikes the void
> As the stone head that is never given the seven apertures
> Commands the growing picture of our knowledge
> What swelling movements from flowers
> Which defy shaping and naming
> That have made everything explainable?
> We suddenly see so many door handles
> That lead us to courts and bowers
> Where you, rising once again, with postures of a relief
> So stun us that we have to restrain
> Rivers, forests, and villages from being washed away
> And the longing of soldiers on the only towers
> From dissolving into a season, dissolving

Into the soundless roaring of a fall
When the paths of woodcutters
Slowly and silently
Reach the yearlong clouds

Fugue

[*Fu-ko*]

I

North wind   can I bear this one more year?
Streets shivering along the walls
Romances in cold sorrows from the frontiers
Remind me of these:
Patience of mountains   Erratic breath of outlands
Chronic neighing of Tartar horses
Bonfires in war and farming in spring
Plants that transcend all knowing
Immaculate snowfalls   Grand cathedrals and palaces
All plunge into the scandals of gods
That follow our youthful days
The song goes:
    The moon will rise
    The sun will sink
Please be quick   And do not get lost in the sun
Have you forgotten the oracle of the dragon?
It may slip again from the jade balcony
Into this only aspen among
Compacted houses   Yesterday
Or today? (I am not yet sure)
Beside the river or the deep-flowing water
              or the dark-shimmering rushes
I see a cloud of crows gather around a drifting of lives
                But where to?
The winds bring the barking of dogs into winding back
      alleys
The poets are dead   The Vixen comes in silk

Is the one-eyed seer still living?
The winds roar   In the cold streets in the flying dust
I can still recognize this is the bus to my native land
Tables mats and wines proudly invite me
To see the stars—fugitive ideas on flowers
And intentions in myths
                    We go sightseeing

                            II

My feet my hands collide together   In the rushing coach
Stumps upheld the fleshy body of winter
In the rush the fire burns the lucent days of the past
In the rush the boulevard tempers the lucent days of the past
A line of thatched huts and flying birds embrace
My skyward solitude   I go in search of
Vespers and festivals within a tent   A beach
A kitten   rains in apricot days   and smoke from wild ferns
That occurred in the first frost shortly after my vigorous
      hands
Caressed a holy face
          He stood up
Imitating the ancient prophet:
                        By the Twelve Branches
                    It comes true
                    It comes true
I wait for you and bring you to see the dynasties of T'ang
      Yü Hsia
      Shang Chou

The earth holds wallowing memories
      the great book read into the world
      the child on stretching plains
      the giant of uprising ranges
The earth holds wallowing memories

Glimmering Mars strolls over our gardens
A man with disheveled hair sings:

I want to see the land of Lu
Mount Kuei hides it
And I have no axe or hatchet
What can I do to Mount Kuei?
Warm the southerly winds
Soothe our woes the southerly winds
Increase our gains the southerly winds
In early winter
In whispers
In sickbed
The fire burns the lucent days of the past
The boulevard tempers the lucent days of the past
We drink to the flowering chrysanthemum   make a flute
   from reeds
And play a stanza from the fugitive song

III

Do you not see people seek for their children
the embryo of man?
Do you not see people seek from sudden falls
an ode of stone?
Do you not see people seek in the jingling of spears
communion with the heavens?
Against the maple the willow the wind and the wine of a
   poet
There is the speech of cliffs   the hurrah of the sea
The soundless pit of sky as we now remember
A spring turns into a pond
   or gets into plants
   or gets into human bodies
   regardless of reality
   regardless of the Great Void
We simply walk down the steps   No monsoon
Nor omened events coming on
We brood over a tale: A peach or a desire
Which spoils the moral of the celestial court? O how boring
Let me tell you the charm of a white mouse. . . .
But on craggy precipices

Or on rocky ruins of a long wall
What can we make of the world?
                    We have ourselves admired
Millions of flowers trees bays and waters
What can we make of the world?
        We have again come across
Rimes meters rhythms tones ballads etc.
What can we make of the world?
Board a congested bus   stand beside the streets
Look here and there   wait for a butterfly
Wait for a supreme seer wait for a knight on horseback
Pass by
            How many faces
            How many names
Flouted by trees and buildings
        Longingly I think of my friends
        I stop and scratch my head
Night brings down a galaxy of chilling rain.

Yeh Shan

Narcissus

[*Shui-hsien-hua*]

Stars gone cry out silently behind us.
We argue bitterly over nothing;
Lie down; and in the lullaby
I count stars as they fall into the bottom of the valley,
           turn into fireflies,
Float by our ankles of flower shadows.

Alas, perhaps deserted mountains and wild ford—
And we share one boat:

Glide down Time's long river;
Flash across seven oceans.
A thousand years: one dream. Immense waves.
Turning my head: you have two temples of star flowers.
Narcissus looks down at himself from Greek Classics.
—Today's stars cry out silently behind us.
We sit down facing each other beneath the north window.
In the dark we pass around yellowing letters to read.

Strawberry Fields in Summer

[*Hsia-t'ien-ti ts'ao-mei-ch'ang*]

Diggers rest beneath trees.
Tree shadows slowly slant eastward.
Searchers of butterfly orchids are clambering

A snow white precipice. Forests in the distance
Look as if growing in a previous century.
Small birds clamor, like a waterfall
A waterfall without any sense of seasons.

I sit inside a small cabin, watching
Several acres of strawberries.
You know, these are several acres of sweetness!
Summer love congeals into
A full valley of juicy red.

And the sun becomes whiter and whiter.
Cicadas' buzz gets more and more on our nerves:
Echoes all four directions; in them
Some degree of primitive sadness.
But mountains and valleys of juicy red
Are no longer the strawberries of former times.

Variation

[*Pien-tsou*]

Wait for warm winds to cool
Like waiting for torrential rain at year's end
Like peeking at bird-singing beyond windbreaks by the res-
    ervoir.
This is us, boring stars.

In a different kind of time
Stillness, compared to pursuit,
Is wearier. This is us.
Foolish sunflowers' ambiguous gaze
Golden silence
And abundance like autumn harvest
Bundled along the river.

As to those initiated by chance,
Or cries of hawks and orioles
All related to bows and arrows,
This is you, floating
In the midst of evening mist
Above green mountains.

Wounds: A Song

[*Shang-hen-chih ko*]

You have never supposed you would
Live in that city.
Some bridges, some dead spirits'
Rags and remains. O will-o'-the-wisp!
A bee-raising, flower-growing brewery.
And we meet again, weep at
Cars and torrential rain flashing by.

Because these are only odors and gestures.
Some strange blending, exuding from dust:
Mirror   dust   mirror   dust
Burning you within the reflected sadness, leaping into
Fresh flower's palm and treads. Until yourself
Like plants in pieces and rotting.
You see yourself undress in stream's nostalgia
Undress and sink. Scattering images—
These are not scales, nor hairs, nor annual rings felled.
Sudden flare of an evening, supposition of night.

TRANSLATED BY YIP WAI-LIM

A Short Bibliography

HISTORICAL AND LITERARY BACKGROUND

Chow Tse-tsung. *The May Fourth Movement: Intellectual Revolution in Modern China.* Cambridge: Harvard University Press, 1960.

Fairbank, John King. *The United States and China.* Cambridge: Harvard University Press, 1962.

Liu, James J. Y. *The Chinese Knight-Errant.* Chicago: University of Chicago Press, 1967. Tales, novels, and plays on chivalric themes are among the materials analyzed in this study.

Liu Wu-chi. *Introduction to Chinese Literature.* Bloomington: Indiana University Press, 1966.

McAleavy, Henry. *The Modern History of China.* New York: Praeger, 1967. Nineteenth and twentieth centuries.

PREMODERN POETRY AND PROSE

Lin Yutang. *The Importance of Living.* New York: John Day, 1937.

Mote, F. W. *The Poet Kao Ch'i, 1336-1374.* Princeton: Princeton University Press, 1962.

Nivison, David S. *The Life and Thought of Chang Hsüeh-ch'eng (1738-1801).* Stanford: Stanford University Press, 1966. A rare glimpse into the intellectual world of the classical scholars of late imperial China.

Schlepp, Wayne. *San-ch'ü, Its Technique and Imagery.* Madison: University of Wisconsin Press, 1970.

Shen Fu. *Chapters from a Floating Life.* Translated by Shirley M. Black. Oxford: Oxford University Press, 1960.

Waley, Arthur. *Yüan Mei.* London: George Allen and Unwin, 1956.

DRAMA

Hung Shen. *The Palace of Eternal Youth.* Translated by Yang Hsien-yi and Gladys Yang. Peking: Foreign Languages Press, 1955.

Scott, A. C. *Traditional Chinese Plays.* Madison: University of Wisconsin Press, 1967. Two popular Peking opera texts: *Ssu Lang Visits His Mother* and *The Butterfly Dream.*

Yao Hsin-nung. *The Malice of Empire.* Translated by Jeremy Ingalls. Berkeley: University of California Press, 1970.

TRADITIONAL FICTION

Bauer, Wolfgang and Herbert Franke. *The Golden Casket.* Translated from the German by Christopher Levenson. Harmondsworth: Penguin Books, 1964. Translations of Chinese novellas in the classical style.

Birch, Cyril. *Stories from a Ming Collection.* New York: Grove Press (Evergreen), 1958.

Egerton, Clement. *The Golden Lotus.* 4 vols. New York: Paragon Book Gallery, 1962. Complete translation of *Chin P'ing Mei* into English and Latin.

Giles, Herbert A. *Strange Stories from a Chinese Studio.* 2 vols. London: T. W. Laurie, 1916.

Hsia, C. T. *The Classic Chinese Novel.* New York: Columbia University Press, 1968. Critical analyses of six major works, including *Monkey* and *Red Chamber Dream.*

Lin Tai-yi. *Flowers in the Mirror.* Berkeley: University of California Press, 1966. Translation of the novel *Ching hua yüan,* by Li Ju-chen.

McHugh, Florence and Isabel. *The Dream of the Red Chamber.* New York: Pantheon Books, 1958. English translation of the German abridgement by Franz Kuhn.

Miall, Bernard. *Chin P'ing Mei.* New York: Putnam's (Capricorn Books), 1962. English translation of the German abridgement by Franz Kuhn.

Shadick, Harold. *The Travels of Lao Ts'an.* Translation of the novel *Lao-ts'an yu-chi,* by Liu O. Ithaca: Cornell University Press, 1952.

Waley, Arthur. *Monkey*. New York: Grove Press (Evergreen), 1958.
Wu Ching-tzu. *The Scholars*. Translated by Yang Hsien-yi and Gladys Yang. Peking: Foreign Languages Press, 1957.

MODERN FICTION

Chang, Eileen. *Rice-Sprout Song*. New York: Scribner's, 1955.
———. *The Rouge of the North*. London: Cassell, 1967.
Hsia, C. T. *A History of Modern Chinese Fiction, 1917–1957*. New Haven: Yale University Press, 1961.
———. *Twentieth Century Chinese Stories*. New York: Columbia University Press, 1972.
Lao She. *Rickshaw Boy*. Translated by Evan King. New York: Reynal and Hitchcock, 1945.
———. *The Quest for Love of Lao Lee*. Translation of *Li-hun*, by Helena Kuo. New York: Reynal and Hitchcock, 1948.
Lu Hsün. *Selected Stories*. Translated by Yang Hsien-yi and Gladys Yang. Peking: Foreign Languages Press, 1963.
Mao Tun. *Midnight*. Translated by Hsü Meng-hsiung and A. C. Barnes. Peking: Foreign Languages Press, 1957.
Pa Chin. *The Family*. Translated by Sidney Shapiro. Peking: Foreign Languages Press, 1964.
Shen Ts'ung-wen. *The Chinese Earth*. Fourteen stories, translated by Ching Ti and Robert Payne. London: George Allen and Unwin, 1947.
Snow, Edgar. *Living China*. New York: Reynal and Hitchcock, 1936.
Wang Chi-chen. *Contemporary Chinese Stories*. New York: Columbia University Press, 1948.
Yuan Chia-hua and Robert Payne. *Contemporary Chinese Short Stories*. Levittown, N.Y.: Transatlantic Arts, 1946.

MODERN POETRY

Acton, Harold and Chen Shih-hsiang. *Modern Chinese Poetry*. London: Duckworth, 1936.
Hsu Kai-yu. *Twentieth Century Chinese Poetry*. Ithaca: Cornell University Press, 1970.
Yip Wai-lim. *Modern Chinese Poetry: Twenty Poets from the Republic of China, 1955–1965*. Iowa City: University of Iowa Press, 1970.

COMMUNIST WRITERS

Birch, Cyril. *Chinese Communist Literature*. New York: Praeger, 1963.
Critical essays by eleven scholars.

Chao Shu-li. *The Rhymes of Li Yu-tsai*. Translated by Gladys Yang.
Peking: Foreign Languages Press, 1955.

Chou Li-po. *Great Changes in a Mountain Village*. Translated by
Derek Bryan. Peking: Foreign Languages Press, 1961.

Jenner, W. J. F. *Modern Chinese Stories*. Oxford: Oxford University
Press, 1970.

Ting Ling. *The Sun Shines over the Sangkan River*. Translated by Yang
Hsien-yi and Gladys Yang. Peking: Foreign Languages Press,
1953.